Maclure of New Harmony

Maclure

of New Harmony

SCIENTIST

PROGRESSIVE EDUCATOR

RADICAL PHILANTHROPIST

❋

Leonard Warren

INDIANA UNIVERSITY PRESS

Bloomington & Indianapolis

This book is a publication of

Indiana University Press
601 North Morton Street
Bloomington, IN 47404-3797 USA

www.iupress.indiana.edu

Telephone orders   800-842-6796
Fax orders   812-855-7931
Orders by e-mail   iuporder@indiana.edu

The paper used in this publication meets
the minimum requirements of American
National Standard for Information Sciences—Permanence of Paper for Printed
Library Materials, ANSI Z39.48-1984.

Manufactured in the United States of
America

Library of Congress Cataloging-in-
Publication Data

Warren, Leonard, date-
  Maclure of New Harmony: scientist,
progressive educator, radical philanthro-
pist/Leonard Warren.
    p. cm.
  Includes bibliographical references and
index.
  ISBN 978-0-253-35326-9 (cloth: alk. pa-
per) 1. McClure, William, 1763–1840. 2.
Geologists—United States—Biography.
3. Geological surveys—United States—
History—19th century. 4. Educators—
United States—Biography. 5. Educational
change—United States—History—19th
century. 6. Social reformers—United
States—Biography. 7. New Harmony
(Ind.)—History—19th century. 8.
Utopias—United States—History—19th
century. 9. United States—Social condi-
tions—To 1865. I. Title.
  E340.M16W37 2009
  973.5092—dc22
  [B]
                                2008051604

1 2 3 4 5 14 13 12 11 10 09

To those who are gone

Sydney A. Warren

Irving A. Warren

Bernice K. Warren

Edith Ennis

Jim Sprague

John M. Buchanan

Jay Lash

Alan Epstein

Sol Erulkar

Jean-Claude Jardillier

Bert BuAime (William Wharton)

CONTENTS

ACKNOWLEDGMENTS

While we may lament the past neglect of William Maclure's contributions in the recounting of the history of American science and education, we can now take comfort in the superb archival work of J. Percy Moore, Arthur Bestor, Josephine M. Elliott, Gerald Lee Gutek, and John S. Doskey, who have all gone a long way in redressing the inattention. The present work, the first formal biography of William Maclure, would have been almost impossible to accomplish without their efforts. Upon reading Maclure's unedited writing, it soon becomes apparent that he was seriously deficient in the secrets of orthography, spelling, and grammar. However numerous the errors, the reader is rarely misled by them, and so the many quotations of Maclure used in the present work have been left unaltered. Some of Maclure's quotations used here were corrected by his contemporaries.

My wonder never ceases at the richness of historical records cradled in Philadelphia institutions and the helpfulness of those who guard their treasures. I wish to thank Earle E. Spamer (now at the American Philosophical Society) and Robert Peck of the Academy of Natural Sciences of Philadelphia, Roy Goodman and Valerie Lutz of the American Philosophical Society, Nina Long and Leslie Pope of the Wistar Institute Library and Archive, the librarians at the Van Pelt Library of the University of Pennsylvania, the Library Company of Philadelphia, and the Historical Society of Pennsylvania. I wish to thank Sherry Graves and Frank Smith of the Working Men's Institute in New Harmony. Katherine N. Norton,

Matthew Person, and Colleen Hurter of the Marine Biological Laboratory library and archives in Woods Hole, Massachusetts, have been a constant source of help and guidance. I am grateful to Anthony Lucente of the Wistar Institute, who has been an indispensable guide and lifesaver in my struggle to master the computer.

I am indebted to Russel E. Kaufman of the Wistar Institute of Anatomy and Biology, and Joseph Sanger and John Epstein of the Department of Cell and Developmental Biology, University of Pennsylvania Medical School, for their generous support. Finally, I hardly know where to begin in expressing my appreciation for my wife, Eve, for her encouragement and advice.

CHRONOLOGY

1763 Born in Ayr, Scotland, on October 27.

1778 Visits the United States.

1782 Second visit to United States to make business connections; returns to England as a member of a trading company.

Extensive travel in Europe during the next decade as a merchant.

1796 Establishes a lumber business in Virginia, settles in Philadelphia, becomes an American citizen; extensive commercial activity in England and the United States that extends into the early 1800s.

1799 Member of the American Philosophical Society (APS).

1800 Extensive travels through Europe as a geologist.

1803 Member of the United States Commission to settle claims of American citizens against the French.

1804 Visits Pestalozzi's radically progressive school in Yverdon, Switzerland, and realizes that this mode of education is central in the struggle for social reform.

Geological exploration of France and Spain.

Visits Joseph Neef's Pestalozzian school in Paris and brings him to Philadelphia.

1808 First Pestalozzian school established in the United States by Neef.

Geological studies in the United States.

Presents landmark paper at APS on *Observations on the Geology of the United States Explanatory for Geological Map*. Published in *Transactions of the APS*.

1809 Maclure publishes *Geology of the United States*.

Extensive travel through Russia, Poland, and Europe until 1815.

1812 Becomes a member of the Academy of Natural Sciences of Philadelphia (ANSP).

1815 Exploration of West Indies with Charles-Alexandre Lesueur.

1816   Settles in Philadelphia and explores the northeastern United States.

1817   Elected president of ANSP. Provides a printing
       press to publish the *Journal of the ANSP*.

1818   Sponsors and participates in expedition to Florida and Georgia.

       Extensive travels through France, Italy, Spain,
       and Great Britain for seven years.

       Publishes revised *Observations*.

1819   Meets Madame Marie Duclos Fretageot.

       Becomes president of the American Geological Society.

1820   Purchases land in Spain with an intention to settle there and
       establish industrial and agricultural schools for the poor.

1823   Liberal Spanish government overthrown, and his land confiscated.

1824   Leaves Spain. Visits Robert Owen in New Lanark.

1825   Returns to the United States where he participates in geological
       explorations with Thomas Say, Charles-Alexandre Lesueur, and others.

       Joins Owen in his New Harmony venture.

       Sails down the Ohio River to New Harmony on the *Boatload
       of Knowledge*, accompanied by naturalists and teachers from
       Philadelphia. Establishes manual training and trade schools,
       a scientific center, and a library in New Harmony.

1826   Winters in New Orleans.

1827   Chaos in New Harmony with collapse of Owen-Maclure
       "partnership." Visits Mexico with Thomas Say.

1828   Returns to Mexico, where he resides until his death.

       Maclure's schools and affairs in New Harmony managed by
       Madame Fretageot and Thomas Say until their deaths.

1831   Publishes *Opinions*.

1833   Madame Fretageot visits Maclure in Mexico; she dies of cholera.

1834   Thomas Say dies in New Harmony.

       Residing in Mexico, aging, ill, and uncertain about plans for
       his estate, which he changes frequently. Generously provides
       the ANSP with money for a new building and his library.

1835   Earmarks the bulk of his estate for the creation
       and support of free public libraries.

1837   Rejuvenates Working Men's Institute and library.

1840   Dies at San Angel, Mexico, March 23.

Maclure of New Harmony

Prologue

Almost every human being who has walked the face of the earth has come and gone without an identifiable trace. "Numberless infinity of soules" live on in their descendants, leaving no record of themselves as unique individuals, with wondrous experience and knowledge accumulated over a lifetime, who then perished. There are, however, the select few, the people who have been canonized to become an integral part of popular thought and culture, whose names are known to all.

Far greater in number are the heroes who in their time were widely known for their achievements, but are now largely forgotten. Their remarkable contributions are unheralded today, memory of them has fallen away, and they only come to life occasionally, if by chance the written record, what little there is of it, is scrutinized. We are able to learn something about members of this multitude through records maintained in archives, always available to the curious. William Maclure (1763–1840), a peculiarly elusive soul, was one of these special people who today is almost unknown. A successful merchant, he retired a wealthy man in his early thirties to become a seminal geologist and a philanthropist, and then in a stunning change of direction went on to try to set right the social injustices of the world through education of the young.

His achievements will be revealed by a telling of his story.

✳

ONE

Origins and the Making of a Life

THE DESIRE TO KNOW THE SECRETS OF THE WORLD

The Royal Burgh of Ayr, a port near Glasgow and an ancient center of agriculture and commerce, was home to about 4,000 people in the mid-eighteenth century. The town lies in a rolling green region by the sea, the black hills of Arran looming in the distance. Widely known as Robert Burns's country, the locale is remarkable for its many extraordinary sons who made their mark in the world.[1] One of these was William Maclure, born on October 27, 1763. His father, David McClure, a merchant, like many other Scots, carried on an export-import business with North America that fell on hard times during the American Revolution, but William's early life cannot be said to be ruled by poverty and deprivation.[2] He was one of twelve children, half of whom survived—William and two brothers, Alexander (1765?–1850?) and John (1771?–1834?), and three sisters, Anna (1766–1834), Margaret (1768–1839), and Helen, who was the only Maclure who married. She and her husband, David Hunter, had seven children, and when she died, William assumed responsibility for his nieces and nephews.[3]

He had, in fact, been baptized James, but for reasons unknown, changed his name to William and his family name to Maclure, a change copied by his siblings.[4] There is little question that William was the dominant member of the family who brought his siblings to America and arranged for them to spend their later years in New Harmony, Indiana. But despite the solicitude, he admitted to a friend that they gave him little pleasure. Insanity seemed to have run in the family. John, whom William called a "weaker brother," ended his days in a mental hospital in Lexington, Kentucky. As many as three of Helen's children were afflicted with significant mental instability, and Margaret was considered highly emotional, "ethereal," and "nonsensical."[5] The suggestion has been made that William may not have had children for fear of perpetuating this family trait.[6] Alexander proved to be a difficult, incompetent businessman, responsible for financial losses that were covered by William, the only member of the family capable of earning a living.[7] Relations between William and Alexander and his religious sister, Anna, were always strained; they openly disapproved of their brother's philanthropy, and they taxed William to the extreme.[8] The family story is one of a generous brother plagued by demanding siblings—worrisome financial millstones who continued to carry on their mischief, even after William's death. The troubled relationship with his siblings may provide some insight into William's silence about his parents; they simply disappear from his story.

Little is known of Maclure's formal education except that it was meager, nor do we know what sort of student he was. Since the family was not without means, William was tutored privately in his early years by a young clergyman, then educated in a public school in Ayr, instructed by a Mr. Douglas who was knowledgeable in the classics, mathematics, and science. From his later pronouncements, Maclure benefited from learning "practical facts" and mastering science and natural history, while he belittled his classical education, as he did English education in general with its bias toward classical and clerical instruction which reflected the tastes of the ruling class and was directed toward the middle-class student. Maclure thundered that the classics drilled into young minds were the remnants of an outworn tradition, myths of the "perfection" of the Greek democracies and the Roman republic, false because they were the progeny of unstable, unrepresentative political systems, "wandering in licentious anarchy," and the prey of "petty tyrants." Their age was barbarous, he felt, and could not measure up to "the present advanced state of civilization."[9]

Classical education had left Maclure "ignorant as a pig of anything useful," and what he had learned after years of schooling could now be acquired in six to eight months of proper education—the waste of it all![10] It did little or nothing to educate the children of the poor, to teach them "useful" information that would equip them to acquire their fair share of the nation's wealth, and it probably did not even prepare Maclure for a life in business. He considered it "an original sin" that classical education was being transferred from Europe to American schools.[11] His later involvement in the establishment of schools and libraries unquestionably derives from his own unsatisfactory scholastic experience, which laid the foundation for his radical thinking.

Maclure ended his formal instruction without going to a university, which left him with woefully inadequate chirographic skills—his writing often indecipherable, becoming smaller and smaller as time went on. It also left this intelligent man with remarkably little talent for grammar, spelling, and punctuation.[12] Indeed, for someone who read and wrote extensively, these failings were so pronounced and pervasive that they suggest a pathology or perhaps a lasting protest against his reviled classical education. Still, his extensive writings reveal an adequate vocabulary and an unadorned, forceful, polemical style of a man with a message, so that his intent was readily comprehensible. He was impatient to enter the practical world in which he would make his fortune, and if he did not excel as a schoolboy, he quickly took to commerce.

Maclure's implacable stance against religion and the clergy probably arose early, in reaction to the teaching of the Calvinist Church of Scotland (Presbyterian), which preached predestination, that man was born corrupt, steeped in sin, and that the only hope of salvation lay in a total dependence on God. To Maclure, formal religion that dominated the education of the young was a "delusion" that "led the human intellect astray, through the mysterious wilderness of deception, by the cunning intrigues of church and State." As a deist, he saw another world, one in which many people suffered terribly through no fault of their own, at the hands of a merciless upper class, abetted by the religious establishment. Significantly, he never mentioned any church affiliation for himself or his family, and he never explicitly revealed his personal view about God or the question of His existence. As for an afterlife, he asserted that he knew "nothing beyond the grave."[13] Religion had little to offer—possibly an ineffective ethical voice, but little more. Morals and ethics based on the golden rule, the Sermon on the Mount, and the teaching of Christ could be better taught in the school.

Although he undoubtedly learned from his father, he never acknowledged receiving any help or encouragement from him—a puzzling silence that suggests some difficulties between them, and changing his name from James McClure to William Maclure would signify rejection. Furthermore, in Maclure's mature, radical philosophy, the family unit was an obstacle to the education of children and the realization of a utopian society, a view that, though formulated through careful reasoning, must strongly derive from the conflict within his own family. As for family pride, he considered it "an extensive delusion," but this did not dissuade him from looking after family members.

With his rather unhappy upbringing, he could not wait to put his life in Scotland behind him. Evidently there was no real identification with Ayr and Scotland. Once he left the country of his birth and youth, he never mentioned or reminisced about it, and conversely, Ayr seemed unaware of its remarkable son despite his great success as a merchant, philanthropist, and scientist.[14] Maclure is not mentioned in Dunlop's book on Ayr, which lists and extols its native sons and the many luminaries it gave to the world. Perhaps they chose to ignore him because of his rebellious attitude toward traditional values—his radical political, social, and religious views. Maclure seems to have led a fugitive existence, a stateless, deracinated voyager, always on the go, visiting and residing in one country after another. He chose to become an American citizen while living the life of an American expatriate, and yet someone who met him in Paris in 1802 wrote: "William Maclure, who though Scotch by birth ... was thoroughly Americanized,"[15] no doubt because of his egalitarian principles and faith in the common man. According to Maclure, these derived mainly from British influences—"the old root from which we spring ... set down in a fruitfull Virgin soil, unpoluted by antient Superstition or prejudices. We had only the deffects to conquer we brought with us."[16]

Details about Maclure's youth are almost unknown. While William was still in his teens, the family moved to Glasgow and then to Liverpool, presumably for reasons of business. In 1778, when a mere fifteen years of age, William and his father visited America during the revolution. Although nothing is known of this trip, it is possible that his father was trying to salvage the remains of his business, which depended on free intercourse between England and America.

The New World must have impressed William favorably because, four years later, when he had just come of age and could act independently, he made a second visit, spending some time in New York for the purpose of exploring means of earning a living in the newly minted, independent Republic, and he probably established important business contacts, perhaps with the help of family connections, but this is not known. He returned to London as a member of the firm Miller, Hart and Co., which like other firms involved in overseas trade shipped manufactured goods such as textiles, hardware, and utensils to America, where they were wholesalers. Maclure was an energetic, aggressive merchant, for not only did he manage the European end of the business, he also supervised the firm's offices in New York and Richmond, Virginia. He then established a lumber business in Norfolk, Virginia (1782), that was run by a clerk—an operation independent of the New York firm. He may also have had business dealings in Canada.[17] The record is patchy, for little is known about the details of his business. He left no account of the nature of his commercial dealings that would explain just how he made a considerable fortune within a decade. With all his growing scientific and social awareness, it remains a puzzle where he found time to nurture his varied interests with such great success.

Between 1782 and 1797 Maclure was preoccupied with making money. Reminiscing, he wrote that he had retired from commerce in 1797.[18] Yet it is known that between 1796 and 1805 he founded trading firms in Philadelphia and Richmond. After years of mercantile experience during which he established a network of buyers and sellers, Maclure's commercial affairs were so well organized, they could be carried on by agents with only occasional consultation and instruction, the hallmark of a competent manager and administrator. As his involvement in commerce faded, his later enterprises were probably more investments than active participation in business. He was traveling extensively in Europe (1800–1808), entering seriously into geological study and collecting mineral specimens as he roamed from "the Mediterranean Sea to the Baltic and from the British Isles to Bohemia."[19]

A mercantile venture such as his was somewhat formulaic and straightforward in operation—buying and selling—with success measured immediately and precisely by profit or loss. His success in business, as evidenced by his fortune, convinced Maclure that he could use the same approach in his later career in the social and educational field, but this assumption was incorrect, and in the end proved costly. His establishment and maintenance of an educational system, with unconventional, experimental schools, and his later involvement in a utopian colony were vastly more complex affairs that could not be run from afar by assistants, however able and devoted. Hands-on direction and supervision were absolutely essential, but Maclure was unwilling to operate this way, insisting on the modus operandi that had been so successful in business.

Maclure's education never ceased, for he bears signs of the brilliant autodidact, reminiscent of Benjamin Franklin, a cosmopolite with experience in business. Similarities between the two men abound. Both were successful businessmen who retired early. Both were deists, profoundly critical of religion. Both became scientists, founded libraries and schools, and committed themselves to public service after they retired. Maclure read extensively, interacted with intellectuals and outstanding thinkers of the Enlightenment (often radical) in Europe and America, attended lectures in various countries, and became expert on disparate topics, derived partly from books but mostly from direct experience and by talking to people, and he tended to seize upon information that supported his ideas. Constant travel in Europe and America and his geological field studies left less opportunity for formal education. From information acquired, he arrived at firm opinions about science, education, and social and economic theory, expressed in later years in print, in a forthright manner in letters and journals, and in his *Opinions on Various Subjects,* a remarkable compendium of writings.

He had many axes to grind, and as he aged his views hardened into a bracing, bullying, argumentative style. He tended to pontificate at every opportunity and speak in maxims, and his later letters and writings were sometimes repetitive and tedious. Deficient in thoughtful, historical perspective, he derided historical study that would have added depth to his understanding. Not one to indulge in extended abstract thinking, he complained to President Jefferson that he could not understand the writings of Kant, and that in any event, it was of no use.[20] Maclure's colleague Samuel George Morton said of him, "Mr. Maclure's mind was devoted to matters of fact, seldom indulging in hypothesis, and never yielding himself, at least in his writings, to purely imaginative reflections."[21]

Contrasting characteristics abound in Maclure, a man who sought out and explored countries in dreadful turmoil that would discourage business, a wealthy man whose radical opinions could not have endeared him to his associates and upper-middle-class friends. He was able to afford anything he desired, but he lived frugally, deploring the materialism of

Americans. Having given up commerce, a good part of his life was devoted to the study of rocks and minerals—emblematic of the inanimate and the eternally stable—while at the same time engaging in the volatile affairs of humankind; perhaps one was a tonic for the other.

Although travel at the time was arduous and sometimes dangerous, he coursed the length and breadth of Europe, crossed the Atlantic Ocean twenty-two times, and traversed the Alleghenies over fifty times. There is uncertainty about how much time he actually spent in America during his earlier years. The whereabouts of this roving Scotsman, especially before 1805 when he began keeping a travel journal, are difficult to establish and can only be determined by the place of origin, the dates of his letters and articles, and the comments of his colleagues; what can be patched to-gether is spotty and not particularly informative.[22] On the other hand, he sometimes kept a record of the people he encountered, the inns he visited, their quality, the cost of food and lodgings, and the rocks and minerals he shipped to museums.[23]

Maclure as a young man must have learned valuable lessons in politics and economics by witnessing the American Revolution and the establish-ment of a promising democratic system of government that presided over thirteen states—to him, an exciting experiment. The American model "confirmed and consolidated all my democratic principles" so sharply in contrast to the rigid, authoritarian societies of Europe. There, many revolutions ended up with a new form of despotism, while the American Revolution led to the founding of an independent republic, amenable to the advancement of ordinary, industrious working men and women (and their children). Maclure saw greater promise in America, a land of abun-dant natural resources where there was no feudal tradition, where there was far more fluidity of social and economic classes, a greater possibility for an equitable distribution of wealth, and legal and constitutional guar-antees to protect the weak and the vulnerable. The temper of the American people had provided him with some assurance of success. And yet what he found in the newborn republic sometimes caused him to despair. At the turn of the nineteenth century, there was virtually no science in the country, and none was taught—"the Natural Sciences were almost as well understood by our Indians, as by the civilized inhabitants of our states"— and agricultural, manufacturing, and mining practices were primitive, far behind those of England. He had to look to the future.

With a rapidly expanding population, new fortunes could be made based on so much "empty" land and untapped natural resources. In 1830, looking back he wrote, "The fruits of freedom, augmented the resources of the country, far beyond anything before.... The last forty years experience of the United States, places freedom in a superior point of view to anything that could be imagined, and the rapidity of their progress compared with anything that preceded it staggers belief."[24] Captivated by the notion of American "exceptionalism," he filled his writings with praise for the United States as the most enlightened nation on earth. By contrast, European societies were presided over by stifling monarchies, beset by waste and corruption, and bolstered by religious establishments. As he aged, he saw even less hope for them.

Maclure declared, with some pride, that he had personally witnessed every significant revolution of his time, five in all, a claim which implies that he did not happen to encounter them by chance but rather had sought them out and studied them closely.[25] In periods such as these, his outspoken social and religious views must have taken hold, nurturing this idealistic but pragmatic reformer. Great social and political upheavals educated Maclure, but as far as is known he never actively participated in any of them, and as much as he responded to these heated movements in England, France, Spain, and Ireland, he carried on business as usual—his primary concern.

Maclure's earliest public expression of radical thought seems to have been in 1819 when he was fifty-five—rather late in life—although he expressed his dissenting views earlier in his travel diaries and made known to some friends his sympathy for the French Revolution and English radical thought in the last decade of the eighteenth century. He was on the best of terms with the geologist Benjamin Silliman of Yale, a staid, religious gentleman who didn't want to rock any boats, earnestly trying to reconcile the findings of geology with scripture, equating geological epochs with events in the Bible. This was an exercise that displeased Maclure. But not wanting to offend, rather than call Silliman to task, he gently stated that his proposal "is perhaps, as good a solution of what is completely out of our reach, as any other."[26]

At times, Maclure sounds like a doctrinaire Marxist (before Marx) in his vehement denunciation of formal religion and the privileged moneyed class that repressed the suffering mass of people. Unlike Marx, he held to the principle of private property, which he justified as a means by which responsible owners can better society—an idealistic view that had been promoted by Edmund Burke. Despite his stance as a pragmatic, truculent Philistine, many of his colleagues may not have been fully aware of his radical thinking, for in his direct dealings with people he was discreet, not confrontational, a gracious and generous gentleman, an admirer of the theater and opera, and a collector of prints. This cultured, seditious businessman was truly an anomaly. His "respectable" friends saw him not as a pariah but as an interesting and intelligent companion; Morton wrote politely of his "startling sentiments." Undoubtedly had he been less wealthy, his reception would have been less gracious. Although Maclure understood the problems of society in radical terms, he was in fact steeped in the values and attitudes held by most Americans from the beginning of its history—belief in private property, a free market, freedom of thought, individualism, and optimism about human nature.

Maclure lived in Paris during the height of the "Terror," the year of Louis XVI's execution, an epochal event for which Maclure shed few tears. Throughout the revolution and the years of Napoleonic dominion, he shuttled back and forth to London and traveled throughout Europe without interference. There is no evidence that he took an active part in the upheaval and endangered himself, as some other foreigners did, like Thomas Paine and Thomas Cooper. He observed and cheered from the sidelines, and much of his time was spent trying to free his brother John from a French jail into which he had been thrown by the revolutionary authorities, for reasons unknown. John languished in detention until 1794, when Robespierre was deposed and the revolutionary fever abated.

Maclure rarely spoke of the horrors unleashed by the revolution; he did not approve of the "Terror," which took 40,000 lives and ultimately consumed the reformers. The revolution, born of the extreme wretchedness of the populace and the inflexibility of the rulers, had resulted in important reforms, but in the end, all this was betrayed by Napoleon's seizure of power, followed later by the restoration of the venal Bourbon monarchy, a "distressful" event that induced a despairing Maclure to write in 1821: "The French are further removed from liberty than they were in the year 1788," and their leaders are "digging their own graves."[27]

The revolution was of such interest to Maclure that he acquired a major collection of revolutionary memorabilia for an American library—at

least 25,000 items that included pamphlets, journals of important partici-
pants, reports of the Tribunate, decrees, minutes of meetings, and financial
accounts—a treasure trove of information about the inner workings of the
uprising.[28]

Maclure spent some of 1793 and 1794 in Belfast, Ireland, witnessing major anti-English riots following the defeat of a home rule bill in
the House of Commons that would have emancipated Catholics—the
vast majority of the populace. Inspired no doubt by the outcome of the
American Revolution, and emboldened by Jacobin sentiment of Liberty,
Equality, and Fraternity, Irish Catholics protested their egregious lack of
representation—indeed, they were debarred by the English from institutions of higher learning and from any positions in government.[29] By 1798,
a full-blown civil war had erupted.

To him, revolutions were experiments in the way people redressed
their grievances—the more entrenched, inflexible, and absolute the controlling authority, with its hereditary privileges, the greater the violence
that followed when the have-nots took power, and he felt that violence in
certain circumstances was justified when there was no alternative. However, in countries with similar injustices but with stronger democratic
traditions, a peaceful solution could be implemented through the appropriate education of the young. A dominant, "useful," productive majority
with expertise and an enlightened attitude could be created that could
legitimately assume control through their vote. Education was the key, and
when Maclure came upon a school in Switzerland run by the revolutionary
originator of a progressive form of education, Johann Heinrich Pestalozzi,
he recognized immediately that this new method of educating poor children was a feasible way of solving many, if not all, of society's problems.
He had been provided with a strategy by which the ills of society could be
eliminated, and he would lose no time attempting to act. His dissatisfactions with both present education and the social order were wed, and he
planned to change both.

It is remarkable how little Maclure revealed of his personal life, or who
his associates were, or which thinkers influenced him—surprising, since
he wrote so many letters and commentaries and never hesitated to pass
judgment and express opinions on a wide range of subjects. The few words
there are about his brothers and sisters are mere complaints and irritations. Maclure rarely cites any of the outstanding political and economic

writers, radical or conservative, who may have influenced his thinking, nor do we know if he personally interacted with radicals and revolutionaries in London and Paris. Utilitarian and Enlightenment principles, central to Maclure's thinking, may very well have been shaped by contact with Jeremy Bentham in London and liberal thinkers in Paris. Surely as the host of bounteous dinners, and as a frequent dinner guest in London and Paris, he must have conversed with the leading intellectuals and reformers of the day and learned so much, but he remains almost silent about these encounters: so many brilliant conversations are lost forever.

His colleagues described him as "amiable," "affable and communicative," and "kind," having a "bold and original mind . . . a fondness for innovation," and "without dissimulation or disguise."[30] He was also described as "brilliant" and possessing "noble" views.[31] A range of judgments have been made by more modern authors who from their reading of the man have concluded that he was a "a complex mixture of down-to-earth pragmatism and visionary idealism" and that he could be "totally illogical."[32] Other scholars viewed him as having a "vehement nature," as "complicated, dogmatic," and as "hasty, dictatorial, [and] prone to take people at face value," who later grew "self-indulgent . . . testy and suspicious.[33] The disparity in judgments between those who knew him personally and those who studied him after his death gives some idea of the difficulty of really understanding this man. Later evaluations benefited from the larger picture, though they are based on his behavior at a time when he was a lonely, sickly man in Mexico, picturing himself a sorely tested victim. Yet all these bits and pieces do not comprise the whole of this elusive man.

As a very young man he was described as a "tall, red-haired Scot," while in his forties he was pictured as an attractive man, blue-eyed, fair-haired, almost six feet tall, with a "large head and a forehead, high and expanded," and his nose "aquiline," of a "naturally robust frame . . . capable of much endurance of privation and fatigue," which he attributed chiefly to his simple diet. Overall, "his collective features were expressive of that undisturbed serenity of mind which was a conspicuous trait of his character."[34] Despite his affability, few if any people really knew him well or could consider him a close friend, although he did have innumerable acquaintances.

It is probably no accident that an appreciation of Maclure's appearance and true nature eludes viewers of his portraits painted by Sully and

Northcote, two highly competent artists of the day, for neither seemed able to penetrate the shell that surrounded him. Northcote portrays Maclure as a Byronic hero, and perhaps this is not unjustified, for Byron and Maclure were comparable, fabulous contemporaries—driving, ambitious, and given to travel. Byron was a half Scot who grew up in Scotland, as did Maclure; both were charismatic, radical activists of great talent who were deeply affected by their unsatisfactory early education. However, there were notable differences in their sexuality: while Byron was promiscuous with both male and female partners, Maclure seems strangely sexless.[35] Although he was always accompanied by a young man in his geological expeditions, a situation that entails close living, there was never a hint of sexual involvement. One senses a reserve in the Northcote portrait of Maclure, a detachment that is peculiarly inconsistent with his intense involvement in the promotion of his philosophy, and yet there is a glint of proud purpose in his eyes.

He never married. Perhaps it would have been a hindrance to his incessant travel, and though he could be charming, in truth there was little humor in him, and a lonely melancholy underlies his life. A serious, commonsensical kind of a man, his interest in food was spartan. He was frugal in eating and drinking for reasons of health, leading one to conclude that there was something of the "dour Scot" in him, resistant to the idea of pleasure and damning the idle. On a pleasant trip to Mexico, where among the passengers were four "very agreeable ladies" enjoying themselves, he thundered like a wrathful Calvinist about the "eternal round of physical indulgences, the cancer of enjoyment, which anihilates the pleasure they were intended to nourish. The creature of ignorance and source of most of our diseases, the [delusion] of fashion, the idol of caprice and imagination." In contrast, he prescribed "the more simple road of reason and utility" because it was "more pleasant and lasting, rendering the labor of providing fessts [feasts] luxuries as unessary as the practice of consuming them are vicious, and contrary to Nature as well as to happiness."[36] Rather a wet blanket at the party.

Maclure is a curious exemplar of a strong man with a powerful sense of his own worth who is reticent about discussing himself, his considerable worldly goods, and his accomplishments. While he thought deeply about the problems beleaguering society, he was not introspective, and was uninterested in examining his own life and letting others know about it. After Maclure's death, Samuel George Morton of the Academy of Natural

Sciences of Philadelphia, who interacted extensively with Maclure, had to request the most elementary information about his past from Maclure's brother Alexander in order to write an obituary, a work of twenty-seven short pages and the only contemporary account of the man.[37] Here and there are brief references to Maclure. The information provides the barest outline of his early life known with certainty. In Maclure's remembrance, Morton wrote that he was "singularly mild and unostentatious in his manner; and though a man of strong feelings, he seldom allowed his temper to triumph over his judgment. Cautious in his intimacies, and firm in his friendships, time and circumstances in no degree weakened the affections of his earlier years."[38] He was surprisingly modest for a man who had succeeded by his own efforts and abilities, refusing to place his portrait in the frontispiece of his three-volume work, *Opinions*. Viewing the world, its institutions, and its foibles with a brutal, uncompromising honesty, he considered "reputation as a bubble, not worth the trouble of keeping afloat."[39]

Settling in America to become an American citizen most certainly was a great upheaval in his life, and retiring from business was a radical change. How would this vigorous man fill the days of his new life? Not one to drift, Maclure considered his choices and came to a clear decision. In a letter in which he discusses retirement, he wrote that for one's health, if for no other reason, one must continue to be useful and to have a plan. Referring to his own experience, he seemed to say that he had deliberately picked the fields of geology and of educational reform because these would permit him to be of benefit to society in a relatively direct manner, and at the same time they were of compelling interest to him. Off-handedly, however, he jested that his motivation was selfishness based on the degree of enjoyment he derived from his choice. Never an idle man who would be in danger of falling into bad habits, he chose "rock-hunting" rather than "deer or partridge hunting." Intensely restless, a man of action who did not believe in half measures, his urge to travel may have determined his choice of life's work, for in his first life he was to some extent a traveling salesman, and after retirement he became an accomplished field geologist who explored two continents.[40]

Politics as practiced in England and America with their party systems, patronage, and corruption, aided by a dishonest, biased press, disgusted Maclure.[41] Yet, despite his intense dissatisfactions, so extensively detailed in his essays and letters, zealous in his views, he was unwilling to take part in partisan politics to counter the abuse, and in fact he seemed to be deficient in the skills of the politician. This lack of direct involvement is typical of Maclure, reflecting his desire to remain aloof and to let others (delegated agents) become involved. His restless travel may be a reflection of his craving for independence that he would not compromise.[42] He abhorred entanglement, usually distancing himself from the site of action—always elsewhere—the invisible man exerting influence and control through letters posted from afar, from Mexico and Europe to New Harmony and Philadelphia. Perhaps one of the underlying motivations for Maclure's remarkable philanthropy was that the simple expenditure of funds allowed him to be "useful," without untidy, direct engagement.

Although Maclure held views that would have condemned him as a menace to Britain and France, there is no suggestion that he came to America for political asylum, as did so many other Scottish and English political radicals of the time—like Joseph Priestley, a victim of British repression, le comte de Volney, who fled French denunciation, and Thomas Paine, who fled for his life from both countries. Maclure was happy to move to the United States, not only because of his outrage at Europe's failings and America's promise but also for reasons of business.

Maclure was, in fact, a Jeffersonian republican, who believed that a democratic republic consisting of separate states was the best possible form of government. In an essay written in 1830, he exulted in the achievements of the very early republic, for "after the revolution, before the people were burdened with federal expenses, the States under their economical governments and free trade, recovered the losses and destruction of the revolutionary war, so as to lay a foundation for an unprecedented prosperity in the annals of mankind."[43] He was opposed to John Adams and Alexander Hamilton, Federalists whose goal was to establish an overriding central government that would levy taxes, dominate the will of the states, and might not be unhappy with a monarch of their own choosing.

Becoming an American, however, did little to change his habit of traveling back and forth to Great Britain and continental Europe. After 1800, he coursed the length and breadth of Europe as a one-man expedition, and he also roamed widely in the United States, always gathering information firsthand and informing his hosts of what he had learned elsewhere. In a world of imperfect communications, he was extremely knowledgeable, a fount of facts, stories, and opinions about the latest political, scientific, and economic tendencies on both sides of the Atlantic, and as a man of integrity, graciously bearing the authority of wealth and science, influential Europeans and Americans, including Thomas Jefferson, listened to what he had to say. And so this charming host and dinner guest, an addition to any salon, shuttled the latest information between the continents and from one part of America to another.

✳

TWO

Philadelphia (1796–1800)

Maclure came to the United States in 1796, became an American citizen, and settled in Philadelphia, with business interests in Richmond, Virginia. At the time of Maclure's arrival, Philadelphia was America's leading city and at the pinnacle of its glory, the second largest English-speaking city in the world, the commercial and financial center, and the political capital of the United States. As a former merchant, Maclure was undoubtedly cognizant of the fact that Philadelphia was by far the leading port for international trade in the country. The city had initiated trade with the Orient in 1784, and by 1801 almost half of the total imports from the East came to this port.[1]

Le duc de Liancourt, a French visitor, was effusive in his admiration of the city: "Philadelphia is not only the most beautiful city in the United States, it is one of the most beautiful in the world." It was a city of upright Quakers who could also boast of the most lavish entertainments and gatherings of society, often comparable to those of Europe which so troubled John Adams and Joseph Priestley.[2] A naïve Chateaubriand was shocked by the luxury and extravagance he encountered, for he had come to America as an exile expecting to find a state of honest simplicity in the mode of the early Roman republic.[3] It must have been clear to a cosmopolitan, social activist like Maclure that Pennsylvania was the most multicultural and democratic of all the former British colonies, and it was particularly attractive because it was not theocratic in its tendencies, as was New England, nor did it have great landowning families, as did New York and Virginia—reminiscent of European monarchies.

Still, it did have an elite, an aristocracy that deemed itself superior to all others in the young republic. An English traveler found that "among the uppermost circles in Philadelphia, pride, haughtiness, and ostentation are conspicuous," and he had little good to say about its lower orders, whom he found inhospitable and impolite. In order to convince strangers that they were free and independent souls, they were "surly" and "wanting in good manners."[4] Perhaps this upper class was more acceptable to Maclure because many of them, although wealthy and powerful, came from a Quaker background, which he so much admired, and its members were "useful" intellectual leaders in the community. He could not condemn Philadelphians for their wealth alone because, after all, he himself was wealthy.

The intellectual life of Philadelphia, where the spirit of Benjamin Franklin still lingered, was unequaled in America. Thomas Jefferson, a man interested in natural history, was vice president of the United States and president of the American Philosophical Society, considered the home of the intellectual elite of the new republic. One of the many institutions Franklin helped found, the Publick Academy in the City of Philadelphia, had become the University of Pennsylvania. The Library Company of Philadelphia graced the city, making Philadelphia's library facilities the largest in the nation. Benjamin Rush, a native son, was an exemplar of the American Enlightenment, the most famous physician in America, "father" of American psychiatry, signer of the Declaration of Independence, and the man who suggested to his friend Thomas Paine that he write *Common Sense*. Charles Willson Peale's Museum, a repository of natural treasures that was looked upon as one of the wonders of the world, was housed in the American Philosophical Society's headquarters on Chestnut Street. Patently, Maclure did not suffer intellectual isolation in his chosen city.

Maclure became a member of Philadelphia's intelligentsia, and his colleagues—chemists, architects, lawyers, linguists, naturalists, and university professors—kept him informed of the latest currents of thought. A hospitable man, he hosted lively dinners, one of which was attended by Jefferson, whom he had befriended in Richmond. Besides Jefferson, guests at one dinner party included Julian Ursyn Niemcewicz, a Polish traveler who recorded the evening's discussions. Other guests were le comte de Volney, an enlightened French scholar and traveler, expert in geography, geology, sociology, and linguistics, who lived with Maclure for a while, and Dr. Giambattista Scandella, a Venetian exile with an interest in natural history who found refuge in Philadelphia and also lived in Maclure's home. Volney, an influential thinker, was an important conduit of the French Enlightenment in America who made a great impression on Jefferson.

The evening proved to be one of "instructive and interesting conversation" about such matters as the cultivation of wild oats and rice and the existence of wild horses—"Spanish runaways"—west of the Mississippi River.[5] Articulate, widely traveled, and knowledgeable, Maclure would not have been out of place in this select group, dedicated to the knowledge and understanding of their rational world. Years later Jefferson wrote to Maclure that he had fond memories of that evening. A library was to be established in Charlottesville that he hoped would attract Maclure to spend time there, while making Monticello his headquarters.[6]

In 1799 Maclure was elected to membership in the American Philosophical Society. He is known to have attended the Society's meetings while residing in Philadelphia in 1808–1809; at one he read his seminal paper on the geology of the United States.[7] The APS was the very heart of the intellectual life of the city where the exchange of ideas between physicians, lawyers, businessmen, and natural scientists took place. The arts, literature, and history were also topics of discussion but were of secondary interest. Conservative exclusivity gave rise to an assembly of outsiders— impoverished young freethinkers, radicals, and socialists who, having been ignored or rejected by the APS, founded the Academy of Natural Sciences of Philadelphia (1812), where science was freely and vigorously pursued. The Academy, more to Maclure's taste, was to benefit and in fact survive through his largesse.

Even before he settled in America, Maclure had developed an interest in natural history and science. A special delight in the subject is evident in his declaration that "a naturalist is never without healthful, and respectable, as well as useful occupation, which strews the path of life with flowers."[8] He was an amateur in an America among many such amateurs, for the rise of professional science and the full-time specialized scientist were a few decades off.[9] Maclure's first years in Philadelphia, which lasted until 1800 when he returned to Europe for a prolonged visit, were spent cultivating the intellectual elite and taking part in biological and geological field trips with knowledgeable companions like Dr. Scandella and

Thomas Peter Smith, a young geologist and chemist. Collecting minerals and geological and fossil specimens was undoubtedly of enormous heuristic importance to these eager students. Fashionable gentleman of the time often took pride in their collections of fossils and rocks and kept up with the literature, such as it was.

As part of his education, Maclure traveled about rural Pennsylvania, New Jersey, Virginia, and upper New York, with the requisite stop at Niagara Falls. Some field trips were described by Niemcewicz and Maclure—trips to the Pennsylvania and New Jersey countryside around Philadelphia, the Pine Barrens and coast of New Jersey, and the iron forges in Bucks County. In some instances, their expeditions began at Maclure's home, and after walking the entire day—an almost leisurely, Pickwickian ramble—they would spend the nights at inns along the way. Assiduous students, they observed and noted everything in sight, carrying with them books that they studied when inclement weather prevented exploration. As amateurs in the early age of scientific exploration and experimentation, where description was sufficient, they were wanting in knowledge and system, content to collect, describe, and classify as best they could the numerous plants, animals, minerals, and to describe rock formations they happened upon in this fresh and unexamined New World. They made personal discoveries that completed or confirmed the record, looking to Europe for innovative interpretations and explanations.

Upon returning to Philadelphia, they shared their experiences with others so that the general base of knowledge was enhanced—by word of mouth and to some extent by publication in journals such as the *Medical Repository* and *Silliman's Journal.* Interest in the field of natural history and science broadened as the overall level of scientific experience grew, facilitated by an increase in wealth that permitted individuals to devote more of their time to study. Within a few decades a body of professional scientists and scientific institutions, with technical vocabularies and publications, sprang up throughout the country.

Although Maclure had a broad range of interests in natural history, he concentrated on geology and mineralogy. Traveling and gathering facts over many years, he became an expert on the natural resources in America and Europe. By 1808, when he returned to the United States, he was operating at the level of a professional, able to complete and publish *Observations of the Geology of the United States,* a work considered to be a major contribution to American geology that justified his encomium, the "father" of American geology. Maclure and his companions, with their far-ranging interests, also studied local economies and the behavior of the rural populace. Social, economic, and scientific matters were constantly falling under their scrutiny, and they educated themselves mainly through firsthand experience rather than through books and other publications.[10]

In one of his explorations of Pennsylvania, Maclure befriended Joseph Priestley, an extraordinary English Unitarian minister and scientist, famous for the discovery of oxygen. A radical, he had fled to Philadelphia and settled in Northumberland, Pennsylvania, after a Birmingham mob had destroyed his home and laboratory (1791). During their visit, Maclure and his friends induced this famous man to come along on a botanical and geological expedition. Perhaps here, together in intimate contact, Maclure was exposed to Priestley's radical political and theological thought. Happily, Priestley found the fieldwork of natural history to be an "amusement" and a "novelty," and if he kept at it for a few weeks, he would begin to "learn it and appreciate it"; the outing was a temporary escape from "books, and even chemistry."[11]

As the year 1798 came to a close, Maclure and Dr. Scandella visited Richmond, Virginia, where they happened to meet Benjamin Henry Latrobe. Maclure had first seen Latrobe in the lobby of a hotel in Richmond and, upon inquiring about the stranger, was warned that "he was a crazy man who gathered weeds and stones in the woods," an answer that indicates the general level of appreciation of natural science by the citizenry at the time. Latrobe, a recent immigrant from England, was a brilliant if difficult man, an engineer and architect, later considered by some as the "founder" of both professions in America. Maclure made his acquaintance and "found him a man of merit, who did more in less time, than I had known done by anyone before."[12] He especially admired him because not only did Latrobe know theory, he was also a practical architect who knew how to lay bricks. In return, Latrobe had the highest regard for Maclure, expressed in a letter to Scandella—"There are few men whom I esteem and love as much as I love him."[13] A first-class naturalist, Latrobe published several original papers on natural history in the *Transactions of the APS* and was inducted into the APS with Maclure. Together, the two men studied the coalfields, soil, and stratification of rocks in Virginia.[14]

Latrobe was precisely the kind of educated, "useful" man that Maclure admired, and he was glad to help him. He induced Latrobe to move to Philadelphia, where he lived with Maclure until he was settled on his own. With Maclure's support, Latrobe flourished. He was introduced to influential citizens, prospective clients, and the most prominent intellectuals in Philadelphia. Scandella, Volney, Maclure, and Latrobe formed a convivial circle of friends that sometimes included Jefferson. As an engineer Latrobe designed the municipal water supply of Philadelphia, and as an architect he designed many important buildings in Philadelphia. Later appointed surveyor of the public buildings of the United States, he directed the completion of the Capitol building and the White House before they were burned by the British in the War of 1812.

Though a constant voyager, traveling extensively throughout Europe and America, Maclure based his affairs in Philadelphia and Paris. After he retired from active commercial activity, he entrusted his affairs in Philadelphia to a business manager and agent. Maclure then devoted most of his time to philanthropic, educational, and scientific concerns, making his views known in numerous essays—many of which were collected in *Opinions on Various Subjects, Dedicated to the Industrious Producers,* which he published himself in the 1830s. His compulsion to travel, observe, and learn was not only in his nature, it had been indispensable for his business interests early in his career, and this provided the financial means by which he could pursue his later passions.

The disparity in wealth between rich and poor that he came upon in his travels convinced him that the equalization of wealth and power between economic classes was the major task of the day. Maclure seemed to live in a constant state of disgruntlement that found expression in almost all discussion, especially about politics and economics. However preoccupied he was with geology, the strategy by which wealth and power could be fairly distributed among all members of society was the central question of his life, and the means by which this could be brought about came in the course of his travels when he was introduced to Johann Heinrich Pestalozzi and his radically new system of education.

THREE

✳

Political and Economic Philosophy

Without dissimulation or disguise . . . he aimed at an intellectual
exaltation which, to common observation at least, seems incompatible
with the wants and impulses of our nature.

Samuel George Morton, *"A Memoir of William Maclure, Esq."*

The seeds of Maclure's radicalism can be traced to his early experience. He seems to have been a privileged but disaffected, unhappy young man who judged the world around him to be flagrantly unjust, and most of his formal education a waste of time. In all probability the ground was prepared by witnessing the suffering of workers in his native Scotland during the early Industrial Revolution. While factory owners prospered, the workers were savaged. Small farmers, driven from the countryside by the landowning aristocracy, migrated to dreary, gray towns where they worked in factories from dawn to dusk. Wages were kept at a subsistence level, and in time of crisis and economic dislocation the workers suffered even more. Later, Maclure's suspicions became certainties as he traveled throughout Europe, seeking support for his convictions, which he found in abundance. Ludicrously, he observed and formulated strategies to alleviate the misery of the working class while running his business and making a fortune.

Yet he seemed reluctant to express his views fully in print. In 1808 he wrote in his diary: "Prejudice is the support of bigotry and tyranny. Ignorance is the chains of slavery and the stronghold of oppression. Those who endeavor to enlighten the masses will make enemies of that swarm of impostors who live by the stupidity and ignorance of the people."[1] Humankind must be saved from itself. His hardening convictions were increasingly expressed as maxims.

He frequently published outspoken essays and commentaries on these matters in *The Disseminator of Useful Knowledge* (1828–), and in his wide-ranging, three-volume opus, *Opinions on Various Subjects, Dedicated to the Industrious Producers,* appearing between 1831 and 1838.[2] Some discussions were based on John Gray's writings, which were so radical Maclure feared Gray would not be published in any American journal, and so he himself had Gray's lectures on human happiness published in Philadelphia.[3]

Maclure was influenced by the brilliant and prolific thinkers of the Scottish Enlightenment. From Hume he inherited both critical, skeptical reasoning and a commonsensical viewpoint. Much of what Maclure has to say about economics and its impact on culture and morality echoes Adam Smith. They both approved of private ownership of property and preached a laissez-faire private enterprise by which people would increase the public well-being and bring about an equitable distribution of wealth through self-interest, creating and taking advantage of opportunity, without government interference. Yet they remained aware of the potential evil that could come from unrestricted capitalism. Harmful, antisocial activity (such as speculation and the formation of monopolies) would have to be thwarted. Both men supported unrestricted free trade, both felt that economic freedom was the foundation of political liberty, and both favored a universal educational system.

Underlying Maclure's view of society was his belief that "society in every stage of civilization, is divided into two great classes or parties, viz those who labour with their hands, and *produce,* therefore called the *productive* class; and those who, from the accumulation of industry, hereditary power, or pillage, have acquired a sufficiency to live without labour ... and have been called the *nonproductive.*" It is the people who work who have created "all the revenue of every society," four-fifths of which finds its way into the pockets of the nonproducers. Indeed, according to Gray, if the producers kept most of the wealth they produced, they would only have to work a few hours each day, with the remaining time devoted to "leisure and moral improvement."[4] The interest of the governors, who are rich and nonproductive, is "opposite, and contradictory" to that of the governed, the laborer, an arrangement that is not "casual"; its origins lie in the "nature and organization of mankind."[5]

Maclure's thinking was based on the fact that the productive working class, by far the largest part of the populace, had always been powerless to keep its fair share of the wealth it created, because those who govern, motivated by self-interest, maintain control by the laws they promulgate and their ownership of the means of production. They exploit the laborer by managing the legal and banking systems, the military, police, the press, and the process of education. Through their ability to levy indirect taxes and create tax exemptions, they force the productive class to pay for their follies. The religious establishment is an important part of this exploitative process. Maclure makes the critical point that exploitation can take place whether the government is democratic or not. So long as the people are ignorant, even in a democracy, the elected leaders can be little better than despots and monarchs who do not have the interests of the masses at heart and are incapable of satisfying the needs of the people. A small group is in control that is willing and able to exploit the majority.[6]

How can society be reformed to eliminate the great disparity in wealth, power, and privilege and redistribute property between the small minority of "nonproducers" and the great majority of "producers"? According to Maclure, "Property is the foundation of most of the qualities, good or bad, of society. Divide it into nearly equal portions, you divide knowledge and power, which constitute freedom, and a due proportion of those ... ingredients, forms a mixture that enables all reasonable beings to participate in the greatest possible happiness they are capable of enjoying."[7] Maclure came to believe that the answer was proper education of the masses living in a democratic society with universal suffrage. Educated to know what their own interests are, they would elect representatives who would control the rich minority by legislation, which would assure the majority that its interests were carefully guarded. When a majority could be obtained in the legislatures, radical reform in all the civil, fiscal, general and particular laws, rules and regulations would take place, and a socially responsible distribution of private wealth would ensue.[8]

The process did not require confiscation of wealth and property by force. Maclure was zealous, but not bloody-minded, for he wanted an

equality "not by depressing the usurped superiority of the privileged orders . . . but by the elevation of the most useful classes."[9] Effective reform
could only come from the bottom up, as opposed to the view that those at
the top, the oligarchs, could be changed by persuasive argument, which
in Maclure's opinion remained in the realm of ineffective "liberal" theory,
promoted by men of property; rights have never been bestowed upon the
poor from above, without conflict. According to Maclure, true reform
could only come from the efforts of working people, in their overwhelming numbers, looking after their own interests—"none but the millions
can benefit the millions"—but it troubled him that the millions were slow
to perceive the way to remedy their miserable state. Fifty years had passed
since the birth of the United States without the workers realizing that the
vote of an enlightened electorate was critically important. Reform and the
"diffusion of wealth" would take time and, in fact, was not inevitable.[10]

He believed that the greatest promise for real reform lay in the United
States, the hope of the civilized world, despite the denial of citizenship to
native Americans, the existence of slavery, and the disadvantaged status of
women. It was a young country without a crippling feudal tradition, dedicated to the noble ideals of freedom, equality, and suffrage, codified in a
written constitution designed to thwart future despotism. Enlightenment
theory was now put into practice for the first time in a democratic country
permeated with a sense of optimism, opportunity, and inevitable progress,
where the possibility of instituting public education and redistributing
wealth was greatest. As Maclure wrote, "On the success of the working
class' experiment, is staked the happiness of the civilized world."[11] Still,
Maclure noted with some concern that class differences had increased
in the United States during the 1820s. An oligarchy of wealthy men had
arisen, and the rights of workers were in a more precarious state than in
the first decade of the new century. He feared for true democracy and was
convinced that the forces of corruption and deterioration were always
present and poised to assert themselves, even in a country with a constitution and an elective system of checks and balances.

Reform would not be easy. Maclure urged workers to ignore the ridicule heaped on them by the elite (John Adams, Alexander Hamilton, and
the Federalists) for their noble aspirations. They must remain steadfast
and focused on their goal, and they must withstand the powerful forces
arrayed against them, keeping in mind that in the future, no one would be

happy in a society that deprives a group of its rights—it would be "against nature."

In countries with hardened authoritarian governments and an abused, deeply unhappy citizenry, Maclure was not averse to revolution and the use of force if there was no other way. But resort to violence was a tragedy that was to be avoided if possible. "A mild, legal and moral revolution through the medium of the ballot box" was always preferable.[12] In one of Maclure's essays in which he discussed revolution, he appealed to those who would deny the worker their due share: "We can gain nothing by anarchy and confusion, therefore [we] will not produce it ourselves or permit you to do it. We do not want to shed your blood, and shall take care that you be not permitted to shed ours. We are the millions, possessed of sufficient physical force, moral courage and political power, to protect our rights."[13] Underlying the message there rests confidence—and a warning. With revolutionary, barricade fervor he exhorted the masses: "The millions, in all countries, have toiled and labored long enough for the benefit of their masters: it is high time they should begin to do something for themselves, before they may be deprived of the means [by] the universal suffrage."[14]

Despite the fact that Maclure, a radical, was not a true revolutionary in deed, he saw that without the ballot box there was no way to rid the country of an inflexible, entrenched, autocratic regime with its supporting religious and military establishments. Given the hardened positions of the classes in France, he felt that the Revolution would "permit the millions to enjoy a little more of their own property than had been allowed them," and later, commenting on the status of French people in 1835, he observed "an immense progress toward equality in the short time during and since the Revolution, entirely owing to some of the impediments to the free circulation of property and knowledge being removed."[15] In fact, Maclure believed that the French Revolution achieved what education could bring about in a democratic society with universal suffrage.

Dwelling upon the positive accomplishments of the Revolution, Maclure looked to events in France rather than England for the solution to the pressing social problems of the time, refusing to condemn the Revolution as did most English and many Americans. To him, the recurring appeal by the ruling class to avoid trouble in the "public interest" was a ploy to promote their own selfish interests. He was heartened by what the Revolution had achieved—the end of tyranny, the destruction of the old aristocracy and the feudal system, the profound weakening of the church, and the betterment of the lives of the peasants. Maclure was pleased to see an end to tithes levied by the church and the loss of lands and hereditary privileges by the aristocracy. He never ceased to admire the constitution written by the Constitutional Assembly, and he felt that out of the chaos arose something of a meritocracy (in keeping with Enlightenment principles) which opened up opportunities for large numbers of people, hitherto excluded from the system. To Maclure, the French Revolution was one of the great events in the history of humankind, for it was the first time that the mass of people changed the course of their lives through political action, providing them with hope that power could belong to all—the very foundation of democracy. Maclure declared, "An equality of property has been produced in France by the equal and impartial laws of their revolution, such as never before."[16]

Maclure did not want a state of anarchy, "the bastard brother of liberty," although he thought it was of some value because it "taught the millions to take care of themselves." The nightmare of anarchy would become a reality if the working classes dismantled the existing system after "influential rulers of every country, by their extravagance, pillage, and misrule, force the people to take the management of their affairs, as has happened lately more than once.... they [will] have none but themselves to blame for the consequences that will certainly fall on them."[17] He was sufficiently hardheaded to see that if the laboring class gained too much power, democratic government might be overthrown, and mob rule would prevail. Countervailing forces were needed to create a balance of knowledge, property, and power between groups with different interests, and where the balance existed one found the greatest happiness for all. At the same time, he recognized the need in this mix for educated individuals without venal interests.

A realist who was aware of the weaknesses of humankind, he knew that power corrupts and that representatives elected by the workers, with their newly acquired power, would soon become consumers and would begin to identify with the elite. He wanted a strong system that would minimize the damage that could be done by the weakness of men entrenched in positions of trust. This could be achieved by careful selection of representatives, term limits in power (no more than two sessions), frequent elections, and salaries that were in line with those of the people they represented.[18]

A profound distrust of government control and a belief in private property might give rise to the cynical view that there was a self-serving element in his lofty views. But to Maclure, the question was not one of ownership but what the individual does with wealth and how it was acquired. The making of a fortune was moral and honorable if it was spent on the improvement of society. To Maclure, the real enemies were those greedy members of the wealthy class who maintained their worldly goods and their "undeserved power and advantage" by abusing their position, noting especially the "absurdity of inherited wealth" that continued the injustice from one generation to the next.

Like many contemporary liberal social thinkers, he considered the masses benign and government corrupt, with great potential for evil enrichment. Maclure's skepticism of government was extreme because "rulers of a free people are as effective in proportion to their general and useful knowledge," which almost without exception they lacked. Among all the leaders, only Jefferson knew anything about science, which Maclure believed was at the very foundation of the future success of the republic. Despairingly he commented, "Unfortunately all governments that has yet existed, has attended to everything in proportion to their inutility, and left the most useful in total neglect, which requires the aid of the people's purse which the rulers too often consider as their own and forget what they were placed in power for."[19]

He condemned the notion that some citizens were unworthy of the right to vote (women, black people, and those without property). Although Maclure and Jefferson cannot be considered populists, they did advocate universal suffrage because they had an abiding confidence in the good sense of the people. And yet Maclure's faith in the common man sometimes faltered, for he also expressed the opinion that the masses must be "controlled" until they are properly educated to think rationally. On observing that citizens of Lyons were "happy and content" to see the last of Napoleon, whom he admired, Maclure concluded that these people were "dissatisfied and ... must be kept under a strong government, and suppressed."[20] These sentiments would suggest that Maclure was less interested in bringing about a truly democratic form of government than he was in advancing his social and economic views through education. Although he spoke of reform through universal suffrage of an enlightened electorate to achieve his aims, it would seem that a despotic form of government would do for the present. However, the democratic approach was preferred. Whichever path was taken would depend on the social and psychological state of the people involved and the level of enlightenment of the monarch. Unfortunately, all extant monarchs were unacceptable to Maclure, and the only reservation he had about his admired Napoleon was that he did not appreciate Pestalozzian education. Maclure's demons were inequality of wealth and power among the people, corruption in government, and incompetent governance, all of which were to be eradicated by one means or another.

One of the major tenets of socialism is collective or governmental ownership and direction of the means of production and distribution of goods produced and property held in common. Although Maclure has been called a utopian socialist, and was a significant actor in the movement's history at New Harmony, Indiana, in fact, the label cannot be applied to him. Some of his beliefs are part of the socialist dogma, such as his faith in the virtuous working man, but most are not. He believed in free enterprise and in private property; that the skilled and productive should be paid more; and that everyone should receive their fair share according to how productive they were and to what extent they were able to use what they earn for the social good. Distribution should be equitable rather than equal, a process that would become exceedingly complex in a burgeoning industrial economy with its great wealth and profits, where the line between public and private was growing increasingly important. Maclure did not seem to expand on this question, though he himself attempted to live by the noble standards he advocated. Neither did he clearly discuss in any practical detail the distribution of wealth and the question of cooperative ownership. He formulated a political and economic system, an eclectic collection of notions, that had as its aim social justice in a utopia of his own definition, to be brought about through a democratic government that renewed itself by the vote of well-educated "producers."[21] This was the key to Maclure's "radical" program of reform.

In his call for change, his denunciations were sometimes intemperate. This rich ex-merchant sounded like an overheated revolutionary, demanding the redistribution of wealth—a demand that if satisfied would act against his material interest. He considered himself a model for the enlightened possessor of worldly goods, and as a useful and "productive citizen" he distanced himself from the corrupt, ostentatious rich by denying himself what money can buy, proclaiming that in order to advance his cause, "I have ceased all gratification from the physical appetites." For many years he was an ascetic, moderate in his eating habits, and a teetotaler, living frugally and spending almost nothing on himself. When he bought houses in Paris and in New Harmony, he permitted them to be used as schools for boys and girls and as residences for visitors. In Philadelphia, he set up a printing press that printed the Academy's journal in his home. In line with David Hume's notion that "man is a bundle of habits," Maclure believed that for a lifetime of benefit, the early education of children must impart habits of moderation, and that enjoyment of the physical appetites should be limited.[22]

Maclure seemed to think that he could inspire reform (at least in part) by setting himself up as an exemplar of the virtuous rich man—a model for others—who would change the world through the judicious expenditure of his wealth, honestly acquired. Maclure's astonishing philanthropy and generosity did not spring from charitable feelings or kindheartedness but from a philosophic principle. Wealth entailed private responsibility, and the reward for the moral philanthropist was the privilege of retaining control of the redistribution process, bypassing government intervention. However indirect, this was the means by which a producer was justified in owning a larger part of what he or she produced, and he claimed that he enjoyed giving away his wealth more than he enjoyed accumulating it.

The events taking place in Great Britain, France, and the United States during the 1790s and early nineteenth century, witnessed by Maclure firsthand, tempered his thinking. The fury of the French Revolution and the shattering of the ancient social order alarmed the English establishment and emboldened English radicals in the early nineteenth century to broadcast their views through the publication of pamphlets, lectures, and public meetings. What was happening in Paris had important consequences for the rest of the world. Maclure, in Paris and London during this time, exposed to articulate political and social activists, was most certainly sympathetic to their cause and their ideas, which resonated in his essays for the rest of his life. But, however his notions fit in with those of other thinkers and leaders, there is little certain knowledge of whom he knew among these people and what books he read.[23] We judge only by his later radical pronouncements on political philosophy, religion, and economics.

In Paris, where Maclure spent most of his time, his friends were liberal, if not radical. They included le comte de Volney, befriended while an émigré in Philadelphia, and Jefferson's friend Joel Barlow, a liberal expatriate American in Paris, a poet who belonged to a society dedicated to the reform of the English Parliament.[24] Another reformer he probably knew in London was Maurice Margarot, a politically active London merchant who was indicted in the 1790s by a judge of the High Court determined to find him guilty of seditious practices; he was transported to Australia for fourteen years. Margarot was a member of the Corresponding Society of London, which "under the pretence of reforming parliament [demanding universal suffrage and annual parliaments], was evidently of a dangerous and destructive tendency, with a deliberate and determined intention to disturb the peace of the community, and to subvert the constitution of the country." Maclure admired the Corresponding Society, which "imitated" their French counterpart and was considered by the English "the avowed enemies of this country who at present usurp the government of France."[25] The proceedings of this case were recorded and published in New York and Philadelphia.

An important radical voice raised at that time was William Godwin's, the extremely popular author of *Enquiry Concerning Political Justice,* a work that set forth the notion that politics emerged from ethics and that the two were inextricably linked. Any person interested in social and political questions had to read Godwin or attend his lectures, and this Maclure most certainly did when he was living in London. Like Maclure, Godwin was a utilitarian with libertarian views who argued that the production and distribution of goods should be entirely free of government supervision or control.[26] Maclure may have also had contact with the radical thinker Francis Place, and he definitely conversed with, and was influenced by the utilitarian Jeremy Bentham, whose views on education, equality of women, and the participation of the masses in government were similar to his own. Maclure's writings are heavily indebted to Bentham's thinking, and in fact Maclure considered himself a Benthamite who believed that happiness would be maximized in a society in which the classes lived in harmony and where there was equality in knowledge, property, and power.[27]

Maclure not only witnessed the debates for representative government in Britain. He also spent much time in France, where he was undoubtedly influenced by the physiocrats whose liberal economic theories were much like those of Adam Smith on such matters as the essentiality of improvements of agricultural techniques, the stability of farm prices, and unrestricted freedom of trade. Simplified schemes of taxation proposed by the physiocrats, based on land value (later advocated by Henry George in the United States), were repeatedly mentioned by Maclure in his writings. Direct taxation was the "most just and equitable mode" because "everyone pays in proportion to what he possesses," while indirect taxation is based on consumption, placing an unfair burden on those who can least afford it—"always unjust and often cruel; falling heavier on the poor man than the rich." Maclure also objected to indirect taxation because it was an uncertain form of income that required a larger number of people to collect the taxes, inevitably increasing the possibility of corruption, and abuse of power. The fact that indirect taxes were levied by every "aristocratic and despotic government" was proof enough for Maclure that "it serves their purpose and facilitates their tyranny."[28] He deplored the situation in Europe where the church, aristocracy, and landowners were able to evade taxation by one manipulation or another, while the burden fell on the lower orders to finance the excesses of the monarchies in their military adventures.

In an ideal state, the size and power of the central government was to be as small as possible consistent with effective governance, because in Maclure's view (and Jefferson's), humans were so easily corrupted by the power inherent in government, especially in the centralized operations of the federal executive branch. To minimize this danger, Maclure advocated that even lesser offices be decided by annual elections, so that elected representatives would be replaced before they became entrenched, controlling wealth that was not theirs. Electing representatives for long periods of time (six years) was equivalent to granting them a hereditary privilege. Those who ruled would lose contact with those who were ruled and would escape their close scrutiny. Smaller government and lower taxes, as advocated by Maclure, would reduce the incentive and opportunity for abuse.[29] In Maclure's opinion, history had shown that a central government was more susceptible to seizure by a despot. A democratic federation of "the smallest aggregates of political societies into a social body, bound together by their mutual interest" as seen in the New England townships was least likely to be subverted. Townships cooperated with one another to serve their own ends and not those of an elite.[30]

Maclure was uneasy with a federalism that "imitates the centralism of the aristocracies of Europe, so far as to collect taxes, raise armies, and maintain their own courts of law and judiciary with jurisdiction over every state of the Union."[31] While Maclure realized that federation was necessary, he remained wary of the encroachment of Washington's authority over the twenty-four states because edicts from Washington could have disastrous consequences. When a centralized government borrows money or prints paper money, it assumes a debt, deplored by Maclure because "it mortgages posterity without its consent," and in the end, it is the productive class that pays off the larger part of that obligation; this was the case following the War of 1812.[32] During the American Revolution, a centralized government in Philadelphia had printed paper money at will, without backing by specie; the value of the paper soon plummeted, causing untold pain and turmoil. Maclure was critical, but he must have been aware of the dilemma of the young republic, in which his desired state legislatures were so dominant they had crippled the operation of the Congress and the federal government, depriving them of their rightful ability to levy taxes to prosecute the war, and so they were forced to print money. This untenable situation was remedied at the Philadelphia Convention of 1787, when the dominance of the federal government over the states was established, making governance of the nation effective by enabling the government to tax and provide itself with an income and to regulate the currency.[33] However, Maclure felt that the constitution, which he admired in part, led to too great a centralization of power. It was a "passive, wordy, and undefined document" that "does not work well in practice," giving rise to endless debate, and setting the central government and state legislatures on a "collision course" with respect to functions best left to the states. Clearly, a proper distribution of power was needed. He thought highly of the Swiss model of federation of cantons, a democratic system in which a restrained aristocracy had a place and a federal government had jurisdiction only in foreign affairs.[34]

Maclure envisioned a world in which there was no need for conscription, or a standing military establishment, or fear of war. During the French Revolution the soldier and the citizen were closely allied and held a common interest, and so a national guard came into being—"a free militia, who elect their own officers"; this was the only kind of military establishment that was compatible with freedom. While Maclure gloried in the relative freedom from tyranny, corruption, and oppression in the United States, he was troubled by its standing army (and a military school), a potential source of despotic usurpation of power, as had happened in Mexico.[35]

When Maclure came to the United States, the Industrial Revolution was in its infancy, helped along by the immigration of skilled industrial workers from England and Scotland who sought to escape the desperate conditions in the old country. What had happened in England and Scotland was now beginning to take place in the New World. Despite the anti-industrial, anti-urban sentiments of Presidents Jefferson and Jackson, the march of industrial capitalism was relentless, creating great riches for a few. As the wealth of the nation grew, the disparity in the distribution of wealth between workers and owners increased. In such a society, a disproportionate fraction of the profits that accrued from labor-saving devices (which were rapidly being invented) were going to the owners, both in Europe and the United States.[36] Whatever the liability, Maclure recognized that the growth of industrialism and trade was inexorable, and he never saw it per se as the villain (nor machines as instruments of the devil).

According to Maclure, inequality in America was due "to the injustice of those in power, granting exclusive monopolies to stock, land and bank speculations, the profits of which enrich the few at the expense of the many."[37] Even the "free press" in a democracy was rendered impotent because the rich had the power to buy and control it.[38] His letters and essays are filled with accusations against "monopolizing bank charters" and lawyers "filling their pockets with bank and other corporation fees."[39] He insisted that the chartering of banks, by those in power handing monopolistic power to the few, leading to their enrichment, should be abolished.[40] Chartered banks held the "exclusive privilege of coining paper money... without personal responsibility or limitation of dividend."[41] Unhappily, Maclure saw his adopted country following the path of undemocratic Europe in this regard, and he spoke of the young republic in agonized terms—"this half barbarian country only emerging from 300 years bondage to a foreign despotism."[42]

Still, at the turn of the century, hope was high for true reform in the United States, a young, confident confederation of republics, notwithstanding that a vocal, conservative establishment, the Federalists, was in control, fearful of Jacobin excesses and without enthusiasm for the education of the mob. Its most important member, John Adams, described the masses as "the common Herd of mankind," and he believed that "an aristocracy of wealth must exist in every society, founded upon the industry of the few and the laziness of the many."[43]

Not surprisingly, Maclure called the Federalist faction the "aristocracy" with monarchical tendencies, possessing many of the same detested characteristics of their European counterparts. He saw the Federalists as an alliance of merchants, big money interests, and landowners: "With us they take the name Federalists because they advocate a union of the states, and would have made the country a monarchy if they had not been outvoted [by presidents Jefferson and Madison].... They detested the French Revolution because it abolished the hereditary powers, privilege and monopoly which they meant to create in their own favor at home."[44] But there was a crucial difference between ordinary Europeans and Americans, for the latter were not burdened with a feudal past and were far less servile or passive to abuse.

Maclure considered labor unions in the 1820s important, but inadequate to counter the massive forces that the elite could muster to maintain their dominance—the church, control of the legislative process, the legal system, the military and police, the press, and the educational system. He had come to realize that the critical strategy in the class war was to teach workers to be cognizant of their own best interest, thereby creating an enlightened electorate in a democracy with universal suffrage. Only then could they control political leadership and legislation so that those laws which Maclure deemed "arbitrary," pertaining to the distribution of wealth, could be changed and simplified. Maclure believed that at the present time "two-thirds of the legislative enactments [interfere] with the management of individual affairs, favoring one class at the expense of another."[45]

Maclure applauded legal reform, with simplification of the law "that no man understands," as a means of remedying many ills, although this could only be brought about by first reforming education.[46] Redress would never take place by reform from above, through the good offices of liberal thinkers and activists.[47] An elaborate system of laws was in place that had been derived from English common law, called an "absurd injustice" by Bentham. It was beyond the scope of the common man, for justice was expensive, requiring the payment of lawyers' fees and taxes on legal documents that workers could not afford. In France, a major achievement that had emerged from twenty-five years of turmoil was the adoption of the Napoleonic Code, which at one stroke made the law relatively simple, clear, and comprehensible to the average man and was conducive to social equality. The "French Law" was less susceptible to the self-serving manipulations of lawyers and judges, who inevitably represented the interests of the ruling class.[48] According to Maclure, the strongest argument for the Napoleonic Code was that lawyers were opposed to it.[49] Maclure frequently argued against the principle of hereditary power, which depended on physical force and was "opposite and contrary to elective power."[50] He pressed for the elimination of the law of primogeniture and for wealth to be equally distributed among surviving children.

Abuses of the economic system, monopolistic practice, indirect taxation, national debt, the printing of money, all of which were extant in America, became an obsession with Maclure. His commentary grew fierce and unrelenting, especially in his later years in Mexico, where, as a semi-invalid, he had little else to do but read about what was happening back home, and brood over the dishonest manipulations suffered by the worker in a supposedly democratic republic. In his numerous letters, between accounts of his health and living conditions, his plans, and practical advice to the ANSP on such a matter as the building of an observatory to study the heavens, he would suddenly launch into windy, ideological diatribes with a ferocity that bordered on the incoherent, and his tendency to express himself in maxims and pronouncements escalated. Sometimes orthography, grammar, punctuation, syntax, and spelling were casualties: "that the great inequality of property, knowledge, and power introduced by civilization as far as it has yet gone is the cause and origin of most of the evils, troubles, and miseries, which torment humanity and that the equalization those three essentials of freedom was the shortest route to reform the vices, crimes, and misfortune, of the millions and that the equalization of knowledge was the only part that an individual could prudently attempt and that by raising the masses of industrious producers by the diffusion of useful knowledge the only mode of accomplishing the equality on which the freedom and happiness of our species depends." Maclure had fashioned an impressionistic overview of his credo.

Samuel George Morton, the quiet, rather staid vice president of the Academy of Natural Sciences of Philadelphia, to whom this particular letter was addressed, must have heard Maclure's rhetoric many times.[51] Morton and his conservative colleagues were certainly not in sympathy with most of Maclure's views. Yet they politely listened without public comment, no doubt because along with the tirade came munificent contributions to the Academy—far greater than they were prepared (or able) to match. Dutifully, these honorable men did Maclure's bidding, and in a letter he thanked them for "distributing my opinions to the different libraries, clubs and meetings of the working classes."[52]

As a man with a strong scientific interest, Maclure considered the great socioeconomic events in terms of eternal and simplifying principles and laws, which were so useful in describing the natural world. He felt that he could foretell events by the exercise of reason. For instance, he was confident that free human activity, left to its own devices, would result in the equal division of property among groups—a natural law.[53] If knowledge and property are divided equally among groups, an equitable division of power will follow, resulting in the greatest freedom and happiness for all.[54] Although the greater part of Maclure's writing was of a dire and gloomy nature, the consequence of repeated setbacks, his outlook for the future of the human race was surprisingly optimistic and rosy.

FOUR

✳

European Sojourn (1800–1808)

At the turn of the nineteenth century, Maclure left Philadelphia for Europe, where he remained until 1808. These were troubled years, when Napoleon Bonaparte, emperor of France, overran Europe, and Britain prepared for an invasion. With all the turmoil, armies and navies dashing back and forth, momentous battles being fought on land and sea, and governments fleeing the French, Maclure still went about his business, meandering the countryside collecting rocks and minerals and recording his experiences in notebooks.

The reason for Maclure's move to Europe is unknown, as it was for many of his seemingly sudden and idiosyncratic relocations. Perhaps this sophisticated cosmopolite could take only so much of provincial America, despite his allegiance to the New World. It is also likely that after taking part in many field trips in the United States, he became particularly interested in geology, and recognizing the absence of geological instruction in the United States, he wanted to complete his education in Europe with its great geologists and schools of geology. Many years later, when he was a recognized geologist, he wrote that he had hoped that his European explorations would enable him to construct a geologic map of Europe, as he later did of the United States. But this task was thwarted by the complexity of the geology of Europe with its confusing pattern of intersecting mountain ranges and its many volcanoes—too ambitious an undertaking for one man.[1]

We learn from a letter to Thomas Jefferson that in the summer of 1801, he had visited Denmark, Sweden, Norway, Prussia, and parts of Germany and France, and that after residing in Paris for a few months, he had left for England. In Paris he had met with their mutual friend Volney. Although French politics had become so complicated—"beyond my comprehension"—Maclure informed Jefferson that the conditions of the poor in France were much improved, the houses of the rich were in a state of disrepair, and property was now more equitably distributed. Five months later he wrote Jefferson again, and after informing him that he had been to Germany and the Rhine, he launched into a discussion of farming practices, the properties of soil, and the growing of tobacco in Germany and Virginia. He continued with a lecture on economics, banking, and paper money—earnest matters indeed![2] Through constant correspondence, Americans learned much about what was going on in Europe, and conversely Maclure must have been a knowledgeable source of information for Europeans.

While visiting Sweden, Maclure visited the laboratory of the eminent chemist Jöns Jacob Berzelius, a pioneering scientist involved in electrochemical theory, the notion of atomic and molecular weights, and chemical composition—the very foundation of modern chemistry (and geology). Although Maclure had an "inordinate appetite for experience" in order to know "the secrets of the world,"[3] in fact, painstaking experimentation, necessary for the validation of new theories in the furtherance of science, was not Maclure's approach (as it was for Berzelius), for it did not suit his restless temperament. There is little doubt that Maclure was thoughtful and creative. But his classrooms were rock formations as well as factories, chemical works, and mines—instruments of the burgeoning Industrial Revolution—not the laboratory.

Although travel was slow and isolating and communication was poor, a worldwide network of well-informed people with broad interests thrived as an agency for the free flow of information. One of the important networks centered around Thomas Jefferson, who seemed to attract countless able people, American and European. Young Americans streamed to Europe on grand tours for one or two years before settling down to serious family matters, not only to lead the good life away from parental control and societal scrutiny but also to acquire cultural polish and advanced training in special fields of interest. They gravitated to London and Paris, despite Bonaparte's plan to invade England (brought to a hasty end by the British navy at Trafalgar in 1805). Paris was the center of advanced thinking, the home of major figures in science and art, and conveniently close to all other intellectual and artistic centers.

In the running battle between England and France, the newborn United States wisely adopted a neutral stance, for it was hardly in a position to fight a war. While its foreign trade grew, and the populace began to flow into the hinterland, especially to the southeast, its ships became the victims of hostile seizure by England and France (each for its own reason), both of whom were rather contemptuous of the upstart republic, its pretensions, and its feeble military capabilities. With the signing of Jay's Treaty in 1794, England and the United States ended their hostilities, and American citizens were permitted to seek redress for their wartime losses. But active conflict on the high seas escalated into an undeclared war between the United States and France, part of a feared Anglo-American coalition, during which American goods were seized by French naval vessels and privateers (1797–99). After costly defeats of the French fleet inflicted by the American and British navies, a besieged Bonaparte thought it best to neutralize the Americans, freeing him to concentrate his forces against Great Britain. In 1800, he offered to recompense American shippers for their losses, and accordingly a "Spoliation Commission" was formed consisting of three Americans whose charge was to review claims by Americans against the French government for compensation "for supplies, for embargoes and prizes made at sea."

Traveling about Europe, Americans developed useful relationships based on common experience, and these often continued after their return home. If information about Europe was needed, or some task was to be undertaken in Europe, official or not, there were always Americans in place to volunteer their services. Frederick Hall, a professor of mathematics at Middlebury College in Vermont, who spent time in Paris, was a self-appointed operative who recruited young Americans to visit Europe and to perform a service, if needed.[4]

Through correspondence, Maclure had let Jefferson know that he was always available to render help to his country, and the time had come to do so. Jefferson appointed Maclure to be head of the Spoliation Commission, along with James F. Mercer of Virginia and Isaac Cox Barnet of New Jersey.[5] The three were to scrutinize all documents submitted, check proof of American citizenship, and examine papers verifying the ownership and value of lost goods. A list of 314 approved claims was submitted to Robert R. Livingston, the American minister to France, and to a special envoy, James Monroe.[6] Livingston was the intermediary who was to present the tally to the French government, but serious conflicts arose. Large claims by desperate people (with influential friends) were involved, accusations were made of preferential treatment for some claimants, rules of procedure were questioned, records were incomplete, and many of the judgments made were somewhat arbitrary and of questionable merit. Livingston was fearful that unsubstantiated or dishonest claims would discredit the entire proceeding, which would result in humiliating rejection by the French, and so he repeatedly conferred with the French authorities regarding what claims they would accept. He complained to the commissioners that they were keeping him in the dark, while the commissioners felt that Livingston was meddling in their operation. Arguments between Livingston and the commissioners ensued, accusations about corruption, incompetence, and dishonesty were hurled, and at one point Maclure, who seemed to be the most vociferous, was removed (briefly) from the commission.

After almost two years, the entire affair ended, largely in failure and confusion. Maclure felt compelled to defend his honor by presenting his side of the story. The result was *To the People of the United States* (1807), a full account of the proceedings by Maclure, case by case, complete with letters between the committee and Mr. Livingston documenting the fact that the three men on the board were scrupulous in the discharge of their responsibilities and were completely free of any wrongdoing.[7] In fact, a touchy Maclure seems to have protested too much in his attempt to dispel any hint of irregularity, failure, or futility hanging over the affair. His exaggerated response to Livingston's jurisdiction may very well reflect Maclure's own intolerance of authority, his sense of personal honor, and his craving for independence; as he stated, "Independence has been my hobby Horse." His bridling under the hand of schoolmasters, along with a craving for travel, suggest that he was driven by a need for freedom that surfaced during this trying imbroglio.

After two years of conflict and frustration, an unburdened Maclure was ready for the exhilaration of geological exploration. While the making of money was not particularly enjoyable to him, wealth gave him the independence he desired and the power to do good. He spent his fortune as he pleased, traveling and studying rock formations.[8]

He left Paris in June 1805, accompanied by Joseph C. Cabell, an intelligent young man from a prominent Virginia family. Cabell had been in Europe since 1803 for "reasons of health," probably suffering from tuberculosis, which was rampant at the time. He was also completing and polishing his education, so he did well coming under the influence of Maclure. Despite being fifteen years his senior and paying all expenses, Maclure did not try to dominate the young man, nor did he ever attempt to intimidate any of his other younger companions; this was not his way. Cabell could do no better than to explore Europe with Maclure, whose primary focus at the time was the geology and the natural resources of every country they visited.

The two men set out from Paris for the Auvergne in central France, traveling in Maclure's cabriolet.[9] The Auvergne was an enchanting backwoods, so remote that there were ancient inhabitants there who did not speak or understand French, their origins lost in time. Extinct volcanoes in the form of elevations known as *puys* abounded—a land covered with rivers of lava, basaltic rock, and granite. Here they hoped to determine whether basalt was of volcanic origin, for if it was, it would support the theory that the surface of the earth was shaped by fiery eruptions and erosion. Both men wrote diaries that were often amusing and filled with information.[10] Time was spent studying the natural baths of Le Mont Dore, known since Roman times. Several days, including July 4, were spent in Clermont [-Ferrand], the largest town in the area, near which the marquis de Lafayette was born and where his chateau was situated. Maclure comments that there were 4,000 whores in the town, a remarkable number considering the relatively small population of Clermont and of the Auvergne itself. This remarkable number was unquestionably an exaggeration, as was Abigail Adam's claim that there were 52,000 prostitutes in Paris. Repeatedly overcharged, cheated, and furnished with decrepit horses by the local country folk, they pushed on over terrible roads, usually finishing their days in deplorable inns. They examined rock formations, wielding their hammers like blacksmiths to gather samples of rock, under whose weight their carriage groaned, and from time to time they packed up boxes of mineral and rock samples weighing hundreds of pounds for shipment to Paris and ultimately to Philadelphia and New Haven. At times they were racked with cold, soaked with rain, or baked by the sun, but they continued, with the advice and help of local authorities, gentry, and scientists to whom they had letters of introduction.

Nothing escaped their scrutiny. Aside from an endless commentary on the rocks and minerals found in specific places, they wrote about the agriculture and viniculture, the nature of the soil, and the crops grown in different regions. Such matters as the price of food and wine, the cost of labor, and the state of well-being of workmen, as well as the rates charged by inns, their condition, and the quality of the food served, did not escape their close attention. Sometimes their meals were bizarre—on one occasion they noted that breakfast consisted of cherries and milk. Maclure's liberal political and social views are apparent from his comments, and Cabell's remarks suggest that the two travelers were in sympathy. They noted that since the Revolution most people were better off, and there was a reasonably equitable distribution of goods in Clermont: "This place did not suffer much during the Revolution: not more than three or four persons having been guillotined, and that from downright folly." Offhanded, anticlerical remarks are sprinkled throughout Maclure's narrative, as he found further evidence of the greed and perfidy of priests.

From the Auvergne they traveled east, sometimes on foot, to Valence on the Rhone River, the Val d'Isère to Grenoble, Mont Blanc, Chamonix, Grenoble, Geneva, Val d'Aosta in Italy, and the Alps, and then they were off to "priest-ridden" Zermatt in Switzerland, continuing the marathon through Switzerland. It becomes apparent that Maclure and Cabell were uncommonly determined travelers with a set agenda. After an expedition that had lasted three and a half months, they returned to Paris through Burgundy, having collected a ton of rocks and recorded their experiences in detail in two full journals.[11]

Upon his return to Paris, Maclure bought a modest house at 20 Rue des Brodeurs, Faubourg Saint-Germain, where he established a school. His home also became a social center for visiting Americans, a place where they could make contact with French and European scientists and thinkers. Frederick Hall was a guest at one of Maclure's dinners, and he carefully observed his host. Hall was impressed by Maclure, for unlike most Americans, he had "quit the counting house" to turn to a higher pursuit—geology. Hall wrote that Maclure had a "strong intellect" but regrettably had little refined elegance. Indeed, Maclure did not hide his disdain for classical education, which even Hall admitted "too often debilitates while it polishes." He looked upon Maclure as a diamond in the rough, a man who possessed the requisite strength and endurance to be a field geologist "who enkindles in my bosom the flame of national pride." To him, Maclure was a gracious host and conversationalist, a vastly experienced practical field geologist with a broadly ranging mind and strong opinions. His eulogy concluded, "He entertains his friends in a style which does equal credit to the philosopher, the economist, and the man of fortunes."[12]

With Paris as home base, Maclure undertook several geological expeditions. From July to October 1806, he, along with Jean-François Berger, a Swiss geologist, embarked on a geological tour of the Vosges Mountains of eastern France, Switzerland, and northern Italy. A year later he began an extensive tour of southern France, accompanied by a Mr. Rodas.[13] The difficult journey, beset by terrible hardships, started on November 3, 1807, in Maclure's cabriolet, and the destination was Spain, which they reached in early February. Again, their focus was on the collection and shipping of rocks and minerals and the study of the strata in which they lay. Maclure's myriad interests are revealed in his discussions of weather patterns, the nature of the soil and the crops it yielded in every region, coal mines and quarries, the smelting of lead, silver, and copper, the distillation of wine, the production of rose water and perfumes, the manufacture of soap, and health spas that featured warm baths.

Of special interest to him was the nature of the people they came across, isolated in different regions—almost separate nations. Some groups were prosperous and civil, while others were filthy, ignorant, and dishonest. The people believed that potatoes were a source of disease and would not eat them, and to Maclure's disapproval, potatoes were fed to pigs. Maclure seemed to be suspicious of physicians, and in light of their ignorance and ineffectiveness and his own experience, he felt sufficiently authoritative to make judgments in medical matters. He noted that in some regions goiter was common among women but not in men, which the locals ascribed to the drinking water, a notion he derided.[14] In Perpignan, he came to realize that when the ditches were filled with water, people came down with "fall fever," which at the time was caused by a "miasma" (probably malaria or yellow fever, spread by mosquitoes, whose larvae grew in ditch water).

Maclure's hatreds were uncomplicated and unrelenting. He never failed to denounce the Catholic Church. In Aurillac, the priests "labor hard in their calling for the propagation of ignorance, superstition, and hypocracy." In Narbonne: "I visited the works of ancient folly, filled with modern stupidity and hypocracy. That is, the cathedral and another church, almost filled with people of all ranks. There are many sorts of ancient vanity, inscriptions on stone, etc. which are examined by antiquarians with great and a kind of enthusiastic veneration. All that can be learned by them is that a people called Romans extended their rapine to this country and had knowledge enough of the arts to cut letters on stone." In one stroke Maclure ardently expressed his contempt for religion, classical antiquity, and historical study, views that may or may not have been valid or justified. His incessant eruption of diatribes is surprising for such a worldly, learned man.

By contrast, his approach to the natural world, and particularly to geology and mineralogy, was thoughtful, somewhat skeptical, and reasoned. He could see the good on both sides of an issue, and was willing to compromise or abandon a view that could not be supported by fact. Like many scientists (and nonscientists), Maclure had a mind that was compartmentalized: the professional part was analytical and rational, and the other part was emotional and zealous. The two components were kept separate, but occasionally joined in an uneasy marriage, which made a hash of subtle, complex issues.

By the time the explorers had arrived in Montpellier, Mr. Rodas, exhausted and bored, seems to have had enough of Maclure's taxing regimen. He was replaced by Mathieu Tondi, an Italian political liberal, a talented geologist, mineralogist, and natural historian who later became a professor at the University of Naples. Tondi and Maclure left Perpignan and arrived in Spain in late January 1808—his first visit. Dealing with perverse, incompetent, and corrupt customs officials at the border was a distasteful business, even with official permits and documents furnished by Maclure's friend George William Erving, the American consul in Madrid. These failed to confer privileges on the bearer, which only confirmed for Maclure the evil of big government and the corruption and incompetence of its representatives. As they traveled south in their carriage along the Mediterranean coast toward Barcelona, they took note of certain kinds of rocks and the patterns of stratification, especially around Montserrat. The travelers found much to admire in coastal Spain—the beauty of the land, cared for and cultivated by an energetic people, and a thriving textile industry.[15]

Displeased by the ignorance of the Spanish upper classes and the dominance of the Catholic Church, Maclure vented his disgust: "All the people are drove by the physical impulse to make children; few are actuated by the moral, pleasurable sensation of forming men. Prejudice is the support of bigotry and tyranny. Ignorance is the chains of slavery and the stronghold of oppression. Those who endeavor to enlighten the masses will make enemies of that swarm of impostors who live by the ignorance and stupidity of the people."[16]

Maclure was appalled at what he saw in remote, isolated areas where barbaric people picked lice off of each other during social intercourse, "savage and insolent . . . more the insolence of slaves than the independence of free men." Adding to the discomfort of bitter winter weather were the bad roads, the inhospitable inns without beds, and execrable food. Maclure was outraged by an innkeeper's refusal on a very cold night to provide an extra blanket for an ailing Tondi, and he complained of their lying, overcharging, and even stealing. It was not difficult for Maclure to make a list of what he considered stupidities—their primitive ploughs, their black hats, which collect heat under the blazing sun, and their shoes, which rapidly fall apart with wear. Reluctant to give credit to anything associated with a Church-dominated, authoritarian Spain, he found much to criticize in the cathedrals at Granada and Malaga, which he portrayed as "exhibiting much labor and little taste"; whatever was good in them had been taken from the Arabs and the Moors. According to Maclure, the old Muslim culture of Spain was far in advance of the Christian culture that displaced it, particularly evident in Granada with its exotic treasures of Moorish arts and crafts and its beautiful gardens.

On their way to Valencia, they came upon the small town of Murveidro, which (once again) triggered a denunciation of the classic world that scholars so admired: "This place was called Sagunto by the Romans who left the marks of their tyranny in a fortification at the top of a hill. . . . Some testimony of their barbarity and cruelty is to be seen in the remains of an amphitheater; the scene of blood and slaughter where the mangled members of men and beasts were indiscriminately scattered over the horrid stage to please and amuse a people who were called civilized."[17]

Valencia was one of the most advanced cities in Spain, with an academy of design and mathematics. Here he met educated people who were well acquainted with the literature of the French Enlightenment, were knowledgeable about practical geology, and were collectors of minerals and rocks. But he could not help observing that "the town is full of beggars and priests who are constant companions. The one is the cause, and the other the effect, of idleness and hypocrisy. The nobles here keep a distance from the other classes."[18]

His overall assessment of the Spanish was sour and damning. "Every work in Spain proves the total want of science or talent in the officers and rich orders of society. There is not so great a difference as has been supposed between the common sense of the great mass of the people and of their neighbors on the other side of the Pyrenees. . . . However the difference between the two nations is immense as far as the knowledge of the rich . . . is concerned. In Spain, all the people are nearly on a par of ignorance, with almost the same dose of prejudice and bigotry as in France. The few are well-informed, although the many are ignorant. Strangers are always brought into contact with the few and seldom [taken] into the society of the great mass of the people."[19]

With a keen and unforgiving eye, Maclure evaluated the peculiarities and imperfections of the societies he came upon, his passionately held beliefs serving as a stern frame of reference. His singular view was so rigid and constricting, it did not allow for a balance of conflicting ideas, so necessary when attempting to evaluate complex human behavior. No doubt, what he described had a certain validity, as limited as is the perception of one man, but one cannot help feeling that what he was looking for, and chose to comment upon, was limited. As biased as he was, it is something of a relief when he writes favorably about cultivated, helpful acquaintances, sunny, well-tended vineyards, and orderly farms run by hardworking people.

After examining mines and rock formations along the way, Maclure reached Cadiz on May 23, 1808, the last stop in his survey of Spain. He had heard vague rumblings about war, but now he could see ships of the British navy offshore with a cargo of 4,000 troops ready to land and drive out occupying French forces. He was particularly critical of the operation because the naval blockade "strangles commerce and all maritime communications. . . . Britain, by impoverishing their neighbors with whom they are at war, ruins her own customers and curtails her own trade" with Europe and the United States.[20] Evidence for this greatest of economic sins was the enormous amount of unsold natural products, as manufactured goods piled up in British warehouses and the severe depression of 1807–1808 played out. Since goods such as clothing were denied to North Americans, Americans began to manufacture their own, making themselves self-sufficient and competitive with British manufacturers.

The area around Cadiz was also in the grip of a yellow fever epidemic following a wet spring and a warm summer; some said the affliction was imported from the United States. The cause, of course, was utterly unknown, but Maclure, attempting a scientific analysis of a medical problem, wrote of "hatch[ing] the eggs of contagion which lay dormant." Such a conclusion was unhelpful, reflecting the ignorance of the time. The form of the disease in southern Spain seemed particularly virulent, often killing patients in four or five hours, a catastrophe that caused enormous social disruption and rendered the ministrations of physicians almost useless.

Maclure was happy to escape from a Spain rife with war and disease, a troubled land fought over by two foreign armies, and largely innocent of geological and mineralogical science—disciplines perceived as a threat to religious dogma. Still, he reveled in Spain's benign weather, and despite his relentless criticism, he considered Spain promising enough to return in 1821.

The route of his return to the United States is unknown; he may have sailed directly from a Spanish or Portuguese port, or he may have first traveled to Paris to tend to his collection of specimens. Maclure, now a thoroughly experienced geologist and mineralogist, was well prepared and eager to start a geological survey of the entire United States—from the Atlantic Ocean to the Mississippi River, and from the St. Lawrence River to the Gulf of Mexico. The outcome would be a monumental work that would thrust Maclure into the front rank of American geologists, and in Europe the achievement redounded to the credit of Maclure and the United States.

※

FIVE

The Maclurean Era of American Geology

Retiring from commerce in his early thirties, Maclure took up geological study and exploration to fill his hours because "it has always appeared to me that the science of geology was one of the simplest and easiest to acquire: the number of names to be learned is small, and the present nomenclature although rather generic than specific, is not difficult."[1] Geology entailed travel, which satisfied his wanderlust, and as a man of commerce, he was keenly aware of geology's relevance to mining and agriculture; geological inquiry was prelude to commercial exploitation.

His interest in geology developed during his early days in Philadelphia, where he had carried out some geological field studies—a rank novice and amateur. But, in fact, as with so many crucial elements in his story, the origins of his interest in geology, precisely when his interest in geology became serious, and the details of his geological education remain unknown. It is likely that after taking part in many field trips in the United States and recognizing his professional inadequacy, he felt it necessary to acquire a geological education, and this advancement could only be achieved in Europe.

Science was not part of the culture of the time in America. Rather, America was a land of pragmatists who demanded an immediate return for their labor, which was hardly possible with so new a subject as geology.

A vigorous democratic spirit found expression in practical achievement. As de Tocqueville wrote: "In America the purely practical part of science is admirably understood, and careful attention is paid to the theoretical portion which is immediately requisite to application. On this head, the Americans always display a clear, free, original and inventive power of mind. But hardly anyone in the United States devotes himself to the essentially theoretical and abstract portion of human knowledge."[2] Even an enlightened intellect like Jefferson had little appreciation of the promise of geology.[3]

Maclure was a kind of hybrid, an internationalist with European roots in geology, and so he was not entirely a pragmatic rock collector. He was also concerned with larger problems such as the structure and significance of volcanoes and the origin of basalt. He berated his countrymen for ignoring what they thought was not useful, for not being interested in the "nature and properties of rocks" and where they are situated on the surface of the earth. Indeed, "even now . . . [the learned and the unlearned] treat such investigations with contempt as beneath their notice." Why this should be so, he found puzzling, but as a budding radical social reformer, which Maclure became, he hinted darkly that the answer lay in "the nature and origin of the power of the few, over the many."[4]

Around 1800, the study of geology in America was in a backward state, almost no systematic work was being done, and opportunities for training in America were virtually nonexistent. This at a time when in Europe the scientific discipline of geology was maturing and becoming more technical and detailed with a language of its own, so that training to become a professional geologist required prolonged study; the tinkering amateur was marginalized, and Americans could only follow the great geological debates from afar. At the time, little or no science of any kind was included in the curricula of American or English colleges, whose task was to prepare young men to become doctors, lawyers, and clergymen, and it was hoped that other students would benefit from exposure to the classics.[5]

The explicit reasons for Maclure's eight-year visit to Europe (1800–1808) are conjectural, as it was for many of his seemingly sudden and idiosyncratic relocations. Many years later, he wrote that he had hoped that his European explorations would enable him to construct a geologic map of Europe, but this was not to be.[6]

It is almost certain that he attended some lectures by Abraham G. Werner, professor of mineralogy at the School of Mines at Freiburg, a brilliant teacher who offered him the elements of the emerging science of geology at a descriptive level—the "facts" strung together by an accessible narrative, all of which could be mastered by the diligent.[7] His education seemed to be unstructured and informal as he picked up information here and there, viewed collections, read books which he was constantly buying, and conversed with those with geological knowledge. He spent time learning in Edinburgh, London, and Paris, and he told a friend, Duke Bernhard, that he had spent 1802 in Berlin associating with "learned men."[8] He just soaked up information as best he could, and he continued to do so throughout his life.

He also did as much fieldwork as time would permit, and by the end of his first extended European sojourn in 1808, he had investigated the geology, mineralogy, and natural resources of almost every European country—from Russia to Ireland and from the Baltic to the Mediterranean—usually in the company of a geologist whose expenses were paid by Maclure. From time to time he shipped boxes of rocks and minerals to the United States for distribution among the earliest American museums and collections.[9]

Painstaking experimentation, necessary for the validation of new theories in the furtherance of science, was not Maclure's approach, for it did not suit his restless temperament. There is little doubt that Maclure was thoughtful and creative, but his classrooms were rock formations, factories, chemical works, and mines—instruments of the burgeoning Industrial Revolution—not the laboratory.

Maclure's active years correspond precisely with the period when great controversies were being resolved about the formation of the earth's surface, and geological theories were taking on their modern form, all born of a truly international effort (1780 to 1840). As data accumulated and physical principles were revealed, wild speculations about the origin and nature of the earth were no longer accepted. Cosmogonies were proposed that were increasingly validated by their consistency with verifiable facts and the laws of chemistry and physics. Around the turn of the nineteenth century, two dominant theories about the formation of the earth's surface emerged, and in the lively controversy between them, important progress was made that led to our present understanding of the subject.

Geological information had been accumulating throughout the eighteenth century, and to this store was added new data, provided by observers in the service of one theoretical school or another. By the time the polemical fireworks had died down, an enormous amount of reliable geological knowledge had been gathered, some by Maclure, which outlived the theories that had given rise to the search. The field itself was solidly established, despite the fact that so little of the earth's surface had been explored and so little was known about the nature of the interior of the earth. Geology became a fully scientific discipline, as had chemistry and physics, both of which were exploited by geologists to broaden and deepen their understanding. Maclure's first lessons in geology, taught by Europeans, were learned during the excitement of these times, and underlying his investigations was the hope of providing evidence in support of one theory or the other.

Almost all scientific cosmogonists were in agreement that the earth began as a molten ball which cooled to form a stiff, unmoving crust that surrounded a hot core, and that as the earth cooled, the core shrank so that the crust was crumpled into ridges, mountain ranges, valleys, and ocean basins. Through the work of William Smith, the "father of British Geology," major advances in the fields of stratigraphy and paleontology were made, both in theory and in methodology. Smith, like Maclure, was particularly interested in applied geology for the service of humankind. Both were concerned with methods for the processing of ores, the detailed examination of coal beds, and the discovery of the best materials for the construction of roads and canals. One of Smith's greatest contributions was to associate the time of extinction of living forms with the time when a geologic stratum containing their remains was laid down. Through this association, strata from widely different locations were identified as being of the same time. It was a great honor for Maclure to be called the William Smith of America for laying out and describing the great geologic regions of the United States. But even so, Maclure never gained the recognition he deserved from Europeans for his pioneering work in geological cartography.

That the earth's surface had been shaped by cataclysmic processes was evident, recounted in folklore and scripture, and its systematic study became the substance of geology. Aspects of this dynamic process had been described in the biblical Noachian flood and could be accounted for by winds, rain, and volcanoes. Abraham Werner, one of the illustrious men who founded modern geology, proposed that the earth's crust was shaped by the physical properties and movement of water—a "Neptunist" theory. A "Plutonic" view of the early history of the earth was held by another major geological thinker, James Hutton of Edinburgh. Since Maclure became a geologist at the height of the controversy between the two paradigms, his basic ideas and his thinking about geology were shaped by them.

According to the Neptunist theory, a Universal Ocean covered the earth, including the mountains, and from this vast amount of fluid various sediments precipitated or crystallized in succession, five stages in all, to form different strata that were uniform over the entire globe, so that strata of different continents were comparable. Fish appeared at the time of the second stage, and in the third, when mammals appeared, there were repeated recessions of water to expose land, followed by flooding. In a fifth (final) period, the waters receded, and volcanic action was evident, which Werner believed was due to the ignition of coal. As the waters subsided, rivers as we know them were left behind.

Werner's idea had the merit of taking into account the sequential creation of different levels of living beings—fish, mammals, and the final crowning creation, the human, a scheme that was not incompatible with the biblical story and also with the theory of "the Great Chain of Being." His theory also embodied the notion of successive extinctions caused by repeated flooding (catastrophes), which would account for the fossils in many strata that were rapidly coming to light.[10]

The picture was elegant and relatively simple, a fine narrative that imparted a sense of chronology to the earth's story. As a mineralogist, Werner impressed on his students the importance of studying the properties of minerals. Since he was a charismatic lecturer and made geology fascinating, he drew devoted followers from every country, and his speculations became very popular. Religious people felt that there was much in the theory that supported the biblical account of the earth's creation in six days, and the biblical age of the earth (6,000 years) was not challenged; the Noachian Deluge of the Bible was not incompatible with Werner's theory.

Although Werner's theory purported to be based on reliable information, and seemed to be consistent with much of the available geological data, it embodied suppositions and conjectures based on unknowable facts from a remote past, and it was incompatible with many new observations. The theory never considered in realistic terms the question of the times involved to effect the proposed changes, nor could it explain why strata of older primary rock were sometimes found overlying younger classes of rock, nor could it account for commonly encountered folded, vertical, and inclined strata. The question of the existence of enormous amounts of water capable of covering the entire globe, and its fate as the water level receded to expose submerged continents with their mountains, was never addressed in a satisfactory way. The theory claimed to be a global explication of the formation of the earth's surface, but it was based on the geology of only a small area around Freiberg in Saxony with which Werner was familiar, a country without evidence of volcanoes. Maclure, who spent some time with Werner, admired him, but he was guarded in his acceptance of his geologic scheme because it did not accord with his own experience. In fact, Maclure himself, a young man, had examined far more of the earth's surface than had Werner.

Despite the Neptunists' vigorous advocacy, in time this ingenious but essentially static view was found wanting and was largely forgotten as increasing amounts of data were found to be inconsistent with the basic tenets of the scheme. Werner's classification of rocks had merit, though somewhat confusing, but he was wrong about the origin and structure of rocks and, more specifically, the aqueous origin of granite and basalt. Yet despite these shortcomings, Werner's great contributions were to stress the importance of classifying and identifying minerals in geology, to provide a chronological substructure to geological thinking, and to affirm the stratified nature of the earth's surface.

A challenging, more rigorous conceptual scheme of the formation of the earth's surface, called Plutonism, was proposed by James Hutton of Edinburgh in his Theory of the Earth (1795). Closely guided by his own observations and by what was known, this former physician and farmer with a keen interest in chemistry concluded that the major shaping force of the earth's surface was the internal heat of the planet, not water as the Neptunists claimed. Heat in the core of the planet led to the building up of great pressures and to the irregular lifting up of land masses to disrupt uniform strata that had formed by sedimentation of materials in the vast oceans, part of a continuous cycle that extended back into distant time and was operative at the present time. Shockingly incompatible with Mosaic geology, Hutton, a deist (a believer in "natural" religion), wrote: "We are thus led to see a circulation in the matter of this globe, and a system of beautiful oeconomy in the works of nature." Just as there were unanswered questions dogging the Neptunists, so were there bothersome loopholes in Plutonic theorizing concerning the origin of the earth's heat—some believed that it was created by the burning of subterranean coal.

Contrary to Neptunist theory, mountains above sea level had come into being by an uplifting process rather than by exposure after recession of the sea. Volcanic activity, caused by the buildup of internal pressure, disrupted the earth's surface structure, followed by the erosive forces of wind and water in the form of rain, ice, and the flow of rivers. Thus the surface of the earth was subjected to a cyclic building up and wearing down process—upheaval, erosion, and catastrophe (volcanic eruptions, earthquakes, and floods)—that could account for the irregularities and constant reshaping of the surface strata. Titanic forces were arrayed in a dynamic equilibrium, in contrast to the Neptunist notion of relatively stable layers at the earth's surface, revealed as the waters receded.[11] Plutonist theory also accounted for the association of basalt with volcanoes and the great masses of granite found in the deeper layers of the earth, both existing at one time in a molten state. Further, over vast periods of time, persistent weathering and erosion created deposits of sandstone, limestone, clay, and pebbles. Hutton and Werner differed radically in their views of the origins and ages of various rocks. Werner believed, erroneously, that basalt had little to do with the flow of lava from volcanoes. The oldest and most primitive rocks, which Werner postulated were formed by chemical precipitation, were correctly identified by Hutton to be of igneous origin (heat and pressure).

The Plutonic theory was a more encompassing, dynamic concept of the earth's formation—an ongoing process, with forces always at work, small changes taking place over immense periods, without beginning or end. Hutton's radical notions aroused opposition not only from Neptunists on scientific grounds but also from the establishment, both religious and conservative, who sensed that its spirit, if not its origin, echoed the ominous turmoil of the French Revolution—a disorderly conflict between opposing political and social forces that threatened the natural stability presided over by the Creator. Certain aspects of Plutonist theory were amenable to testing and were, in fact, supported by experiments in which the formation of igneous rock was mimicked by melting rocks under conditions of controlled heat and pressure, and then cooling the melt to form crystalline material or masses of slag with the properties of commonly found igneous rock (granite), the crystalline structure of which depended on the rate of cooling. Geological problems could be studied and solved in the laboratory—certainly a modern approach.

An ever-increasing amount of evidence undermined the basic tenets of the Neptunist position, calling into question Werner's dubious notion of unique and discrete periods of geologic time. Increasingly, Hutton's theory looked more reasonable and was more amenable to confirmation by geological studies. In the mid-nineteenth century the theory was expanded and transformed into a Uniformitarian view by Sir Charles Lyell. Central to the Uniformitarian idea was the dynamic equilibrium of the earth's surface, which existed in the remote past and is ongoing, so that the process could be studied at the present time. But most important of all, Uniformitarianism expanded the time frame of existence from 6,000 years, when the earth and man were created together, to an unimaginable dimension that permitted the formulation of cosmological and biological theories of evolution.

Opposing the Uniformitarians were the Catastrophists with their Wernerian underpinnings whose major proponents were Georges Cuvier in France and William Buckland in England. Lyell contended that the advocates of this "unscientific" theory were susceptible to speculative theorizing, erroneously defending assignments of geological time spans that resembled those of the Bible. He argued that the great scriptural deluge, unique catastrophes, and miraculous interventions should no longer be invoked as shaping forces.[12] The Uniformitarians prevailed, but the Catastrophists did make important contributions to world geology. Some reputable geologists preferred to include elements of both theories in the formulation of their own geological views, and as the nineteenth century unfolded, there was an accommodation and a meshing of the two major approaches to the study of geology. Broad speculation was dampened by close examination of reliable geological data, and new information provided answers to the questions that had been proposed by a disappearing breed of cosmogonists.

William Maclure began his geological career when these great debates were going on, and they continued during his years of active geological exploration. At a time of uncertainty about the most basic issues of geology, his thinking and his strategies were most certainly molded by the controversy.

The breadth of Maclure's practical geological experience in the field was virtually unrivalled. He roamed from one country to another, his curiosity increasing as he conversed with the local intelligentsia and inspected geological formations, mines, and volcanoes. He collected vast numbers of specimens of rocks and minerals that ultimately found their way into the collections of the Academy of Natural Sciences of Philadelphia and Yale University, among others, and by the time he died, there was hardly an important mineralogical collection in the United States that was not beholden to him for his gifts.

A restless man of action, Maclure wanted to get to the bottom of things in a hurry, to "seize the great and prominent outlines of nature" rather than dwell on the "accidental deviations" and "supposed exceptions of the great laws of nature." The future economic potential of his findings was paramount.[13] He did concede, however, that ultimately the painstaking gathering of facts might prove the most valuable strategy, and on several occasions he stated that the description of rocks was "the most essential part of Geology."[14] It was, however, an "exhausting" approach that Maclure was too impatient to employ.

Maclure was an experienced field man, closely examining mines and surface outcroppings of strata, rocks, and minerals, acquiring intimate knowledge of the geological distribution of rocks in a large part of the country. Rather than construct theories about how and why there came to exist various rock formations, he chose to describe the nature of rocks and minerals that he found, their precise location and extent, and neighboring formations. The work was informative and almost always correct. The study was carried out over the entire United States as it was known then—the eastern half of the present United States between the Atlantic Ocean to just beyond the Mississippi River (including Missouri, Arkansas, and Louisiana), and from the St. Lawrence River and the Great Lakes in the north to the Gulf of Mexico.

From Maclure's piecemeal education emerged an expertise and authority in geology that found expression in his classic Observations on the Geology of the United States, with a colored geological map of the region east of the Mississippi River. He published this book scarcely a year after returning to the United States in 1808. To do this he must have worked at a furious pace, studying the geology of the New England and mid-Atlantic states as well as the rock formations of Georgia. That he wrote Observations after less than one year of study in the United States, aided no doubt by his vast geological experience in Europe, was truly a remarkable feat.[15] In his career he crossed the Allegheny Mountains twenty-two times and suffered great hardship in the remotest parts of the land to gain firsthand geological knowledge.

Observations, which first appeared in the Transactions of the American Philosophical Society in 1809, has been considered a landmark in American geology that inspired a whole generation of young Americans at a time when geology was emerging as a separate discipline, a branch of natural history. The work was translated into French in 1811 and became well known in French circles.[16] Maclure's comprehensive map was widely used by other authors in their publications, and so it was very influential in the formative years of geological study in America.

Observations begins by recognizing two general approaches to geological practice. The first is to exhaustively examine a small area of the earth's surface for the kind of rocks found, their positions, and the geologic formations present. By systematizing the detailed observations and correlating the information with that from other small areas, an enormous amount of data would be acquired, from which a larger view of a region would emerge. Because of the shades of differences between different set classes of rocks and minerals from different areas, "an extensive and intricate nomenclature" would be required with "long and voluminous descriptions." This approach, which also required detailed chemical analysis of rocks and minerals, about which Maclure knew little, did not suit his temperament at all. He shunned this approach, which he thought "would be like the portrait painter dwelling on the accidental pimple of a fine face."

Maclure adopted a ranging, comprehensive approach to geological study that would render unnecessary "embarrassing description," and he justified his broad approach to field geology by stating that what he did could not be "understood by microscopic investigations or the minute analysis of insulated rocks and detached masses."

Despite its deficiencies, he preferred to begin "with the great outlines, trace the limits which divide the principal classes of rocks, and their relative situations and extents," and from this followed his colored geological map of the United States. His book and later writings reveal that he had a grand conception of the structure of the North American continent, the changes it had undergone (including glaciation), and the resultant consequences for plants and animals. An innovative feature of the book was the inclusion of a plate with five figures, each a cross-section of the eastern half of the United States, traversing the Appalachians, with towns and geographic sites through which each section passed, precisely defined.[17]

In Maclure's outline of North America, the "primitive class prevails, both in the mountains and in the lowlands, decreasing gradually as it proceeds south" (colored orange on his map). This huge, elongated band, running from the northeast to the south and west, was bounded on the

east by alluvial plains (yellow) that reached the Atlantic Ocean, while
to the west "it serves as a foundation to that immense superstructure of
transition and secondary rocks forming the great chain of mountains"
(red). The boundaries of each of the great classes of rock were outlined in
some detail, and it is apparent that Maclure was speaking from firsthand
experience as he described the type of rocks in each class and their extent,
locating boundaries with considerable precision. In many instances he
equated the type and distribution of rocks and minerals in America with
those in specific sites in Europe, information that reflects his extensive
experience and his global view of geology.

Maclure, neither an orthodox Neptunist nor a Plutonist, recognized
that some of his own observations were at odds with Neptunist ideas,
and so he was circumspect in his support.[18] Still, Maclure was regarded
as a follower of Werner because his *Observations* was generally credited
with introducing Wernerian classification and terminology to the United
States. In his *Observations of the Geology of the United States*, Maclure wrote
of Werner: "Although subject to all the errors inseparable from systems
founded upon a speculative theory of origin, the system of Werner is still
the best and most comprehensive that has yet been formed," an opinion
that was reiterated in several of his papers.[19] But he was not averse to making changes in Werner's system and placing rocks in different categories
when his experience compelled him to do so. Although the nomenclature was sometimes inconsistent, and even in error, and would surely be
changed, Maclure realized that "some of our young geologists fascinated
perhaps by the brilliant wake of some Europeans, appear willing to ex-
plode the received artificial divisions," but he himself found them useful;
they were "best understood," and each class was "well defined."[20] His re-
classifications of rocks into classes and orders were presented in detail in
his major publications over several years.[21]

Maclure's approach was Baconian, not deeply concerned with speculation and the heated Plutonist-Neptunist controversy, seeing no advantage in the replacement of one speculative theory by another without the
guidance of new facts. He seemed to have little patience with the impassioned advocates of either side of the debate—his position was skeptical
and critical. Maclure cautioned his readers about the dangerous appeal of
theorizing, for "the pleasure of indulging the imagination is so superior to
that derived from the labour and drudgery of observation." In agreement

with his colleague Benjamin Silliman, it was crucial that the tension that arises between fact and interpretation be minimized. As much as possible, thinking should be "untinged by the false colouring of systems," alluding to the Neptunist-Plutonist debates, and "visionary and baseless speculation concerning the origin of the globe."[22]

Maclure and other geologists attempted to resolve the Neptunian-Plutonist dispute by closely examining volcanoes and volcanic rocks, which they believed were the key to the resolution of the problem.[23] If basalt was found to be of aqueous origin, the Neptunists' position would be validated. However, Maclure frequently found basalt united with lava (which clearly was of volcanic origin), and so he concluded that both basalt and lava had the same volcanic origin and were not a precipitant in line with Neptunist theory.[24] Others had come to the same conclusion, and chemical analysis indicated that basalt and lava were identical. By 1817, many of Werner's ideas about the role of water in the fashioning of the earth's surface had been challenged, and they became obstacles to the advancement of American geology. By this time Maclure's thinking had clearly shifted toward the Uniformitarian (Plutonist) position, and he now had some idea of the vastness of geological time and of the history of the earth as a molten ball that was cooling down.

In 1823, he wrote, "Now that Werner is dead, [the theory of the formation of the earth's surface] is likely to swing as far in the opposite direction, and scorch our globe with fire, as unmercifully as the Neptunians inundated it with water."[25] According to Maclure, there was strong evidence that the earth's crust was shaped by both fire and water. In fact, he had a broader, more accommodating approach to the problems of geology than did Werner, and he even wrote about "Werner's error" in claiming that the earth's crust was formed "solely by the agency of water."[26] Maclure believed that the zealous partisanship in the controversy emerged as much from nongeologic factors as from detailed geologic argument. In his view the mature opinion of a geologist largely depended on whether his early exposure was to volcanoes or to flatlands.

He raised objections to both Neptunist and Plutonist dogma; on the one hand, he states that an impossible 2,000 to 3,000 times the existing amount of water would be needed to dissolve the solids of the earth as proposed by Werner, and he asked where all the water went that would uncover mountain ranges and whole continents? After observing lakes in

Switzerland and their surrounding strata, he could find no evidence for an ancient ebbing and flowing of water over a 2,000- to 3,000-foot range.

Challenging the Plutonists he asked what had happened to all the heat released by solidifying molten rock necessary to form the entire earth's crust. Explicitly, he stated that no one event was responsible for the earth's landscape, and he categorically dismissed any Creator theory. It was not an "absurdity" to think that the earth was as eternal as the sun and the stars, "the origin of which we shall most probably find it difficult to explain." "I have always thought that the changes on our globe depend more on the coincidence of a great many partial causes and changes rather than on any one great sweeping agent which would have wrought up the whole in seven days, as Moses made the creation." He noted that "nature has many ways of acting," that "an immensity remains to be examined" because we have been asking pertinent questions for only a few years—since "only yesterday"—and "much as we have lately done, an immensity remains yet to be examined."[27]

Observations was an important influence on aspiring young American geologists who learned their basic systematic thinking about geology from Werner through Maclure. Maclure classified rocks and minerals according to the descriptive "German" system of Werner, because it was peculiarly suited for use in North America with its vast and defined fields of rocks and, most important, its relative freedom from irregularities and disturbances.[28] Because of this, he felt that the simpler North American geology would provide a sterner test for the validity of the Wernerian system, and that European geologists, recognizing the superiority of American geology with its regular and undisturbed stratifications, would flock to study it, as "Greece and Italy are just now [visited] by antiquarians."[29] In fact, the accessibility of American geology, and its significance for agriculture, mining, and the construction of railroads, attracted young Americans of great ability, and by the midcentury the American geological enterprise, nourished by numerous state geological surveys, was second to none.

By the second decade of the nineteenth century, Maclure was pleased to see a marked growth in interest in geology in America because "the useful application of the substances found on the earth's surface, to arts, manufactures and science" had become apparent to all. He emphasized the practical advantages that would come from geological studies, the profit that would come from knowledge, and the loss of money that would befall the ignorant.

Geological knowledge about the locations of valuable materials (coal, tin, gypsum, etc.), and where they would *not* be found, could be used to save time and money. Maclure was intensely interested in the nature of ores and minerals and their location—the "principal object of geology."

The extensive anthracite beds of Pennsylvania and the use of anthracite in the smelting of iron ore were of particular interest to him. In a letter to Benjamin Silliman in 1826, he predicted that once the technique of smelting was perfected, these natural resources would "render the state the most productive in the Union" and make the United States "one of the greatest iron countries on the globe."[30] Indeed, it was this source of energy that made Pennsylvania a powerhouse and provided Philadelphia with the means to become the leading American manufacturing city during the early Industrial Revolution.

Study of rocks and soil could inform the constructors of buildings and roads about the fitness of the earth to support the structures they built; glass and brick makers and agriculturists would profit from a knowledge of what lay underneath their feet. To Maclure it was obvious that useful information for the creation of wealth and the enhancement of the social good was what should be taught in schools, especially "when it is considered, that less than half the time necessary to give a smattering of any of the dead languages at our academies, would be more than sufficient to give our youth a complete knowledge of the common and useful applications of earth and rocks."[31] The chapter on rocks and soil in *Observations* ends almost eloquently: "On looking back to the probable past, without going so far as to interfere with any of the present general laws of nature, it may occur, that before all this alluvial, secondary or transitional had been rolled about, pounded up and mixed by the rains and rivers, united with the various operations of vegetable and animal production, the state of this earth most probably was different, when the first lichen began to accelerate the progress of decomposition on the surface of the first rock."[32]

In keeping with Maclure's utilitarian philosophy, a major portion of his treatise was devoted to geology as applied to agriculture. He dwelt on the properties of different kinds of soil formed over great periods of time by the decomposition, dissolution, and mixture of various classes of rocks, with a further addition of decaying organic matter. He compared them according to their capacities to retain water and heat, their solubility, and their ability to anchor and promote growth of vegetation. His preoccupation with such matters is evidenced in a letter of congratulations to Thomas Jefferson in 1801 for becoming president. His salutation was quickly followed by a dissertation on agricultural practices, climatic conditions, and the nature of the soil of Germany and the Rhine valley, which he had just visited, topics which were of vital interest to both men.[33]

Having summarized the kinds and origins of soils in *Observations*, Maclure used the information to assess the agricultural and economic potential of every region and state of the Union, starting with New England and ending with the Louisiana Territory. His analysis took into account the effect of such factors as climate, rivers, and soil fertility on the number of people that could be supported in every region. Recognizing the need for land management, he deplored the practice of wanton clearing of forest land, and he warned that, without trees, the soil could not hold water and would heat up, which in turn would affect the climate and decrease agricultural productivity. He discussed the fertilization of soil and intelligent farming methods that do not exhaust and ruin the soil, the cost of construction and benefits of canals for the transportation of coal and farm produce to markets, and the impact of geology on the economically important navigation of coastal waters, inlets, and rivers.

Toward the end of *Observations*, Maclure's grand, geopolitical view of America took on an ideological hue in his discussion of the productivity of the land. An important part of his calculations dealt with the number of productive workers necessary to support nonproductive people (anyone who did not work for a living). In essence, he separated the population of the United States into two groups, each living in their own country, each with a different outlook. Those living to the west of the Allegheny Mountains formed a newer, less established, and more egalitarian group, who enjoyed a natural protection from foreign invasion in the interior of the continent, while those to the east of the mountains, in a land with a long coastline, were vulnerable to foreign attack, inducing them to maintain an army and navy at great expense, with higher taxes. Inevitably a military establishment would appear, which in the past had "always produced the ruin of free and equal representative government."[34] Maclure felt that those in the West were more likely to establish a government representative of the majority, unlike in the East, where the governance of the older, more established states is "founded on a representation of property, and liable to be governed by the few or the minority"—a fate that in time would probably befall the West. A more democratic United States did in fact come into existence in the Midwest, populated by settlers who had no future in Virginia and New York with their aristocratic landowners and from other regions where the poor soil had been exhausted.[35] Maclure's stated preference for the West and his distaste for the city were important factors that prompted his later association with Robert Owen and the utopian colony, New Harmony, in southwestern Indiana. Maclure wrote that "large mercantile towns are sinks of great corruption, vice, and money," which engender hatred "aggravated by the existence of slavery."[36] On the other hand, he envisioned the sunny, fertile Mississippi valley as the breadbasket of the country, supporting a population that would reach 200 million.

Observations, a work that gathered together many facts and opinions, had the good fortune to appear at the right moment in American history, and it was the most important work on North American geology published in the first quarter of the nineteenth century. Maclure sent Jefferson a copy of the book, which he dutifully read "with as much pleasure as I could expect to receive from writings in a branch of science with which I am so little familiar," and he found it praiseworthy. Jefferson had "neglected" geological theory because he was unable to accept the proposal that "little . . . scratches of 100 feet deep into the crust of a globe of 8,000 miles diameter could authorize conjecture as to its internal structure." But the president commended Maclure for sticking to the truly "useful" part of geology—the distribution of rocks and minerals in the United States. How American![37]

Observations was hailed as a landmark achievement, but some found fault with the work. Amos Eaton, the only professor at Rensselaer Institute in Troy, New York, and a major figure in geology who ranked with Maclure as a field geologist, was ungenerous in his praise. He found the book a "heterogeneous thing," noting that its classification of American rocks and strata was found wanting, although its map was useful. Balancing negative comments with praise, he admitted that as a geologist, Maclure (along with himself) was "the best I know of" and that he appreciated the practical applications of his book. Eaton believed that *Observations* initiated major progress in geographical geology in the United States.[38]

Sir Charles Lyell judged Maclure to be an accurate observer, while Benjamin Silliman spoke of him in the most respectful terms, placing him in the company of the greatest geologists of his day, which included Abraham Werner. He pointed out that in his "Herculean labour," Maclure had studied far more of the earth's surface than did Werner, and there were few, if any, geologists who had studied so much of Europe and North and Central America as had Maclure.[39] *The Edinburgh Review* called *Observations* an "excellent" publication and its author "thoroughly conversant with his subject." *Observations* was an "interesting" and "instructive" sketch of a large part of North America. Despite a patronizing tone, the overall judgment was sufficiently positive to secure Maclure's reputation. To have an American work reviewed in a European journal and translated into French was in itself an achievement.[40]

Observations was well reviewed by Constantine Samuel Rafinesque, a brilliant but controversial polymath. Treating the book kindly, he lauded Maclure for his "zeal, assiduity, perspicuity, liberality, utility, and an early attention to this important subject," and found the book praiseworthy for its attempt to relate geology to agriculture and mining and for its insistence that this information should be taught in schools. However, he felt that there was too little mention of the fossils in the surface structure of the earth.[41] The criticism was valid, for Maclure seemed to display relatively little interest in fossils and paleontology. While he studied rock formations, he made no original contributions to paleontology, perhaps because the discipline was almost entirely speculative, and there was little of economic benefit in the fossil remains of animals. Still, in his honor, a genus of a Silurian spiral shell was named after him.[42]

Maclure continued his geologic explorations of the United States and published a revised edition in 1818 in the *Transactions of the American Philosophical Society*.[43] This was probably the most comprehensive geologic survey and map in the world at the time, a work that marked the zenith of Maclure's geological efforts. The making of such an extensive map was remarkable, for as late as 1829, Maclure could write that "there is no geological map of a whole country on the continent of Europe, and the maps of all the partial basins and patches of mountains yet published would scarcely cover the surface of the state of New York or Pennsylvania."[44] Maclure's great achievement, according to Silliman, was that he had "struck out the grand outline of North American geographical geology." To do this, he carried out his work mostly unassisted, suffering hunger, thirst, and exposure in the wilds and the rude incomprehension of the frontier people.[45]

The monograph was really the first broad, systematic inventory of American geology, and befitting his role as a leader, Maclure was deputizing future geologists to fill in the details—a starting point of modern geology in the United States that justified Maclure's reputation as the "father of American geology." A century later, Maclure was honored by the historian George P. Merrill, who proclaimed the period of geological study in the United States between 1785 and 1819 the Maclurean era.[46] Maclure was also well known through his letters to his fellow geologist and friend Benjamin Silliman, editor of the *American Journal of Sciences*, who dutifully published almost anything he had to say, for Maclure was the president of the American Geological Society. The reputation of this munificent geologist was also enhanced by two notable papers, one on the geology of the West Indian islands,[47] and another on the formation of rocks.[48]

Though few in number in the first decades of the nineteenth century, those with an interest in geology were distributed widely throughout America, forming a nationwide network whose members communicated with one another through letters, publications, visits, and lectures, but there were too few dedicated American geologists to constitute a professional association. This cooperative arrangement was especially suited to the peripatetic Maclure, who was able to communicate directly with so many of his colleagues. Since he had studied geological formations in several countries, there were almost no geologists in the world with his broad experience and knowledge, and so Maclure became an invaluable member of a national and international network, who picked up and imparted the latest information wherever he went.

The young science of geology grew slowly in America because higher education had been a casualty of the Revolution, and from the very beginning of the republic, the government was reluctant to support "private pursuits," which included science in general and geological surveys in particular. President Jefferson and his successors warned that government funding would not be forthcoming and was not to be depended on; the raising of money would best be left to the individual states and to private individuals.

The first organized attempt in the United States to teach students to become geologists dates from 1802 when Benjamin Silliman, twenty-two years of age and recently graduated from law, was appointed professor of chemistry and natural science at Yale College. After educating himself in geology and chemistry at the University of Pennsylvania and in Europe, where he purchased books and instruments, he was ready to begin lecturing in 1804, and he reported on the mineralogy of the New Haven area.[49]

Recognizing the need for instruction in geology in the United States, Maclure hired a young geologist from Paris, S. Godon, to lecture in Boston and Philadelphia.[50] Interest grew, and in 1807 James Mease published an ambitious 500-page book on the geology of the United States. By 1816 there were enough students and aspiring geologists to ensure the success of the first substantial American textbook of mineralogy and geology, *Elementary Treatise on Mineralogy and Geology* by Parker Cleaveland, a primer that incorporated Maclure's work and was taken seriously by Europeans.

It was not until 1819 that the American Geological Society was founded by Benjamin Silliman, with William Maclure as president, to promote geological study, and in 1830, government-sponsored geologic surveys were organized. As the Nestor of American geology, Maclure's was a respected voice, passing judgment on various publications and expressing opinions in Silliman's *American Journal of Science* and in the *Journal of the Academy of Natural Sciences of Philadelphia*. His articles were widely read, and some were translated into German and published as a kind of survey of American geology and mineralogy.[51]

In 1825 Maclure wrote to Benjamin Silliman, "To collect facts without being warped by an attachment to systems is the surest mode of advancing geology, as well as all other sciences; and it gives me pleasure to see our young geologists so far on the right road. They have proved that they are fit to walk alone and to make the best use of their senses."[52] By midcentury America was turning out geologists of international stature, and American geology was on a par with European geology, the first discipline to attain this distinction, and the rise was in no small part due to Maclure's efforts. Just after Maclure's death, the Rogers brothers published a work on the origin of the Appalachian range, the first major, seminal geological study by Americans, one which European geologists studied carefully.[53]

Maclure's mode of operation in geology was different from that which he employed in commerce and education. In the diligent pursuit of his geologic interests, he acted alone or with a single helper; he himself did the work. In his other interests, he exhibited a chief executive officer's mentality, almost always an absentee, making decisions and engaging others to help effect his plans. Quite clearly, Maclure was a hardheaded rationalist, a skeptic who insisted on separating the knowable from the unknowable, which "like everything else out of reach of our senses" consists of "mere suppositions." But as he aged and became less physically active, he tended to theorize more freely, and he expressed his long-held views in essays and articles that were published in his *Opinions* of 1831–38.

The Enlightenment had enlivened Maclure's thought, and its pronouncements suffused his thinking: "There is nothing fixed or stationary in nature; all is in motion, either increasing or decreasing . . . [only] the laws of motion are fixed and unalterable." He challenged the religious notion of immutability: "Do not the changes and variations which take place every day, every year, denote any thing but fixity in the habit of our species? Moses genealogy of the earth and all upon it, being created in six days, about five or six thousand years ago, was generally received as incontrovertible fact, that no one dared to doubt; now geology has progressed so far as to investigate many changes, both in animate and inanimate matter, as to raise great doubts when, if ever, the earth was made, and to encourage the anti-christian suppositions of the naturalist. . . . The earth and all that is on it must either be from eternity or was made. As far as our observations have gone, there are perpetual changes but no principles of a creation or something out of nothing."[54]

In his writings of the 1830s, Maclure's comments on recent findings in geology and paleontology reveal a considerable understanding of change in biological forms and extinction. "We find the remains of animals and perhaps vegetables, in a form which does not at present exist, and some of the animals at present existing . . . which affords some reason to suppose that there has been a succession of animals, and, perhaps vegetable life, produced on or near the surface of the earth." The location of fossil remains suggested to him that there were earlier and later forms of life, some existing after others had ceased to exist. Maclure was deeply impressed by the immensity of coal beds derived from ancient plant life, and based on the antiquity of strata in which the remains of fish could be identified, he maintained that fish were the most ancient of all animals, whereas humans had appeared on the world scene only recently—"one of the last formations"—because human "relics" could not be found in deeper strata where the remains of ancient animals, "thousands of millions of years" of age, are located.[55] Maclure was not alone in this kind of thinking, all of which predated Darwin's work (1859). However, there was never a hint of the mechanism by which change took place—natural selection, as proposed by Darwin.

Maclure was sympathetic to the idea of directionality in Lamarckian evolution: "Nature began with the most simple, and gradually proceeded to the more complicated and perfect [man]," but he admitted that he was indulging in speculation, against which he was on guard. Yet one could not deny that differences existed between petrified bones and the bones of comparable nineteenth-century animals, and that even the nature of disease changed in time. Since nature has produced new species of plants and animals in the past, he asked, why shouldn't the process be going on at the present time?[56]

Painfully aware of the flawed nature of humans, he hoped that if inevitable change had brought humankind this far, in time humans would "progress towards perfection of intellect by civilization." Progress should be rapid, as judged by the increase in volume of the skulls of the most advanced human beings (Europeans), compared to those of "savages" (nonwhite), all taking place in a relatively short period of time. Maclure cited the results of Samuel G. Morton, who had measured the cranial volumes of humans of every "race" and found that the white European had the greatest volume, obviously reflecting brain size and intelligence, a conclusion that reinforced common prejudice. Morton, a respected scientist in Philadelphia, had amassed the largest collection of human skulls in the world (many provided by Maclure when he resided in Mexico), and with these, he carried out much-cited investigations. His studies, now known to be in error in their methodology and damaging in their conclusions, were to a large degree the foundation of scientific racism in America and Europe.[57] Maclure's pious hope for rapid improvement of humans was strongly influenced by a flawed study.

Maclure had broken with his mercantile past to concentrate on geology, a seemingly undeveloped, abstruse subject, upon which he imposed an economic bias. Having made his fortune over two decades as a merchant and established himself in America as one of its leading geologists, he was in the privileged position of a generous patron. He aimed to promote the study of natural history by supporting young investigators, scientific institutions, and expeditions at a time when they received little help from government; his timely support proved to be invaluable in the development of American science. His other major concern was social: he burned to improve the lot of suffering humankind. Maclure was enraged that the great majority of people everywhere were being exploited by a minority, and he was obsessed with the desire to remedy the situation.

✳

SIX

Introduction of Progressive Education to the United States

I have considered ignorance as the cause of all the miseries and errors of mankind and have used all my endeavors to reduce the quantity of that truly diabolical evil.

Maclure to Madame Marie Duclos Fretageot, May 22, 1820

Maclure frequently wrote that the only firm foundation of freedom lay in the "equal division of property and knowledge and power" in which workers have their "proportion of the cake."[1] Despite their overwhelming majority, the workers lacked influence and power even in a democratic state with universal suffrage because they did not know what their best interests were, the consequence of their inadequate education; they were ignorant, and ignorant people are easily deceived. Maclure's thinking about education's reformative power became clear only after he came upon the system of education devised by Johann Heinrich Pestalozzi, and his student Philipp Emmanuel von Fellenberg, in Switzerland, and practiced in their schools.

This new chapter in Maclure's thinking about education's role in social reform began in 1804. While in Paris, Maclure became acquainted with Joseph Nicholas Neef, a teacher in an unconventional school for orphans based on Pestalozzi's novel system of educating children. This was the first Pestalozzian school Maclure had encountered, and showing great interest in the system, he was advised to visit Pestalozzi himself whenever he was in Switzerland.[2] Neef had been converted to this new approach to education while recuperating from a serious wound he received in the battle at Arcole in Italy during the Napoleonic wars.[3] He was so taken with Pestalozzi that he spent several years at his school in the canton of Berne teaching orphans, and by so doing Neef became one of many ardent disciples of the master.[4]

In October 1805, while studying the geology of Switzerland, Maclure visited Pestalozzi's school for boys and girls, situated in a large stone castle in Yverdon, a town of 6,000, on Lake Neufchâtel. Truly impressed, Maclure wrote in his diary that the institution he had come upon used "the most rational system of education" he had ever seen, and again, it brought to mind some of his own inadequacies that had resulted from not having had such an education.[5] The visit to this school changed Maclure's life forever, for it provided him with what he thought was a realistic way of using his fortune to eliminate societal inequities. To Maclure, it was an epiphany. The new system would enlighten the children of the "useful" class with "useful" knowledge, imparting to them a sense of confidence, pride, and dignity while providing information that would enable them to earn a respectable living. Surely these students would become thinking, responsible adults who would know what were their own best interests. They would be capable of making rational decisions, and in a democracy with universal suffrage, they would prevail.

Maclure visited Pestalozzi seven times, and on each occasion he spent a few summer months observing, assessing, and discussing the kind of instruction best suited for the masses, with regard to content and method of teaching.[6] Pestalozzi was happy to receive generous financial backing, books, and scientific instruments from Maclure, who assumed the role of a missionary for Pestalozzi, spreading the word and persuading his friends to send their children to Yverdon.[7]

Unfortunately, the task of reform was formidable because "the free circulation of knowledge is opposed by a host of enemies, who by education and interest are drilled to obstruct the dissemination of useful knowledge," and so by controlling education, the minority shaped the thinking of the majority.[8] Maclure was not primarily an educator interested in the reform of education. He was a political radical bent on redistributing wealth and power, and he concluded that this could be done by educating the children of workers, who as adults would constitute an enlightened majority through their elected representatives. In the declarative language of the democratic radical, he proclaimed, "Knowledge is power in political societies, and it is, perhaps, as impossible to keep a well informed people in slavery, as it is to make an ignorant people enjoy the blessings of freedom."[9]

Pestalozzi's school in Yverdon was filled with happy, energetic students who took great pleasure in their "mental labor and study . . . constantly occupied with something useful to themselves and others," and Maclure recalled that he never "heard a cry or any demonstration of pain or displeasure, nor even an angry word from either teacher or pupil." Students and graduates, born into the laboring classes, were uniformly enthusiastic about the school and the system. The difference between this educational experience and that of the conventional school was enormous, one in which students were imprisoned "for four or five hours in the day, to a task of irksome and disgusting study, which nothing but the fear of punishment could force them to perform; after which they are let loose on society for eight hours, full of revenge and retaliation against their jailors." According to Maclure, the "rigors" of this kind of education give rise to "violence . . . rebellious riots . . . mutiny" and "the destruction of other's property."[10] One might conclude that this torrent of evil consequences arose from Maclure's unhappy memories of his own school days.

Always concerned with the burden of the poor, Pestalozzi's focus was on providing children with an education of a practical nature acquired through experience, that would enable them to appreciate their own interests, and this would best be accomplished by teachers who had a full understanding of the lives of misery their students endured. With brilliant insight, he recognized the important role of the child's emotional development in learning, and he was probably the first to "psychologize the instruction of mankind" in an explicit and systematic fashion, providing a framework upon which research and experiments in education could be carried out.[11] His emphasis was on educating the very young, for the earlier a child was exposed to Pestalozzian schooling, the more receptive the child would be thereafter to further instruction. To this end Pestalozzi wrote *A Mother's Manual*, the very foundation of which was that the mind of a child is a *tabula rasa*, differing from that of an adult: "Man is born neither good nor bad but that the disposition to become either good or bad is intimately interwoven with his organization" and that "our education is the only cause of our becoming either good, useful, intelligent, rational, moral, and virtuous beings, or wicked, noxious, ignorant, senseless, superstitious, criminal, and therefore miserable creatures."[12] Essential to the process was a loving, trusting relationship between student and teacher, the consequence of which would be an equality that is the basis of all morality.[13]

Following John Locke's idea that the mind is the product of sensation and that knowledge is acquired through the senses, Pestalozzi insisted that education be based on "sense experience," which is primary, followed by language, which is learned to describe the impressions made on the senses.[14] The early phase of education was essentially nonverbal. Drawing was to come before writing, and conversation before reading. Students first learned through practical application with real objects such as beans or movable letters rather than learning through abstract concepts from books or highly verbal instruction. As students learned how to spin and weave, they were taught the arithmetic required for the task. Boys were expected to master at least one mechanical art such as lithography or typesetting and printing, activities that would also teach them how to spell and provide insights into the structure of language. Students interested in music and singing were encouraged to incorporate them into their daily lives. Field study, in which nature was experienced directly, was a particularly important part of instruction in natural science and not an independent entity. Gymnastics and physical instruction—swimming and ice skating—were essential parts of the curriculum. In his new, uncharted pedagogical approach, there was an experimental aspect to what was taught and encouraged—the dedicated teacher learning as he went along.

Pestalozzi rejected the notion of teaching by rote, especially the memorizing of Greek and Latin classics, an exercise that would overload the child's memory; method was more important than content. His was a "natural" system of learning tailored to the development of the child living in the real world, a process that took time. Perhaps Maclure was so taken with Pestalozzian education and idealized it because he recognized that it was everything that had been denied him. He felt that his own early education had left him with little of value, far less than only one aspect of the many parts of Pestalozzi's system—for instance, the measuring and drawing to scale of gardens which laid the foundation "for a quick, impartial and logical judgment, in deciding on all questions of intricacy and difficulty." Education "ought to be the apprenticeship of life, and children ought to be taught what imperious necessity may force them to practice," and this Pestalozzi attempted to do.[15] The Pestalozzian mode of education had a special appeal for Maclure, for he was a man of action, always on the go, learning by experience and from everyone he encountered. It is no wonder that Maclure chose geology as his life's work, especially research in the field, which necessitated travel and exploration. He was mildly skeptical of bookish geologists who were more taken with theory.

The subject matter to be taught was reduced to its simplest elements, and as the child grasped the basics, more complex elements would be added—"a graduated series of instructions" that was not to be rushed, for learning did not take place by dramatic "jumps or starts, nor giant strides."[16] Students should be allowed to advance at their own speed, and teaching should take place in a loving, homelike environment, one engendering a feeling of emotional security in students that enhanced their capacity to learn, especially from one another. Students and teachers dined together to encourage a warm relationship. Pestalozzi also stressed the importance of active involvement by a supportive family in the child's learning process. The environment provided by such an education would "give the necessary direction and support to the unfolding of a child's faculties."[17]

In this idyllic setting, Pestalozzi was regarded as a kindly father figure who, unlike his predecessors, instructed his pupils in a remarkably permissive environment. He was intensely involved with his charges as illustrated by his description of teaching at his first school in Stans when he was a young man: "We shared our food and drink. I had neither family, friends, nor servants—nothing but them. I was with them in sickness and in health; and when they slept I went last to bed, and yet I was the first to get up. Their clothes and bodies were intolerably filthy, but I looked after both myself." The parents distrusted Pestalozzi, not least because he was not religious and gave no spiritual or moral instruction. However, Pestalozzi believed that these matters were best taught in the home, really the heart of all education, and he was comforted by the fact that the children "felt I was being treated unfairly by their parents, and loved me the more, I think, for it." Despite the warm atmosphere and the intense concern of the teacher for his pupils, the daily schedule was rigorous and exhausting. The day began at 6 AM and ended at 8 PM, the afternoons reserved for "useful" work, with lessons in the morning and evening. Pestalozzi linked study in school with manual labor in the fields and workshops, an aspect of the program that was accentuated and fully developed by Philipp Emmanuel von Fellenberg, a former student of Pestalozzi.

According to Pestalozzi, the parents and townspeople grumbled, but a few months after the school was in operation, "it was evident that the children were all doing well, growing rapidly, and gaining color. The magistrates and ecclesiastics who saw them stated that they had improved almost beyond recognition." An educational commission (1800) reported, "The first thing we noticed was that Pestalozzi's children learned to spell, read, write, and calculate well, arriving in six months at results which an ordinary village schoolmaster would hardly bring them to in three years," and the Council of Public Education in Berne (1802) declared that "Pestalozzi has discovered the real and universal laws of all elementary teaching."[18] He was beloved by all, an amiable, honest man, recognized for his "great heart" and his "genius." Of course, this amazing success was due to the fact that Pestalozzi was an extraordinarily dedicated teacher. But how would the average teacher fare in this system? Maclure recognized that there were few teachers like Pestalozzi, willing to sacrifice themselves as he did.

Pestalozzi goes on: "As soon as [the children] found that they could learn, their zeal was indefatigable; and in a few weeks children who had never before opened a book, and could hardly repeat the pater noster or an ave, would study the whole day long with the keenest interest. . . . What encouraged them most was the thought of not always remaining poor, but at some day taking their place again amongst their fellows, with knowledge and talents that should make them useful, and win them the esteem of other people. They felt that, owing to my care, they made more progress in this respect than other children. They perfectly understood that all they did was but a preparation for their future activity, and they looked forward to happiness as the certain result of their perseverance."[19] Astonishing results such as this, the fruit of Pestalozzi's superhuman devotion as much as his theorizing, must have impressed Maclure and given him reason to hope that society's problems could indeed be solved by education of the young. Surely these children would grow up to be the kind of enlightened adults who would fulfill Maclure's dreams. His essays on education attest to the fact that he was in complete accord with Pestalozzi's "natural" approach, as opposed to the conventional "artificial" system.[20]

Pestalozzi's new philosophy of how children should be taught became widely known through his essays and books. One such was *How Gertrude Teaches Her Children* (1801), a quixotic work that is partly autobiographical, in which the reader is frequently taken into the author's confidence with intimate little confessions. The work bursts with philosophical exposition and letters to colleagues, but it is primarily a teacher's manual.[21] Another important work was *Leonard and Gertrude,* which he wrote in 1781 and published in four volumes between 1781 and 1787. Despite Pestalozzi's occasional lack of clarity in his presentation, the nineteenth century saw widespread adoption of his principles in whole or in part, with reform of the existing educational systems and the establishment of new schools, some supervised by disciples of the master. But not all Pestalozzian schools succeeded; in Paris, these schools languished because they were not favored by Napoleon, who had his wars and other matters to worry about, nor by the Bourbons, who considered the system too revolutionary.[22] Still, it is fair to say that Pestalozzi, the dominant educational theorist of his time, revolutionized pedagogy.[23] The reform of German education, to a significant extent based on Pestalozzi's ideas, has been considered an important factor in Germany's ascendancy in the nineteenth century, and his philosophy was a powerful influence on English, French, and American educators.[24] It is generally acknowledged that "no educator in modern times has more profoundly influenced his contemporaries and immediate successors than Pestalozzi,"[25] and in fact all contemporary, progressive pedagogy began with, and still echoes, Pestalozzian dogma.

Pestalozzi's humane and startlingly "modern" ideas about education, so different from the approach used in conventional schools, elicited enormous interest among those concerned with the teaching of children. Admired by educators and political leaders, they came to the school from every European country to observe its operations. Frederick of Prussia and Czar Alexander of Russia were interested, and the school was visited by Queen Louisa and the kings of Spain, Holland, and Denmark, some of whom enrolled their students.

Fellenberg, a disciple of Pestalozzi, was also important in the formulation of a suitable education for older working-class children. In Fellenberg's school in Hofwyl near Berne, which Maclure visited several times, a large component of their time was spent in physical labor, especially as farmhands in an agricultural institution with workshops for instruction in mechanics, carpentry, cabinetry, and shoemaking, and two hours a day were devoted to letters and music. Maclure approved of Fellenberg's notion that a school should aim to make students self-sufficient with respect to their food, clothing, and education by their own labor, both mental and physical, which were enjoined so that life was made more pleasant and productive. Children were treated as little adults, and the goal was to train and educate both their minds and their bodies, while work should be regarded as recreational, rather than burdensome, and as training for the future; the aim was to produce workers who could think. Based on what he saw, Maclure's hope was to establish Pestalozzi-Fellenberg schools that would prepare working-class children for life, teaching them a craft or trade in industrial schools by which they could earn a living and be happy, productive, and even self-supporting while they learned. He predicted that when these children, steeped in Pestalozzian educational philosophy, grew up and became parents, their children would almost automatically receive a "useful" education at home, and eventually teachers would not be needed.

Fellenberg, an aristocrat and an authoritarian, had no wish to disrupt the social order, and so his school operated on a two-track system, for the poor and the rich. The students mingled, took some instruction in common—mechanics and agriculture—and both performed manual labor and learned to appreciate it. For affluent students, Fellenberg ran a literary institute, where science and horsemanship were stressed, and a boarding school for which they were charged the considerable tuition of $600 per year.[26] In this school there was one teacher for every three students.

The Yverdon school bias was vocational and practical, principally aimed at the children of the poor whose education should increase their pliancy, versatility, and potential while operating within their social class. It should provide greater insight of individuals into themselves and their class in relation to other classes—a principle applicable to all social classes. Members would change their attitudes toward class, but not their class itself, where Pestalozzi believed they would always remain, with little prospect of social mobility. The process would actually contribute to social stability, something greatly desired by the Swiss upper echelon, who feared the social unrest that education might foment. Indeed, Pestalozzi believed that social unrest was the consequence of a poor (non-Pestalozzian) education, a surprising, original conclusion that piqued the curiosity of enlightened leaders throughout Europe who desired both social stability and an educated citizenry. However, according to Maclure's line of thinking, Pestalozzi's system of education would most certainly lead to social unrest, and it would result in the redistribution of wealth and power as the properly educated poor would assume their rightful place in society.

Although troubled by the dreadful state of the Swiss peasant, Pestalozzi was not as politicized or as intensely concerned with the social, economic, and political consequences of his methods as was the doctrinaire Maclure, although he did believe that ultimately society could be reformed and the peasant empowered through education of the young, albeit at a slow pace. The situation in the United States was quite different and would require some rethinking, for this was a land without a feudal tradition, where the people, especially those at the frontier, were ferociously independent.

Robert Owen, founder with Maclure of the New Harmony colony, was so impressed by Fellenberg that he sent his sons, ages fifteen and sixteen, to the Hofwyl college.[27] One of them, Robert Dale Owen, described his experience there as "a marvelous life." Despite the fact that students had come from virtually every country in Europe, many of whom were princes, dukes, and minor nobility, the college was established and run as a democratic republic, with a constitution written, amended, and voted upon by the students. Fellenberg was president, but in fact he was called "foster-father." Teachers never interfered, nor were they considered the "enemy." Punishments were never meted out by authorities, and disciplinary problems were almost nonexistent. There were no rewards, punishments, or class rankings. Students became members of committees, one of which was responsible for tending to the poor in the Hofwyl area. A working, stable, utopian system was established in which aristocrats, converted into republicans without titles, participated in elections for office, but without electioneering. Owen, who later wrote his account after years in the U.S. Congress, declared that this "remarkable" system, based largely on trust and a sense of responsibility, "gave birth to public spirit and to social and civic virtues." However, he admitted that the success of the operation was largely due to its leader, Fellenberg, for after his death the brilliance of the school faded, and it became rather conventional.[28]

An institution such as this was a powerful magnet for Maclure, for in it he could envision the expansion of an idea capable of embracing all of society—both the affluent and laboring classes—providing solutions to many of their problems. He was convinced that Pestalozzi's and Fellenberg's empirical and rationalist system of education, in which "useful," practical knowledge linking mental and physical labor (properly taught) was the means by which the intelligence and industry of a whole segment of society could be harnessed.[29] At this early date, however, Maclure's utopian dreams were unchallenged by the perversity, corruptibility, and self-interest of people he later dealt with in the real world.

Thereafter, Maclure's effort in the field of education centered on establishing and supporting, with his own money, schools for boys and girls grounded on the principles of Pestalozzi and Fellenberg. Maclure insisted that girls as well as boys should be educated and that girls would be welcomed into his schools. Women should "be put on a par of education with the men, and be rendered capable of filling all places of honor and profit that their physical strength enables them to perform, and that the world in its progress towards perfection, will not lose the assistance of the half of our species, by the degraded state in which females are kept."[30]

These schools would serve as templates from which an entire national public school system could be modeled. Tempering his expansive thinking with practical concerns, he stressed that his educational strategy would require enormous sums of money to support the large numbers of teachers needed in the many schools to educate all working-class children. And so, to make the plan feasible, he insisted that expenses be carefully monitored and kept to a minimum. For practical economic reasons he encouraged the popular Lancastrian system of teaching, where one master could teach many pupils through a platoon system in which senior and better students served as monitors to instruct their juniors, as opposed to the conventional system where one master lectured a class. It was a standardized, somewhat superficial, mechanical mode of instruction that could accommodate large numbers of students; most attractive of all, it was relatively inexpensive. Lancastrian education was a concession to the dictates of real life, where there were insufficient numbers of trained teachers, many if not most of whom were unwilling to expend themselves in the teaching process, and few would be emotionally involved enough to create the warm, loving atmosphere that Pestalozzi had provided.

Another departure was in rote learning, with rewards and punishments —necessities in the Lancastrian system, but abhorrent to Pestalozzi, albeit in an ambiguous way. Moreover, the Lancastrian system did not lend itself to the study of nature in the field, a core component of the Pestalozzian method. Thus Maclure's trade-off was to sponsor a no-nonsense institution that was not quite Pestalozzi's joyous school, filled with music, singing, and play. With his burning social agenda, and an appreciation of the resources available, Maclure was willing to compromise—indeed, he was compelled so long as "positive useful knowledge" was imparted to the young; only then would they be prepared for life. As much as the practical-minded Maclure appreciated Pestalozzian-Fellenbergian education, he must have realized that it would have to be modified for American needs, and he surely knew that there would be implacable opposition to a new system of education by a conservative moneyed class, and by organized religion as well, since no provisions were made in the curriculum for religious instruction.

Pestalozzi's system did not address the question of adult education; this was a separate problem. As Maclure wrote, "It was impossible to give any real information to men," for the task of undoing the consequences of a lifetime's learning was formidable. But education of adults to enable them to think for themselves, make reasonable, commonsense judgments, and participate in government was also essential in the creation of his heaven on earth, despite his occasional statements that adults were incapable of learning. Experience had taught him that children could not be educated if the parents, in their ignorance, were unsympathetic and uncooperative. He advocated the formation of clubs in which members would attend lectures, read books to each other, and discuss them for mutual enlightenment, and toward the end of his life, his founding of many libraries in Indiana and Illinois for adults and the Working Men's Institute at New Harmony attested to the importance he placed on adult education.[31]

According to Maclure, just as members of society can be divided into producers and nonproducers, so there are two kinds of education—"the useful and necessary" for the benefit of the producers, and the "ornamental" and "amusing," appropriate for the nonproducers. As a man of science it is of significance that Maclure called useful education "natural," while ornamental education he dubbed "artificial," terms borrowed from biological taxonomy, an important subject, heatedly debated in the early nineteenth century. The "natural" system prevailed—a decisive advance in the development of modern biology. Maclure seemed to lean on the authority of an ascendant science to bolster his views on education.

The Pestalozzian education advocated by Maclure for both boys and girls—the acquisition of "positive knowledge"—was distinctly pragmatic and utilitarian: "The grand object of all beings is happiness, and the principal aim of all species of education, ought to be to put the youth on the straight road to the goal. . . . Education ought to be the apprenticeship of life, and children ought to be taught what imperious necessity may force them to practice when men, always preferring the useful to the ornamental; preparing them to withstand the reverses of fortune. . . . To court pleasure and avoid pain includes the greater part of the motive of human actions; to accomplish which, children ought to be taught to avoid remorse, fear, misery, and ennui."[32]

The art of "drawing and delineation" of real objects, which Maclure considered a language, was equivalent in importance to spoken and written language. It was indispensable for an understanding of "mechanics and natural history," especially in the absence of the objects of study. Chemistry was valuable to the layman for its use in the kitchen in food processing, soap making, dyeing, and candle making. There was no reason to take a complete course in chemistry if one was not going to use it; he left to the professors the theoretical aspects of the subject. The teaching of mathematics, mechanics, geography, and astronomy was of the greatest importance. Natural history was a useful subject because it "instructs us in the various uses we can make of the animate and inanimate bodies that nature has placed round us," and it greatly pleases children while they "acquire the habit of investigation." Maclure held mineralogy and geology, which deal with the substances under people's feet, as the most important for children to master. Botanical instruction should be limited to describing and naming plants, especially those on the farm, while zoological study should be confined to animals that are used for food or that "work for us, or prey on our property."

Subjects to be taught in Maclure's schools were stripped of everything but their "useful" components, which is the knowledge he felt students needed. Familiarity with Latin and Greek was "useless," irrelevant to the lives of the ordinary working person. A hardheaded Maclure disdained Belles Lettres, literature that "disguises the truth." The teaching of history (self-serving stories concocted by the nonproducers), fine art, and literature, which he considered a frivolous exercise favored by the rich, was like "attempting to polish a sponge." Surprisingly, although he was an international traveler who knew several languages, Maclure was also not enthusiastic about instruction in modern languages.[33]

He believed that "a plain simple narrative of facts, got by evidence of the senses, is all the literature that 99/100ths of mankind have occasion for, and the thing most to be guarded against is the exaggerated delusions of the imagination." Broadly, he considered knowledge about things and facts "useful," while knowledge about theories and abstractions was "useless." In this category he dismissed political knowledge as "the science of mere sound words without utility." In a letter to Madame Marie Duclos Fretageot, a French schoolmistress and head of a Pestalozzian school for girls in Philadelphia which he supported, he advised, "The best way is to occupy your pupils so constantly with positive knowledge as not to allow their minds to wander into the region of fiction and imagination."[34] To him, positive knowledge consisted of "truths that don't change with the caprice of fashion or opinion." A relatively silent man, the spoken word was suspect, lending itself to the useless exercise of the imagination. However, he acknowledged the importance of scholarly study by specialists—a second and independent track for the minority.[35]

The rich were satisfied with an educational system that promoted the status quo. According to Maclure, they endowed elite schools that were of no use to the working class—an "absurd, monkish system of education," modeled after English universities that emphasized the classics, a system that was "slavishly" adopted by Americans. He never failed to berate existing universities and colleges,[36] and he did not favor the founding of a national university in Washington because it would only promote "useless" education, a "killing of time" for the children of the rich.

Not only was the existing educational system without benefit to the children of the worker, it did not even provide future administrators and legislators with adequate tools to function effectively in government. Maclure deplored the fact that "there is little or no science in our legislators" and that "of all leading American politicians, only Franklin and Jefferson were literate in science." According to Maclure, "Jefferson was the only scientific man a free people ever put in power." One of the reasons Maclure sympathized with the French Revolution was that many of its leaders were scientists, which assured him that some good would come of it. To Maclure, the rapid advances made by the French were the consequences of "men of science [being] elevated by democracy into power."[37] In 1835, when Maclure was concerned with Central and South American affairs, he expressed admiration for Jose Maria Vargas, president of Venezuela, "an able physician and a man of science" who had promulgated "the most liberal constitution yet in existence," and he proposed him for membership in the ANSP.[38]

Joseph Neef in Paris was Maclure's connection with Pestalozzian philosophy. As a former student at Burgdorf remembered nostalgically, Neef was the embodiment of the Pestalozzian credo: "Our joy reached its climax when our gymnastic master, Neef, with his peculiar charm, took part in it. . . . This Neef was an old soldier . . . with a great beard, a crabbed face, a severe air, a rude exterior, but he was kindness itself. When he marched with the air of a trooper at the head of sixty or eighty children, his great voice thundering a Swiss air, then he enchanted the whole school. Singing was always a true means of recreation at Burgdorf. We sang everywhere, in the open air, when travelling, when walking, in the evening in the court of the castle, and this singing together contributed much to keep up a spirit of good feeling and harmony among us. I should say that Neef, in spite of the rudeness of his exterior, was the pupils' favorite, and for this reason he lived always with them, and felt happiest when amongst them. He played, exercised, walked, bathed, threw stones with the pupils all in a childish spirit; this is how he had such unlimited authority over them. Meanwhile he was not a pedagogue; he only had the heart of one."[39]

Maclure was so much in accord with Pestalozzi's philosophy that he envisioned an entire American educational system based on it, and to initiate the movement he had tried to lure Pestalozzi to the United States. But knowing no English, and feeling too old to learn, Pestalozzi declined. However, he suggested that Joseph Neef might be available. Neef was also reluctant. But not to be put off, Maclure offered to pay passage from Paris to Philadelphia for Neef and his family, guaranteed him a salary of $500 per year for three years, and gave him two years of support to learn English—an offer too good to refuse. Neef, an ardent republican eager to see America, was overwhelmed by Maclure's generosity and accepted the offer—the beginning of a collaboration that lasted many years in Philadelphia and later at New Harmony. Thus was established the first school based on Pestalozzian principles in America. While Maclure revered education for its ability to change society, Neef regarded education as the facilitator of personal development—the liberation of the mind—the two functions complementing each other.

Neef had been flattered by a visit from Napoleon, Talleyrand, and the American ambassador, an event at which Maclure, a guest of the ambassador, first met these great personages. But after watching the children perform, Maclure overheard Talleyrand say to an inattentive Napoleon, "It is too much for us—entirely too free."[40] In fact, Neef was not unhappy to leave Paris, despite his school's modest success. He complained that he was underpaid and lonely in Paris and that the French didn't really understand the Pestalozzian philosophy. As the Napoleonic dictatorship tightened, Neef's republican sentiments grew stronger, and his eagerness to take part in the democratic experiment across the Atlantic grew.[41]

Maclure was the very first to be heard explaining and extolling the Pestalozzian system in the United States. He published several articles (in the form of letters) to the *National Intelligencer and Washington Advertiser* in 1806, Silliman's *American Journal of Science and the Arts,* and the *New-Harmony Gazette* to spread the word about Pestalozzi's approach to education: "The great and fundamental principle is never to attempt to teach children what they cannot comprehend, and to teach them in the exact ratio of their understanding it, without omitting one link in the chain of ratiocination, proceeding always from the known to the unknown, from the most easy to the most difficult, practicing the most extensive and accurate use of all senses, exercising, improving, and perfecting all the mental and corporeal faculties by quickening combination, accelerating and carefully arranging comparison, judiciously and impartially making deductions, summing up the results free from prejudices and cautiously avoiding the delusions of imagination, the constant source of ignorance and error."[42] Although he sometimes did not remain faithful to these goals, he can be credited with introducing a progressive system of education to the New World.

Neef and his family settled in Philadelphia, and in the next few years he learned English. To alert the public about the new system of education that he had brought from Europe, even before he opened his school, Neef wrote a *Sketch of a Plan and Method of Education* (1808). In this book, the first "on the science of education in the new world," printed at Maclure's expense, Pestalozzi's principles and methodology were presented and explained with the aim of enlightening Americans and guiding the parents of prospective students. A paean to Pestalozzi, he insisted that there was nothing new under the sun and that he was simply trying to make the students "learn the old things in a new way" by "inquiry and investigation." The key to the new approach was to awaken the child's interest, which was best done through the direct study of natural history, not through slavish devotion to books.[43] This principle was later echoed by Louis Agassiz in his admonition, "Study nature, not books." Maclure agreed, and he deplored "the superabundant verbiage of books, and the fatiguing task of readers, to turn over 1,000 pages in search of the lines of common sense that might be contained in a few pages, when all that is useless, mysterious, or incomprehensible was abstracted."[44]

To further enlighten the populace about the Pestalozzian way, Neef published his translation of *The Logic of Condillac* (1809), which elucidated the philosophy underlying his pedagogical practice. His third book appeared in 1813, dedicated to teachers, *The Method of Instructing Children Rationally in the Arts of Writing and Reading,* a work filled with examples of teaching, dialogues with students, and general instructions for teachers, all born of firsthand experience.

Although Neef admired Pestalozzi, he introduced important changes as he adapted Pestalozzian notions to education in the United States. Pestalozzi had grown up in a rigid, class-bound society, and this is reflected in his writings. He assumed that social mobility was all but impossible, and so his education was designed to maximize the effectiveness of boys and girls within their class, not to change their social status. People should be judged by their educational achievement, not by their social class. The situation was quite different in the United States, a vast, abundant land with little history. There was almost no hardened class structure, the status at birth was not critically important, and whatever boundaries did exist could readily be crossed. What counted was personal achievement, especially at the frontier of a land of opportunity and an optimistic belief in progress. In America, one was free to choose one's social status—something new in the history of humankind. Clearly, Pestalozzian principles designed for the education of Swiss children could not be applied to American education without changes, and this Neef attempted to do with limited success.[45] The aim of education in America was to instill a faith in the individual that one can achieve anything if one has the ability and is willing to work hard. To succeed, individuals must develop a critical judgment and think for themselves. Most certainly, Maclure approved of these shifts, and he may have contributed to their formulation, but the fact remains that his primary aim was to use education to reform the governance and economics of the country.

By 1809, with Maclure's support, Neef had established a Pestalozzian school for about seventy-five boys between the ages of six and eight, a few miles outside the city at the Falls of the Schuylkill River near the present-day Fairmont Waterworks, then a suburb of Philadelphia. The school consisted of three buildings: a dormitory, a schoolhouse, and a residence that housed Neef, his wife, Eloisa, and their children. Eloisa tended to domestic matters and the business aspects of the enterprise, for Neef was remiss in sending bills. This first Pestalozzian school in America incorporated Fellenberg's system of practical education in the form of manual labor. Most students were from Philadelphia, but several came from cities along the east coast, from Massachusetts to Georgia, and from Kentucky, which suggests that the school and its promising new pedagogical methods were not unknown and that there were parents willing to take a chance, even if most were skeptical of a new, untried system.[46]

From the memoirs of a student who attended the school, it is apparent that Neef was adored by his students and was a worthy disciple of Pestalozzi. Pupils did not use books, nor was the alphabet taught. Instruction in languages, mathematics, and natural sciences was oral, and the reasons for learning these subjects were stressed. Students were constantly enjoying field trips where they were instructed in geology, botany, and agriculture while barefoot and hatless. Maclure closely followed the school's operation and was exceedingly pleased, while others who examined the school were "astonished" at the progress made by students. Its record of turning out accomplished young men, in proportion to its size, purportedly exceeded all other schools. A list of seventy-five graduates compiled by Maclure detailing their subsequent history leaves little doubt that the school turned out many successful individuals.[47] But as Maclure declared, in the end Neef was destroyed: "His success for the first 5 years was his greatest crime with that hord of canibals that pray on humanity and live by the rank growth of ignorance."[48] His enemies said that Neef's only authority was Pestalozzi and himself, and that he would take advice from no one—typical of zealots who believe themselves to be the keepers of the truth. Neef was an impassioned proselytizer, who extolled the benefits of the new system without let-up.

The school did well until 1812, when for unknown reasons Neef decided to move to Village Green, near Chester, Pennsylvania, perhaps because it was deeper in the countryside. But few students enrolled, and financial difficulties mounted until the school was forced to close in 1815, amid rising criticism. Still, testimonials of former students at Village Green, including that of Admiral David G. Farragut, suggest that Neef's teaching was effective and appreciated.

Neef was not socially at ease, and he found it difficult to adapt to American ways. Pestalozzian pedagogy, the major precursor of modern "progressive" educational practice, elicited criticism then that is very much the same as it is now, 200 years later. Many complained that Neef was not enough of a disciplinarian and that his students had too much freedom. Parents were alarmed at his permissiveness and concerned that their children were not reading until they were ten or eleven and hardly even knew what a book was. They insisted that their children learn to read so that they could study American history as well as other subjects. In fact, Pestalozzi, like Maclure, had a low opinion of history and did not want it in his curriculum. His preference for various subjects was highly restricted, which educators and parents deplored. The literary and classical approach to education, so familiar to parents, was being sacrificed to the practical and "useful"—too many walks in the woods and fields, and too much emphasis on physical education. While parents wanted more emphasis on teaching facts (different from Maclure's "useful," hard facts), the aim of the new approach was to teach the child how to think and reason. Perhaps the most serious charge against Neef, one that outraged parents, was that he was an outspoken atheist who neglected religious study of any kind and whose instruction in morality was strictly secular.

While Neef was criticized by conservative forces at this desperate time, he was actively supported and encouraged by Maclure, who was contemptuous of criticism by conventional educators and "ignorant" parents. Maclure was particularly saddened by this lack of success, because he felt that if Neef's school had survived, Pestalozzian education would have become widespread in America—a toehold had been lost. This failure taught Maclure that, above all, patience was needed when attempting to reform education in a major way or to change social attitudes, for the human race makes progress at a "snail's pace," and generations need pass before change is seen.[49]

With the failure of the Village Green school, a Dr. Galt whose two sons were students of Neef persuaded him to establish a Pestalozzian school in Louisville, Kentucky, a town of 5,000. This, too, failed, and after a few years, despondent and in debt, Neef turned to farming in Kentucky to make a living. He and Maclure had started with such great hope for Pestalozzian schools in the United States, but they were now deeply disheartened, for they had made little impact on American education. They had not created a movement with a cadre of followers; instead, they had roused the opposition. Since Neef had insisted that the school be kept small so that he could do all the teaching, no teachers were trained to spread the word. The rebirth of Maclure's and Neef's dream did not occur until a decade later with the establishment of the New Harmony colony on the banks of the Wabash River in 1826 (chapter 13).

Pestalozzi's pedagogy was too promising and important to succeed or fail in the United States on the basis of the efforts of Neef and Maclure alone, but it was they who had introduced Pestalozzi to America. His ideas took hold in various ways, "corrupted" by people who "misinterpreted" him. Only after the Civil War did the Pestalozzian program have a significant impact in the United States through the writings of English educators, since almost no Americans had direct experience in Pestalozzian schools. In the 1830s Amos Bronson Alcott (father of Louisa May Alcott) established a Pestalozzian school in Boston. Conversations he had with children from under seven years of age to twelve on scriptural matters reveal the astonishing capacity of these pupils to think and articulate when guided by a brilliant teacher. The children's wondrous responses and their power of reasoning demonstrate that they had unsuspected, unrealized capabilities that Pestalozzi "discovered" and attempted to bring to light.[50]

Maclure's contribution to public education was notable, but in some ways his views were so far in advance of what was acceptable to parents for their children that his efforts were bound to fail. The same may be said for his efforts in adult education, for he simply expected too much from the poor and the working man. Establishing a model school, and hoping that the world would copy it, was not enough. There never was any sort of broadly based organization to promote his cause.

While it can be said that Maclure was imbued with Pestalozzi's ideas, the schools he supported differed in significant ways from that of the master. Maclure was almost fanatical about imparting verifiable facts, numbers, and statistics, capable of answering important questions, and not open to "interpretation." Although Charles Dickens was probably unaware of Maclure's existence, he came close to capturing him (in some ways) in creating Mr. Gradgrind, a teacher in *Hard Times,* whose mantra was "facts, facts, facts!"

While Pestalozzi was sensitive to the emotional needs of the child, Maclure sacrificed without qualm this important part of Pestalozzi's approach to satisfy his sociopolitical agenda. Maclure was not strong in his understanding of human nature and its subtleties, as suggested by his remoteness and in his relationship with women and his family. Pestalozzi stressed the role of the joyful and loving relationship between teacher and pupil, whereas Maclure gave this relationship scant attention; he seemed to want competence and little else from his teachers and the assurance that children should not be left idle. His aim was to provide a progressive form of teaching, but he was satisfied with imparting myriad useful facts which would require the student to resort to abhorred "rote learning," especially when mere hypothesizing was frowned upon. As much as Maclure disdained rote learning, it is difficult to see how a child could assimilate the vast numbers of facts favored by Maclure's educational system without resorting to rote learning. For practical reasons, he accepted the Lancastrian method of instruction in which education was based on "signals and commands," with students being humiliated for poor performance—anathema to Pestalozzi. This was probably the kind of schooling Maclure had endured for many years, against which he railed, and yet to which he was returning. To Pestalozzi and Maclure, parents were an important part of the educational dynamic, but in practice Maclure simply cut them out of the process, regarding them as a hindrance and a nuisance.

At the time that Neef's educational efforts were being underwritten in the United States, Maclure also maintained a Pestalozzian school in his home at 20 rue des Brodeurs in the Faubourg Saint Germain. A school for boys, it was run by Guillaume Sylvan Casimir Phiquepal d'Arusmont (later called William Phiquepal in the United States). Phiquepal had impressive credentials: a medical degree and training in psychiatry with Philippe Pinel, a major figure in converting asylums for the insane into humane institutions of treatment. Abandoning this field, Phiquepal returned to education to direct Maclure's Pestalozzian school in Paris, where he devised new ways of teaching "useful" subjects such as carpentry, printing, tailoring, shoemaking, barrel making, and blacksmithing. The school was highly praised, but declined in popularity as the oppressive influence of the recently restored Bourbon dynasty grew.[51] Maclure wrote that in Phiquepal's school "boys from eight to ten years old become good mineralogists and chemists, almost equal to the analysis of rocks, and [they] speak and grammatically understand three to four modern languages, mathematics in all its branches, are good arithmeticians, and in short, before the arrival of that critical time, the age of puberty, they will possess more useful knowledge than they could have had by the old system at the age of thirty or forty"—a remarkably rosy picture.[52] However, enrollment was low because the French seemed resistant to change and reluctant to adopt a radical new method of educating their children that did not include religious instruction.

Maclure aroused the suspicion of the royalist government of France, for his Parisian friends were largely liberal and were looked upon as subversive. Six of Maclure's essays for the *Revue Encyclopédique,* edited by his friend Marc-Antoine Jullien, had been rejected by the Bourbon censor because they were too radical. No wonder, for in one of the rejected essays he wrote of "the incompatibility of the two powers, hereditary and elective, to exist peaceably in the same body politic."[53] Years later he published the essays in the United States in his *Opinions* (1831–38) and had them translated into Spanish. When, in 1820, French officials did not allow Pestalozzi's books into the country for Phiquepal's use, Maclure commented, "Not a ray of light is permitted to disturb the Political and religious obscurity of the Royal French Kingdom from without, and I fear that the internal light is mere moonshine."[54] Adding to Maclure's troubles, Phiquepal proved to be vain, difficult, and undependable. It was not long before Maclure gave up trying to enlighten the French and transferred his hopes to Spain, with its new liberal government, and to America, whose people he considered "more usefully rational."

Fortunately, Phiquepal's assistant, Madame Fretageot, rapidly assumed the role of Maclure's reliable agent and confidante. Maclure's relationship with her had begun in the spring of 1819, when they were introduced by his colleague, Isaac Cox Barnet, the American consul in Paris. A French woman who was destined to play a major part in Maclure's efforts to bring Pestalozzi's system of education to the United States, she had run a boardinghouse for girls in Philadelphia and had returned to France when her parents died. Attracted to each other, Maclure and Madame soon formed a close relationship.

The couple passed the summer in Paris, a time of close discussion about social problems, philanthropy, and educational philosophy, during which they came to know each other well, he the inspirational teacher, instructor in the English language, potential employer and benefactor. She was caught up in his dreams, her expectations fueled by the man and his ideas, and by her own admission, the experience left a lasting glow that is evident in her adoring letters. While Maclure spent the next winter in the south of France ameliorating his "gout, rheumatism, and gravel," Madame Fretageot, left to pine for her hero, moved into his home on the rue des Brodeurs and prepared herself by continuing to learn English and other subjects, useful for tasks Maclure would assign her. In one of her letters to Maclure early on, she wrote, "You made me compliment about my english writing. Was you not my master? This dear master, when in these amiable evenings gave me not only english lessons but all what is reassonable and free of error flowed from his lips like pure water issues from a rock. How happy I was then."[55] While her writings in English became serviceable, they were invariably spotted with errors in grammar and spelling, as were those of her master. Maclure, who was often away, kept in constant touch with Madame Fretageot by mail between 1820 and 1833. She was his most trusted agent, and she kept him fully informed about how his interests fared.[56]

Born in 1783 near Lyon, she had married Joseph Fretageot, a veteran of Napoleon's army, a survivor of the retreat from Moscow, and for the remainder of his life a semi-invalid. A lapsed Catholic, Madame Fretageot had been unhappily married, and without qualm she had left her husband to go to America to teach, leaving their son, Achille, in Paris. Later, as a teenager, Achille came to New Harmony, Indiana, to finish his education. Since Madame Fretageot and Maclure were close, almost uxorial, and her unbounded affection and admiration for him was no secret, rumor had it that they were intimate and that Achille was their illegitimate child. But as reasonable as this supposition might seem, it was without foundation, for Achille was born long before Madame and Maclure ever met.[57]

She worshipped Maclure, but there was a great disparity in their ages, she being thirty-six and he, fifty-six.[58] Maclure had the very highest regard for her and made her a partner in their efforts, as their close relationship, apparently nonsexual, continued. Maclure's diplomatic skills are evident in their extensive correspondence, as he gingerly turned aside the eager advances of this determined woman—without giving offence. She seemed to laughingly accept Maclure's diagnosis that her feelings toward him resulted from a mental illness, to which she responded that it was one from which she would never recover. It would seem that this loyal, reliable, and selfless woman sought, above all, the consummation of Maclure's plans for education. When Madame Fretageot wanted to purchase a house in Philadelphia, Maclure warned her not to buy it in her name because her husband (in France) could make a claim on it. It would be far wiser to have Maclure the owner. Fortunate to have such an assistant, he treated her kindly, and when she later provoked him by going over to the opposition (briefly teaching in a competing school), he was angered, but soon forgave her.

At first she assisted in the Pestalozzian school run by William Phiquepal. Maclure had hoped that she would run a girls school on her own in Paris, but the plan was abandoned. In 1821 Madame left for America to establish a progressive Pestalozzian school in Philadelphia to be underwritten by Maclure. In 1824, Phiquepal conceded defeat after royalist French authorities made teaching too difficult for him. Maclure had been constantly troubled by his school for boys in Paris, run by Phiquepal, assisted by Auguste Comte, a young philosopher, hired as a gymnastics teacher (later to become famous as the author of *Positivism*). He had wanted to bring Comte to Spain, where he was trying to establish another school, and then to the United States, but the plan fell through.[59] The Paris school, floundering in a hostile climate, was ultimately abandoned, and Maclure brought Phiquepal to America, as he had Neef and Madame Fretageot.[60]

Maclure now had little doubt that reform in the education of children, so necessary for a workable democracy, had the greatest chance of success in the United States where there was stability and promise because of its independent, prosperous "middling and labouring or productive classes." He wrote, "I consider Philadelphia at the top of civilization in the United States, and the United States at the top of the civilized world."[61]

While in Paris, Madame continued to express her feelings toward Maclure, who was spending the winter in the south of Spain: "O my dear friend! If I could hold your hand in mine this dumb language should be better understood than words. Am I not to be pitied being obliged to live so far from you?"[62] In another letter, she broke down: "It is indeed a pleasure for me to do things for . . . the most amiable, the most beloved, the most cherished of men. When my thoughts are turned on your side (it is very often) my eyes are full of tears, my heart is broken of sorrow because I cannot see you, I cannot hold your hand in mine. You don't know such privation."[63] There was no measured response to such an appeal, and so Maclure ignored her entreaties and filled his letters with much praise, advice about purchases, handling of specimens for shipment to America, and warnings about dealing with certain people. The letter was the ideal vehicle for Maclure's inclination to lecture and instruct, and this he did profusely, ending lengthy disquisitions with a cool, "Remain with much affection, sincerely."

Her heart-wrenching pleas unanswered, they were sometimes reduced to "my dear friend," or "I love you in spite of all," but they never disappeared. Indeed, outbursts surfaced from time to time between proper expressions of praise for his admirable qualities. In late July 1821, lonely and anxious in Le Havre, waiting for a wind to take her to America, she wrote to him in Spain: "The more I know you the more I love you, my beloved friend. You have condemned me to live far from you. It is a continual regret, a continual grief, and my sorrow shall end only when we reunite."[64] Maclure was indeed fortunate in enlisting the services of this loyal, selfless, intelligent woman, who was willing to sublimate her passion for the fulfillment of his grand plans.

The relationship of Maclure and Madame and the nature of Maclure's sexuality have given rise to considerable speculation. Despite the profession of love and admiration in Madame's letters, there is nothing in any of them that even hints that there was ever sexual union—no memories or fond musings, and surely a bold, almost desperate Madame Fretageot would not have hesitated to remind him of specific moments in her private communications. But the intimacy of the sexual relationship is unknown to this day. Modern sensibility prompts examination of Maclure's sexuality. He seemed to be asexual, but with the suspicion that there was perhaps an unexpressed homosexual element (as far as is known)—in the manner of Henry James or John Singer Sargent. True, he always traveled in the company of a young male assistant, but there is not the slightest hint of anything other than friendship and mentorship. As a prominent man with strong and unpopular opinions, Maclure had enemies, and some of the young men with whom he traveled left him disgruntled for financial and other reasons, but there was never the slightest suggestion of impropriety on Maclure's part in the extensive writings of his companions or adversaries. As far as is known, there were no rumors or gossip. On the other hand, there were numerous outrageous allegations—probably untrue—concerning Maclure and Madame.

Having failed in her attempts to visit Maclure in Spain, Madame Fretageot left France in July 1821 for America.[65] Maclure thought it best that she settle in Philadelphia, "freest from the speculative prejudices of Religion and Politics," but certainly not Boston, which was "one of the last places I would recommend as being One of the most illiberal and bigoted cities in the Union."[66] He seems to have developed an antipathy to New England, looking upon it as the least likely place in America where Pestalozzian education would succeed, and he even disparaged her hiring New England teachers, for the "darkest corners" of their minds were slow to see "the light of reason"— perhaps a response to their religious heritage and John Adams's aggressive federalism and illiberal pronouncements about the common man.[67]

Madame Fretageot was contented to leave Paris and Phiquepal's failing school to strike out on her own once again. At times Phiquepal was impossible to deal with; in her words, he was incompetent, arrogant, touchy, and nasty, although there were instances when she praised him to the heavens. In her last month in Paris, Madame Fretageot had dictionaries, books, journals, prints, telescopes, and microscopes sent to Philadelphia for her use and for a school for boys in Germantown sponsored by Reuben Haines, an influential Quaker who kept an eye on Madame's school for Maclure.[68] Generously supported, she purchased whatever supplies and equipment she needed, including an organ and a new kind of printing press. However generous he was, Maclure wanted his agents to be prudent in their buying, saving money by buying good secondhand apparatus. Always on the lookout for equipment that would be of help, he sent a pressure cooker to the Philadelphia school that "makes soup in 30 minutes and boils bone to softness," but he cautioned her to heed the safety valve to prevent an explosion. Along with supplies and equipment came a generous amount of advice—from the best flour to use for bread, to the sole use of cheaper and healthier iron pots and utensils, to the avoidance of copper pots, and the best exercise and diet for children. He warned Madame that acid sauces should not be allowed to stand in earthenware pots because harmful acetate of lead would leach out. Maclure was a fount of useful information and advice, lofty or mundane.

He urged Madame Fretageot to hire women teachers, as he felt women were equal to, if not better than, men because of "their superior good sense." He considered prejudice against women participating in all trades and occupations as "the remains of barbarity," and he deplored the waste incurred by excluding them from productive work. By contrast, Quaker women were "treated like reasonable beings, and is perhaps the cause of their superior good sense and intellectual acquirements."[69] Maclure was partial to the enlightened view that "the station that women hold in society has been with some justice considered a good barometer of civilization. In the savage state, they are slaves to the physical force of men. Society loses the services of half its population, for if women are given the same opportunities as men, they will perform equally as well."[70] While we applaud Maclure for his views about equality of gender, we are put off by his favoring the hiring of women because three could be had for the price of one man. Madame Fretageot, however, objected to the hiring of three women teachers because, she felt, they would be constantly wrangling and out of her control, while she was confident that she could handle a single male. Maclure was pleased with the success of her school in Philadelphia, which operated at capacity—about thirty-two students.

Cultivated Philadelphia Quakers like William Price and his brother Philip, a young physician, tutored by Madame Fretageot, were taken with the Pestalozzian approach to education to become her fervent supporters. Madame's financial needs were met by Maclure through his business agent in Philadelphia. Madame Fretageot's school at 240 Filbert Street seemed to be particularly attractive to Quakers, and it had as students the daughters of Reuben Haines, William Duane, the editor of the *Jeffersonian Philadelphia Aurora,* and John Griscom, a Columbia University professor of chemistry.[71] Griscom, a Quaker, had visited Pestalozzi's school in Switzerland and Robert Owen's schools in New Lanark, Scotland, and had been impressed by them. While they were all enthusiastic about establishing a Pestalozzian school in America and assisting Madame, conservative Quakers were displeased with Madame's curriculum, which lacked religious study. To answer the complaint, pupils were taken to liberal Quaker (Hicksite) services on Sundays. This was something of a compromise by a diplomatic Madame Fretageot, who knew how to handle parents and their dissatisfactions, and as she said, she always left them "satisfied."[72] A gruff Joseph Neef had failed because he lacked diplomatic skills and was incapable of finding a middle ground.[73]

From time to time, Charles-Alexandre Lesueur and John James Audubon were enlisted as instructors in art,[74] and the nearby Peale's Museum of Natural History provided the children with instructive outings. Madame's school soon became financially self-sufficient,[75] and required relocation to a larger building, and by April 1824, she was making a profit of $1,000 per year, which she set aside to repay Maclure's investment, offering the profit to him for any purpose that he cared to suggest. Eager to please, she begged him to return from Spain to see for himself how well his school was doing. For a person convinced that this new method of education would be the salvation of society, Madame's achievement and the approval of prominent Quakers whom Maclure admired must have been particularly encouraging, fully justifying his belief that women were the equal of men as teachers and as directors of schools. Madame was highly respected in the city, gaining many friends and allies, and it was through her, and the writings of Robert Owen that she had brought to America from Europe, that several Philadelphians were converted to the educational and social views of the English socialist reformer Owen, who was soon to arrive on American shores.[76]

Madame's school in Philadelphia lasted four years, until her departure for New Harmony, Indiana, under Maclure's auspices, at the end of 1825. But in the meantime resentment grew in an American society that cherished its religion. As Maclure's agent, it was she who bore the brunt of Philadelphia's hostility to his antagonism toward religion. Maclure's exalted view of the openminded, tolerant American had led him to expect better. The response of this pragmatic man was to advise Madame Fretageot to be circumspect about religious matters. Privately they regarded themselves as a righteous, persecuted minority of two, and their letters were colored by the intimacy of the besieged. They would never forget what happened to poor, brutally honest Neef, master of a defunct school, whose "ennimies were the ennimies of the propagation of Knowledge . . . they will stop at nothing to ruin you," and Maclure likened what happened to Neef to Napoleon's imprisonment on the island of Elba.[77] Neef's failure troubled Maclure because he believed that his school had been successful, graduating a remarkable number of leading citizens; its failure gave heart to the enemies of educational reform.

However much Maclure cursed the rich, he was restrained in his public proclamations. In America, Neef had translated from the French a work by Condillac on education which many Americans would find offensive, and he had added an advertisement for his school, thereby linking the two. Apparently Maclure felt that the notice was impolitic, not suitable for American ears, and so he advised Madame Fretageot to omit it in the printing. He was also unhappy that Neef had mentioned his name in his book, calling it imprudent, for now his "name [was] exemplified for atheistical and Deistical ideas" by those who did not even know him.[78] If Maclure wanted to be an anonymous force (an unrealistic wish), perhaps in part because of a self-effacing modesty, this position changed during his later New Harmony and Mexican years when he published his radical and inflammatory political essays for all to see.

An extraordinary man of goodwill and imbued with his concern for humanity, Maclure was among the first of the great American philanthropists. He attempted to bring Pestalozzi's pedagogic principles and mode of teaching to France, America, and Spain, with the expectation that educational reform would lead to the amelioration of society's problems—a daunting mission that was not well managed. In the end, the venture unraveled because the program was looked upon by those in power as a threat to the social order, and it never succeeded in fully winning the confidence and cooperation of the working and middle classes nor the sympathy of the enlightened members of the upper class. However, many a nineteenth-century child gratefully benefited from Maclure's dream.

✳

SEVEN

The Grand Tour of Europe (1809–1815)

Maclure spent the better part of two years in America (1808–1809), during which he launched extensive explorations that enabled him to create his masterwork, *Observations on the Geology of the United States of North America*.[1] With the manuscript ready for publication, he was off again for Europe, where he spent the next six years, leaving but supporting a Pestalozzian school in Philadelphia, run by Joseph Neef. In essence, he was an immigrant American expatriate whose studies took him from one end of Europe to the other. He seemed to live for travel in order to see everything for himself, with occasional stops in major centers like Paris, London, and Stockholm, where he would converse with geologists and natural historians, examine rock collections, and dispatch specimens to America. In between, he rested from the stress and inconvenience of travel.

A pattern soon became evident in his journal entries—accurate and dispassionate geological descriptions alternating with heated polemics on all other subjects—jeremiads about the corruption of human beings and their societies by both power and poverty, each in its own way. Constant references to such matters as the enlightenment of society, the unequal distribution of wealth among the social classes, and governance of the people punctuate his diaries, his bitterest commentary being reserved for countries with the greatest poverty which were the worst abusers of power—Russia and Italy. In fact, his eyewitness accounts provide valuable information about Maclure himself, society in the early nineteenth century, and the difficulties endured by the traveler.

November 1809 found Maclure in Uppsala, where he spent four months ferreting out information about northern lands. According to Maclure, the University of Uppsala provided an education bereft of utility, whose students were ignorant and devoted to the pursuit of pleasure. There was such a notable absence of books and so little interest in reading, especially of a scientific nature, that he wondered, "How long will common sense be banished from the system of education?"

In Stockholm he lived in two small rooms in a modest hotel with a servant, to spare himself when he felt overworked, and he maintained a careful account of his personal expenses, which were kept to a minimum. A frugal man with simple tastes, who frowned on any display of affluence, he shunned travel in the grand style as would befit someone of his economic status. Arduous journeys devoid of civilized comforts, with an element of danger, must have given him a sense of meaningful service and sacrifice, as it might a soldier in a military operation. He had a particular admiration for the Swedish people because despite the inadequacy of their soil and a poor climate, their "poverty is joined by moral excellence, where honesty and probity pervade and elevate the millions to a much greater degree of happiness."[2]

With letters of introduction, Maclure befriended several notable Scandinavian chemists—Johan Afzelius of Uppsala and Jöns Jacob Berzelius of Stockholm—as well as prominent engineers, canal builders, and local statesmen. He conversed with them, visited nearby sites of geological interest, mines, iron foundries, tanneries, cobalt and chemical manufacturing plants, and the water supply of Stockholm. Hearing of Maclure's interest and expertise in the Pestalozzian approach to education, the Prince Royal, Karl August, consulted him to determine the applicability of the system to Sweden, which at the time was in need of educational reform. The meeting was in the form of an audience, the prince questioning Maclure in the presence of fifty officers—not quite a relaxed affair.[3]

In a changing world, rife with revolutionary thinking, of special interest was the formula by which the government, the upper class, the church, and the peasantry were each allotted land according to the new Swedish constitution. Evenhandedness was Maclure's test of worth, and not unexpectedly he was dissatisfied, for the peasants were once again bested by the rich and powerful, there being too much power, property, and privilege in the hands of the few. But even so, he was impressed by the rights actually bestowed on the peasantry. Still, he remained skeptical of politics.

The gathering of mineral and rock specimens for American institutions was a major justification for Maclure's travels. To acquire specimens he was compelled to deal with local suppliers, who in Sweden charged exorbitant prices so that only the very rich could afford to be collectors. He was outraged by the monopolies of suppliers that prevented prospective buyers from visiting sites where certain rocks abounded, destroyed material in order to keep the prices high, and sometimes sold common rocks at outlandish prices. Maclure grumbled that these "mineral merchants" were "men who pretend to science, warping and distorting the truth to serve the purpose of their trade."[4]

He found that practically no one he met in Europe knew anything about the United States, and he could not find a map of the United States in all of Sweden, in Spain outside of Madrid or in France outside of Paris. Maps could be purchased in Germany, however, even in small villages, perhaps reflecting a tradition of German emigration to the United States. Maclure's view of the Swedish people was at times inconsistent. At one point he labeled the people of Stockholm apathetic, without curiosity or energy. A "love of amusement infringes much upon the thinking powers and few of them go deep into any investigation . . . and they skim lightly over the most profound subject."[5] Yet he conceded that the people had both "good sense and moderation" and that their rate of literacy was high.

Maclure emerges from his chronicle as a sober man who disapproved of smoking and drinking, whose mission was so compelling, he had little time for humor or amorous encounters—at least none can be discerned in his diary. His explicit description of a massage and wash by a young Swedish woman intimates that he was capable of being aroused, although the experience itself is related in a dry, almost clinical style. No naughty asides or ribaldry here, just precise information!

Leaving Sweden, he traveled north along the Gulf of Bothnia to Lapland, and then southeast through Finland to St. Petersburg, conveyed by sled, carriage, or cart—not an easy journey, battling north winds and blinding snow. Although a victim of poor, jolting, slippery roads, sometimes in unbearable subzero weather, he persisted in doing what he always did—investigate mines, forests, rock formations, and the local populace (among whom were Laplanders with their great herds of reindeer).

As he journeyed through Finland, the Russian influence increased, as judged by the degraded state of the people and their miserable lives. "The rays of reason seem to diminish. The rosy clear faces of the Swedes and Finns began to disappear and a sallow, weather beaten face prevails. . . . The open, smiling countenances which brightened up with the smallest mark of civility are [now] succeeded by a sullen, contracted visage, fixed and immovable by anything but fear. Even the horses begin to participate and they are meager, balk, and require the whip."[6] As he neared St. Petersburg, he noted that the misery of both people and horses increased even more, and "a mixture of fear and hatred predominate[d]." He could find nothing to please him. The dirty inns run by coarse, villainous cheats were "the worst in Europe." The rooms were sometimes without furniture, obliging Maclure to sleep on the floor. The food was "dreadful," and he was "scarcely able to get a drink of water." The staff refused to perform any service unless they were paid in advance.

Finally, on March 30, 1810, he reached St. Petersburg, but only after a hassle at the border, where passports were taken and copied, the original to be returned at some indeterminate time. In order for this to happen, it was necessary to advertise in a daily newspaper that one was leaving the country, to hire an agent to do the paperwork, and to participate in official rigmarole that took over one month. Fearful and paranoid, officials were afraid that foreigners might sneak out of the country. The best hotels in the city were not only expensive; they were also fully occupied. So Maclure settled for four modest rooms, a "tolerable" arrangement in the Hotel du Nord, where he hired a servant. At times the hotel obtained its water for cooking and brewing tea from a nearby canal, sickening its guests.

In spite of all this, St. Petersburg was "magnificent," with large buildings, squares, and streets crowded with horse-drawn carriages. The immense pillars of the cathedral and churches and the furniture inlaid with semiprecious stones were dazzling Byzantine treasures, many of which, designed by French and Italian architects, were deteriorating and falling apart. Maclure deplored the fact that anything pleasing and useful was of foreign design, but Russia, since the time of Peter the Great, emerging from a profound barbarism, admired, copied, and adapted western ways while denigrating local creations and overlooked the creativity of native artists and craftsmen.

The variety of people, "their show and eastern parade," was "not to be found in other European capitals." The magnificent collection of paintings in the Hermitage he found inspiring, and as was his habit, he inspected the cabinets of rocks and minerals, animals, fossils, and shells at the Academy of Sciences and the School of Mines. While Maclure could not or would not mix with the lower orders of citizens, he spent many enjoyable moments at the English Club and the German Club, where one could mingle with expatriate Europeans and the "better classes" of Russians, including the nobility. Visitors could dine, read a variety of newspapers, play billiards, and chat.

If Maclure was unhappy about so much of what he had seen in Sweden, visiting Russia was a descent into hell. His notebook, which becomes more and more detailed, is a litany of almost unrelieved criticism. Through letters of introduction, he befriended and dined with the rich and the powerful and toured their mines and factories. Although he identified with his hosts and to some extent entered their world, he shrank from almost all other Russians because he thought them craven, grasping, and hostile— there seemed to be no "civilized" people in the middle. He had entered a feudal world, with an unbridgeable chasm between rich and poor, the likes of which he had never seen before.

A resolute defender of the French Revolution, in Russia he was confronted by, and was often at the mercy of, the kind of unpleasant, unattractive people—the oppressed—who had taken part in that violent insurrection, and he was compelled to reexamine his feelings toward them. To his credit, under duress, he could still properly evaluate their grievances and the injustices they were forced to suffer. What was utterly unacceptable to him was the indifference of the upper classes to the misery and wretchedness of the masses, who were in fact slaves—serfs—deprived of all rights. It was estimated that in a total population of 22 million males, 9 million were serfs. This was an unstable, precarious state that rendered education useless and would not improve until nobles and great landed proprietors understood that it was in their own interest to improve the situation. Maclure was very much aware of the similarities between life in Russia and the state of the French just before their revolution.

What troubled Maclure when he visited Russian factories was their utter inefficiency, the carelessness of the workers, and the waste. Workers with no hope of improving their lot were uninterested in their work and shockingly ignorant of what they were doing. As soon as the supervisor turned his back, they would stop working. In response, the Panopticon was introduced, which enabled masters to watch workers without being seen. Interestingly enough, Jeremy Bentham, the utilitarian, was enthused about the device, believing that secret observation would make steady workers out of the lazy, and he tried to have it introduced into England. But Maclure saw no good end in sight for this deplorable practice. "No progress is to be made by chaining the great mass of productive labor to ignorance and bad habits of bondage.... Anything which is left to their mental care depreciates immediately."[7] He was not speaking only of the Russian masses; the same applied to "our negroes" in America.

At the time of Maclure's visit in 1810, the Industrial Revolution was well under way in England, and from there it arrived in Russia through émigré mechanics, engineers, and entrepreneurs who, using steam power to manufacture everything from steam engines to glass products, hoped to make their fortune in this backward land of cheap labor and potential markets. Maclure met many of these men, and he visited their factories—a distillery for the production of vodka, a textile mill, and a porcelain factory where he proved to be sufficiently knowledgeable to suggest improvements in their technology. Wherever there was direction and supervision by western Europeans, operations were satisfactory, but as soon as they departed, there was near-catastrophe. The same hopeless condition held true for agriculture, specifically the inefficient cultivation of tobacco and cotton and the ignorant dismissal of the potato. Maclure could only conclude that despite the abundance and high quality of their natural resources, promising enterprises fell apart because the workers had no stake in what was going on in their country.

From time to time, Maclure's hatred of religious establishments found expression as he encountered the Eastern Orthodox Church and its priests, with their "mysterious, incomprehensible dogmas... [and] contrivances." The fervor of the masses at times of religious festivals was viewed by Maclure as a study in the profound faith of a people burdened with a sense of hopelessness. Religious services, "one of those superstitious farces [which] is acted out in all the Greek churches," was described by him in mocking tones: "Their bowing and crossing themselves, which they continue for hours together, and the vast number of people of all descriptions at this pantomimical exercise, gives such a ridiculous appearance to the whole that it is difficult from refraining from laughing... [yet] all of their churches were filled the whole night."[8]

Inflation had run rampant for years in Russia, and the country was afloat in paper money. The government was desperately trying to introduce economic reform to stabilize the economy, calling in paper money, offering crown lands to families, with mortgages at reasonable rates, and setting up a schedule of taxes. But the problems were systemic, vast in scale, and corruption was extensive. As for the legal system, it was primitive, operating "without defined law." The purveyance of arbitrary justice by corrupt judges was brutal and riddled with extortion and bribery. Public discipline consisted of whipping, and within the home the stick was used liberally. It is no wonder then that the brutalized lower orders with whom Maclure was forced to deal in his travels, operating at a near-subsistence level, were almost without exception surly, hostile, and dishonest. They had to be bribed to perform a service and often had to be paid beyond an agreed-upon price. A defining moment came when Maclure bought a new carriage with a one-year warranty. Within six hours the coach fell apart, and when he returned it to the coach maker, he was charged "an extravagant price" for repairs.

There is little record of Maclure's mid-June visit to Moscow, and what scant information there is only reaffirms his views on the dreadful state of Russia. By mid-August Maclure had reached Odessa where, as in the rest of Russia, tyranny and its consequences prevailed: "It would be a curious calculation to make of how much security, comfort, and happiness the great men lose for the pleasure of having it in their power to tyrannize. 'Tis a costly pleasure which they would be much better without. The ease and affluence of the British nobility, so superior in comfort to all of those on the continent, ought to have learned them a lesson. That is, that their interest is inseparable from the whole, and whatever regulation injures the great mass of the people injures equally the profits and privileges of the superior orders."[9]

It was in southern Russia and Odessa that Maclure first encountered Jews, and he described them at unusual length. Maclure was confident in the accuracy of his characterizations and his objectivity, and when he encountered towns "filled with Jews," often living under trying circumstances, he set down his impressions dispassionately, observing them as he would a tribe of primitive people. Struck by their beards, earlocks, and caftans, he described them as "an ugly, ill-made race" who suffered from too much inbreeding. They were "the most polite and hospitable people in the country, and for money they will render you any service you require"—something you could not buy with "money or civility" from the "natives." They constantly overcharged him for the rental of horses when he could not obtain them from the more conventional post stations, but he found that having paid an exorbitant rental, he could depend on the agreement made.

Jews in eastern Europe, who were just being liberated from ghettos by Napoleon in his eastward march, were obliged to make their living as best they could. Maclure approved of the liberation: "The elevation of the Jews by Napoleon to their rank amongst men is an act that will be productive of immense benefit in time. . . . They will lose many of their bad habits when they find consideration attached to character in proportion to the action of the individual . . . as the charitable Christians have done for so many centuries. That is, ever since they were the majority and had the power to persecute."[10] He also wrote, "The Jews can all read and write and are really the best informed people in the country, and of course their morals are better." This Maclure believed to be so because they were a free people. By contrast, he described the native Russians living in deplorable squalor as wretched thieves, insolent drunks, responsive only to beatings— "Ignorance is a bad servant and a worse master. 'Tis the devil of the bible and the evil spirit of all other religions."[11]

Forbidden from owning land, and blocked from entering professions or becoming farmers, Jews became entrepreneurs, peddling, milling, managing great estates, lending money, and at times indulging in business practices that were not entirely legal or ethical. Maclure observed that Jews, living in harsh societies of masters and slaves, sometimes took on the exploitative manners of the masters while adopting the rough and devious habits of the slaves. He was very much aware of bigotry and the degrading effect it had on all concerned.

Maclure entered Poland through Galicia, which had recently been taken over by Joseph II of Austria. The Napoleonic Civil Code had been adopted, giving peasants land and legal rights, the serfs had been freed, and conditions in the country had generally been improved, even though feudal attitudes persisted. The roads were good, people spoke civilly to each other, and there were potatoes in the fields. When bribery was necessary to retrieve his passport, Maclure ascribed it to the fact that they were still too close to Russia—a rare glimmer of humor in Maclure's odyssey.

In Warsaw, Maclure visited Julian Ursyn Niemcewicz, his Polish friend from Philadelphia with whom he had explored the Pennsylvania countryside. Niemcewicz had lived with Maclure, and now he returned the hospitality; they dined together every day and met the local intelligentsia, whom Maclure found "well-informed and polite" and capable of great sacrifices for their country. As a respected patriot, his well-known host provided an invaluable entrée into Polish society.

Maclure's visit to Russia and Poland was now at an end. His last entry in journal 10 was made on August 14, 1810, in Cracow. Despite all the aggravation and hardships, enough to discourage lesser mortals, Maclure had pressed on with his geological mission, as he broadened his experience in natural and social history. Few if any geologists had the vast, firsthand knowledge of this inveterate traveler, nor were there many that had such a complete knowledge about the natural resources of so many lands.

A gap of one year in the written record follows Maclure's visit to Russia and Poland. His next journal (no. 11) began on August 18, 1811, in Basel. There is reason to believe that before this time, Maclure spent the early part of the winter in Paris and the latter part in the south of France, interrupted by a visit to the United States, at a time when crossing the Atlantic Ocean was not without its risks and hardships. Returning to Europe once again, it is likely that he spent time in Belgium, Luxembourg, and western Germany, from which he sent home specimens, and then he was off to Basel, where the new journal commences.[12] An understanding of Maclure's philosophy can be gleaned from his diaries, which provide endless examples of his views, the basis for his predictable judgments about what he experienced. What he saw reaffirmed his strongly held beliefs. All this was later set down in essays in his *Opinions*.

The pilgrimage recorded in journal 11 resembles those described previously except that there is far more geology and less discourse on personal and social matters. While traveling, he was always the field geologist, describing massive formations and the regional distribution of rocks, with a view to reconciling the Werner-Hutton debate—water or fire as the dominant factor in shaping the earth's surface. The fossil remains of elephant, rhinoceros, and hippopotamus found in Tuscany, an intriguing oddity of great potential significance, commanded his (and everyone's) attention. As in his other journals, there are commentaries on an astonishing array of subjects, from farming, manufacturing, architecture, and building materials to details of the culture of oysters—truly an impressive display of interests and erudition. Because travel in Europe (compared with Russia) was civilized, he was less distracted from his geological investigations. As was his habit, Maclure was accompanied by a geologist, a M. Menard, probably from Geneva. From Maclure's remarks, he was irritated with Menard—"fatigued by the minutia of Mr. Menard's mode of examination" and the "multiplicity of his general and extensive inquiries, nine-tenths of which do not interest me," and so after two weeks, he suggested that they each go their own way. Maclure paid Menard 1,000 francs and bade him farewell.

Switzerland was a land of good roads, polite border officers, and friendly people who invited him into their spotless homes. However, some parts of the country were poorer than others, and Geneva he found to be "a dirty little town." Maclure was struck by the astonishing differences in the people from one region or valley to another—differences in their physiognomy, clothing, and level of prosperity, a somewhat loosely controlled study which confirmed his views on the influence of environment on human behavior. Matters other than geology caught his attention, such as the prevalence of goiter among women, especially in deep valleys of Switzerland that were subject to flooding, and a high incidence of cretinism near Evian.

Entries he made in his journal while in Neufchâtel illuminate Maclure's notions about governmental authority. The town had prospered while there was an "absence of political constraint" and an independence permitted by the controlling Prussian government. National and international trade had enriched them, but now with the various embargoes during the Napoleonic wars, there was a serious decline in foreign commerce, leaving local trade, which was small, as their only source of income. Their desperate condition confirmed Maclure's belief that the worst thing about war is that it puts an end to free commercial intercourse. It beggared those who were blockaded, and it harmed the restraining power which had hitherto enriched itself through international trade.

Maclure was deeply suspicious of governmental authority that could be wielded by officials, important or petty, elected or appointed, because invariably they made costly mistakes such as declaring war (something Thomas Jefferson avoided at all costs).[13] He was skeptical of nationalistic ardor, and while he was especially heedful of the welfare of the masses, his writings reveal that he was an elitist who really did not trust or even like them. He thought them ignorant, unthinking, and easily misled. But despite this, he often expressed his faith in the common man. Clearly not a populist, Maclure knew what was best for the people.

He preferred to write about larger themes and the powerful people who run countries, but he never discussed partisan politics in any detail or the sort of rousing, timely matters and national concerns that fill newspapers. Although he called them despots, Maclure admired strong, effective leaders such as Frederick the Great and Leopold II of Austria, who were perceived as improving the lot of their subjects. He claimed that the masses do better when power is placed in the hands of a single man rather than in the hands of a privileged few, implying that there is a greater chance that a group of people will form a corrupt oligarchy than that a single ruler will abuse his power—a questionable assumption. Citing Napoleon as an example of an enlightened, "benevolent" despot who could institute change to better the lives of his countrymen, he theorized that a single ruler had a greater chance of effecting change by decree. Although this might be true, a despot such as Napoleon could make bad judgments, such as his policy on education, according to Maclure.

Whenever Maclure was confronted by authority, he bristled, and the slightest affront provoked a diatribe on the abuse of power. Crossing into France, "the gendarmerie make their appearance . . . they represent that extinguisher of that last ray of personal liberty; that concatenation of power which embraces the most minute ramification of society, and which loads . . . all the weight of the imperial mantle upon the most insignificant individual in the social order. Whether it adds to the security of those in power is a doubt." While he felt that the people were comforted by the belief that there were some restraining powers on the authorities, "such limits are absolutely incompatible with any species of police."[14]

After two weeks of geological exploration in the French Alps, Maclure crossed the Simplon pass into Italy, where almost every daily journal entry began with "Fine weather."[15] While he was pleased with the variety of rocks and rock formations in the region, the native population did not particularly appeal to him. Being a rather formal, restrained individual, much like a proper English gentleman, he differed strikingly from the easygoing Italians, whom he considered irresponsible, undisciplined, undependable, and much too fun-loving. They would grate on the sensibilities of a rather humorless, work-driven traveler who rarely departed from his agenda, and so Maclure's journal is filled with pejorative comments that probably were never meant to be published. In contrast, he had great admiration for the French and believed they would never behave as badly as the Italians.

Maclure was struck by the intense regionalism of the country—one small area or town so different from its neighbor. In Milan he found strong anti-French sentiment, not only because of Napoleon's anti-Catholic pronouncements, which roused the clergy, but also because the invading French had conscripted young males for service in Russia where almost all perished. The Milanese, taken with opera and theater, were not particularly interested in science. Still, Maclure was able to befriend several local savants with worthwhile cabinets of curiosities. Noting how the "churches were filled with men and women of all classes," he found it impossible to understand how the Catholic Church could have such a command of the people: "I fear the reaction of superstition may produce the persecuting ages of bigotry again."

As he proceeded eastward across a populous northern Italy, noting its dominant geological features, he again found himself sleeping in filthy rooms with beds infested with bedbugs, and in the "best hotel" near Brescia he was "tormented" by fleas and vermin, even as he wrote. Outside, the noise, singing, and bustle went on "the whole night." Maclure noticed that all those who entered Brescia paid a tax at the gate, which he deemed "an unprofitable mode of raising tax." The imposition caused much inconvenience and delay for those people who, in order to get on with their business, felt it worthwhile to pay this small amount. Those in power preferred this mode of taxation because a large bureaucracy was required to oversee this seemingly innocuous process, and in carrying out its tasks, "the greater part of the population" were brought "within their grasp" and placed "under the lash of every subaltern. . . . By increasing the list of artificial crimes, they have more to punish or pardon as they see fit."[16]

Maclure proceeded to Verona, which was now part of the Napoleonic empire. In a time of general upheaval, and suffering from a want of trade, some groups were losing their power and others were benefiting—"the nobles and privileged orders are much injured by the annihilation of the feudal system and the taking away of their judiciary privileges." Lawyers and judges complained of the "exactitude" of the recently introduced Napoleonic Code of Law, but Maclure approved of the Code because it curbed the Bar and the Bench from deviating from prescribed law to help their friends.[17] In Verona, there was an exceptionally large number of beggars, which Maclure linked to "the influence of the Church" and an increase in the "quantum of Christianity." To him, beggars "are the troops in the pay of the church and are always in proportion to their revenue and influence."[18] In the lengthy anti-Catholic polemic that followed, Maclure was gladdened by his somewhat erroneous perception that the Christian religion was on its "death bed."[19]

After two months of geological exploration in the Alps and Tyrol, he arrived in Trieste, "a well-built little town with houses like palaces" that could boast of an impressive exchange, a customhouse, warehouses, many churches, and two synagogues. The town reflected a former prosperity, destroyed by the French occupation. But now, with its "sorry merchants" gone and producing nothing, it was a mere fishing village and a tourist center.

Maclure's response to Venice was not the usual one of exhilaration and wonderment. Rather, he could only note the serious difficulties that such a city had to face—it was of "singular appearance as it is literally placed in the water without any appearance of land," beset with terrible engineering problems and economics and a ruinous cost of maintenance. He wondered how such a city could survive. The "Lords of Venice," an "improvident" group, had lost their position and generally were in a "state of misery," but they remained hopeful for a return to the old days when they had "places and power," which were now in the hands of a new set of wealthy merchants.[20] The streets were crowded with beggars, poverty was rife, churches were full as were the prisons, and executions were common. His comments on wondrous landmarks such as the Cathedral of St. Mark and the Palace of the Doges were perfunctory and technical in nature. Maclure, used to the deferential treatment of French bankers, found Venetian bankers offensive—"scarcely polite," acting as if his credit was doubtful.

Maclure traveled south along the Apennines, visiting Mantua, Modena, and Bologna, and arrived in Florence at the end of November. Descending from the Apennines, he found the roads so poor and "wretchedly planned" that their passage was far more difficult than crossing the Simplon Pass, which was three times higher. Maclure's explanation was dictated by his detestation of the ancient world: "'Tis probable that in making the road they followed those barbarians, the Romans, who considered the heights the best situated for best seizing and securing their plunder. War and pillage was their trade and the end and object of all their amusements and public works. 'Tis a query whether any good can arise from copying them. I know nothing either useful or convenient in which they had made much progress, except architecture and statuary, most of which was more for show than utility."[21] There is only occasional mention of the magnificent art and architecture that adorned Florence and all of Italy. When Maclure was unhappy, he was most reluctant and ungenerous in his praise.

Still, as he first approached Florence, he could not help being impressed by the magnificent entrance, the views on the streets, and the buildings and churches built "on the grand scale," recalling the sublime era of the Medici, a time of strong leadership. But he found the city without bookstores, the library without readers, and maps of Tuscany unavailable. Inexplicably, the city abounded in hospitals, and while there were six theaters, there were no schools or colleges. "Everything seems calculated to draw the attention and prevent reflection. It seems to have been the principal aim of all those aristocracies, called Republics in Italy, to divert the attention of the people by music, operas, balls, carnivals, etc., from any serious exercise of the mental facilities. Thoughtlessness and lack of foresight being of course the leading characteristic of the mass of the people, and hospitals and poorhouses the remedy."[22] Maclure's final words about Florence, which close journal 13, are harsh and certainly would not have pleased the Italians: "The arts are everything here, and nature is not worth examining. Music is all. . . . When they attempt anything serious it must be sweetened by a considerable dose of the burlesque or the hearers would sleep over it. What a happy disposition for the longevity of all absurd habits. What plastic matter for the mold of the politician."[23]

Maclure arrived in Rome on December 19, 1812, where he spent almost a month but left almost no record of the visit. The day after he arrived, "I was occupied in visiting the remains of Roman grandeur scattered among the filth and rubbish of the present race. The rubbish was being cleared away by "all those who will work," but they did so "with a bad grace," and he predicted that "they will not learn to be industrious." The city abounded in thieves and pickpockets, one of whom robbed Maclure while in a church. The city lacked "theaters or any amusement except the conservatoires which are nothing but card parties." The few geologists in the city did not impress Maclure, nor were their rock and mineral collections notable. He found "little or no science," and "after the antiques, natural history forms but a small part of their occupation."[24] Maclure refused to be impressed.

Naples and the surrounding countryside provided Maclure with a choice opportunity for examining volcanoes, so that much of his time was spent doing geological fieldwork. Pompeii was examined with a Mr. Lastera (Charles Philbert, comte de Lasteyrie-Dusaillant), a remarkable French aristocrat of liberal leanings who had fled the Revolution and, upon returning to France, brought with him the technology of lithographic printing. An agreeable man, this "élève of the French Revolution" was greatly admired by Maclure and became his companion for the remainder of his stay in Italy.

Observing the lower orders of Neapolitan society, Maclure, known for his own spartan diet, was appalled by how little food they lived on and how little they worked or desired to work. In a "state of barbarity in which the chains of the feudal system has left this country, it is one day's useful labor and three days of idleness and roguery of every kind which renders them unfit for any honest or steady employment."[25] "I cant help remarking the propensity to lying which pervades the whole mass of the people. 'Tis impossible to believe anything they say. . . . They have an apathy and stupidity which reduces them much below the civilization of hogs. . . . That apathy is implanted in them by their education by universal example and fortified by the few wants which the climate renders positively necessary. In this state of animalization, the weak and much neglected moral side of their nature is a slave to the physical passions and appetites."[26]

If Maclure judged a people by how salvageable they were, by education and enlightened law, Italians in general, and more specifically Neapolitans, were low on his scale, and they became fair game for his merciless judgments. Maclure had become hopelessly discontented, and objective analysis disappeared entirely from his writing. He so detested the Neapolitans and their culture that his account became an ugly, tiresome screed, over thirty pages in length, based on his six-week visit; an approving word about anything can hardly be found. The reader's thoughts and patience descend to the petty—does Maclure really enjoy suffering at their hands, in their city? Why doesn't he leave if things are that bad? After all, he was not compelled to visit or to wallow in this intolerable situation. He remained because of Naples's surrounding volcanoes, and it provided him with satisfying verification of his beliefs, geological and social. In Naples, degradation of society had been brought about by incompetent leaders who through ignorance, selfishness, greed, and indifference could not create or sustain a viable economy to satisfy the needs of all the people. Two imperfect groups—governors and governed—brought out the worst in each other. The education of both the masses and the governing classes was nonexistent or badly wanting, prompting him to declare that there was little possibility of salvation for this society. Their only hope of redemption was through education. He noted that in a few places where a superior form of education could be found, the conditions of the masses improved, and the lying, cheating, laziness, begging, and apathy declined; therefore, these traits were not inborn.

The wondrous monuments, the objects of local creation, and anything of ancient origin drew his scorn. He had little to say about Paestum with its astonishing triad of almost intact Greek temples (recently uncovered), except for some technical statements about the stone with which they were built, and he noted that the structures were in "tolerable conservation." One Sunday, at Cape Miseno near Naples, he was shown "as great wonders some ancient cisterns which if made by moderns would not attract the attention of the most foolish inquirer. . . . I don't find anything worthy of imitation in any of their works, and wasting much useful time both to themselves and their readers, I consider the whole tribe of antiquarians as a drag on the progress of useful knowledge."[27] In the same spirit, he wrote, "I do not recollect ever to have found the resemblance of convenience, comfort or utility in anything ancient."[28] More to his taste was the visit to a plant that distilled sulfur and alum from heated earth. He discussed the economics of the process and made recommendations that would reduce the cost of production.

Clearly, Maclure reveals himself to be the "modern" man—a Philistine —pragmatic, unappreciative, and even intolerant of anything outside his own sphere of interest (however broad). But it is also likely that Italians behaved badly in Maclure's eyes because they sensed that their guest was a difficult man, impossible to please. Still, Maclure was not entirely the hopeless philistine without interest in the arts, for he purchased a case of sixty volumes in folio and 100 "drawings in water colors of figures and vases," and in Venice he bought 1,000 books for shipment home. One might label Maclure a cranky zealot, persistent in complaint, in response to egregiously corrupt governments, self-aggrandizing despots, and beggary in the presence of an opulent Church.

Homeward bound, the farther north he traveled, the more his outlook brightened. The countryside around Stradella near Pavia he found "charming," and he noted a different physiognomy in the people—Swiss mixed with Italian. "They are well-clothed and have an air of independence." But the gaiety of Italians, their love of dance and music, in light of their poverty and bare subsistence, seemed to discomfit Maclure—"what enters by their ears seems only to effect [*sic*] their heels"; he used the word *gaiety* rather mockingly. An earnest Scot, Maclure seemed to feel that to overcome the serious defects of southern people, they had to be governed by northerners, specifically the French, who would impose a discipline on their behavior and their affairs. An enlightened leader would not permit the dreadful authority of predatory feudal barons in southern Italy whom Maclure called "pests to society," against whom people banded together to protect themselves: "In Calabria, thirteen hundred privileged assassins executed the orders of that feudal band, and it required all the energy of the French military to eradicate them."[29]

Maclure was a Francophile, and he felt more at home in France than in Italy. Although he deplored the excesses of the "Terror" and the ensuing chaos, the French Revolution had rid the country of an entrenched aristocracy and a detested religious establishment. As for the Napoleonic era, he spoke frequently of the benefits it bestowed on ordinary people, sounding like an apologist for the regime. Napoleon had simplified the law, and he had reformed and improved public education (although it was still defective, according to Maclure). Maclure believed that it would take the authority of the French Empire to introduce uniformity of weights and measures, at present in a confused state. He cited a peasant in Tuscany who favored French rule because now the "laws were plain and promptly executed" whereas under the former government "the litigation and impunity of crime rewarded rogues at the expense of the honest man." Occupying Italy, Napoleon raised taxes (anathema to Maclure), *but* he balanced this by eliminating church tithes; he conscripted young men into the army, *but* they would pick up practical and useful knowledge and learn by seeing more of the world; conscription caused a shortage of labor, *but* with a languishing Church, many young men who would have become priests could now enter the labor market and do *useful* work. Maclure's comments about conscripted troops were always upbeat.

On May 9, 1812, he arrived in Turin, and then entered France by way of Mont Cenis Pass, studying the complex geological structure of the Alps as he went along. There was now more geology, and there were fewer complaints in his diary. To his surprise, there was no barrier at the border crossing, which spared him the aggravation of dealing with officious guards. After reaching Lyons, he sent off 250 pounds of rocks that had been hauled over the Alps in his carriage, drawn by "two old horses." In Lyons he found "little or no science," for it was all in Paris. "The monopoly of Paris has retarded, and will still retard, the civilization of France," and this overcentralization exacerbated by Napoleon still persists almost undiminished at the beginning of the twenty-first century. He also noted that "Paris is the regulator of the rest of France, and as long as fiddling and dancing, poets, and *marchands de modes* are the sovereigns of the capital there is not much chance [of] civilization progressing in the provinces."[30]

Maclure continued west to the Auvergne, where for a second time he studied the extinct volcanoes around Puy de Dôme and Clermont-Ferrand in the Auvergne. His conclusion was that the basalt and lava of these volcanoes were identical to those of distant Vesuvius and Etna. Clearly basalt and lava were of volcanic origin, often overlying masses of gneiss and granite. Maclure attended the classic theater in Clermont-Ferrand, which he denounced as "the *ne plus ultra* of pedagogism," for it extolled the perfection of the ancient Greeks. Sentimental German theater was more to his liking because it "affects and interests those who have not quit of all their natural feelings and whose affections, passions, pastimes" are "not shaped and fashioned by the mode of the day." He was not interested in the trials of ancient princes, kings, and "conquerors of the earth."[31] Maclure implied that the impulses that engendered the horrors of the French Revolution—zealotry, intolerance, and superstition, which arise from irrational thinking—are closely related to those that give rise to the Church: "Perhaps nine-tenths of the horrors of the Revolution were owing to the superstitious revenge of the priests. . . . 'Tis certain that where there was the least superstition, there was always the least bloodshed."[32]

According to Maclure, slavery to fashion was just another expression of the stupidity and corruption of the populace, and he had no difficulty identifying the latest Paris fashion in cities such as Lyons, Bordeaux, and Limoges: "What an immense difference in the ideas of different people in respect to ornament and elegance. What an immense difference in the same people at different periods. . . . With the capricious belles of Paris even the dress of last month is frightful this month. . . . There is no test or measure but the heated imaginations of the idle and capricious; the hair style takes the form of a hog or handsaw, long hair or short, full of powder and grease, accumulated to a monstrous bulk, or shaved close to the head." Choking with disdain, he growls, "Yet these same people require all the power of absolute government to prevent them from throwing all their filth out of their windows on the head of the first person that passes, . . . wear dirty shirts and dirty clothing, and never think of a bath."[33]

Wherever Maclure traveled, he could see that the Industrial Revolution was taking root, even in provincial France where change came slowly. He wrote of steam engines in mining operations, water and steam power in wool spinning, and the efficiency of the steamboat as measured by the amount of fuel necessary to travel one mile. The idea of invention, improvement, and progress was beginning to blossom in the early nineteenth century, and it became evident to Maclure that new machines (often American) were far more efficient than those he had seen in the French provinces. Restless, entrepreneurial Americans were beginning to analyze and improve conventional farming and industrial procedures and to invent devices, such as a wool comber, with a view to making production more efficient and profitable. But workers in the French provinces hung on to the old ways and were slow to change. For instance, Maclure came upon weavers in Macon who refused to use looms with a newly invented fly shuttle that was vastly superior to the "clumsy shuttle" with which they were familiar.

On July 4, 1812, our peripatetic geologist arrived at his home on the rue des Brodeurs in Paris, where he resided for one year. Almost nothing is known about Maclure's activities during this time, which ended with another three-month geological tour of France and Switzerland at the beginning of July 1813.[34] Traveling eastward, roughly following the Seine, he crossed the border into Switzerland. Once again Maclure visited Pestalozzi's school in Yverdon, which was to him a shrine.

Scattered throughout his journals are references to Napoleon, reaffirming his admiration for the French emperor, which was derived largely from his hatred of the old, privileged aristocratic class of France. In journal 19 there is an impassioned defense of Napoleon that leaves no doubt about where Maclure's sympathies lie. At the end of January 1814, Paris was rife with rumors and "the stupid nonsense of fear, folly, and treason" as allied forces of Britain, the German states, and Russia were closing in on France to remove Napoleon and reinstate the monarchy—a nightmare for Maclure. He mocked those who believed "that nothing less than a miracle can prevent [France's] humiliation and conquest." Maclure was confident that Napoleon would teach them a lesson, for his forces had hitherto been remarkably successful: "The last winter ought to have given them some idea of what the Emperor of France would do, and that this ought to have convinced everyone that if he permitted those savage hordes to approach the center of civilization it was because he knew it was the most economical manner of bringing about their total destruction." Praising the high state of French military preparedness, he could not believe that "such a country with such a chief is to be overrun by a few bands of barbarians, congregated together by their common fear. . . . How fortunate for France and even for Europe that they are under the control of such a master whose superiority awes them into compliance with his commands. He has given the people a freedom they have never known, and now some of them are taking advantage of the liberty which has been granted them by the magnanimous generosity of the man they absurdly call a tyrant."[35]

Europeans beyond the borders of France, including many of Maclure's colleagues, thought Napoleon was the devil incarnate. But to Maclure, Napoleonic reform was the first feasible step in the destruction of old privilege and abuse and the unmasking of subterfuge. He believed that the vast majority of people were incapable of realizing that any freedom they thought they had was an illusion. Even in Switzerland, where each canton is governed by elected representatives, "the stupid people by always re-electing the same representatives have no benefit by it, and the government is a complete aristocracy in the hands of a few influential families."[36] These people could enact oppressive legislation that no tyrant dare impose. Maclure was incensed by the thought that kings such as Louis XIV who bled their subjects dry were considered beneficent because from time to time they handed out a few alms to the people. The villains were the aristocrats and the rich who now found life under Napoleon intolerable.

Maclure's attitude toward the European common people in their present state was one of noblesse oblige. Since they had only the slightest appreciation of their rights and were easily misled, they had to be looked after, to be saved from themselves. It followed, therefore, that they needed a strong, beneficent leader, and so, despite his antiauthoritarian, democratic instincts, Maclure was perfectly willing to accept Napoleon, an absolute dictator, whom he forgave because he was abhorred by the ruling classes of Europe and was able to realize many of the ideals Maclure cherished (although some historians argue that many of the changes implemented by Napoleon were already launched by the revolutionary government before he seized power). Never mind that by the time he was exiled to St. Helena, Napoleon was responsible for the deaths of multitudes. Maclure was willing to accept a deplorable means to achieve a desired end. He might have approved of Robespierre had this man satisfied Maclure's ideal of social and economic reform.

In the United States, Maclure's view was one where Jeffersonian republicans were set against Federalists, an alliance of merchants, big money interests, and landowners: "With us they take the name Federalists because they advocate a union of the states, and would have made the country a monarchy if they had not been outvoted [by presidents Jefferson and Madison].... They detested the French Revolution because it abolished the hereditary powers, privilege and monopoly which they meant to create in their own favor at home."[37]

Maclure's diaries are invaluable historical documents, for they provide a vivid picture of European life, especially in the hinterlands during the tumultuous early nineteenth century. He undertook his travels with an open mind as far as geology, mining, and manufacturing were concerned, but his ideas about the structure of society, its governance, its business, and religious practice were inflexible and sometimes contradictory. What he observed and learned invariably confirmed what he already knew to be the truth, only dimly altered by the constant jolt of new experiences and by the insults and challenges suffered by a traveler in foreign lands.

In January 1814, Maclure and his friend George W. Erving, American minister to Spain, left Paris on another expedition, taking the road to Fontainebleau, and then to Bordeaux, where they stayed throughout February. Bordeaux was a city of business dedicated to trade with Britain that had seen better days and was now in limbo. Unfortunately, it was also a city with "no books and no science." At the time, the Duke of Wellington's army was approaching the city, and capture was certain. Panic ensued, a flood of refugees fled the city, and Maclure prudently accompanied them, geologizing all the way to Montaubon and eastern France.

One of Maclure's cardinal rules of trade and commerce was that anything that hinders free trade is evil, and to this end he had no difficulty providing examples of harm that had been done by government interference and war. While in Bordeaux, it pained Maclure to see so few trading vessels and so little evidence of activity in a harbor that was formerly alive with ships filled with cargo, sailing to and from England. What galled him was that the Bordelais merchants and wine producers were still somewhat friendly with the English and willing to suffer a loss of trade while waiting for the English to defeat Napoleon. They knew who their enemy was.

There is almost no record for one and a half months, until Maclure traveled to Burgundy. Just south of Lyons, on April 25, he happened to come upon Napoleon, who was on his way to Elba, no doubt with an allied escort. His hero "looked more calm and composed than I have ever seen him. He was in good health and apparently superior to his misfortunes." While passing south through Lyons, Napoleon bought a large number of books, presumably to pass the long hours in exile. He was particularly interested in those that were critical of him—perhaps to learn why he had failed.

By May 9, 1814, Maclure reached Fontainebleau, the end of his journey. There is little record at this point, but it is probable that he spent the winter of 1814–15 in Paris at an exciting time when the Bourbon king, Louis XVIII, was restored to the throne, Napoleon escaped from Elba, and the Hundred Days ensued, during which the king fled to Ghent and returned only after Napoleon's hastily assembled volunteer army was defeated at Waterloo.

While in Paris in 1815, Maclure met Charles-Alexandre Lesueur, a young naturalist and talented artist who had just returned from a three-year expedition to the Australian coast from which he brought over 100,000 specimens, 2,500 of which were previously unknown, and many fine drawings—an outstanding accomplishment that was lauded by Cuvier and other important members of the Parisian scientific community. Lesueur was just the kind of exceptional talent that Maclure wanted to cultivate and recruit for whatever project he had in mind, one of which was to stock America with first-rate scientific and artistic talent. Maclure made a generous offer of financial support for Lesueur to come to America. Lesueur had not wanted to leave Paris, but Napoleon had just met his Waterloo, and as a man without financial resources, Lesueur could not depend on the new regime in France for support. He agreed to be taken under Maclure's wing for a period of two years, and so began his extended visit to the United States.

In August 1815, Lesueur accompanied Maclure as artist and naturalist on a three-month tour of England, and then, with two Pestalozzian teachers in tow, they departed from Falmouth, England, for the West Indies, where Maclure carried out a geologic survey of numerous Caribbean islands—from the Barbados to the Virgin Islands. He concluded that they were volcanic in origin, "probably thrown up from the bottom of the ocean."[38] The travelers arrived in New York, spent a month in Philadelphia, and then were off on a summer tour through Maryland, Pennsylvania, New York, and the New England states—an exhilarating introduction to the United States for the young Frenchman. They returned to Philadelphia in October 1816, where they took up residence at 104 South Front Street, which Maclure named Bachelor Hall. Settling in Philadelphia, with Maclure's backing, Lesueur became an extremely prolific engraver who introduced lithography to American publishing. Elected to membership of both the APS and the ANSP, he earned a living as curator at the Academy's museum and as an art teacher.

Maclure kept a diary only during his travels, and so he left little record of his activities and thoughts between 1815 and 1820 while in America. He supervised the republication of his great geological works, *Observations on the Geology of the United States,* in its final, expanded form, and he wrote "Observations on the Geology of the West India Islands" and "Essay on the Formation of Rocks," publications that marked the high point of his scientific career. A leading position in American geology was affirmed in 1819 by his election to the presidency of the newborn American Geological Society.

Although Maclure had often proven his robustness by his strenuous expeditions across Europe, and especially by enduring a freezing Russian winter, he was now in his fifties and ailing. For the remainder of his life he contrived to manage his affairs from southern climates, because he learned through experience that cold winters did not suit him. During the winter of 1816–17 in Philadelphia, he had suffered from the cold, which had created "a kind of alternation of gout or rheumatism and gravel." Next winter, in the warmth of Florida and the islands off Georgia, he was free of physical distress, as he was in southern France, but when he had moved north to Paris, his medical problems had returned in full force. Clearly, warm weather suited him best, and if his health was maintained, he felt that he could carry out his ambitious plans of educating the children of the poor, from bases with a mild climate in southern Spain and in Mexico .

Maclure continued his dogged travel and geological exploration, visiting and revisiting corners of Europe that must have provided him with a sense of having seen everything (although never enough to formulate a comprehensive view of the geology of Europe). Paris was his European headquarters at a time when Louis XVIII had been reinstated by the victors of Waterloo. The monarch and a retinue of ultra-royalists assumed authority as if the Revolution had never occurred. They had learned nothing, insisting on all their long held privileges, and once again they egregiously abused their power—an outrage to Maclure and his liberal friends. Maclure was especially incensed by royalists who had made fortunes taking advantage of their privileged position. He regarded them as particularly "dangerous," to be distinguished from true aristocrats with inherited wealth who were so "stupid and ineffective" ("spoiled children ... with violent and unruly passions"); these people could be managed and distracted from their "mad schemes."[39] Maclure grew tired of the cold of France and northern Europe, and wanting to be "out of hearing of the noise of the chains that so many aristocrats were endeavoring to forge for the poor, blind people," Maclure left Paris for Madrid.[40] Having to cope with the monarchy and a royalist government was so distasteful to him, he was leaving the country and would not even consider settling in the remote south of France. Once again, Maclure withdrew himself from what he knew to be the heart of the action.

The intolerance and the lack of independent spirit of the people he encountered was a great disappointment to him, in view of the glorious march of the French Enlightenment that had so recently swept over Europe, eliminating tyrannical regimes in its wake. Alas, the people under the monarchy were now mired in "darkness and barbarizm," and he agreed with a fellow traveler that " ¼ of the French nation are [now] paid by government to oppress the other ¾." The relentless growth of bureaucracy would ensure that France would be the last European country to enjoy good government,[41] and at the time, it was certainly not ready to accept a new kind of progressive education. For the present, Maclure was glad to see the last of France.

✳

EIGHT

Patron of the Natural Sciences

It was in the *Transactions of the American Philosophical Society* that Maclure first published his *Observations on the Geology of the United States of America*. The APS had a national reputation that attested to the vigor of the young nation. The APS was a magnet that drew books, specimens, documents, and oddities to its museum, archive, and growing library—indispensable assets for the scholar. Maclure had been a member of the APS since 1799, and he was a member of its council from 1818 to 1829. Whenever he was in Philadelphia, he attended its meetings, but as a relative newcomer who was frequently absent from the city, he was probably not considered a true Philadelphian, nor was he in the inner circle of power. Clearly, few of the elite would be sympathetic with his social agenda and his strong antireligious views.

Maclure's Philadelphia was a city with a patrician class that ran the affairs of the community. Some of its members were the major figures in the American Philosophical Society, the University of Pennsylvania, and various other cultural organizations, almost as a birthright. The fifty-year-old APS was the emblem of respectability, a forum for discussion and the presentation of original work, mostly of a descriptive nature. Looking to the old country for inspiration and a benchmark, the APS, whose roster contained some outstanding learned men, aspired to become the young republic's answer to the Royal Society, but in fact it was only a pale reflection of that august group.

In time, a select group within the Society itself, the Wistar Party, gathered to itself even more influence, so that a small core of members became the leaders of the larger membership and of the practice of science in the city. Maclure never belonged to the Wistar Party. This inner group, which possessed a quiet confidence that brooked no opposition, was largely based on wealth, family connections, and social standing, and rarely on great intellectual achievement alone. A nod from one of the elect meant acceptance or rejection. Wealth itself would not suffice: the Philadelphia merchant and banker Stephen Girard, probably the richest man in the United States at the time, who had set up a hospital and personally cared for yellow fever victims in the epidemic of 1793, was blackballed because of his uncouth manners.

Passion for natural science has never been confined to a select few, and so, as the decades passed in the new nineteenth century, a growing assembly of intense and talented young men took shape—botanists, chemists, and apothecaries, all but one self-taught. Many were considered undesirable because of their radical political and antireligious beliefs, but what distinguished them was their acute lack of money, and all of these black marks clearly rendered them ineligible for membership in the APS. In January 1812, they met at the apothecary shop of John Speakman, a Quaker and radical social reformer, to organize what was to become the Academy of Natural Sciences of Philadelphia. Maclure was closely associated with the Academy, favoring it over the APS, and he became its major benefactor over many years.[1]

The group held no ambitious illusions that they were the progenitors of a great new professional organization, nor did they fully appreciate the value of their interest in botany and entomology to agriculture or the value of geology to the extraction of the earth's treasures. Quite simply, these sons of the Enlightenment hoped to take part in "the advancement and diffusion of useful, liberal, human knowledge." This was truly an amateur group, without grand pretensions, with little thought of interaction with other groups interested in natural history or with any governmental body, but it did have an interest in educating the public. Its small library and museum were only to be used by members, but as the Academy prospered, there was a significant broadening of their aspirations, promoted and supported by Maclure.

The ANSP was clearly an institution out of favor with the elite, and so it received no financial support at a time when government did not provide funds for any form of research, nor did it support educational institutions.

The early years of the ANSP were shaky, operating perilously close to a state of bankruptcy before Maclure's active participation, but however threadbare, the Academy always had a library and a museum. In their struggle to survive, a few members organized lectures and entire courses in botany, crystallography, and chemistry, to be attended by the public upon payment of a modest fee, and some courses were especially designed to appeal to women. The lectures proved to be enormously popular and had to be repeated to meet demand. Not only did the educational effort satisfy one of the explicit aims of the Academy—to inform the public about science—it also provided a modest income for certain members of the Academy and for the Academy itself.

With growing success, the Academy was compelled to move into larger quarters for meetings, to house an ever-burgeoning library and museum. As the unsavory reputation for radicalism, socialism, and atheism of the Academy declined, membership increased from the original seven in 1812 to about fifty in 1815, with fifty corresponding members. The Academy had saved itself by bypassing the elite powers and reaching out to a public that was quick to respond. By 1817, the Academy was stable enough to adopt a constitution and be chartered by the State of Pennsylvania. But despite all these signs of success, its financial status was still precarious. Until 1817, there were several other worthy associations in Philadelphia whose struggle for survival was hardly different from that of the Academy, but they all withered, while the Academy survived because of the generous support of William Maclure, whose commitment to the Academy imparted a luster that lifted its reputation in the eyes of the Philadelphia community.

Maclure was not in the city at the time the ANSP was founded, nor when he was proposed for membership in 1812. Because members wanted to maintain the active interest of this imposing and beneficent man, they elected him president of the ANSP in December 1817 and each year thereafter until his death in 1840. The Academy's first president, the chemist and crystallographer Gerard Troost, now struggling to make a living, was only too happy to make way for Maclure. Although the ANSP lacked the social status of the APS, Maclure chose to devote himself to this organization because it was the most intellectually exciting at the time, and perhaps with his business experience he felt that he could set the young Academy on a firm foundation and mold it to his liking. Moreover, the organization was composed of young men with whom he liked to interact and could encourage by a promise of financial support—for them and the Academy. As an earnest senior companion, he liked to expound on any subject at hand. The English visitor Frances Trollope recounted a chance meeting with Maclure: "In the shop of Miss C**** I was introduced to Mr. M'Clure, a venerable personage, of gentlemanlike appearance, who in the course of five minutes propounded as many axioms, as 'Ignorance is the only devil,' 'Man makes his own existence,' and the like."[2] What more appreciative audience could Maclure have than the eager members of the Academy, who were a captive audience?

Since Maclure was traveling most of the time and always involved with other matters, he was in effect an absentee president. The affairs of the Academy were handled by the vice president, George Ord, and later by Samuel George Morton, with whom Maclure was in frequent contact. He had a lively involvement with the Academy, considering what was best for it, even when its radicalism had vanished and it was run by establishment figures. Maclure could always be relied on to contribute generously to special projects and when crises arose. He had joined this struggling organization because he was drawn to the unorthodox, freethinking views of some of its members, their social concerns, and their antireligious bias— the very things that had made the Philadelphia establishment less attractive. Still, he never referred to the APS or its members in disparaging terms, perhaps because despite their exclusivity and patrician bearing they were dedicated to a republican form of government, and many of them were productive citizens whose opinions on government, business, and economics were similar to his own.

Maclure had come to Philadelphia as a man of paradox. He was the most famous American geologist of his day, with vast experience and knowledge, and his extensive travels in the Romantic age of Byron and Humboldt could only elicit feelings of wonder. An egalitarian, radical internationalist, he was the perpetual outsider whose wealth and unequalled generosity won him entrée into exalted circles. There was no one remotely as philanthropic as Maclure; his was a largesse that augmented the mystique that enveloped him. With the bearing of a gentleman, however liberal and provocative his views, he rarely if ever indulged in direct confrontation, and so he must have confounded proper Philadelphians.

In the early nineteenth century in the United States, there was almost no opportunity for earning a living as a natural scientist, unless one could survive by teaching. Paid positions in research were almost nonexistent.

Charles-Alexandre Lesueur, who was brought to America by Maclure in 1815 and who lived in Philadelphia for nine years, earned a living by teaching painting and drawing, and he did scientific work, engraving, and color printing only when he found time. Thomas Say, the greatest American naturalist of his time and the unifying force who ensured the cohesiveness of the group, was forced to live a life of beggary and near-starvation to pursue his interest in nature. It was no wonder that parents discouraged their sons from taking a serious interest in natural history, for there was little future in it, and of what use was it? To his great credit, at this formative time, Maclure supported the work of Lesueur, Say, and other naturalists, offering them a glimmer of hope that they could be supported as they followed their interest and practiced their profession.

Maclure was an important presence in the Academy. Members were grateful for his timely gifts of money, specimens, and books that he kept sending from afar, but beyond this, they respected him for his achievements, his contributions to geology, and his vast knowledge. Morton said of him: "Wherever we turn our eyes we behold the proofs of his talent, his zeal, his munificence," and the Academy probably would not have survived without him.[3] Even the troublesome physician Richard Harlan, whose social and scientific outlook differed from Maclure's in many ways, seemed to have revered him, for in 1835 he dedicated his *Medical and Physical Researches* to Maclure with the words "Admiration of your intellectual endowments— esteem for your private virtues—and grateful recollection of your munificent donations to public institutions devoted to science ... [your] friendship ... and brilliant efforts in the department of science." Of course, there may have been an element of sycophancy in this tribute. In the same vein, conservative members of the Academy, who would not be disposed to listen to offensive, radical, and antireligious pronouncements, must have kept silent for fear of offending their great benefactor.

In keeping with his passion for improving the lot of society through education, Maclure insisted that the museum and library of the Academy be made available for public use, that it should provide a place for public lectures (especially on Sundays), and that the library and museum must be open most days of the week. Particularly important to him was the exposure of children to the excitement of natural history.[4]

As the Academy prospered and its membership increased, it was obliged to move to larger quarters to house its ever-growing collections and its expanding library. From the apothecary's shop it had established itself in a more permanent home in 1814 which it quickly outgrew, so that in 1826 the Academy moved to larger quarters, a move disparaged by some members of the Academy. Maclure himself felt that since cities had seen their best days, the Academy would find itself in the midst of a wilderness, "with foxes looking out of the windows" as Philadelphia faded away.[5] In like manner, he deplored the building of canals and railways because there would never be enough transportable produce and goods to make them profitable, even in 50 or 100 years.[6] These opinions reflected Jefferson's anti-urban sentiment and his belief that the course of the United States was westward, as the East declined. But the city flourished, and by 1839 the Academy, now with 200 members, was compelled to construct an even larger building, toward which Maclure contributed the great sum of $20,000, and every year thereafter the Academy could count on a donation of $1,000, in addition to gifts of books and specimens.

As early as 1817, when Maclure became president of the Academy, it was becoming a substantial institution, and to fulfill one of its aims of diffusing knowledge, at Maclure's urging it began publishing its own journal which would serve as an outlet for the work of its members and scientists from the rest of the country. Maclure purchased a used printing press and type for the Academy which he and members of the Academy operated in Maclure's home to print a new publication, the *Journal of the Academy of Natural Sciences of Philadelphia*.[7] The journal was one of the very first publications devoted to natural science in America, and it was of particular value because it publicized the works of Academy and American authors both at home and in Europe. The Academy could now boast of a weighty scientific journal, and it acquired a prestige that began to attract wealthy and prominent members of Philadelphia society, decidedly enhancing its chances of survival.

Thomas Say and Thomas Nuttall, both outstanding naturalists of limited financial means and members of the ANSP, enjoyed Maclure's largesse (which even extended to the support of the painter John Vanderlyn, whom he had encountered in Rome). Nuttall, ever grateful, named the Osage orange tree *Maclura pomiforma* in honor of his patron.[8] Whenever Maclure was in Paris or London, he haunted bookshops, picking up current and classic volumes on science, natural history, and the arts, and by 1819 he had contributed 1,500 volumes to the Academy's library, making it one of the best in America. By the time of his death in 1840, he had provided the library with more than 5,200 books, some rare and priceless, which unquestionably broadened the intellectual horizon and international outlook of the membership.[9] Recognizing Thomas Say's outstanding ability, Maclure was always on the lookout for books that would be of special interest to him.[10]

Maclure needed little inducement to organize expeditions. Within a few months of his "settling" in Philadelphia in 1817, he spent a month with Thomas Say, Charles-Alexandre Lesueur, and Gerard Troost, studying the geology and natural history of New Jersey and Pennsylvania. Soon after he was elected president of the ANSP, the Academy sponsored an expedition to Georgia and eastern Florida, organized and paid for by Maclure (winter of 1817–18). The group included Maclure and three members of the ANSP—Thomas Say, Titian Ramsay Peale, and George Ord, a wealthy merchant and vice president of the Academy who took along a servant and his hunting dogs.[11] Maclure and Say traveled by carriage to Charleston and boarded a steamboat to Savannah, Georgia, where they joined Ord and Peale, the eighteen-year-old naturalist and illustrator (son of Charles Willson Peale, the remarkable Philadelphia museum builder and artist). Proceeding south in a thirty-ton sloop hired by Maclure, the group visited the Sea Islands off the Georgia coast and then sailed to the mouth of the St. Johns River in northeastern Florida.[12]

The organizing of the expedition was sudden and spontaneous, an example of Maclure's precipitate decision to travel. Say was asked to join the expedition only a few weeks before they embarked for the South. Each member of the expedition, an expert in a field, was to examine in Florida what he had been studying in other parts of the United States, and in this sense the enterprise could hardly fail. A major aim was to explore the St Johns and Mosquito rivers to collect specimens of Florida flora and fauna, as well as rocks and minerals, and with Say on board, this goal was pursued with great vigor. While Say gathered insects, snails, and shells, Peale and Ord shot everything in sight for food and for their collections.[13] The insects collected were included in Say's *American Entomology*, a classic work dedicated to William Maclure. Many new species of plants, birds, insects, and crustaceans were described, and the data collected was recorded in publications. The specimens gathered provided Titian Peale and the etcher and engraver Lesueur with abundant objects for study for several years. The group inspected large Indian mounds, which were sketched by Peale, who also collected birds for his father's museum.[14] Having covered a portion of northeast Florida, they sailed up the coast of Georgia to Savannah and re-connoitered numerous islands along the way.[15] Beset with invitations to visit isolated estates and plantations, where they mingled with the local gentry, shot alligators, and dined on parakeets, their scientific efforts became so compromised, Maclure was compelled to call a halt to further hospitality.

The group continued to Charleston, South Carolina, where Maclure boarded a steamboat for home, having had enough of seasickness on a small sloop. His activities on this trip were limited, because as an "old man" in his fifties, nursing his "rheumatism," he declined to accompany the young men on some of their strenuous excursions. He discovered, however, that the warm climate of Florida alleviated his suffering from the "rheumatism," which afflicted him during winter months in northern cities.[16] The project, deemed very productive, was a happy, adventurous escape from a Philadelphia winter. An unfamiliar kind of wilderness had confronted the young naturalists, a world of nature hitherto unknown to them, rich in unfamiliar biological forms, and to add to the excitement, they were very much aware that they were following in the footsteps of the legendary John and William Bartram, kinsmen of Say. This was reason enough for having participated, and in fact Say would have wanted to remain longer.[17] The expedition was the first ever to be sponsored by the Academy, a prototype for others organized by private institutions, which contributed to the establishment of natural history and biological systematics in the United States and to the building of museums of natural history.

There may have been a clandestine motivation for the venture, although to the young members of the Academy, exposure to the natural riches of Florida was reason enough to have participated. Florida was under a teetering Spanish jurisdiction that was rapidly losing its authority at a time when ownership of the region was in the process of being transferred to the United States (which actually took place in 1819). It has been suggested that Maclure was acting for his good friend, the American diplomat George William Erving, who had been sent to Spain to purchase Florida. With so much wealth derived from sugar cane being extracted from the Caribbean area, mostly flowing to Europe, Florida was of great strategic importance to the young republic. Perhaps the expedition was a cover for Maclure to gather information for Erving and the American government about just what they were buying.[18] Through Erving's contacts in influential Spanish circles, and perhaps through Maclure's own Spanish contacts, he was able to obtain a passport with the king's seal, a commanding entrée that local Spanish officials, usually uncooperative, unhesitatingly honored. The land was virtually lawless, a haven for pirates, runaway slaves, and Indians whose hostility to Americans had been inflamed by the Spanish. Ever-present danger probably shortened the expedition and limited its reach.

With the success of the Academy, its library and collections rivaled those of the senior APS, and its enlarging membership began to dilute the old, early members who had been so unacceptable to the APS. Old Philadelphia and Pennsylvanian names, and those who wanted to be associated with them, became more common—Morton, Harlan, Ord, Haldeman, Collins, Haines, Biddle, Vaughan, and Vaux. Despite Maclure's views, everyone was pleased to have this generous man as their president, especially since he was so rarely in Philadelphia. Within the Academy there were now very active leaders of independent means, with links to the APS, to Philadelphia society, and to European scientists.

Approval of American work by European savants was their highest aim, and friendship with European natural scientists was cultivated in an attempt to disparage the notion that Americans were uninterested in research of a theoretical nature or even capable of doing it.[19] A deep-seated notion of American exceptionalism nestled uneasily with a sense of intellectual (and artistic) inferiority, and so most American workers seemed resigned to the fact that the great scientific advances would be made in Europe, after which Americans would fill in the details. But perceptions of native ability were changing, and confidence was growing because of such prestigious advocates as Maclure.

There were a few individuals who dedicated their lives to the systematic study of nature. Differences between two emerging groups within the Academy—dedicated natural scientists and dabblers—were brought to a head by Richard Harlan's *Fauna Americana,* a work that was guided by a rigorous classification of animals, living and in fossil form, grounded in the systematics of Linnaeus. The book was for the specialist, not for the general membership, and it was received with some unease by the generalists who felt that the study of plants and animals should devolve on the larger picture—descriptive but without too much detail, easily accessible—nor should studies of this kind depend heavily on rigorous taxonomic rules, which would only confuse everyone. The amateur gentleman naturalists and artists would be left behind, for this newer kind of study of nature would necessitate intense study, analysis, and background knowledge, required of the dedicated professional who was developing a specialized, technical language, meaningful only to the few.[20] The problem of rigorous taxonomy was especially relevant in an age of exploration of Africa, Asia, and the Americas that led to an explosive increase in the number of genuinely new species of plants and animals.

Because of the rapid expansion of knowledge taking place, the new guard realized that those involved in the study of natural science must become specialized in order to become effective contributors whose quality of work would compare favorably with Europeans. According to their lights, the proper foundation for natural history was based on a consistent classification with a standardization of nomenclature of the many new plants and animals being discovered and described. Unfortunately, they were slow to change from the simpler Linnaean system, which had become obsolete, to the more advanced French "natural system" of classification, whose earliest advocates in America (among others) were Correa da Serra, Portuguese consul in Philadelphia (a botanist), and Constantine Samuel Rafinesque.[21]

The specialists wanted to convert the Academy's journal from a "popular science" magazine that could be read by the amateur, to a technical, scientific publication of record, relatively free of fanciful speculation. Despite the fact that this change alienated members who felt the journal should present comprehensive and comprehensible articles readily accessible to all, in the end the revised journal proved to be an important and successful publication that enhanced the reputation of the Academy and attracted new members. The Academy prospered, and a new spirit of professionalism was born as it took on a more rigorous, critical cast at a time when trained scientists were appearing in increasing numbers.[22] By the time of Maclure's death in 1840, American science had taken on its modern form, and the word *scientist* had been coined by William Whewell (1834).

The direction of the Academy became clear as papers from established investigators of the old school were rejected, an effective way of regulating the direction and quality of science, but perceived nevertheless as hostile acts that exacerbated the conflict between the two groups. Even Thomas Say's manuscripts were now rejected by the publications committee of the Academy on the basis of the new criteria. Vitriolic contests for priority in the naming of new species arose between members of the two groups—in the field of reptiles between Thomas Say and Richard Harlan, and in ornithol-

ogy between Lucien Bonaparte and George Ord. All was not pacific within
the ruling group of the Academy, for bitter arguments were constantly erupting, at times spilling into print. Harlan refused to allow Audubon (a prime
example of a great artist doing inferior science) and some of his friends into
the Academy, contrary to the wishes of Ord and his associates.[23]

Those whose membership and whose work had been rejected by the
Academy responded by forming a new society in January 1827. The Maclurean
Lyceum of the Arts and Science put forth its own publication, *Contributions of
the Maclurian Lyceum to the Arts and Science,* which was open to all. The use
of Maclure's name by the breakaway society was an obvious ploy to obtain
his financial and moral support, but in fact he never gave them enthusiastic
encouragement, nor did he ever attend a meeting. He was not in a generous
mood, for he had just lost a good part of his fortune in Spain and was now far
away in Indiana and Mexico, concerned with other matters. While he continued to support the Academy in a substantial way and remained its head, his
sympathy for an organization that bore his name extended only to sending
rock and mineral specimens for a prospective museum. It would seem that
as a major figure in both organizations, on good terms with all members, he
would be a cohesive force that could keep together two competing groups,
but he preferred not to get involved. Maclure, the absentee leader, chose to
operate above the fray, and he was silent on most of the specific problems
facing the Academy. His major interest was in making the Academy an instrument of public education in order to eliminate ignorance with regard to
science—a crucial part of his effort to reform society.

But the Academy saw itself as an agent for the gathering and diffusion
of knowledge, not as an official organization with set positions or policies on
questions that might be introduced into public discourse. Its members could
not be classified as professional scientists, for they were part-time workers
who earned nothing from their science, nor were they experimentalists—
Morton and Harlan were prominent physicians while Ord was a chandler.
Maclure himself was a blend of the professional and the amateur. Still, in the
long view, attention to standards and quality of publications and an emphasis on the specialized nature of their investigations were prerequisites for
the establishment and shaping of professional science in the United States.
In time, the language of science used in the journals would become increasingly arcane, and knowledge would grow at such an ever-increasing rate
that in order to cope, the field of natural history would become separated

into branches of science—geology, botany, and zoology—each employing the principles of mathematics, physics, and chemistry. The Academy itself, which was generalist in origin and in tendency, was challenged by specialist organizations, each with its own journal.

In the end, Maclure's social agenda, his approach to the study of nature, his practice of science, and his views on the uses of knowledge did less than it could to convert the ANSP into a modern scientific institution dedicated to experimental work. He was less concerned with the growth of scientific knowledge through research than in enlightening the people through an appropriate education with a view to redistributing wealth and power so that social injustice would be eliminated. In his opinion, the Academy should be an instrument of teaching whereby newly acquired scientific information could counter the dogma of religion associated with so much human suffering, and bring a new society into being.

For all his talent and drive, Maclure was not an exemplar of the emerging modern scientist. Not really a professional scientist, he was a brilliant polymath, spreading himself thinly but concentrating on geology at a descriptive and geographic level, usually with an eye to assessing the mineral wealth of a region and establishing the nature and productivity of a soil. He was very much respected, but his distant voice did not carry as much weight in the Academy as it should have, and he was not a force in the transition of the organization from its original amateur form to one suitable for the evolving modern scientific age in which professional scientists would keep politics, the problems of society, and social reform out of the scientific agenda.[24] It is probably no coincidence that the rate at which the Academy became a fully professional organization quickened after Maclure's death.

Finally, by helping to establish the New Harmony commune in Indiana, Maclure badly damaged the Academy and the study of natural science in Philadelphia. Paradoxically, while he was providing the Academy with specimens and acting as its major benefactor, he took with him to Indiana its best investigators, to pursue a utopian venture that soon failed, leaving his followers stranded in the marches, unable to fulfill their great potential. Privately, Ord was prompted to write bitter words denouncing Maclure and Robert Owen, the driving forces behind the New Harmony project: "Do they [Say, Lesueur] ever design to quit that stupid establishment called New Harmony? All the men of science with whom I have conversed here and in London, speak with the utmost contempt of Maclure and his projects; and wonder that such men as Say and Lesueur could allow themselves to be humbugged." In the same vein, after the untimely death of Thomas Say, he wrote, "He died last month at New Harmony; a sacrifice to the whims and follies of that old man, Mr. Maclure."[25] In fact, there was some truth to the charges. Maclure was a father figure to Say, who was bound to his benefactor by affection, a sense of loyalty, material need, and common social ideals. His accomplishments were outstanding, but he would have done better if he had remained in Philadelphia rather than struggle in the hinterland.

Maclure was devoted to the Academy, and he remained its president for the remainder of his life, as he attempted to fulfill his responsibilities from afar. This was not, however, his most compelling mission, which, aside from geological exploration, was to institute a remedy for society's problems—Pestalozzian education for the children of the masses.

✳

NINE

Spanish Years and Return to America

Maclure's first encounter with Spain was on a five-month geological expedition in 1808. Spain was occupied by Bonaparte's forces, while offshore a threatening British navy blockaded the country, a worrisome situation that did not seem to trouble or impede Maclure's agenda. Crossing the Pyrenees from France, studying rock formations, gathering specimens of rocks and minerals, and at the same time observing the people, their government, their customs, agriculture, and industries. His judgment of the nation was mixed. He was appalled by the ignorance and arrogance of the aristocratic class, the wretchedness of the peasants, and the power of the Catholic Church. At the same time he was impressed by the sunny quality of the people and their well tended vineyards. But above all, he found southern Spain's climate irresistible, because it relieved him of the tormenting rheumatism he suffered in northern climates. While he favored the nations of the north because of their social and political nature, he was drawn to those with balmy climates—Spain, and later Mexico—on the grounds of health.

In 1820, disgusted with the failure of his schools in Paris and the resistance of the French to new ideas in education, Maclure was eager to relocate to Spain, not only to escape Parisian winters but also to establish Pestalozzian schools for poor boys and girls. He arrived at Madrid from France at the end of 1820, where the weather was cold and variable. Craving warmth, he pushed on to southern Spain, a terribly backward region, and it was here that he decided to establish his educational program.[1] In his first visit to Spain he had made important friends who could protect him, and now a decade or so later, he felt that this was the country most amenable to educational reform along Pestalozzian, Fellenbergian, and Lancastrian lines.

A liberal constitution, inspired by the French Revolution, "at least some centuries in advance of their state of civilization," had been adopted by the Spanish parliament (the Cortes), in 1812. The constitution retained the Church and the Bourbon monarch, Ferdinand VII (thrust upon Spain by the European powers), but greatly restricted their power. However, in 1814, the king repealed the constitution and seized control of the country, and he so mismanaged it in the next five years that the country was almost brought to ruin. Revolts and uprisings led to a revolution that ended with the reinstatement of a liberal, democratic government, dedicated to the preservation of the constitution, while Ferdinand, once again, was allowed to remain king, but with limited powers.

Maclure was delighted that many of these events took place while he was in Spain, having arrived at the beginning of a three-year period of reform government—the "Liberal Triennium"—which witnessed a slow but steady improvement in the state of Spanish society, the curtailment of the power of the Church, and reform of the military. A national militia under civilian control was created that distinguished itself by defeating a superior counterrevolutionary force in July 1822. Maclure believed that the restored constitutional, representative government was the best government in Europe and that the country's capital, Madrid, was the only democratic city on the continent.[2] Subsequent events revealed that Maclure's optimism was unjustified, and it proved costly.

Despite promising signs, the country remained in a constant state of unrest, always threatened by the forces of reaction "headed by the king, who [is] at work, day and night to create rebellion, bloodshed, and destruction over the whole country . . . to smother the constitution," and who is "buying and bribing all the rogues of Spain to cut throats." According to Maclure, bandits who held up the mail were paid to create havoc, and this prevented him at times from making geological field trips for fear of being kidnapped and held for ransom.[3] Maclure found the Spanish people "ignorant as any people upon the earth," but he was heartened by their energy, humanity, and sense of confidence that encouraged them to assert their rights, however little they actually understood. They were a stabilizing force in a state of anarchy, which permitted a kind of freedom. Bolstering his optimism was the ineffectiveness and extreme ignorance of the "higher orders" of Spain, scarcely better than that of the masses, so that their authority was lame—"the indolence and imbecility of those who possess property reduces their exertions to zero"—and so, strangely, it would seem that the power and knowledge that usually derives from property was more equally distributed between the classes. In Maclure's opinion, a dangerous state of anarchy prevailed that was offset by the "pride and dignity" of the Spanish lower classes.[4]

As the year 1822 ended, Maclure was settled in Alicante, which was to be the site of his major educational effort. Maclure was optimistic about his prospects in southern Spain, but the lack of intellectual stimulation in the provinces troubled him. He did not miss the "foibles" of those who lived in big cities—"a constant round of shows, theatres, fairs, and crouds," which made them unhappy when they were not available.[5] He complained that he lived like a "hermit," for there were few with whom he could converse, probably because his spoken Spanish was limited, and most of those with whom he could communicate were royalists, conservative and religious. In his judgment there were almost no scientists or "gentlemen" with an interest in science in Spain.[6] However, his relative isolation provided time to devote to nursing his health, acquiring property, planning schools, exploring geological formations, and sending off cases of mineral and rock specimens to friends and institutions in America.

The weather of Alicante was so agreeable, even in winter, that Maclure came to believe that living there would add "8 or 10 years" to his life. Warmth was of such benefit to this aging, weakening man that his thinking about climate went far beyond the personal, taking on an importance in the life of society and nations and meriting frequent comment. According to Maclure, a warm sunny climate was responsible for the admirable qualities of the average people of Spain (and Mexico), which prompted him to write a highly speculative work on the effect of climate on forms of government. His thesis, quite simplistic, was that countries with warm climate—a "perpetual spring"—with fertile soil, such as in the tropics, produce an abundance of food with less labor. The result is that people become "thoughtless," averse to protest and revolt, and consequently they are easy prey for secular and religious tyrants. After covering the globe, in a country-by-country analysis, he boldly concluded that "no free government has ever originated under such climates." Furthermore, "Europe is the favorite climate for the perfecting of the human species, both as to government, and everything else." Maclure was convinced that the great progress Europeans had made in creating a superior civilization was owed in large measure to their climate. They were blessed with freedom from "alternate and rapid extremes of heat and cold." His "scientific" arguments abound in tortured, questionable suppositions, as he skips from Russia to China, Africa, Hindustan, South America, Turkey, and the Cape of Good Hope. In essence, his learned discussion largely reflects the ethnocentric prejudices of his time.[7]

The liberal spirit in Spain at the moment favored Maclure's plan for establishing schools, but the constitutional government in power necessary for their implementation was plagued by political intrigue and turmoil. While Maclure was buoyant about the future of Spain, Madame Fretageot, now in Philadelphia, was prophetic in her worry that money invested in that country would be at risk. She warned him repeatedly about the ever-present dangers in Spain and cautioned that a warm climate should not be enough to keep him in that unsettled place.[8]

To promote his views, Maclure planned to bring to Spain a printing press from France, along with two American printers, and to popularize Pestalozzi's method of education, he had Joseph Neef's book *Sketch of a Plan and Method of Education* translated into Spanish, a book he had first published in Philadelphia. His own essays for the *Revue Encyclopédique*, which had been banned in France as too radical, were translated into Spanish. Maclure seemed to be settling down in Spain, as suggested by his detailed arrangement with a Madrid bank to facilitate his financial transactions and by the establishment of a network of friends—scientists, businessmen, manufacturers, and politicians. He invested in a silk factory in Valencia with an eye on the American market, and he became interested in the manufacture of soap and sulfur. He also attempted to manufacture farming implements in Spain, rather than import them from England. Though "retired" from business, he could not resist the lure of trade. Maclure's geologic and commercial interests shared common ground in mining, a means by which Spain could become a part of the modern, industrial world, but unfortunately the chance of success in ventures such as these was small because the country was much too underdeveloped.[9]

Entertaining the idea of constructing a geological map of Spain, Maclure studied the geology of the Alicante region, and he assessed the mineral riches that might be exploited. But as anarchy grew, lawlessness increased, reducing and eventually ending his explorations.[10] Maclure kept busy corresponding with prominent members of the Geological Society of London, and he sent books and journals to Philadelphia, often operating through agents like Obadiah Rich, a bibliophile and a former U.S. consul in Valencia, who was always on the lookout for materials that would be of interest to Maclure and of value to American libraries.

Maclure was becoming fully identified with the Spanish, whose language he learned to read and write. A Spanish romance, *Eusebio* by Don Pedro Montengon, a tale in four volumes about Quakers in Philadelphia, was praised by Maclure as "the most common sense on education I ever saw in print," and he sent the book to Madame's school. By reading this appealing story, students would become familiar with the Spanish language, which Maclure thought was the most important foreign language for Americans to acquire, especially because Spanish colonies in the western world were gaining their independence.[11]

In July 1822, a major threat to the constitutional government was overcome when 6,000 guards of the king failed to seize power after hatching "a plan to murder all the militia and liberals, and plunder Madrid."[12] To complicate matters, the possibility weighed heavily on the liberal faction that invasion by an alliance of European monarchies, with the return to real power of the treacherous Ferdinand, could occur at any time. Still, Maclure felt that his investment in Spanish bonds issued by the legitimate government had not been a mistake; it was like buying a lottery ticket—one cannot gain if one does not take a risk. At Maclure's urging, his friend George William Erving had also invested in Spain's future by buying bonds. A former American representative in Madrid, Erving was not as sanguine, despite earlier assurances by his highly placed Spanish friends that bonds and loans would always be honored, for according to these knowledgeable people, politics and finances were separate entities in Spain. Despite the looming threat, Maclure bought more Spanish bonds in February 1821 and even as late as January 1, 1824. Amazingly optimistic, Maclure wrote an encouraging article, "Spanish Bonds," for the *London Daily Chronicle* (November 1822), giving assurances that the Spanish government and the bonds it had issued were sound and that the state of affairs in Spain was not that bad and would gradually improve. This confident note did not impress Erving, who increasingly brooded that all was lost.[13]

Maclure was dismayed by the widespread poverty of a good but passive people in a country with a "depraved" upper class. Corruption and looting of the government, a legacy of the former royalist regime, were prevalent, the national debt was growing, and the country's finances were labyrinthine, all pointing to an impending failure of the constitutional government; remedy entailed the collection of taxes, decrease of the tax burden on the poor, and the cutting of government spending—all unlikely to take place. Maclure must have known what was going on, but if he had his worries, he kept them to himself. He and Erving looked to each other for assurance, but the two men began regretting they had ever purchased Spanish rather than French bonds. Being liberals with similar views on politics and education, they balked at investing their money in despotic Bourbon France. In the end, the judgment of Madame Fretageot proved sounder than that of Maclure.

If he thought the United States was so amenable to reform, why did he not return to get personally involved in establishing schools that would bring on the millennium? In response to appeals to return to America by Madame and others, Maclure offered the weak excuse that it was unnecessary for him to be in Philadelphia because "my letters are of great deal more service than my presence," for they can be reread and studied.[14] If he returned to Philadelphia his effectiveness would be diminished by ill health ("Rumatics, gravel &&&...") that would surely befall him. He could not endure the cold northern winters, and those parts of the United States that had a climate comparable to southern Spain were tainted by the "barbarous institution of slavery," which he could not abide. Later, when he was driven out of Spain and had returned to North America, he chose to live in Mexico where the twin sins of slavery and despotism had been vanquished. There was no place for slavery, that "horror of nature" in a free society, and he claimed that three-quarters of Americans disapproved of this "monopoly of the aristocracy," which was not only immoral but also economically unprofitable.[15]

Perhaps he thought it best at the time to avoid direct contact with Madame Fretageot, retaining her absolute loyalty while eluding as much as possible the fire of her bold declarations of love. For the same reason he may have directed her toward Philadelphia and away from Spain where he wanted to settle. Perhaps he remained in Europe because he found the people more to his liking, and at the same time he could send back specimens, books, educational material, and even "wine, oil, raisins, almonds, figues &" from farms he was purchasing.[16] We can only guess at the true reasons.

Once again, Maclure distanced himself from the scene of action in Paris and Philadelphia, a tendency that can explain why his grand plans were never fully realized. Novales, a Spanish historian, states that though in his way Maclure was a fervent social revolutionary, today Maclure's name is unknown in Spain. His goals were overly ambitious and could never be reached in the world in which he lived, for he demanded radical change in the patterns of belief and behavior of ordinary people. He tried to force success with money, perhaps convinced that his impassioned belief, which he endlessly proclaimed in print, could substitute for personal, direct involvement—he was always somewhere else.

According to Maclure, when he arrived in a democratic Spain, even its relatively stable government, bent on reform, did not seem to fully appreciate the benefit of a "rational and useful" system of education as he saw it. Funding for a few secular Lancastrian schools in Spain was seriously inadequate, while disconcertingly, money was lavished on "60 priest schools where the children are 6 or 8 years in learning what they would do in 6 mos by the Lancaster methode."[17] Wanting to participate in the building of his newly adopted country, he endeared himself to the governor of Alicante province by contributing to the salary of the master of a liberal Lancastrian school for poor children, and he sought out suitable teachers of Pestalozzian persuasion who could be rendered more effective by having senior pupils teach their younger colleagues according to the Lancastrian platoon plan.[18] For the present, Maclure favored the Lancastrian system because it was less costly and required fewer skilled teachers, while the more teacher-intensive and superior Pestalozzi method would be incorporated as conditions permitted. Clearly in conflict with Pestalozzian principles, the Lancastrian method used rewards, punishment, and humiliation of students to impart knowledge, and its monitors left much to be desired in terms of time of direct contact with students. Maclure also proposed that schools should operate through the summer months, so as not to waste empty schools and students' time.

Land and property in and around Alicante and the town of Orihuela, confiscated from the Church, was eagerly purchased at bargain prices at public auction by Maclure, to be used for Pestalozzian schools and for an agricultural college where poor Spanish boys would be taught the best way to cultivate the soil.[19] In January 1823, Maclure wrote Madame Fretageot,

"I have bought ⅔ of an extensive tract of land consisting of from 12,000 to 15,000 acres [San Gines], one olive plantation & vines && of from 120 to 200 acres [Hacienda de Coix del Carmen], and another a short league from this with a large home and 100 acres of vines, almond & figue trees &&&, which will make a delightfull & healthy summer residence [Grosmana farm], and a convenient house in the town with about 20 rooms in it, fountain, Terras covered with &&, all for about 4 years rent of your house on Chestnut Street."[20] The twenty-room house in Alicante, Calle del Lobo, no. 7 (Wolf Street) was the only property not formerly owned by the Church. There was a convent and about ten houses on the large tract of land with excellent soil at San Gines, twelve miles south of Orihuela. One-third of this estate was owned by a friend, Robert Montgomery, whose mortgage on the property was held by Maclure. Maclure used approximately $50,000 in government bonds, which he had purchased in 1820, to pay for the properties, an investment of a small fortune at a time when he was confident that the existing liberal authority, abiding by the constitution, would last. To effect the purchase, he negotiated with the Crédito Público (a government agency known for its corruption), which had been set up to deal with confiscated church property.[21]

Despite persistent threats to the existing government, Maclure held the somewhat rosy and naïve view that despotism in Spain and Europe was on the wane. While in Madrid in July 1822, he had witnessed a major disorderly counterrevolution ("royalist machinations"), extending from Cadiz to Madrid, that involved shameless betrayals and the revolt of the military, an affair that had ended when a resurgent Ferdinand was defeated once again and had meekly pledged an oath of fealty to a constitution he loathed, which was designed to keep him in check. According to Maclure, the humane qualities exhibited by the Spanish people during and after this ordeal were exemplary; their capital remained calm, and they did not seek revenge on the wrongdoers. While Maclure was impressed by their behavior, Madame Fretageot in America, concerned about Maclure's safety and his investments, persisted in her warnings and pleaded with him to return to the United States, if for no other reason than that her students, indoctrinated with the notion of Maclure's godlike qualities, anxiously awaited him. But he was determined to fulfill his mission in Spain.

Maclure seems to have been playing a dangerous game. He still owned Spanish bonds of considerable value and had bought confiscated land and property in a country with an unstable government rife with political unrest. Threatening French troops, just inside the border, were controlled by a Bourbon king of France and supported by a somewhat diminished Church that was still in place and ready to rise again to reclaim all that it had lost. But Maclure felt that the French were bluffing and would not invade Spain; they only wanted to frighten the Spanish liberals—a gross miscalculation. Despite this alarming situation, Maclure was calm and seemed unworried by "trifling rebellions, all squashed," and by reactionary forces that were "losing their influence" on the Spanish people. Indeed, he proclaimed that Spain was the most peaceful place in Europe, and despotism would soon be swept away! However, there were moments when he did express some concern, probably resigned to whatever befell him, because even if he desired to extricate himself from his commitments, it was too late to do so.

Six months after his purchases, during the summer of 1823, when the various factions of the constitutional government were at each other's throats, when corruption in government was flagrant, and the royalist forces appeared to be gathering strength, Maclure seemed to think that all he had to do to avoid molestation was to be "agreeable" and keep his opinions to himself. Somehow, these would confer an immunity, enabling him to meld with the ruling classes and go on with his business, which was in fact bent on their destruction. With his experience in handling people, he believed that he could be above all the politics and strife of the time. His radical views tended to be for his acquaintances' ears only, and not for broadcast, but in fact he was unrealistic in believing that the existing powers would be ignorant of them, since some were published.[22] Authorities would have no difficulty deciding whether to investigate and rid themselves of a foreigner with numerous liberal friends and the buyer of confiscated Church property.[23] Maclure underestimated the ferociousness of Spanish reactionaries and the long memory of the Church, defending their privilege, fortune, and faith.

Maclure misjudged and ignored what was apparent to many less astute individuals.[24] Viewing matters in terms of black or white, conviction distorted his judgment. If political decisions or actions were seen as favoring his views, he was inordinately buoyant and optimistic, success building upon success. But if they challenged his views, there was no charity whatsoever for them—"the protectors of ignorance." The fundamental idea that overwhelmed Maclure's thinking and critical judgement was that "useful" education was an unstoppable cure-all, and ignorance was the basis of all evil.

There was little time for Maclure to set up schools and put his farms and vineyards in order before events put an end to his plans. He had made a promising start by acquiring land and buildings, but he had great difficulty hiring teachers and recruiting students, and he ran into frustrating delays. A plan to populate his agricultural school at Coix del Carmen with sixty orphans proved unachievable. His grand hope for this school by which local outmoded farming practices would be replaced by efficient American methods and the latest farming implements was never realized. An industrial school that he set up was provided with tools from Philadelphia, and he attempted to establish a Lancastrian school in Alicante. Plans were made for the establishment of a Fellenbergian school independent of the agricultural and industrial schools, but time was running out, and in fact, little progress was made.[25]

The axe fell in the last few months of 1823. French forces invaded and occupied Spain, and its constitutional government was terminated as the country descended into a state of anarchy. The way was now ripe for Ferdinand to seize power, which he did by shameful treachery, and a reign of terror began that shocked liberals throughout Europe. Ferdinand broke his promise of amnesty, hung liberal leaders, jailed and exiled thousands, including all those who were in government in the previous three years. The king's confessor was made secretary of state, and with pious pronouncements, the Inquisition was revived to cleanse the land of its sinners.[26]

Madame Fretageot received a letter from Maclure in January 1824 in which, after reviewing a variety of his usual concerns about his schools, he informed her almost casually, "They have confiscated and have taken from me upwards of 10,000 acres of good land with many houses &&&, but if they give me back what I paid for it and acknowledge their just debts I shall not lose much. If on the contrary they make a national Bankrupcy and cancell all claims upon them, I shall (or rather my heirs and executors) will loose from 30,000 to 40,000 dollars." Inexorably, a total loss did befall him, the Church further benefiting by taking back a newly renovated convent. He assured Madame that possible losses in Spain would have little impact on his style of living, for his material needs were minimal—his expense for food and drink was only twenty-four cents a day.[27]

He also informed her that he was leaving Spain as soon as possible, and since travel by land was dangerous, he was attempting to make arrangements to travel by ship. Unable to book passage to America from Spain, Maclure planned to travel to Ireland, knowing that leaving Spain probably meant forfeiting his investments. Whatever interests remained were attended by Robert Montgomery and Obadiah Rich, established expatriate Americans who chose to stay because they were married with families. Maclure's remaining assets were transferred to a bank in Madrid, and with the help of a Spanish lawyer, he continued for the next decade to press for the return of confiscated lands, properties and other assets which, as expressed in his will and letters to Samuel G. Morton, he wanted to leave to the Academy of Natural Sciences of Philadelphia. Maclure was anxious that even after his death, his wealth should be used to promote the maximum social good. If money was recovered, it was to be "applied to the useful knowledge and instruction of the working classes or manual laborers who gain their bread by the sweat of their brow, in the State of Pennsylvania."[28] To this end, he had drawn up a will in Spain in 1823, which he amended in 1833 and again in 1839, each with a different set of trustees, confident that his friends would honor his wishes, especially George W. Erving and John Speakman, liberals with a faith in education and a political philosophy similar to his own.[29] Unfortunately, by the time of his death in 1840, his holdings in Spain and France had so declined in value, there was little from abroad to distribute, but his holdings in the United States were substantial.

Before returning to America, he wanted to visit Great Britain to see those of his old friends who were "yet on the surface," while dismissive of those who were "by their own imprudence. . . . below the sode [sod] sometime, all owing to the defect in education," a rather cryptic and uncharitable remark.[30] Maclure, downhearted, wrote to his friend Benjamin Silliman, "Fatigued and tired with the injustice, cruelty, oppression, and folly of despotism, I left Alicante,"[31] and after shipping off his possessions, he departed from Gibraltar. An "unpleasant" thirty-five days were suffered aboard the *Robert* before he reached Newry, Ireland. His companion on board was a priest, trained in Spain, "who was the most ignorant young man I have met with." This was understandable because church authorities forbade any but theological reading and even censored the priest's mail. He was the product of "a despotism which is designed to produce a brutal ignorance unheard of." Maclure took it upon himself to help "awaken [him] from a metaphysical dream" by providing Neef's book on Pestalozzian education in which religion played no part.[32]

As was his habit, he explored geologic formations while on his way to Dublin, a city of "liberal although rather extravagant spirit" but without scientists in the vicinity. There were grand public buildings, but they stood uneasily amid the poverty of the masses. Still, he was pleased to find evidence of social awakening and so many liberal men who were interested in the reform of education, who listened to him carefully, in marked contrast to many in Europe and the United States who thought him "a Utopian reformer who is spending his money like a fool."[33]

Tirelessly, he studied the architecture, the courts and legal system, the Dublin Exchange, prisons, a botanical garden, various manufactories, printing establishments, stone quarries, regional mines, and Lancastrian schools—a mighty range of interests that he commented upon with broad insight. He visited the Giant's Causeway where he gathered specimens of basalt, but he was forbidden by authorities to ship sacred soil and rocks from this site out of the country. After a whirlwind two weeks in Dublin he proceeded to Belfast, where the pattern was repeated. In Belfast, with large populations of Protestants and Catholics, a "war" between the two groups "increased the public spirit and public exertions of both, particularly in education. . . . Both are forced to teach [students] to read, write, and count."[34]

After a pleasant trip lasting fifteen hours on a "swift steamboat," he arrived at Greenock, Scotland, and then proceeded to bustling Glasgow, "a handsome town," but with an "atmosphere saturated with smoke and dust," and "everyone elbowing you in the streets, and all of them anxious pigs of business."[35] Again, he visited factories with machinery of the latest design—printing presses and power looms—and he was entertained by several scientists and businessmen. Catching up on the latest advances, Maclure's visit to Scotland made him realize how much progress had been made in science and technology during the years he had been buried in backward Spain. This was no sentimental journey to his past; although he was close to his hometown of Ayr and made frequent excursions to the surrounding area, apparently he did not visit the town, nor did he refer to his roots in the region—the scene of his childhood and education.

Next on his agenda was the Mecca of social reform, New Lanark, where he met its architect, the charismatic Robert Owen, and was deeply impressed by "the order, happiness, and comfort that pervades the whole of Mr. Owen's establishment"—textile mills and schools.[36] The meeting was truly fateful, the beginning of a relationship that—for better, but mostly for worse—changed the course of Maclure's life. He reveled in the joy and happiness of the children in Owen's schools which had all but eliminated religious instruction and had adopted so much of Pestalozzi and Fellenberg, "grafted" onto the Lancastrian system—perfectly in accord with Maclure's views. Visits to Owen's schools and his experience with New Lanark workers, "cheerful, modest, and orderly," confirmed Maclure's high opinion of Owen's efforts.[37]

The "grandeur and magnificence" of Edinburgh and its buildings moved Maclure. As a distinguished geologist, he was able to meet many important scientists, including Robert Jameson, professor of natural history at Edinburgh, the leader of Wernerian geologists in Scotland. After a busy two weeks, he left for London on the steamboat *Soho,* which as a modern man he found to be an "expeditious and pleasant" means of travel.

Having been away from London for almost a decade, he was struck by its high cost of living, its sophistication, luxury, and wealth, where shopkeepers took off entire weekends. Clearly, there was excitement in the air and signs of "progress" everywhere, to which Maclure responded. The potential of the steam engine was impressed upon him by an American expatriate, Jacob Perkins, an inventor and entrepreneur who applied the power generated by high pressure steam to the manufacture of coins, the printing of money, and the tanning of leather. Perkins was currently devising a new form of steamboat which undoubtedly would replace the sailing ship. There was no end to the practical applications of steam pressure. Maclure was fascinated by Perkins's driving, creative mind: "Mr. P cannot stop, he must go on inventing—the force of habit. This is another proof that we are the children of habit and circumstance."[38]

London was a hive of reform-minded, liberal journalists and activists—John Bowring and Charles Maclean, whom Maclure knew well, John Black, Francis Place, James P. Greaves, a mystic and major advocate of Pestalozzian education in Great Britain, and George Birbeck, the founder and president of the London Mechanics Institution, a model for Maclure's future Working Men's Institute in New Harmony. He knew all these men, and although their conversations were never recorded, without a doubt they broadened his social and political thinking, and in return they received copies of his essays on political economy and politics, one of which, published in the *Morning Chronicle,* was commented upon favorably by Francis Place.[39] On several occasions he spent hours conversing with Jeremy Bentham, "a cheerful old man, full of good ideas, and a liberal." Maclure provided him with information about the United States, but again his diary and letters provide almost no substantive information about their discussions.[40] Maclure managed to visit hospitals, Greaves' Infant School, bookstores, and instrument makers, and he tended to the financial affairs and education of his difficult nieces and nephew in Britain, the children of his deceased sister Helen (Mrs. David Hunter). Because members of the family were susceptible to consumption, he urged them to move to a southern climate—at his expense.

In September 1824, he encountered Robert Owen in London on his way to the United States. Despite his enormous successes, Owen had been deposed by his partners in the textile mill and had fallen into financial difficulties. Owen was accompanied by Richard Flower, an agent through whom he was to buy Harmonie, a village with 20,000 acres of land on the Wabash River in Indiana. The millenarian religious colony, built by 2,000 German settlers, had been founded and led by Father George Rapp. Owen's plan was to buy the entire village outright and convert it to a secular utopian community based on social and economic principles that would remedy humankind's terrible problems and give rise to "a new moral world." Maclure was enthralled by the prospect. 'Tis the best field experiment on earth, and I am rejoiced to find that he has chosen it. . . . It gives me great hopes in the success of my experimental farms [at Alicante]."[41] Maclure's enthusiasm was more than matched by his colleagues in Philadelphia, who had zealously read Owen's literature and were anxious to join the procession to New Harmony. One wonders how, after having his property confiscated and fleeing Spain, Maclure could muster enthusiasm for another great, costly, and risky social experiment. Realistically, he had little hope of recouping his losses in Spain, but he continued to make claims through agents.

After three weeks in London, Maclure departed for Paris, where he remained until the spring, busying himself with his far-flung affairs through a very active correspondence with friends and associates. Throughout the fall and winter he was the victim of poor health, suffering from "intermittent fever" and hot and cold "fits" that were sometimes "violent." In January 1825, he had colic, followed by stoppage of urine, apparently due to stone and gravel, which required frequent catheterizations by a physician who was hired to live with Maclure; by February, his condition had improved.

With much regret, Maclure shut down his Paris operation. William Phiquepal finally closed his school on the rue des Brodeurs, and with "fifty packages of prints, instruments, books &c" he sailed from Le Havre to

Philadelphia, accompanied by Madame Fretageot's son, Achille, and three other students whom he was training to be Pestalozzian teachers, as well as operators of printing presses.[42] With the sale of his house, his Parisian headquarters, Maclure felt there was little to hold him in Europe. In poor health, ejected from Spain, and cutting an important link with Paris, with deplorable royalist regimes in France and Spain, Maclure had good reason to be depressed. Yet there were some small satisfactions; in Paris, he noted an Osage tree, *Maclura,* named in his honor by Thomas Nuttall, and he was greatly pleased when Henry Seybert, a brilliant young American mineralogist who had attended Neef's Pestalozzian school in Philadelphia, assigned the name *maclurite* to a variant of the mineral *chondrodite.*[43]

In June 1825, Maclure sailed for New York, declaring that he was glad to quit Europe: "Since the plots and conspiracies of the great and privileges orders, against the peace, comforts and happiness of the industrious productive classes, have succeeded in Europe, I am mortified beyond measure at the recollection that I belong to the species and am forced for consolation to extend my view across the Atlantic, and hope to return to America that I may be an eye witness to the prosperity of the United States and enjoy the gratifying sensation of beholding man in the most dignified attitude which he has yet attained." His aim was "to assist a little in that great general good" by establishing schools designed "to teach the pupil to avoid *remorse, fear, misery, and ennui,*" no doubt all that he had suffered.[44]

A fervent American patriot, Maclure was well aware of the country's deficiencies, for which he prescribed remedies in the light of his own radical views. While he was relentless and uncompromising in his criticisms of Europe, he was charitable in his judgments about America. Comparing the relatively lowly state of American achievement at the time of the American Revolution, he marveled at how far the United States had come along in science, industry, and the arts. According to a prejudiced but not uncritical Maclure, "there were more naturalists scattered over every corner of our Union than are to be found in all Europe."[45] And this he claimed was due to the freedom enjoyed by the people, even though equality was still lacking; yet the inequality in America was not as extreme as in Europe. It was tantalizing for Maclure to consider what wonders would be realized in America if property, knowledge, and power were to be equally divided among *all.*[46]

Maclure arrived in Philadelphia in July 1825, anxiously welcomed by Madame Fretageot, Thomas Say, and other members of the Academy, all

Owen converts, and eager to join forces with him to make utopian New Harmony a reality. It was, in fact, Madame Fretageot who had been in direct contact with Owen, distributing his literature and spreading the word about his vaulting philosophy—well before Maclure's arrival.[47]

A month was spent in discussion, with a somewhat cautious, restrained Maclure trying to dampen Madame Fretageot's extreme enthusiasm. Although he had seen what Owen had created in New Lanark and was enthusiastic about Owen's social goals, he was not totally convinced that his project was workable. Perhaps the major source of Maclure's doubts was personal; there was something about Owen's overwhelming, uncritically optimistic enthusiasm (not unlike Maclure's own) that made Maclure hesitate. He would have liked to wait a year or so to see how well Owen succeeded before committing himself—a remarkably wise path, which if taken would have saved Maclure time, torment, and a lot of money. As it turned out, Maclure walked into a buzz saw.

Meanwhile, he organized and underwrote a monthlong scientific expedition with members of the Academy—Say, Lesueur, Troost, Reuben Haines, James Carmalt, and William Price—to explore southeastern Pennsylvania, New Jersey, and New York in a leisurely way, an idyll that was described by Haines.[48] They traveled by coach, dining and sleeping at inns along the way. While Say caught insects, Lesueur sketched, and Troost and Maclure studied iron forges, mills, and the geology of each region, enthralled by the enormous deposits of coal in Pennsylvania. Maclure had not lost his intense curiosity about the structure and composition of the earth, wherever he was. As in his European travels, he seemed to wake up each morning determined to learn something new and perhaps useful.

When the group returned to Philadelphia in November, Maclure had still not quite decided whether to join Owen. But a very persuasive Owen, who was visiting Philadelphia at the time, and Maclure's eager coterie convinced him that this was the chance of a lifetime. By late November 1825, Maclure had committed himself to the venture, and within a few weeks he was going west on a keelboat he had purchased, drifting down the Ohio River to the promised land.

Gallery

William Maclure, by C. W. Peale, 1818. The Academy of
Natural Sciences, Ewell Sale Stewart Library and the Albert
M. Greenfield Digital Imaging Center for Collections.

Thomas Say, by C. W. Peale, 1819. The Academy of Natural
Sciences, Ewell Sale Stewart Library and the Albert M.
Greenfield Digital Imaging Center for Collections.

Portrait of Charles Alexandre Lesueur, by C. W. Peale, 1818. The Academy of Natural Sciences, Ewell Sale Stewart Library and the Albert M. Greenfield Digital Imaging Center for Collections.

Madame Marie Duclos Fretageot. Artist unknown. Courtesy
of the Lebrecht Music and Arts Library, London.

JOHN HENRY PESTALOZZI

Johann Heinrich Pestalozzi. Library of Congress, LC-DIG-pga-00128.

Robert Owen. The Warren J. Samuels
Portrait Collection at Duke University.

Joseph Neef, by David Dale Owen. Courtesy of the Workingmen's Institute.

Frances Wright, by Henry Inman, 1824. "There was a majesty about her." Walt Whitman. Oil on canvas, negative #38842. Collection of the New-York Historical Society.

View of New Harmony by Karl Bodmer, 1832. Joslyn Art Museum, Omaha.

New Harmony on the Wabash River (watercolor), Karl Bodmer, 1832–1833.

New Harmony on the Wabash. New-Harmony am Wabash. New-Harmony sur le Wabash. Engraving for the illustrated *Travels in the Interior of North America between 1832–34* by Prince Maximilian Alexander Philipp Zu Wied-Neuweid, published in two volumes by Ackermann, London, 1843.

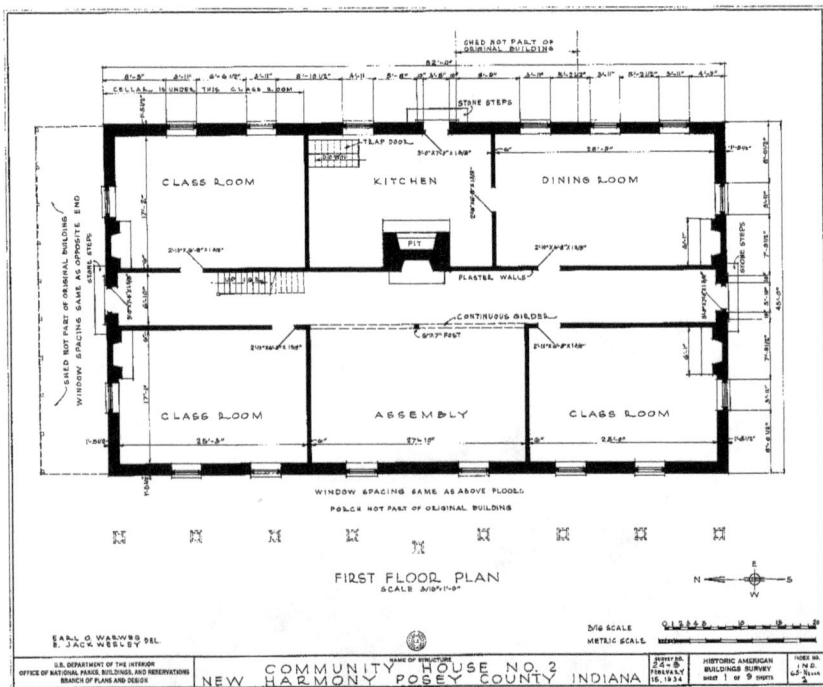

Rappite Community House No. 2. Photograph by Homer Fauntleroy,
April 7, 1934. (a.) Rappite Community House No. 2, plan of the first
floor. (b.) Rappite Community House No. 2, plan of the second
floor. (c.) Rappite Community House No. 2, plan of the third floor.
Historic American Buildings Survey (Library of Congress).

SECOND FLOOR PLAN
SCALE 3/16"=1'-0"

DORMITORY TEACHERS ROOM TEACHERS ROOM DORMITORY

CORRIDOR

PLASTER WALL

DORMITORY TEACHERS ROOM TEACHERS ROOM DORMITORY

SAME NOT PART OF ORIGINAL BUILDING — WINDOW SPACING SAME AS OPPOSITE END

WINDOW SPACING SAME AS OPPOSITE SIDE.
PORCH NOT PART OF ORIGINAL BUILDING

N E W S

3/16"SCALE
METRIC SCALE

0 1 2 3 4 5   10   15   20

EARL O. WARWEG DEL.
E. JACK WESLEY

U.S. DEPARTMENT OF THE INTERIOR
OFFICE OF NATIONAL PARKS, BUILDINGS, AND RESERVATIONS
BRANCH OF PLANS AND DESIGN

NAME OF STRUCTURE
COMMUNITY HOUSE NO. 2
NEW HARMONY POSEY COUNTY INDIANA

SURVEY NO.
24-5
FEBRUARY
19, 1934

HISTORIC AMERICAN
BUILDINGS SURVEY
SHEET 2 OF 9 SHEETS

INDEX NO.
IND.
65-Harm

THIRD FLOOR PLAN
SCALE 3/16"=1'-0"

DORMERS CENTER OVER WINDOWS BELOW
BUILDING LINE 2

BREAK IN CEILING

DORMITORY TEACHERS ROOM TEACHERS ROOM DORMITORY

BRACING BEAMS OVER.
GIRDER OVER. TRUSS OVER.

CORRIDOR

GIRDER OVER. TRUSS OVER.
BRACING BEAMS OVER.

DORMITORY TEACHERS ROOM TEACHERS ROOM DORMITORY

BREAK IN CEILING
BUILDING LINE 2

WINDOWS CENTER OVER THOSE BELOW

SEE SECTION FOR DETAIL OF FRAMING

N E W S

3/16"SCALE
METRIC SCALE

0 1 2 3 4 5   10   15   20

EARL O. WARWEG DEL.
E. JACK WESLEY

U.S. DEPARTMENT OF THE INTERIOR
OFFICE OF NATIONAL PARKS, BUILDINGS, AND RESERVATIONS
BRANCH OF PLANS AND DESIGN

NAME OF STRUCTURE
COMMUNITY HOUSE NO. 2
NEW HARMONY POSEY COUNTY INDIANA

SURVEY NO.
24-5
FEBRUARY
19, 1934

HISTORIC AMERICAN
BUILDINGS SURVEY
SHEET 3 OF 9 SHEETS

INDEX NO.
IND.
65-Harm

Rappite House on Granary Street in New Harmony. Historic American Buildings Survey (Library of Congress).

✳

TEN

Robert Owen, Maclure, and the Utopian Commune

We have it in our power to begin the world over again

Thomas Paine, Common Sense

In the eighteenth century, the unfolding of the scientific spirit and the growing appetite for new knowledge were taken as harbingers of a better world; rational analysis based on sound information would be humanity's salvation. Sadly, events proved otherwise, for there still remained the vagaries of human nature, moral and intellectual inadequacy, and an ignorance that frustrated hopes for a heavenly kingdom on earth. With all the political turmoil, most of the dreadful oligarchies remained in place, and in France a revolution that was cheered by liberal thinkers because it was guided by the promise of reason and the Enlightenment descended into a hell of its own—as one despot was replaced by a murderous band of ideologues, who in turn were replaced by Napoleon Bonaparte, a dictator responsible for the deaths of millions.

Where did hope for a better future lie? Some intellectuals sought solace in the blandishments of the Romantic movement, while others began to formulate ideas about humane, cooperative, and egalitarian societies. For hundreds of years, people living under intolerable conditions had devised cooperative, communalistic schemes, some strange and mystic, others based on traditional religious beliefs, to escape the brutalities of the world. But, alas, at best they met with little success.

In the late eighteenth century, a new political-economic entity took form, a juggernaut called the Industrial Revolution, with its huge economic benefits and its terrible human devastation. While it was the means by which fabulous wealth was created, it was also peculiarly susceptible to manipulation by the rich and powerful few who were empowered to exploit the many—the workers. In the United States, the situation was made worse throughout the nineteenth century by the immigration of throngs of impoverished Europeans and by the failure of the Jeffersonian agrarian movement, which led to the overcrowding of cities by the dispossessed. While Jacksonian populist democracy held the promise of an answer to the wretched problems of society, it was overwhelmed by a dynamic, exploitative capitalism where the dollar was king.

In Maclure's time, revolution in France had shaken the world, and with the weakening of the old systems, continued turmoil inspired thinking about new social and political arrangements—blueprints for the building of a just society. Three major socialist systems evolved that may be considered transitional in the early history of socialist thinking—Saint-Simonian, Fourierist, and Owenite—each of which influenced Maclure, as reflected in his writing. All proposed in practical terms the creation of utopian socialist communities based on principles that promoted shared commitment and countered individualism and economic competitiveness, which were at the foundation of society's devastating problems. Although they did not advocate revolutionary violence, they had little regard for politics or for existing governmental systems. They fervently believed that education was one of the keys to change. The dream of socialism was for the producers of the world to attain control of their destiny.[1]

One socialist plan was proposed by Claude-Henri de Rouvroy, comte de Saint-Simon, the impoverished descendent of Saint-Simon, the man who had recorded the events of Louis XIV's court at Versailles. He had fought in the American Revolution and returned to France, only to lose his fortune during the French Revolution (and through unwise financial speculation). A man of brilliant historical insight and a visionary, he had witnessed the young Industrial Revolution and had seen its potential for both the creation of wealth and the disruption of society. He wrote of the coming industrial age, in which a new society would arise, organized and controlled by captains of industry, while scientists and savants would tend to society's spiritual needs. Saint-Simon recognized what he believed to be the religious nature of the human being, and while deeply critical of Christianity as it was practiced, he incorporated religious elements, its language and symbolism, into his program. In essence, he wished to create an "industrial religion" in which followers were exhorted to "love one another." Saint-Simon attempted to fuse science with Christianity to form a "New Christianity" in which heaven on earth would be created by a humanized industry. The new "rational" system was hierarchical in nature, utilitarian in spirit, and insistent on an "equality of privilege." Saint-Simon proposed to do away with competition, inheritance, and the military, and women were to have rights and privileges equal to those of men. Whether private ownership of property should continue was not clearly addressed. The influence of the Saint-Simonian doctrine was far-reaching.

Saint-Simon died in 1825, but he left an organization, a cult, whose able, selfless apostles, some with financial means, dedicated themselves to the spread of his doctrine. Ultimately, the movement lost momentum, and enthusiasm abated, but it was a major wellspring of the modern socialist movement and of utopian thought, with many of its ideas seeping into progressive and radical thinking, almost unacknowledged. Karl Marx considered Saint-Simon "among the most fertile thinkers of any age," who "foreshadowed much that we of later days are able to establish on a firm foundation." Surprisingly, the Saint-Simonians' leadership consisted of the scions of important families—brilliant, effective speakers who were influential in the promotion of industry, commerce, communications, railways, and finance. The line of authority in the Saint-Simonian organization gave rise to the view that, in fact, the movement was antidemocratic, for rule was not established by vote but imposed from above through apostles who consulted with Saint-Simon or his successors as if they were popes. In such a system, private property was always in jeopardy.

Maclure and his circle of European and American intellectuals were most certainly influenced by Saint-Simon with his emphasis on the role of science and industry in reorganizing society along lines that they believed would remove the egregious consequences of industrial capitalism.[2] Saint-Simon had visited Maclure when he lived in Paris, and Maclure had bought his publications and sent them to the library at New Harmony.[3] However, Maclure, a practical man who believed that "an ounce of practice is worth 100 tons of theory," was not entirely satisfied with the Saint-Simonians, who were famous for their endless discussions and exquisite theorizing—a French proclivity.

Another scheme to reorganize society was conceived by Charles Fourier, who had learned much from Robert Owen, with whom Maclure was to join forces.[4] Aside from bizarre, apocalyptic pronouncements, some absurd, Fourier strove to design an ideal ambience for people who he believed are by nature good but who are demeaned by debased institutions and a corrupting environment. His ideal society would consist of self-contained units of about 1,750 people who owned their own property and traded their excess goods with other units, all striving for a society of equal opportunity and privilege that included women. Believing in the harmony of the universe, love and respect for fellow humans were to govern interactions in a society free of poverty, violence, and coercion.[5]

Maclure's thinking about how to improve the well-being of humankind was profoundly influenced by John Gray's *Lecture on Human Happiness* (1825).[6] This young economist analyzed in detail the numbers of each class of people and their incomes in England and Ireland in 1812. Gray concluded that working people, who were in the great majority, were being deprived of 80 percent of what they produced, and that the rich were rich because they were constantly feeding off the poor. This was an early, clear exposition of the division of society into two groups opposing one another—*producers* and *consumers*—with an attendant class war.[7] Thereafter, in all writings on the numerous problems of society, Maclure divided people into *producers* and *consumers*. Maclure was in London at the time that Gray's words induced London workmen to band together and raise money by selling shares to finance cooperative communities that would protect them from the tyranny of an exploitative system. One such assembly, the London Cooperative Society, drew up Articles of Agreement to create communities in which there would be equality of gender and the assurance of "individual freedom of opinion on all subjects of human knowledge."[8]

That Maclure was influenced by Gray's polemic is apparent in a letter he sent to Benjamin Silliman in which he glowingly endorsed the establishment of Gray-inspired cooperative societies in England and in the United States, at a time when the New Harmony colony was just being formed in 1825.[9] According to Maclure, such reorganized societies would "remedy the evil, by enabling the industrious producer to retain a far greater proportion of the produce of his labour, and removing the necessity of his working more than a few hours in the day, to obtain every necessary comfort, leaving the rest of his time for moral improvement and recreation." Since the individual could not fight a "well disciplined antagonist," the only solution was to organize, to form a "coalition of those useful and industrious producers to retain as much of their own, for their consumption and benefit." The new society would remove "the temptation to avarice, cheating, and crime." All would eat "at the same table" and "cook in the same kitchen," and women would be "placed on an equality with men." In this ideal world, "by a mutual guarantee of all the necessaries and conveniences of life," the new society would "annihilate the competition and struggle for riches and power, and that lust for dominion and command, which is the cause of envy, malice, hatred, cruelty, and of most of the miseries of mankind." Maclure did not advocate violence or the incitement of "violent antisocial passions" in the hearts of men. Although he had made a fortune as a merchant, he turned against commerce, and his own merchant class ("the merchant has an interest in opposition to that of all others").

To the list of major influences on Maclure's thinking can be added Robert Owen, and unlike the others, the influence was energized by prolonged and intense interaction between the two men. Maclure's association with Owen began in 1824, when Owen was thinking about founding a utopian community, New Harmony in Indiana, which Maclure felt might provide the ideal, controlled environment in which his schools might flourish. Owen is particularly important in Maclure's story because he provided him with an entirely new ambience in which to pursue his aims. Maclure probably would have continued with his strategy of establishing schools here and there, struggling in precarious environments, if he had not come under Robert Owen's spell.

Owen was one of the great heroes of the working class at the beginning of the nineteenth century when workers in the factories of Great Britain experienced wretched poverty, insecurity, and dissatisfaction that led to crime, drunkenness, and grave social and medical problems. A remarkable man, he emphasized the need for a comprehensive reorganization of social institutions and is credited with the founding of British socialism, the trade union movement, cooperative societies, the very first "infant school," and progressive Pestalozzian education in Great Britain.[10] He was responsible for the first labor reform legislation in England designed to alleviate the desperate conditions of the workers. This was the beginning of the end of child labor in Britain, where five- and six-year-olds worked more than twelve hours a day in textile mills under brutal conditions. Friedrich Engels said of Owen: "Every social movement, every real advance in England on behalf of the workers, links itself onto the name of Robert Owen.[11]

Rising from a modest background, Owen was a self-made man. Enormously able and popular, even as a child, he went to work at age nine, climbed his way up the ladder by educating himself through extensive reading, and by his mid-twenties managed and owned a large textile mill (with Quaker associates) at New Lanark, Scotland. It was here that he established his model community in which society was best organized to grapple with the growing abuses of industrial capitalism, especially as it pertained to the textile industry. He proved himself to be a trusted friend of the worker during a crisis provoked by Jefferson's trade embargo, a disaster for English textile mills whose source of raw material (cotton) and customers for finished products quickly vanished. While mill owners closed their mills and discharged the workers without regard for their welfare, Owen continued to pay his employees until trade resumed.

A kindly man, life had taught him that "character was made by circumstance," and like Maclure (and David Hume) he believed that "man is a *bundle of habits*—the child of surrounding circumstances, and that education (the only thing that can distinguish him from the brutes) was the means of producing all the advantages his nature is capable of."[12] Owen is widely quoted as saying that "man's character is made for him, not by him," a credo that is at the base of his entire system of belief.[13] His ambitious program of social reform began with education, and in America he was an early advocate of government sponsorship of public education. Vilified by fellow capitalists, he was known to most people as honest, sincere, dependable, and even-tempered, and as he aged he became increasingly single-minded about the solution to social problems and the abolition of poverty.

Although driven by the need for relief of the poor, Owen's approach was not for workers to seize control of the government nor to confiscate the riches of the capitalist. He did not believe that class struggle was the engine that would drive social reform. By persuasion alone, he planned to establish a new moral world of clean, independent, well-run "industrial villages," happy and free socialist colonies based on utilitarian principles and small enough to obviate the problem of communication. These would be financially independent communities with their own land, existing along-side the government, which would maintain law and order and promote the wealth of the nation. Since human behavior was shaped by the environment, an improvement in human society would follow from Owen's utopian arrangement. A liberal and wealthy man, he reflected the values and attitudes of the upper middle class, who dreaded the social disorder and unrest caused by unemployment and a disgruntled working class. There was a philanthropic component to his urge to reform.

New Lanark was an industrial village that came to be dominated by a textile mill established in 1800 by Robert Owen and his associates. Radical reforms were soon instituted, partly inspired by the Shakers in the United States, a millennial sect who built communities in preparation for the kingdom of God on earth, but Owen wanted to create secular utopias, heralds of a "New Moral World." Within a decade, New Lanark had become a showplace and the inspiration for the founding of more comprehensive communities (Orbiston, New Harmony, and several others on both sides of the Atlantic Ocean) beginning in the 1820s.

New Lanark was an orderly and well-run factory town that was inhabited by contented mill workers, the kind of small, self-supporting community that had been envisioned by Fourier. Maclure looked upon it favorably because it would provide the best environment for the implementation of his educational plans. Working conditions were good, the hours reasonable, and no child under ten was allowed to work in the mill (at the time, a much praised humanitarian policy). In his inspections of factories in various countries, Maclure never commented critically about children working. Child labor, which was commonplace, seems to have been accepted by many humane observers as long as the children were not too young and working conditions were safe and healthy. Homes on clean streets were provided for workers, and the company store sold quality goods and food at fair prices. There seemed to be no limit to what rational, ethical humans could bring about. Through Owen's efforts, 1,000 common laborers were organized into an orderly, productive, cheerful community—an unheard of phenomenon. Owen the "environmentalist" had shown that human nature is in fact malleable, and that if the environment is improved, humans change for the better. Significantly, the performance of every worker was still rated at regular intervals, an evaluation that reveals a strong, paternalistic element and a social stratification, for owners and higher officials were not evaluated on the same terms.

Owen's institution in New Lanark had become famous and was highly praised. He had established in New Lanark the first ever "infant schools" for children, ages eighteen months to six years, which freed the mother for work in the mills. In the coming decade, infant schools became popular in Great Britain. Children six to twelve years of age were taught in another school that was free of competition and of the common practice of flogging. Learning from books was delayed, while singing, dancing, and military exercises (to instill discipline) were emphasized. Military visitors were impressed by the drills, and others were pleased to watch 100 toddlers going through their dance routines in unison. For Owen, the most important function of the school was "to build character."

Curious visitors, high-born and low, came to visit utopian New Lanark, while Owen, now famous, gradually removed himself from daily operations to become a messenger to the world, spreading the tidings of social reform by written and spoken word—a communitarian solution to ubiquitous social problems for which most people wanted a solution. Confiscation of private property was not in his (or Maclure's) agenda, and investors in the profitable New Lanark mills earned 12.5 percent per annum. Owen and Maclure, wealthy men of commerce and manufacturing, seemed to have expressed different opinions about private property at various times. In the end, they believed that satisfactory reform could be achieved without abolishing it. But despite a vast increase in the nation's overall wealth and productivity, the condition of the worker deteriorated. The rich remained rich and the poor, poor.

The New Lanark experiment was a triumph, both profitable and humane, and Owen became widely known and admired as an excellent businessman, a brilliant philanthropist, and a social theorist. He was convinced that communitarian societies such as his could be the basis of extensive social reform, to better the lives of people throughout Europe. As a further step, exploiting scientific knowledge and engineering expertise, machines could be built to do the hard, dirty work. Owen accumulated data showing that in the cotton spinning industry alone, machinery could do the dreary work of millions of manual laborers, and any ensuing unemployment could be dealt with in a system of small utopian communities.[14]

Owen, now a celebrity, toured Europe and spoke and wrote extensively about "a new view of society," but while lionized, he had little success in convincing wealthy Europeans to adopt his model. Disappointed, he returned to New Lanark, where there was growing discontent among his colleagues because he was not tending to business. His Quaker partners also objected to military drill as part of the school curriculum to inculcate discipline, and they disapproved of the neglect of conventional religious teaching. Owen's proposals to Parliament to pass protective legislation for the workers and the poor met with formidable opposition, and when he ran for Parliament, he was defeated by men of property—the only people with the right to vote. In the end, forced out of the textile business, Owen decided that America was the place to test his grand ideas. What made the plan particularly attractive was the possibility that he might join forces with William Maclure, a famous geologist whose social views were the same as his own. Maclure could bring with him experienced Pestalozzian teachers, and being wealthy, he could provide financial support.

Maclure's understanding of society's problems and their remedy was certainly colored by his scientific background, but in its formulaic simplicity it also reflected his relative ignorance of, and contempt for, history. Gray's analysis and plan seemed sound to Maclure, and since the only objection he heard was that it was "impossible! the eternal cry of every thing new," he felt it was "at least worth a fair and impartial trial."[15] Maclure chose to engage in rhetoric, railing against perceived injustices such as indirect taxation, which favored the rich, "useless" establishment schools, and "granting exclusive monopolies to stock, land, and bank speculations."[16] Maclure was prepared to invest his fortune in the reformation of the education of the children of workers and the poor. Children educated according to Maclure (and Pestalozzi) would lead to the equalization of knowledge and power of all classes. As properly educated children developed into enlightened, productive citizens, they would know what their best interests were. Ultimately they would constitute a voting majority that would be the dominant voice in government. This debatable plan was logical, but it underestimated both the inertia of the people and the immense power and influence of those with capital.

Owen believed that beyond education, it was the ideal, cooperative community that molded character and was the venue for social reform. Maclure was attracted to utopian societies because he realized that in such a controlled and ordered environment such as Owen planned, his educational approach based on Pestalozzian pedagogical philosophy would have a greater chance of success than did his struggling educational ventures in the real world of Paris and Philadelphia. There would be a far greater chance in America that parents would be sympathetic to the aims and methods of Pestalozzian schools, although Maclure doubted that they really understood the aims. How much direct effort was made to inform them is uncertain, given his expressed view that it was almost impossible to "reform" adults. What was particularly tempting to Maclure was the opportunity to set up industrial (manual labor) and agricultural schools, which he had wanted to establish in Spain. Once shown how well these schools could function, Maclure had visions of extending the new educational approach to encompass an entire public school system in the United States.[17]

Despite Owen's fame and ready access to intellectual and political leaders, Europeans were beginning to tire of his rhetoric and were unwilling to go along with his radical reorganization of society, providing him with yet another reason for giving up on them. Concluding that society could best be reformed through Fourier-like small communes rather than by the gradual modification of society as it existed, Owen decided this could best be done in the United States, especially on its western frontier where a fluid, democratic spirit was more evident than in the established East and South.[18] His *New View of Society* had been distributed to President Monroe, his cabinet, state governors, and educated Americans, especially in New York and Philadelphia, who knew of him through American and European reviews. The influential Jeffersonian publication *Aurora*, emanating from Philadelphia, wrote favorably about Owen and his ideas, and small Owenite societies dedicated to a communitarian philosophy were established in Philadelphia and in several other cities. Friends of Maclure such as Gerard Troost, former president of the Academy of Natural Sciences of Philadelphia, Thomas Say, John Speakman, and Madame Fretageot responded enthusiastically. Evolving from Enlightenment ideals, Owen's views were enormously appealing to Americans who, within recent memory had fought for freedom and established a system of government that gave promise of a society of equal rights for all, guaranteed by law—an idealistic vision that Owen (and Maclure) praised and wished to build upon.[19]

Owen's decision to relocate to America was made at the time Maclure first met him in Scotland. The encounter buoyed Maclure's spirit, reflected in his enthusiastic letter to Madame Fretageot in the summer of 1824: "I spent 3 or 4 days, the most pleasant of my life, at New Lanark contemplating the vast improvement in society effected by Mr. Robert Owen's courage and perseverance in spite of an inveterate and malignant opposition. I never saw so many Men, Women with happy & contented countenances, nor so orderly, cheerful & sober a Society without any coercion or physical constraint."[20] Maclure began thinking about throwing in his lot with Owen.

Both men were at a difficult turn in their careers, Maclure having suffered a debacle in Spain, and Owen at New Lanark. They were partners in despair at the moment, but not for long, for both were visionaries, bursting with optimism, convinced that they were at the forefront in the creation of a new world. The two men, so passionate in their desire to rid society of its injustices, seemed indomitable with means to experiment with social arrangements.

What Maclure saw at New Lanark encouraged him to continue his efforts to establish schools, especially experimental farming schools, because at New Lanark, a progressive school along Fellenbergian lines was already in place and was successful. Children were learning geography, natural history, statistics, and other subjects that Maclure deemed "useful," while the mills were thriving and profitable, producing a superior product that was in great demand. A progressive education and increased profitability of the factory operated by satisfied workers were linked—the natural result of a new, enlightened philosophy. What really impressed Maclure was the fact that Owen "had succeeded against a powerfull combination of both church and state." If this could be done in Europe, it was certain that it could be accomplished in the United States. Maclure now prepared to sell his house in Paris and return to the United States, "where the sun of science and usefull knowledge has been less obscured by either public or private prejudices."

A few weeks after his visit to Lanark, Maclure wrote to Madame Fretageot that Owen was coming to the United States, where he would "join the purest and most rational Society on the Globe," and that he intended "to make arrangements for one of the most beneficent experiments ever attempted by either public or private, and if it succeeds (which I sincerely wish and hope . . .) will mark an epoch in the history of man that will elevate him far above what he has yet been, or perhaps expects to be."[21] In the 1820s, an age of enthusiasm and great expectations in America, Owen and Maclure were convinced that their mission was of special significance, for at long last they would be able to lead the way to an ideal state of human relations—"a new moral world," unprecedented in the history of mankind.[22] The message was well received in the United States, a land imbued with the idea of change and progress.

✳

ELEVEN

Harmonie to New Harmony

At the time Owen was having difficulties with his Quaker partners in Britain and was beginning to think about a cooperative commune in America, he was approached by an Englishman, Richard Flower, who had settled in Illinois and was a neighbor of a religious commune led by George Rapp. Flower informed Owen that Rapp wanted to sell the entire commune, called Harmonie, on the lower Wabash River.[1] Wanting to save time and effort building a completely new settlement, Owen chose to buy an existing one—and he had the money to do it. The village as described differed from the one he had in mind, but it would do for the present.[2]

Harmonie had been founded by a millennial branch of German Protestant immigrants steeped in mystic spirituality (a Pietistic splinter group of Lutherans from Württemberg, in southwest Germany) led by their pastor, George Rapp, a fundamentalist preacher and a pruner and trainer of plants. He and his followers came to America, settled in Pennsylvania in 1804, and then moved on to the fertile Wabash River valley with ready access to the Mississippi and Ohio rivers, in what was to become the state of Indiana. Here in 1814, they established Harmonie on 20,000 acres of land. Under Rapp's leadership the "ecclesiastical autocracy" prospered, and in ten years they had cleared 2,000 acres of land and had built a town with two churches, forty houses, half in brick and half in wood, a sawmill, a gristmill, a distillery and factories, and log cabins surrounding the town proper. A huge church of brick was built mounted by a steeple bearing a clock with a face eight feet in diameter and bells that tolled the hour and quarter hour, filling the air with sound for seven miles around.

A five-story, thick-walled stone granary was built, with slits for the aeration of stored grain, which prevented spontaneous combustion. Later, the imposing structure was dubbed by neighbors The Fort, and to later generations the slits assumed the function of gun portals. But to the pacific Harmony Society, the fortlike structure had no military significance; it was only a granary. Still, the commune was not without its enemies—jealous neighbors resentful of insular communalists and even hostile Indians— and perhaps the granary, a symbol of strength, was a gentle reminder that a commune in the hinterland was not defenseless.[3] Despite great hardship and the threat of malaria, the commune could boast of great tracts of farmland, an orchard, vineyard, school, library, and greenhouse, and it sold an array of goods, including beer and whiskey. Harmonie became especially well known for its fine wine, whiskey, and woolens.[4]

Some of Rapp's religious doctrine was bizarre, such as the dual (sexual) nature of Adam and the fall of man, justifying a policy of celibacy. As adherents of millenarianism, they believed that after 2,000 years, now approaching, Christ would reappear and life would come to an end, and so there was no purpose in further procreation. He insisted that members of the colony, married or not, be celibate, "a state more pleasing to God." Since Rappites did not seek converts, their commune eventually ceased to exist in 1905.

Esteemed by his followers as a prophet and a saint, he was a man of good nature who exhorted Harmonites to be humble, hardworking, self-sacrificing, and clean. Rapp wanted to sell Harmonie and relocate elsewhere, because he felt that the commune was too far from centers of business and that "the weather did not agree with the Germans." But it is probable that Rapp's flock was becoming too prosperous, contented, and difficult to control.[5] After selling Harmonie to Owen, he and his followers successfully established a new community, Economy, not far from Pittsburgh.

Owen, along with his son William and an associate, Donald Macdonald, a royal engineer and a veteran of Waterloo, arrived in the United States in November 1824 to examine the commune.[6] Owen's fame had preceded him, and so, disembarking in New York, he was met by ardent sympathizers. For two weeks his hours were filled with lectures and discussion. Owen embarked on a lecture tour that he hoped would inspire Americans to join him in doing away with an "ignorant, selfish system" and creating a "New Moral World" that would benefit all people, where value was based on labor. Surely in an as yet unformed and bountiful America he could put to the test the idea that the ills of society stem from a malevolent social environment and a worthless educational system. A charismatic, eloquent man, bursting with enthusiasm, he swayed large audiences across the country with his intoxicating visions and his exhortations of "what was right and what wrong with the world."[7]

Tireless, he was deeply engaged with the intellectual elite and the powerful political leaders of New York City and State, relating his views on how to right the ills of society. He outlined a plan that he estimated would take three years to come to fruition. Virtually everyone of eminence in the state was impressed by this wealthy manufacturer who had seen the light and was attracted by his infectious enthusiasm, despite his radical views and his outspoken condemnation of established religion. Departing from the prevailing views of conservative sectarian religion, he preached that all religions were flawed and that an agnostic belief in pure reason would be their salvation, an openly provocative assertion that his friends wanted him to soften.

Owen was most popular when he was regarded as a philanthropist, but admiration quickly disintegrated when he insisted on labor reform and fair treatment of factory workers and when he criticized established religion and the institution of marriage. His assertion that marriage was "one of the great trinity of evils which have cursed the world ever since the creation of man" could not have endeared him to most audiences. But closer examination reveals that Owen disapproved only of the existing contractual state of marriage sanctioned by the church, because "it obligates the contracting parties to do what they may not be able to perform and because it marks a disposition to enslave one-half of our fellow creatures"; it was unreasonable to "promise never-ending love." Property rights, being what they were, placed the female at a distinct disadvantage.

Owen's motivation in rewriting the conventional marriage contract derived from his insistence on the equality of the sexes and his desire to give women an equal voice in human affairs (including equal opportunity in education). Accordingly, Owen proposed a "natural marriage," which was a businesslike, civil agreement that was not indissoluble. It was "a marriage where a union is formed under those institutions which provide for all parties an equal education, under which they are enabled to acquire an accurate knowledge of themselves and of human nature." Children should not be a barrier to divorce, for they belong to the community where they are raised together. To Owen this kind of marriage was sacred, and its acceptance by any society was a measure of its virtue. Not surprisingly, there were many who accused him of advocating free love, but in fact he believed he was elevating the state of marriage to a new level of morality and sanctity, with true equality of partners.

However much he approved of marriage, Owen felt that there were some undesirable aspects to the union. The instinct of possessiveness and separation from the group, so destructive to communal values, was stronger among married couples than in single individuals, and in a similar vein, he felt that the interests of the family were in conflict with those of the larger association. While he allowed married couples to have their own bedrooms with an alcove in New Harmony, he provided no space for children, who were to be housed in nurseries or boarding schools. Private kitchens were unnecessary because everyone would eat in a common dining hall.[8] It would seem that communal life compelled some sort of redefinition of the marriage relationship. The reasons for the rejection of marriage and sex, commonly found among communitarian sects (Rappites, Shakers), are complex. Certainly they derive in part from old religious doctrine and ascetic practice, as well as from psychological considerations. Owen's marriage was not a happy one, and perhaps he felt that wives were a distraction that reduced the effectiveness of their husbands.

Some members of the establishment who had no sympathy for Owen's plans, and most definitely did not subscribe to his revolutionary doctrines, were still attracted to Owen himself. A few wanted to sell him land on which to build his Utopia. But his destination was Harmonie. The travel journal of Duke Bernhard of Saxe-Weimar-Eisenach reveals that opinions about Owen were varied: "In the eastern states they are not at all partial to him." Americans, touchy about the opinions of Europeans such as Owen, found it "improper" that upon arriving in the United States he boldly proclaimed that "in addition to their many virtues, they [Americans] also had many great failings." He was critical of their dogmatic religious beliefs, and he "presented himself as their reformer." Bernhard noted that while many individuals, including the "highest government officials," regarded him favorably, a few found him to be "somewhat mentally deranged."[9]

Probably the attitude of most Americans toward Owen (a mixture of hope, goodwill, and incredulity) is embodied in the words of a Supreme

Court judge who in a letter to his wife wrote about meeting this "extraordinary man" in Lancaster, Pennsylvania:

> He is a man of large fortune, and the owner of a very extensive cotton manufactory at Lanark. He has now under his control and care about two thousand five hundred persons, who are governed by him without rewards or punishments ("no praise nor blame"; "no merit nor demerit"), upon the single ground that every man will choose that which is for his happiness, if he is instructed as to what it is. I understand that the children of his workmen are all educated by him together, without restraint, playing when they choose, and studying when they choose. His whole scheme is so romantic that it would seem but a dream; and yet he has tried the experiment for twenty years, and it has entirely succeeded. He has come to America to try his plan here. Believing in human perfectibility, he is satisfied that all the existing evils are founded in the institutions of society. He thinks property ought to be held in common, and is so benevolent and yet so visionary an enthusiast that he talks like an inhabitant of Utopia. However he is very simple in his manners and pleasant in his conversation.[10]

Bearing letters of introduction to people he would meet along the way, including Thomas Jefferson, Owen swept into Philadelphia, the home of prized recruits, where he was extolled by the eminent, who besieged him with invitations. In his element, he radiated a blinding belief in his ability to solve the great problems of humankind. Here he met naturalists of liberal, if not radical, persuasion who had already seriously considered founding a utopian colony. The treasured group included John Speakman, Gerhard Troost, Thomas Say, and Charles Alexandre Lesueur, founders or young members of the Academy of Natural Sciences of Philadelphia and recipients of William Maclure's largesse.[11] What was especially appealing to these men who had been struggling to survive in a society that did not support or appreciate their work was Owen's proclamation that in the new commune the special talents of each member would be recognized, that science would be highly valued, and that scientists would be considered on an equal footing with laborers and those with financial means.

Owen visited Madame Fretageot's school, and he bedazzled her. Madame, after leaving Paris in 1821, established a school for girls along Pestalozzian lines in Philadelphia (supported by Maclure), and she had brought Owen's writings with her, which she pressed upon her friends. She proved to be a major voice in enlightening the young members of the Academy of

Natural Sciences of Philadelphia about the benefits of the Owenite plan. Caught up in his enthusiasm once again, she remained a devoted disciple who convinced members of the Academy that Owen was humankind's salvation. Gushing, she wrote Maclure: "The more I know of that man, of his plan and of his high sense, the more I am convinced that we will join in his undertaking."[12] Owen had convinced her that a Pestalozzian school in a big city like Philadelphia would be unable to "counterbalance the evils which surround" it, and so would end in failure, while in the controlled and ideal environment of New Harmony, progress could be made in the proper education of the young.[13] He argued that if the environment in which people lived was improved, people would improve—the building of character would follow from the nature of the community in which people lived and worked, as witnessed in New Lanark, which he himself had created. He was now attempting to duplicate and expand the concept by creating another utopian community.

Maclure soon realized that his own educational strategy for reform could best be implemented in a communitarian society such as New Harmony, which Owen could provide. Without Owen there would never have been a New Harmony community in which Maclure's educational approach to societal reform could be applied. Maclure's background was in commerce, geology, and science, none of which fitted him to grapple with the problems of establishing a communitarian society. Never did he propose to found one, for he became fixed on the notion that social reform begins with education, and education alone. A prolific writer, he published impassioned essays that asserted that inequality of knowledge led to inequality of wealth and control of the means of production.[14]

The necessity of winning over Maclure was important to Owen's plans. As a wealthy man who supported Pestalozzian schools, Maclure employed skilled teachers (Fretageot, Phiquepal, and Neef) and was the patron of young naturalists who could contribute so much to his Utopia. He had enchanted Madame Fretageot, who in lauding Owen made sure that she did not make Maclure jealous. Her letters were filled with praise for Maclure, cajoling, reassuring, and soothing him—"That I owe to you that this happy situation makes it 1000 times greater if you was by me in this moment. . . . I should be crazy for joy." She knew how to handle Maclure.[15]

The triumphant tour continued as Owen arrived in Washington to meet President Monroe, Secretary of State John Quincy Adams (soon to be the sixth president of the United States), and many leading politicians and jurists. Owen, barnstorming around the country, aroused Americans to heed his words, that his social and economic scheme was the answer to the problems that beset their nation. Tireless in addressing anyone who would listen, he even lectured a delegation of Choctaw and Chickasaw chiefs visiting the capital.

Owen's introduction to the United States was a national event, just as it had been at an earlier time in Europe when he was considered the most influential promoter of socialism and social betterment and a vigorous opponent of war (which is "irrational"). Buoyed by such an enthusiastic welcome, a timely anodyne that sustained his hopes, there seemed no better place for his dream to be realized than in America. Americans looked with pride and affirmation at their land of abundance, their inventions and marvels of engineering. But the truth was that despite the spirited reception, when it came to commitment, the moneyed class doubted the practicality of Owen's schemes and was no more supportive of them than were Europeans who had also accorded him a fervent reception. Owen seemed to interpret the enthusiasm of social and political leaders for his message as approval and willingness to adopt his point of view. They listened, and perhaps for a moment they entertained visions of a better world—but only for a moment.

Almost an entire month had been spent touring and creating excitement in the major centers of the East, and now it was time for Owen to proceed to Indiana to inspect and purchase the Rappite colony. Owen, his son William, and Donald Macdonald traveled by coach to Pittsburgh. Since Father Rapp's newly established colony of Economy was only eighteen miles from Pittsburgh, an opportunity to confer with Rapp and to examine his new colony in actual operation could not be missed. Owen, fascinated by Rapp, held lengthy conversations with him about practical and doctrinal matters, and he gathered useful information about the town he would rename New Harmony. Both men were pleased that they had so much in common, although there were critical differences. "Rapp was the pioneer, the pious servant of God, and the practical reformer, deeply concerned about eternal salvation, while Owen was a man of the world with a generous interest in man's material welfare, but not concerned about the world to come."[16] Owen's intent was to convert a religious commune into a secular utopia of his own design.

William Owen and Donald Macdonald disapproved of Rapp's absolute authoritarian style and the grayness of his creation, but as they later inspected what the Rappites had accomplished in Harmonie, they were impressed by what large numbers of plain men and women, working cooperatively under a rigorous leader, could accomplish. While Owen declared that "I have not yet met with more kind-hearted, temperate and industrious citizens, nor found men more sincere, upright and honest in all their dealings, than the Harmonists," William, while not disagreeing with his father, noted their "grave, stolid, often sad German faces," though they "seemed free from anxiety." Material wants had been sufficiently satisfied in this religion-driven autocracy, but "Rapp's disciples had bought this dearly, at the expense of heart and soul." Freedom from want had been earned by an "unquestioned submission to an autocrat who had been commissioned . . . by God Himself."[17] Another visitor wrote that while at Harmonie, he had never seen anyone laugh.

Departing from Pittsburgh, the group continued their journey to Indiana, descending the Ohio River by steamboat and reaching Harmonie in mid-December, three weeks after leaving Washington. They were greeted by Father Rapp's adopted son, Frederick, an architect and the business manager of the Rapp colony. Owen conferred with Frederick and Rapp's agent, Richard Flower, about the details of purchase, and after a week of inspection of the colony's machinery and the buildings and grounds, Owen bought the entire town on January 3, 1825, for $150,000, although in truth, the precise figure paid varies in different accounts.[18] The Owenites who took over Harmonie felt that the German settlers they were replacing were a bit slow. However, Father Rapp was a shrewd dealer, and so it is probable that Owen paid too much. In a letter to Madame Fretageot, Maclure later wrote that fertile land in Ohio could be bought for a fraction of the price Owen paid, an error of judgment which confirmed Maclure's wariness that he should separate his financial obligations from Owen's and that under no circumstances should he be considered Owen's partner.[19]

When the Rappites departed for their new home in Economy, Pennsylvania, as a gesture of goodwill they left sheep, cattle, and some machinery. Owen was now the owner of an entire town, renamed New Harmony, with its brick, frame, and log structures, churches, granary, factories, stores, public buildings, and homes, sufficient for 700 people. The centerpiece of the town was a massive brick church, able to seat 1,000 people. Four wings of the structure extended from an imposing central structure surrounded by twenty-eight large columns. Lovingly built by the Rappites, sacrilegiously it was promptly renamed "the Hall" and used as a school, library, workshop, lecture hall, and recreation center.[20] A school was set up by Owen, which by June had an enrollment of 135 students who were boarded and clothed at Owen's expense.[21]

Amazingly, no sooner had the purchase been completed than Owen hastily departed on a three-month tour, leaving New Harmony to fend for itself under the direction of William Owen and Macdonald. His destination was Washington, the center of power, where his views were described sympathetically by the local newspapers. Again, he was warmly received and granted the high honor of speaking twice in the Hall of Representatives on "A New System of Society." The lectures were attended by Presidents Monroe and Adams, Supreme Court justices, members of the cabinet, and many congressmen. He also conferred with former presidents Jefferson and Madison. The texts of his talks were published in the widely read *National Intelligencer*.[22] In contrast to the virtual rejection of Owen by the British Parliament, the acclaim accorded Owen in America was overwhelming, although little of substance came of it.

Owen continued to tour the United States, spreading the word and advertising for recruits—with too great a success. "The industrious and well-disposed of all nations and creeds" were invited to join New Harmony, and by summer 1825 they were overwhelmed by volunteers from every state and every country of northern Europe. The harvest included a good percentage of the lazy, incompetent, alcoholic misfits of the world, while in New Harmony a desperate lack of housing was fueling disappointment and discontent.[23]

No one knew when Owen would return to New Harmony and what real authority his subordinates had, and many practical questions were left unanswered, such as the choice of members to be admitted to the commune, the use to which specific buildings should be placed, and the assignments of people to work in factories or farms and where they should live. Anxiety grew as drift and discouragement set in. Owen's deputies were besieged by growing numbers of people with many problems and every motivation. It was evident that detailed planning and close attention to myriad details were necessary for New Harmony to succeed, and these were lacking. They seemed to be beneath Owen's regard.

Despite Owen's absences and the unsettled state of New Harmony, the commune was taking shape, and the prospects for such an enterprise were a matter of national discussion. There was no lack of prospective members, including whole families, who presented themselves at the gate, some arriving mainly for the superior education their children would receive. But freeloaders and crackpots were also attracted to this new kind of community. While there were no established procedures or rules for rejecting or accepting newcomers, in Owen's absence no one at New Harmony had the authority to make the harsh decision of refusing admission. All this was taking place before Maclure (perhaps ignorant of or hazily informed about the disorder) had even decided whether he would join Owen.

In mid-April 1825, at the end of an enormously successful 100-day tour, Owen returned to his Eden on the Wabash where he was besieged by 900 supplicants desiring entry. Buoyant and convinced of the ultimate success of his venture, he lectured frequently, and carried away by his own rhetoric, he proclaimed that New Harmony was one of the greatest social experiments ever attempted in history, one that should lead to "universal happiness of the human race." He was about to bring to America a change so sweeping that "all former revolutions in human affairs scarcely deserve the name." This exhilarating declaration must be tempered by the account of a sympathetic but critical visitor. After a lengthy conversation with him, Duke Bernhard sadly reported, "He had no less an expectation than to convert the entire world, to exterminate all evil, to banish all punishment, and in this way prevent all disputes and war."[24] But now the real work had to be done, and the flaws in Owen's ambitious operation became apparent.[25]

Upon his return to New Harmony, Owen established a *Preliminary Committee* to govern the commune, and he proposed a socialist constitution that was adopted within a few weeks (May 1). As sole proprietor, he would appoint a committee of management for the first year, after which members would be elected.[26] In a lengthy lecture in the Hall of New Harmony, he outlined his plan. New members were to bring their earthly goods, and their work would earn them credits upon which they could draw at the public store. New Harmony was dedicated to the idea of free speech and thought in an egalitarian society without gender discrimination, where age and experience would be respected and where expertise would prevail. The overall goal of New Harmony was "to procure the greatest happiness of the members and their children."[27] In New Harmony, society was to be free of quarrels and insult, and public education was to be provided equally for boys and girls, who were to be clothed and boarded at public expense. New Harmony, a showcase and a prototype, was only the first of many communes to be established. Owen looked upon New Harmony as a testing ground, a halfway house on the road to the ideal commune. All would eventually be self-governing after a probationary period, one of transition for people who must "change from the individual to a social system; from single families with separate interests, to communities of many families with one interest." Since old habits were so ingrained, the change would take time.[28] These lofty proposals, reflecting current values, did not pertain to black people. For them, special (and unequal) arrangements would be made; they could be "helpers," in preparation for resettlement elsewhere, including communes in Africa.

A prophet of messianic pronouncements, Owen was at his best expounding on grand visions and laying out a great blueprint for his secular "New Moral World." It has been said that while Rapp was prepared to wait for the millennium and to leave the Second Coming up to the Lord, Owen took on the responsibility of doing so through his own efforts.[29] At the same time, he neglected to attend to the details by which such schemes are brought to fruition in the everyday world. Bestor has clearly described Owen's failure, pointing out that he never addressed in any satisfactory way the question of who should be selected as members, and on what basis they should be chosen, nor did he consider what would be the system of property rights.

The central problem confronting Owen was how to convert a commune where all property was owned by him to one where property was to be held in common, where equality of all citizens would prevail, and where at the same time a fair return on his investment was expected. Owen owned everything, so should new members be considered renters, the benefactors of philanthropy, or employees? Could they buy part of the property and become partners, and what would be the status of the property they brought? His statement that there was to be a "community of property" was inconsistent with others he made which permitted property ownership by individuals at every level of the social stratum, while those at the bottom labored almost as slaves.

Owen, the sole proprietor, appointed four members to the newly established Preliminary Committee, and in three years' time increasing numbers of members would be freely elected to the committee and would operate independently in a new Community of Equality, under the rules and regulations of a constitution set forth by Owen and debated by members of New Harmony. Property could then be purchased by individuals, a sale which seemed to be inconsistent with the frequently proclaimed goal of "common ownership." Members of the committee would be responsible for the operation of New Harmony according to the principles set forth in the constitution. To become a full member with its responsibilities and privileges (education, living arrangements), persons had to agree to the terms of the constitution in writing, and what they would receive thereafter would be determined by the committee.[30] Each family was given a certain number of credits based on its service to the commune, which allowed it to draw whatever food and clothing it needed from a store. A uniform dress for men and women was prescribed. Members were to meet three evenings each week—one evening for discussion of rules and regulations, one evening for concerts, and one evening for dancing. Music recitals usually preceded lectures and orations.

The principles and the rules set down in this and in later constitutions, however ringing with idealism, were often vague, open to interpretation, and inconsistently applied. When openly challenged, one set of rules was abandoned and replaced by others in order to stem a growing dissatisfaction that was becoming apparent as productivity of the commune declined and financial losses, which were covered by Owen, continued to mount. At times he must have envied George Rapp's absolute control of Harmonie, with its disciplined, obedient, and productive members who responded to the word of the Almighty, not to the dictates of reason and deliberation.

Despite unresolved problems, in early June Owen departed New Harmony at short notice, leaving William, Macdonald, and the Preliminary Committee to manage the commune once again. He had begun another tour, visiting large and small cities in the East, lecturing to large audiences, and conferring with presidents. In mid-July 1825, he sailed for England, where he remained until November. There, the distant turmoil and the daily problems of New Harmony hardly concerned him, while much of his time was spent drawing plans for a model village to be built near the old and, to a large extent, to replace it—a spectacular undertaking that was to be realized upon his return. He hired an architect, Stedman Whitwell, to design and construct an expensive model of an ideal community, which he brought to New York, accompanied by another of his sons, Robert Dale Owen, along with the architect. Owen continued to publicize the plan, despite alarmed warnings from William that the new community could not be built: "As for building houses, that is at present out of the question. We have *no lime, no rocks* (ready blasted), *no bricks, no timber, no boards, no shingles,* nothing requisite for buildings, and as to getting them from others, *they are not to be had in the whole country.*"[31] Moreover, the labor required would bring to a stop the normal business of the existing commune. As it was, the community was not productive because of an acute shortage of skilled people to work in the pottery, textiles, and dyeing establishments left by Rapp. But Owen pressed on, ignoring all warnings and advice to the contrary.

Serious dissatisfaction was growing in New Harmony, for the Preliminary Committee was treating members inequitably, based on their financial status. Those who brought capital to the community received benefits from the capital they had invested—hardly an impartial sharing. Terms of compensation were established on an ad hoc basis, sometimes changing, and frequently rendered ambiguous, especially in times of shortages. Many questions remained unanswered. Were productive and unproductive workers to be equally rewarded? How were irresponsible and incompetent people to be treated, and what should be their share? There were complaints that the Preliminary Committee was "despotic," threatening people with expulsion if they did not "cringe" before them, and that they were making "slaves" of free people.[32] Anguished letters were sent back home from Harmonists who had come with great hope and were now bemoaning their miserable physical and mental state in the wilderness. But they were sustained by the knowledge that when Owen returned all would be remedied, and their certainty grew as the time of Owen's return approached at the end of 1825. After nine months, the committee had incurred a loss of $30,000, which Owen was obliged to honor.

A chronic shortage of skilled workers, supervisors, and farmers plagued the commune, so that the farming component of the colony was almost nonexistent, and while no one went hungry, failure to produce a sufficient amount and variety of food resulted in dreadful meals that tested the commitment to New Harmony principles.[33] Unhappy and disaffected, people were preoccupied with governance and valuations, and strife was pervasive. Just before Owen's return, one lady wrote, "Our store is in want of a great number of necessary articles, and nobody is sent on for goods, because they wish to consult Mr. Owen first. We are out of coffee, sugar, sewing cotton, thread, paper, etc, etc."[34] In addition, the textile mills, pottery works, and grist and lumber mills established by the Rappites were operating at far less than capacity or were not functioning at all. Housing was grossly inadequate for the 1,000 inhabitants. New Harmony was clearly not self-sufficient, and yet, despite advertisements in newspapers beseeching people *not* to come, they kept arriving.[35]

Within New Harmony, tensions grew between religious and agnostic members, and some who fervently maintained their Christian beliefs were offended by the blasphemous conversion of the former Rapp church into classrooms and a community hall. Still, all forms of religious belief were permitted, though none were preached.

Class differences became apparent as people began to segregate into distinct groups. Leadership of the commune, such as it was, was compelled to eject the lazy and the troublemakers. Owen had forbidden drinking and had ordered that the Rapp distillery be demolished, much to the dissatisfaction of many workers.[36] But despite the complaints and the departure of some disgruntled members, most members of the commune were reasonably content and willing to remain. All would be set aright when Owen returned from his tours and took control.

Remarkably, Owen kept on sinking his fortune into New Harmony, and he continued to believe that the problems that beset the community would soon be resolved. Owen, a man of great persuasive eloquence, was remarkably optimistic, and when he spoke, dissatisfaction vanished. In direct contact with people, he could draw them together "from all points of the compass, various in habit and disposition, to mix like brethren and sisters."[37]

Still, attitudes toward Owen were changing, criticism in the press was mounting, and he was increasingly challenged during lectures. Owen, a deist, persisted in making provocative, antireligious, antisectarian statements that alienated many who could have helped promote his cause. He was vilified by some as godless, blasphemous, an advocate of free love, and worse. Not only was he reviled by conservative Christians at a time of Christian revivalism in the United States, he was also denounced by capitalists who abhorred any scheme that suggested the idea of common ownership of property. Owen was under siege, and yet he felt, blithely, that all was well and that vexing details would take care of themselves. As later described by Robert Dale Owen, some of Owen's traits were not conducive to diplomatic accommodation: "My father had various arguments in public and private whereby however in my opinion he did not accomplish much. It seems to me that he expresses himself in too vehement and dogmatic a manner and is too general in his criticism of the present system. Such general criticism is not only unjust but it also irritates almost all those who have other ideas. He tends to fall into the same fault which he criticizes in others." Owen seemed surprised that people who disagreed with his father actually applauded him: "But the impression would in my opinion be ten times stronger if my father understood how he ought to talk."[38] After stirring the hearts of Washingtonians with the promise of a new society to come, Owen finally returned to New Harmony in January 1826, welcomed as a savior and bringing with him Maclure and his devoted followers.[39]

TWELVE

✳

A Boatload of Knowledge

Ignorance is the fruitful cause of human misery.

From the masthead of Maclure's Disseminator of Useful Knowledge

As much as he admired Robert Owen and his goals, William Maclure had hesitated about associating with him, perhaps suspecting that he would be unable to cope with this irresistible force of nature. Although he was devoted to the idea of "equality and common property on Mr. Owen's principles" and to Owen's notions about "useful" education, Maclure was wary of his exuberant, messianic dogma, which was divorced from reality.[1] His hesitation also bespeaks an instinctive distrust of a hyperarticulate, overly optimistic prophet with grand schemes (not unlike his own).

He must have sensed, even vaguely, a disturbing deficit in Owen's attention to detail, amounting to irresponsible behavior, and it is difficult to believe that Maclure would commit himself and his money to such a man and such a risky undertaking. Had he not heard about the chaos and unrest in the newly established utopia during the past year? Perhaps he had discounted reports as mere rumors promulgated by those who wanted

New Harmony to fail. He had not forgotten that when he was in the United States in 1817 his own plans for educational reform had met with hostility and indifference—"openly reprobated, as Eutopian and folly, spending my time and money so ridiculousely."[2]

Until the final moments of his capitulation, Maclure showed some reluctance to make a drastic move that involved the transfer of his educational and scientific efforts, a costly disruption affecting so many people, wondering whether perhaps it would be better to concentrate on promoting his schools in Philadelphia.

Owen had visited Philadelphia in March 1825, where several members of the Academy of Natural Sciences were anxious to follow him to New Harmony if their patron Maclure was agreeable. They would be a prize catch for Owen, for if they came, they would instantly establish New Harmony as an important scientific center. Madame Fretageot's enthusiasm for Owen and his great plan was rekindled, prompting her to implore Maclure in Paris to accede to the Philadelphians' wishes.[3] Owen had become the second of her heroes: "the best man explaining a plan which is the best calculated for human happiness. . . . He came and the pleasure I felt when he took me in his arms can be equaled only by the one I will experience when I will have the happiness of taking your hands in mine!" In March 1825, Owen in Philadelphia, surrounded by Madame Fretageot and Maclure's admirers (Say, Speakman, Troost, Phiquepal), sent a letter to Maclure imploring him to hasten home. In this joint letter, Madame Fretageot enthused, "You have no idea of his patience, calmness, benevolence, and kindness towards his fellow creatures, even the most despicable."[4]

In a letter dated July 12, 1825, Madame Fretageot assured Maclure, "Your anxiety concerning Mr. Owen['s] plan is without foundation." In Maclure's reply, he chided her for being too enthusiastic about Owen and suggested that her judgment was impaired. Although he was fascinated by Owen, there were other matters of great concern: "there is two things to be considered and cooly examined. The first is the reasonableness of the plan and the goodness and solidity of the theory, in which I perfectly agree with Mr. Owen and all his most enthousiastical supporters. The second is the most difficult to annalise as the means of putting in practise, because the materials he has to work upon are stubern, crooked, and too often bent in an opposite direction from their owne most evident interest."[5] Even after New Harmony had been operating for one year, Maclure expressed concern about the kind of people being attracted to the commune: "Every-thing I have heard . . . diminishes the little confidence I had in the material he [Owen] has to work upon, and you cannot be too cautiouse of chusing your members, avoiding as much as possible those who have contracted indolent, grumbling, and corrupt habits under the wretched government of the Preliminary Society."[6] He doubted that most members of the com-munity understood Owen's principles.

Owen visited Philadelphia twice in early November 1825 to urge Ma-clure to join his great venture, and in the end Maclure succumbed. Bal-ancing negatives with his admiration for Owen and the prize to be won if New Harmony was a success, he found the possible reward too tempting. Maclure seems to have been almost defenseless against Owen's appeals and the urgency of his own young followers, especially the impassioned Madame Fretageot. On several occasions, he was pressed by Owen him-self to join him, and in the end, after a year of deliberation and extensive discussions, he decided to participate in the New Harmony venture.

To the young, idealistic scientists and teachers associated with Maclure, living in a commune seemed a most attractive model for the elimination of egregious social problems, even in microcosm, and at the same time this new arrangement would relieve them of the intolerable burden of seeking finan-cial support for their unremunerative work. Of modest origins and means, they had little chance of advancement and support in Philadelphia, whereas in New Harmony they would be the honored members of the new society.

The group consisted of Gerhard Troost from Holland, a chemist and crystallographer; John Speakman, an outspoken radical and failed business-man; Thomas Say, the author of classic studies on entomology and conchol-ogy who was considered the "father" of both disciplines in America; and Charles-Alexandre Lesueur, an outstanding naturalist and artist Maclure had brought from France to become a curator at the Academy of Natural Sciences of Philadelphia.[7] Zealous in their admiration of Owen, which was sharpened by Madame Fretageot's aggressive encouragement, they were impatient to start a new life in his utopian colony on the Wabash River.

The Academy of Natural Sciences of Philadelphia was now left in the hands of the local establishment—George Ord, a wealthy man, retired from business, Samuel George Morton and Richard Harlan, successful physi-cians and respected scientists, and an assortment of people who looked with dismay at these superb young men (proto-professional scientists) who were running off into the wilderness, following a spurious dream in which science was to be (mis)used to abolish injustice and poverty. To their credit, some of those who remained in Philadelphia had a clearer idea of where science was heading, and to this end they seized the leadership of the Academy, controlled its publications, and insisted that scientists must specialize.

The loss of several of the Academy's best people was most damaging, and those who remained always resented the defection, especially that of Thomas Say, for he was a brilliant unifying force, respected by all.[8] Paradoxically, Maclure, the man who was financing the abandonment of Philadelphia, continued as the revered head of the Academy, his wishes attended to by those who remained, for the Academy was heavily dependent on his generosity and his specimens.

Once the decision was made, little time was lost in relocating to Indiana. What followed was a hurried settling of Philadelphia affairs so that the trek was able to begin within a few weeks. Speakman and Troost were so anxious to go, they left on their own before the main migration occurred. Maclure and his retinue set out by coach for Pittsburgh on a cold Sunday morning, November 28, 1825. Accompanying him in this trip over the mountains were Thomas Say, Charles-Alexandre Lesueur, Madame Fretageot, her assistant, Lucy Sistare (who later married Say), and Lucy's two sisters. Maclure had planned to hire a steamboat in Pittsburgh to take everyone down the Ohio River to New Harmony, but the low water level precluded travel on such a vessel. In the course of a week, Maclure bought and fitted up a keelboat of shallow draught, eighty-five feet long and fourteen feet wide, capable of carrying at least forty passengers, albeit in somewhat cramped accommodations. The vessel was divided into four parts, the first for six oarsmen, the second section for men, the third for women (named "Paradise"), and the fourth for children, called "purgatoire" by Lesueur. One area was set aside for cooking, and another for dining and general recreation, and two stoves provided heat and warm meals.[9] While the boat was officially named the Philanthropist, an enthused Owen exuberantly dubbed it the Boatload of Knowledge in recognition of the illustrious nature of its passengers, for the "boat contained more learning than ever was before contained in a boat." By learning, Owen did not mean Latin, Greek, and other languages but real knowledge—scientific and "useful." Without question, the boat held some of the ablest instructors of youth that could be found in the United States,[10] who would assure the success of the enterprise as a whole and the educational plan in particular. New Harmony eagerly looked forward to the arrival of this legendary boat bringing science, culture, and art to the West, the jewel atop the crown of this commune that would fairly provide for its members without the torments of the world they had left behind.

Aboard the keelboat were Maclure, Owen and his son Robert Dale, Owen's servant, Say, Lesueur, Madame Fretageot, her son, Achille, and her two young nephews, who had attended Maclure's Pestalozzian school in Philadelphia.[11] They were joined by the three Sistare sisters, William Phiquepal, another Pestalozzian teacher, and his ten students, a Swiss engraver, Cornelius Tiebout, Balthazar Obernesser, who taught art, Dr. Samuel Chase, a chemist, and his wife, Dr. William Price of Philadelphia, a boyhood friend of Say, his wife, sister-in-law, and three children, and a skilled carpenter, John Beal, with his wife and daughter.[12] Donald Macdonald and the English architect Stedman Whitwell caught up with the boat and joined the group later, downstream, after spending time in Washington displaying Whitwell's model of an ideal commune—the future New Harmony—commissioned by Owen; the model had been viewed by President John Quincy Adams. Rounding out the list were several people who had responded to Owen's newspaper advertisements for craftsmen and wanted to take part in the exciting new social experiment. On December 8, the thirty-five passengers and ten crew left Pittsburgh to descend the Allegheny River, with Robert Dale Owen in full throat, singing, "Land of the West, we come to thee, Home of the brave, soil of the free."[13]

The enchanted voyage to the frontier began in high spirits, but they came to a halt on the second day when the boat ran aground, having traveled only sixteen miles. Fortunately, George Rapp's new Economy settlement was only a few miles away, and it took six of their strong men only an hour to free the boat. After visiting Economy, conversing with George Rapp, and inspecting the impressive new commune, they were on their way again, but without Robert Owen, who returned to Pittsburgh with a Mrs. Fisher, supposedly to verify the deeds to New Harmony, but more probably it was an excuse to avoid such a slow and unpredictable form of travel. Owen never rejoined the crew. He traveled to New Harmony aboard the more reliable mail coach, and he welcomed the boat at New Harmony when it arrived many weeks later. The keelboat had lost two passengers but gained others along the way.[14]

Soon the river began to freeze and an icy barrier formed, bringing the boat to a halt, and locking it in for a month at Safe Harbor, eight miles from Beaver, Pennsylvania—nowhere—a situation best described as the storyline of a movie. For some, all was not lost. Young Robert Dale Owen, European-educated and sophisticated, wrote in his diary: "During that month, immensely to my satisfaction I took my first lesson in Western country wood-craft." From "an old hunter of the leather-stocking school," he learned about the forest trees, the proper care of a rifle, and the "habits and haunts of the game." James Fenimore Cooper had come alive from the pages of a book he had read in preparation for the adventure.[15] Owen kept a diary in which his very private opinions were written in German. This perceptive young man thought Madame Fretageot (his admired confidante) "highly remarkable" and of a "truly mannish disposition" who would be invaluable to the New Harmony community. He mentioned Maclure twice in rather unflattering terms: "Mr. M [Maclure] seems to me at times to act somewhat stubbornly and vehemently." The next day he wrote, "It seems to me that Mr. M looks at everything in a much too suspicious manner and manages thereby at times to make difficulties for himself."[16] These descriptions would suggest that Maclure was still having misgivings—even at this late date—about the New Harmony venture and about Owen himself, who had abandoned the ship. The unexpected delays were making Maclure particularly uneasy.

Thomas Say, a quiet, gentle soul, was elected captain. He seemed to have drifted gracefully into a position of authority, becoming an effective leader of the ship and keeper of the accounts, no doubt with Maclure's blessing. His spare time was spent hunting. He also courted Lucy Sistare, later described as "the handsomest and most polished" woman in New Harmony. They married, and she became Say's invaluable assistant, coloring his drawings with great skill. For them, the month in the wild with few responsibilities was a month of romance in Eden. Lesueur, a close friend of Say, was a naturalist with artistic talent, who spent his days sketching the boat, its passengers, and the countryside, leaving a delightful record of the trip and of early America.[17]

Passengers had no alternative but to settle down to a quiet, cozy existence, passing the time listening to piano music, reciting Byron, singing hymns, skating, and foraging for food in the surrounding countryside. In this snowy setting, they read and discussed the intricacies of Charles Fourier, the social theorist, or played cards while the hungry stoves kept the young men chopping wood or making preparations of stuffed animals for the future museum at New Harmony. But some did not fare so well, for many of the women were unhappy living under such primitive conditions. A restless Maclure had enough of enforced inactivity, and after one week he and Madame Fretageot abandoned ship to trek to Beaver, where they hired a wagon to take them to Steubenville, Ohio, and Wheeling, West Virginia.

After being locked in for a month at year's end and growing impatient without their two leaders, Say and others decided to cut a path through the ice that would enable them to move the boat into the navigable central channel of the river. The work was arduous, but within a day they were ready to continue the journey (January 9, 1826). Proceeding down the Ohio, they came to Wheeling, West Virginia, where they found Maclure and Madame Fretageot, who rejoined the ship for the remainder of the trip. Hard oar work by both men and women brought them to Cincinnati, where Owen had preceded them by a week, and then to Louisville, Kentucky. By chance they came across Joseph Neef, who had abandoned school teaching several years previously to farm. Maclure had little difficulty convincing him to sell his faltering venture and join the New Harmony colony. Neef, a skilled Pestalozzian teacher, was a valuable addition to the group, as was his wife, Eloisa, who proved to be an effective manager of schools.

For some passengers the river journey came to an end at Mt. Vernon, Indiana, on the Ohio River a few miles upstream from where the Wabash enters the Ohio. Their arrival on January 23, forty-seven days after leaving Pittsburgh, was celebrated by a banquet. The river was freezing up again, and with the possibility of being ice-bound for another month, only fifteen miles from New Harmony, most passengers were anxious to get to their destination without further rowing or chopping ice. The trip had, for the most part, been an adventure drifting down the river, as in a dream, sometimes singing and dancing in the evening as the keelboat slid past great forests and farms, the river banks dotted with the cabins of friendly pioneer settlers who provided them with milk, eggs, and fowl. Macdonald confided to his diary that "evenings were pleasantly passed in reading and conversation," that his accommodations were "extremely good," and that he enjoyed rowing.[18] There must have been long periods of boredom, as well as moments of stress and terror, when ice on the river broke up with thunderous crashes. For some, this was the adventure of a lifetime.

Half of the passengers completed the trip by wagon, over hills and through dense forest to New Harmony—while others chose to continue the river voyage. The forests were dark and threatening, and what roads there were in the area were treacherous. Robert Owen had arrived at New Harmony on January 12, eleven days before, conferring and lecturing with his usual vigor. His son Robert was so anxious to reach New Harmony that he borrowed a horse and galloped off alone from Mount Vernon, arriving in time to hear his father in the midst of an evening lecture.

Say and Lesueur remained with the keelboat, and proceeded down the Ohio to Shawneetown on the Wabash where they picked up the heavy baggage that had been shipped to New Orleans from New York, and after being transferred to a steamer, they had ascended the Mississippi River. The keelboat with luggage went up the Wabash, a western tributary of the Ohio River coursing between Illinois and Indiana, and soon arrived at New Harmony, 354 miles from Pittsburgh. By the New Orleans route Maclure sent "fifty tons" of books and "philosophic apparatus" purchased in France, so that his educational program could start immediately. William Pelham, a member of the colony, stated that the freight charge was over $1,000, and he claimed that New Harmony would now have "the best Library and best School in the United States."[19]

✳

THIRTEEN

Education in New Harmony

Leaving behind the *Boatload of Knowledge* mired in ice, Robert Owen reached New Harmony in January 1826, almost two weeks ahead of the main body of settlers. His arrival was marked by celebration. Joyful school-children met the prodigy of hope at the edge of town and escorted him to the tavern, where welcoming speeches declared that mankind was at the threshold of a new era. Owen was in his element, arriving in a blaze of glory, a harbinger of great things to come, bringing with him $15,000 worth of goods to restock the town store. He was to remain at New Har-mony for the next eighteen months, his longest stay.[1]

New Harmony, capable of housing about 1,000 people, was laid out as a grid—four east–west streets intersecting six north–south streets at right angles, all spacious and lined with poplar trees. At the center was a square where there were two churches. Small houses, furnished by each newcomer, were made of logs, boards, or bricks, each with a fenced-in gar-den facing onto the streets. There were also some large brick buildings.[2]

Owen's surrogate, his twenty-three-year-old son William, had proven to be a competent leader with a talent for practical management, and to no one's surprise, his father's financial interests were always a prime consider-ation in making decisions. He and members of the Preliminary Commit-tee had guided the affairs of the community with rules and regulations in keeping with a written constitution approved by Owen, and now the great author, idolized by the majority of New Harmonites, had returned to set right all unforeseen difficulties. In a letter to his son in February, William Pelham, a scholarly Virginian and an editor of the *New-Harmony Gazette,* wrote: "He is an extraordinary man—a wonderful man—such a one indeed as the world has never seen. His wisdom, his comprehensive mind, his practical knowledge, but above all his openness, candor & sincerity, have no parallel in ancient or modern history." Pelham was confident that, despite all the "irregularity of effort" of the past half year, New Harmony would be going "like clockwork" within six months.[3] In these heady times, excitement was palpable as people of good will came together to form an ideal society, one that the world had never seen.

Despite misgivings, Maclure now seemed confident that the commune would succeed. After living for two months in New Harmony, he wrote Benjamin Silliman that all was well and that things were "better than expected." He and Thomas Say were engaged in geological and biological investigations of the region. Schools, drawing from a pool of hundreds of youngsters, were already established, where girls as well as boys were taught. Students paid for themselves through their half-day of labor. In this system, the idea of a servant class would not be tolerated. Boys made shoes for themselves and the community, while girls under Madame Fretageot's supervision worked in textile mills, washed, and cooked. Pestalozzian principles were being brought to life in these schools. Great plans were afloat to teach carpentry, weaving, and tailoring. Half-believing that the entire movement was marching forward, Maclure wrote approvingly of the sale of two nearby parcels of land to groups of settlers. The properties were to be jointly held and were never to be sold. Thereby, clones of New Harmony would be established, in keeping with the desired creation of a series of small, cooperating communities.[4] Early on, all seemed well and hopes were high, while flaws were minimized or overlooked.

But it was not long after his arrival that Maclure became critical of the Committee and warned Madame Fretageot to avoid "those who have contracted indolent, grumbling and corrupt habits under the wretched government of the Preliminary Society."[5] Maclure was uneasy about the large number of freeloaders and the shoddy character of so many of the new settlers, and he judged that the commune's finances were in a perilous state that would be difficult to rectify. Maclure's commitment was cautious and measured. His initial financial pledge to New Harmony was only $10,000, a fraction of

Owen's investment, and this money was specified for educational purposes alone. Maclure was aware that Owen had "wasted" money in his operation, and he did not want to be the co-sponsor of bonds that Owen might float, for the new capital might be squandered on useless projects. His strategy was to operate within Owen's larger scheme, confining himself to organizing and supporting schools—paying teachers, supplying them with books and educational materials—and he was also deeply involved with scientific matters.[6]

Feeling semi-insulated, Maclure took charge of education at New Harmony, transferring his educational efforts from a large city to a controlled commune, convinced that both his schools and the commune itself would benefit.[7] Maclure must have felt a great sense of accomplishment creating an important scientific center in the wilderness. According to Maclure, the advancement of science and "useful" knowledge was at the cutting edge of the social reform movement, a cause that he promoted by bringing talented scientists and naturalists to New Harmony, making it at the time the most important scientific center of the West. If nothing else, the presence of such remarkable people on the frontier was a harbinger of the ideal world to come. Maclure, a radical in many ways, must have been looked upon as a new kind of man of science—a man of means with business experience, one who could bring his powerful agencies of education, research, and natural history to bear on social and economic problems. He and his scientific colleagues would also bring to light a wondrous natural world that might serve as a model for nurturing relationships in human affairs. Led by two men of wealth and power, the entire enterprise was esteemed by many.

In the February 15, 1826, issue of the *New-Harmony Gazette*, Maclure described the introduction into America of the Pestalozzian system of education, promoted by both Owen and Maclure, elaborating on the philosophy upon which it was based and its resulting benefits, "a system of education, which has for its object the development of *all* the powers and faculties of man . . . with a view to the increase of our own happiness and that of our children."[8] Maclure took pride in the fact that students in the boys' school were making shoes for themselves and would be making them for the entire community, and soon they would have "work-shops for tailors, carpenters, weavers &c" that would be combined with instruction in arithmetic, mathematics, and nature study, learning best through a combination of mental and physical labors.[9] In this scheme, time was spent not on gymnastics but on learning trades and working in the fields and garden.

With the arrival of the *Boatload of Knowledge* and Maclure's controlling education, attendance increased from 100 students to 140, and later to 400, all taught by experienced Pestalozzian teachers. Maclure himself provided books, instruments, and specimens, and he attended to the feeding and clothing of students. In fact, his aim was for the students to earn their keep, but to do so they had to labor hard and long, their days reminiscent of those in Charles Dickens's academies of education.[10] Mrs. Trollope, author of *Domestic Manners of the Americans,* placed her son Henry (brother of the author Anthony) in the New Harmony school, but she soon withdrew him in a state of exhaustion, brought on by school days that started at 5 AM and ended at 8 PM.[11]

Owen and Maclure, rationalists and utilitarians, were profoundly influenced by the progressive pedagogy of Pestalozzi and Fellenberg, which emphasized the training of students to observe and analyze—an approach more appreciated by Maclure than by Owen. But there were underlying differences in their philosophy of education which led to deep conflict between the two men, neither willing to compromise. The ultimate deterioration of education at New Harmony was part of the general erosion of the utopian experiment, and lay in a failure of practical implementation of programs based on Pestalozzian theory.

Unlike Owen, Maclure was a practicing scientist who believed that "knowledge was a constantly changing product of a scientific process."[12] Owen "believed that knowledge was a fixed body of fact that could be applied scientifically to solve social problems" and that society could be improved through a centralized authority, which could alter the learning environment to impose change on people—a communitarian education.[13] Educating both adults and children was the key to bringing about societal reform and to establishing an egalitarian community where property was to be held in common. The environment would mold the child. To Owen, adult education was a means of indoctrination with his "system," where obedience to the dictates of the leader was fostered—an arrogant, elitist, authoritarian view.

Maclure dismissed this approach, placing his faith in a flexible, democratic society run by properly educated students who by their training would be prepared to take over the operation of government in the future. He insisted that little could be done to change adults by the process of education; instead, his strategy was to focus on instruction of the young to attain freedom of thought in a truly democratic society that was moral and egalitarian and yet driven by self-interest, a profoundly American point of view that championed the individual, an echo of Fourier's principle that the pursuit of self-interest by the individual and hard work lead to social harmony.[14]

Maclure and Owen had some views in common on education, such as the benefits of infant schools, but Maclure dismissed as "visionary" and untested Owen's school for older pupils and adults, where learning would depend almost entirely on brute memorization—"parrot" learning, "by faith rather than observation," and reasoning, where students were not encouraged to form their own opinions or to think for themselves. Owen had always been critical of the independence of thought of pupils in Maclure's schools, attested to by their wildness and lack of discipline (according to Owen). His aim was to have pupils and practical teachers enlighten each other, for "there need be no distinction of teacher and pupil; but all may be regarded as teachers and all as Pupils" in a Lancastrian platoon system as it had been in New Lanark in which older students taught the younger.[15] Owen's plan was to establish schools based on this approach, but individualistic Americans were less amenable to dogmatic instruction than were the children raised in a more rigid European environment. While Owen believed his more authoritarian education would achieve reformation of human society rather quickly, a more cautious Maclure was of the opinion that changing human behavior was a long, slow process, one that would take at least "fifty years."

Both men wanted pupils to be separated from their parents. They aspired to house orphans and other children in boarding schools, isolated from parental influence, so that, according to Maclure, they could be trained to use their reason—a long-range point of view. Maclure believed that only after suitably educated students became parents in a just society could parents be allowed to teach their children, and then the school as an institution would lose its purpose and would wither. Owen, on the other hand, wanted to separate children from their parents as early as possible because he wanted to weaken or destroy familial bonds. To him, the family thwarted the aim of having all members of society regard each other as equals in an ideal, egalitarian society.

Maclure's plan was not only to provide practical education but also, with his background as a geologist, to train the young to become scientists, naturalists, and intellectually curious adults. But Owen felt that this training did not provide a "social education" and would tend to separate people from the spirit and operations of the commune. In Owen's approach, with its emphasis on adult education, the primary aim of educating children was to train them in a narrowly practical way to become integral members of the community. The children of the masses were to be taught occupations and trades to the neglect of education in chemistry, geology, and mineralogy, taught by the scientists and trained Pestalozzian teachers (the literati) Maclure had brought from Philadelphia.

Despite the woes of Owen and the economic and organizational disruptions of New Harmony, the schools established and financed by Maclure and run by his associates functioned reasonably well at first. He was pleased that his educational effort was proceeding in a manner consistent with his philosophy, with a curriculum that was essentially anti-intellectual and devoid of religious content.[16] Teachers kept to the facts, "useless" rhetoric was excluded, and flights of the imagination were regarded with suspicion, for they obfuscated and misled. The capable Madame Fretageot, assisted by Mrs. Neef, taught the children ages two to five and trained the teachers. The "Infant School," based on the school at New Lanark, was the first of its kind in America. Joseph Neef (with his four daughters and one son) was in charge of about 200 students ages five to twelve. William Phiquepal taught teenage boys the "useful" arts and mathematics. They worked from 4:30 AM to 8 PM, learning their lessons and making shoes, hats, pottery, and brooms, thereby earning their keep, according to the practical instruction advocated by Pestalozzi and Fellenberg. In all there were about 400 students.[17]

Maclure's organization was truly remarkable. Not only did it educate the young, emphasizing the development of both the minds and bodies of young boys and girls, it was also partly an institution of biological and geological research (Say, Troost, Lesueur) and a center of vocational training for both sexes. This was probably the first full-time trade school in America. The education provided was superior to anything to be found in the region, and remarkably students were contributing to the support and success of New Harmony by their labors.[18] Boarding of students was stressed, for Maclure desired that children be removed from the corrupting influence of their parents and society in general. Some of the students came from outside the commune, for which tuition of $100 per year was charged.

The school was not without its critics, who claimed that a lack of discipline produced wild, badly behaved children and that the strategy of separating parents from boarded children, whom they saw only once a year, was extreme. Students led a spartan existence, their dress was simple, and their diet usually consisted of a cornmeal mush, molasses, milk, meat, and vegetables. Still, most students remembered their school days with affection.[19] A visitor to New Harmony observed boys working in the garden and fixing fences, while the girls were learning "female employments." He noted, "All the boys and girls have a very healthy look, are cheerful and lively, and by no means bashful. . . . These happy and interesting children were making their youth pass as pleasantly as possible."[20]

The attractiveness of the children's diet was not Maclure's highest priority. Maclure was a gastronomic ascetic who blamed all kinds of ailments on overindulgence of the wrong kinds of food—"we swallow the seeds of $\frac{9}{10}$ of our diseases." He denounced the use of hot red peppers, which had "deranged" his stomach for two weeks, as well as the ingestion of oysters and truffles, and the habit of smoking tobacco. His tendency was to make himself fit by walking, drinking plenty of water, and almost starving himself, advocating the consumption of two very simple meals a day (no dinner), a total of six ounces of meat and six ounces of cornmeal. He seemed to feel that the cheaper the food, the healthier it was, and that rich, expensive foods should be avoided.[21] He himself could get along in perfect health spending fifty cents per day on food, and he pointed out that Arabs enjoyed excellent health and long life because their diet was simple, consisting of "milk, dates, or game," aided by living in a very hot climate.

Quite possibly, Maclure's semi-starvation regimen contributed to his sickly state in later years. Suspicious of the healing ability of physicians, he relied heavily on diet to alleviate disease: "Nothing but starvation can cure, and untill the stomach gets smaller the greatest part of the food put in it ought to be without nourishment. Never fear starving, the idea is ridiculouse." "Health can only be preserved by the greatest moderation in all physical, natural appitites, and to avoid as much as possible the acquiring of artificial ones." He declared that an addiction to fashion was "the most despotic of all tyrannies; always directed by the rich and powerful against the interest of their inferiors."[22]

In June 1826, Maclure sought relief from the organizational turmoil of New Harmony by journeying through Ohio and Kentucky, a trip that lasted four months. He felt secure and encouraged, because he had come to a binding agreement with Owen, and he was pleased that a sound reorganization had taken place in accordance with his suggestions. On one of his customary geological and natural history forays, he sent articles for publication in the *New-Harmony Gazette,* as well as letters of advice and encouragement to Madame Fretageot, warning her of Owen's tricks and alerting her to expect purchases he had made—a piano, sheets of glass, laboratory glassware and equipment, books, cloth for uniforms, and shoes. In return, he received a list of needs (glue, linens, tin) and the latest information about New Harmony.

Maclure's letters reveal his increasing anxiety about Owen's irresponsible behavior and his tendency to incur debt. There was endless talk about Owen's extravagances, the "waste" and needless expenses he has incurred, and how much this might cost him (Maclure) if Madame Fretageot didn't pay attention to the accounts. In these matters she was aided by an "orderly," Joseph Applegath, a former teacher at New Lanark with accounting skills; advice was also to be sought from Thomas Say and Maclure's brother Alexander. Maclure frequently reminded her that his money was earmarked for educational purposes only, and not a penny was to fall into Owen's hands. There is something of the pedant in Maclure, as he counsels: "Take warning from the faults of Mr O, and his loose and incorrect mode of doing business. Keep short accounts and frequent settlements. Never put off till tomorrow what can be done today; and always recolect that foresight is the chief superiority we have over the other animals, and that a Biped without foresight is scarc above the par of a quadriped."[23] Constant communication from afar with a trusted agent was Maclure's imperfect method of maintaining control of his complex affairs. It was a *modus operandi* that avoided the unpleasant task of directly confronting an adversary, which he found difficult.

To some extent the educational enterprise was a haven, essentially apart from the strife that plagued the rest of the community. Maclure was tired of Owen's preaching, which now "meant nothing" to him. His alienation was clearly set down in a letter to Madame Fretageot, dated August 21, 1826: "I only have for the last 6 months tottaly changed my opinion of Mr. Owen's capability to succeed in any undertaking on the high visionary ideas . . . engendered in his brain; and that however willing I might be to spend my money on my own education visions, I'm positively determined to waste none of it on the visions of others.[24] In the end, Maclure could not remain apart from the problems of a failing commune, and before long he was in the midst of the agitation, which required his attendance at innumerable committee meetings and repeated reorganizations of finances and governance. During 1826 the unstable community tottered along, and some settlers, abandoning hope, left for more promising vistas.

Maclure was frequently away from New Harmony, either on geological forays or, as the cold of winter arrived, on prolonged visits to Mexico and the South. Unfortunately, his schools faltered in his absence because of dissension among the teachers, whose wrangling could not be managed from a distance. In the midst of tempests, Madame Fretageot pleaded with Maclure to return to set things right. While Madame Fretageot was lively and charming, she was not entirely an innocent, for she was stubborn and determined and could antagonize her fellow teachers. Disputes arose between Madame and Neef, whom she called intolerable, rigid, and inflexible, and she threatened to leave if he remained.

Phiquepal became a constant source of trouble. His teaching was faulty, he was careless with the precious mineralogical specimens, and he vandalized Maclure's fine prints by cutting off their margins.[25] Indeed, he acted almost insanely as he attempted to isolate his school and "boys" from the rest of the community. Eventually, Maclure came to believe that Phiquepal was "a dangerous mad man . . . the vainest man I ever knew . . . a hare-brained animal," and he warned that he should be watched closely.[26] Maclure labeled Phiquepal's students "half savage" and averse to science, as was their master. He was appalled to find that Achille, Madame Fretageot's teenage son and a student of Phiquepal, did not know how to read or write and was not interested in acquiring these "trifling" skills.[27]

Expert instruction in natural history and science was provided by Thomas Say (biology), whose official position was superintendent of literature, science, and education, Charles-Alexandre Lesueur (art), and Gerhard Troost (chemistry and mineralogy). These men were also carrying on scientific research, publishing their findings, and lecturing adults on scientific subjects. However exalted their activities, they were not really appreciated by Madame Fretageot, who was taxed by practical problems every day, trying to keep Maclure's educational program on track. In a letter to Maclure, she burst out: "If Say was only occupied with the dissection of his Insects, I would consider him just as I do Troost and Lesueur. They are shut up in their cabinet, the former with speculative Mineralogy, the latter with the collection of Fish, Shells, Birds, Drawings, perfectly useless to the happiness of mankind. Yet calculate the expense they carry with them and tell me what benefit will arise from their work to the present and even the future generations. That is the case with all Scientific people. Their knowledge is not only useless (because there is no application of it) but hurtful."[28]

Clearly, this lack of appreciation of science and the hostility to her colleagues' vital interests could only lead to conflict. Maclure, whose efforts in geology were exempt from her criticism because they could be useful, kept silent, for he did appreciate the efforts of Say and Lesueur. Adding to the sting of the rebuke of the scientists was the fact that criticism of such weighty matters had come from a woman who knew very little about these disciplines. American science and natural history were in their infancy and their potential benefits barely comprehended, so Madame Fretageot's antiscientific opinion was probably held by many New Harmonites, certainly by Phiquepal and, according to Maclure, by Owen himself. Owen's view of what science was and what it could and could not do was naïve, in contrast to Maclure's. Although Maclure felt that Madame Fretageot was in error, he did not protest or make an issue of the matter, for her cooperation was indispensable. Thus within the larger, roiling community sat an Education Society in conflict, beset by animosities and sharp differences of opinion.

In an age of enlightenment where words, ideas, and rational discourse were important, there was a clear need for communication between members of the commune, and it was important that a record be kept of what leaders and dissenters in the community thought and said. Since several New Harmonites were highly literate, creating a journal presented no problem. The *New-Harmony Gazette,* a weekly publication of sound literary standards, was established in October 1825, which was designated the founding year—"the first year of mental independence"—an echo of the calendar of the French Revolution. On its masthead were the noble words "If we cannot reconcile all opinions, let us endeavor to unite all hearts." The first issue contained the constitution of New Harmony and the text of a stirring address by Owen that had fired up the entire assembly, and during the next few years the publication provided a record of Owen's and Maclure's thinking. Local news, letters to the editor, articles about communal affairs, and discussions of practical and philosophical consequence were of interest to members of the commune—unifying force. They also had a considerable readership throughout the United States, which was curious about the progress of this highly publicized social experiment. As well as being a publication of enlightenment and abolitionist sentiment, the *Gazette* contained thoughtful discussions about atheism and religious faith.

For both Owen and Maclure, the *Gazette* was a convenient forum in which opinions and concerns about governance of New Harmony could be aired. There were numerous weighty essays on education by Maclure and by Robert Dale Owen, the editor-in-chief, with his brother William and Robert L. Jennings, associate editors.[29] Later, the remarkable feminist Frances Wright served as editor, while William Phiquepal, her future husband, and his students in the New Harmony School of Industry printed the journal.[30] Essays on such disparate matters as the "Vindication of the Rights of Women,"[31] the making of bricks, growing of vines, production of wine, and geological descriptions graced its pages. The initial number contained the first of several articles on the history of New Harmony beginning with the Rapp colony. Other issues were filled with news, announcements, medical matters, cures, reports of the various committees, poetry, excerpts from Volney's and John Gray's works, reprints of articles from various journals such as the *Saturday Evening Post,* advertisements, and homilies—a kind of *Reader's Digest.*

The summer of 1826 was spent traveling about with Thomas Say and young Achille Fretageot, visiting the troubled Owenite community of Yellow Springs, as well as the communities of Xenia, Cincinnati, Columbus, and Springfield, Ohio, and Louisville, Kentucky. Considering himself knowledgeable in the operation of communes, he conferred with the organizers of such ventures that were taking shape in the East and around New Harmony. At the time he had high hopes that the New Harmony school would serve as a model for education in new communities.[32] Yellow Springs, a community inspired by Owen's philosophy, was falling apart just as New Harmony was, and it continued on its downward path despite visits by Owen.[33] The settlement was foundering on the valuation of the contribution of those who had invested their capital in the commune and those who contributed by their labor, a problem that Maclure's mediation and a tentative offer of a loan to Yellow Springs could not resolve.

During the trip Maclure arranged to have the children of some of his friends attend school in New Harmony, and their willingness to do so gave him reason to believe that his approach to education was taking hold in the United States. He also sought out young teachers who might be flexible enough to teach the Pestalozzian method. Troubled and surprised by the hostility toward New Harmony that he encountered in the outside world, his response to the criticism—"lies and slander that were being spread" about the commune (sexual freedom, atheism)—was aggressive. Maclure did not hesitate to come to the community's defense, despite his awareness of New Harmony's troubles and his ongoing struggle with Owen.[34]

Soon after his return from his last four-month tour, Maclure was off to a warmer climate in November 1826, for with the onset of fall and winter he was beginning to suffer from "rheumatism" and a chronic stomach ailment (perhaps an ulcer) that compelled him to relocate to New Orleans. Taking Achille with him, he did not return to New Harmony until May 1827. Descending the Mississippi River by steamboat, Maclure reached New Orleans by December, where he found that a surprising number of people disapproved of New Harmony. He purchased a printing press and copper plates and shipped them to New Harmony so that Lesueur and Say could begin publishing their pioneering works in natural history, and at the same time the press could be used to teach children the useful vocation of typesetting and printing. As was his habit, he made arrangements for cases of specimens to be sent to New Orleans, a community which he deemed to be deficient in science.

On the way south, he had stopped off at Nashoba, a plantation established by Frances "Fanny" Wright and her sister, Camilla, on 2,000 acres of land near Memphis, Tennessee.[35] A brilliant Scotswoman of means, an emphatic voice in support of women's rights and the emancipation of black people, she had come to America in 1819 and was captivated by the new society she encountered. Wright described the new American culture in utopian terms—unlike anything that existed in Europe.[36] In 1824 she returned to the United States to stay, determined to remove its single flaw—slavery. Harmonie, George Rapp's thriving commune, had struck her as a model arrangement for the elimination of slavery, for here she witnessed the creation of a prosperous community, suitably managed by uneducated German peasants. However, her visit to New Harmony, which was always troubled, must have given her more than a hint of the problems that beset such a community of free men and women. Despite the probability that she would encounter the same difficulties, she was determined to push on. In her settlement she would teach black men and women to become self-sufficient farmers and craftsmen who eventually would be capable of purchasing their freedom, thus assuaging slaveholders by the promise of compensation for their "property." The plan had been reviewed by Lafayette himself and had been shown to Alexander Hamilton, John Marshall, and Thomas Jefferson, who approved of it and wished her well.

Slaves were purchased, supervisors were hired, log cabins were built, and farming commenced, but it proved difficult because the soil was poor. After exhausting herself with the roughest kind of physical labor, in unhealthy, malaria-infested Nashoba, after several months, Wright sought rest during the summer in New Harmony. During the respite she formed a warm relationship with Maclure, attracted by his ideas, and thereafter she visited him from time to time—a retreat and an escape. Maclure, who was sympathetic to her aims, felt that she could spend her time to greater advantage at New Harmony, and he urged her to leave Nashoba and let it be run by others. To induce her to do so, he offered to support a school at Nashoba, the kind that would impart useful knowledge of a nonclassical nature and permit students to earn their keep, an education that would be of great use in the preparation of slaves for their freedom. Maclure's sound judgment and his radical social, political, and educational views appealed to her, and his words were echoed in her lectures and writings on the education of boys and girls as the solution to social problems. Dazzled by her spirit and intelligence, Maclure and Madame Fretageot felt that both Wright and New Harmony would be better off if she moved in with them, and perhaps she would serve as a counterforce to Owen's destabilizing activities.

Maclure was greatly impressed by what he saw on his visit to Nashoba. Inexplicably, despite all evidence to the contrary, he concluded that this obviously failing venture was far more orderly and better run than New Harmony, and he was "delighted with the oeconomy, cleanliness, tranquility and excellent arrangement introduced in so short a time amongst slaves"—an orderly group, disciplined and hardworking. He claimed that there was a greater difference between the two communes than there was between the skin colors of whites and blacks. This is where he should have invested his time and money rather than in hapless New Harmony where his efforts were unappreciated.[37] However, Robert Dale Owen and others described Nashoba realistically in far less flattering terms, so that it came as no surprise that within a year the project foundered. Slaves, supervised by a kindly Shaker farmer, refused to work, and the decay of buildings was becoming evident. It is difficult to understand how such an intelligent, worldly man could not see the obvious and could come to such erroneous conclusions. Judgment based on the evidence of the senses seemed to be corrupted by ideology.

Frances Wright's Nashoba colony, whose strategy Maclure considered "a Master piece of Logical reasoning,"[38] prompted him to consider the notion of establishing another colony that would house Wright's black "students" and other "free colored" people, whom he considered "vastly superior to the whites who have got no more education than they." The colony was to be located on 7,400 acres of land he had purchased from Frederick Rapp in the vicinity of New Harmony, but little came of this ambitious plan, probably because such a complicated enterprise could not be established and maintained by an absentee proprietor. Like Owen, Maclure in his enthusiasm seemed to share a remarkable inability to assess the obvious, for he had seen nothing but promise and success. To Maclure, Wright's solution to the problem of slavery was far more acceptable than a much publicized proposal to end slavery in the United States by sending black people to Africa, a notion that he deemed abhorrent ("expensive" and "absurd"), believing instead that they could make a real contribution by remaining, to become free and useful members of the United States.[39]

Terrible scandals concerning Nashoba then erupted. One of the supervisors, James Richardson, lived openly with a black woman and advocated such relationships between consenting adults, something unpalatable to almost all Americans. Camilla, always in the shadow of her sister, was emboldened to publicly belittle the bond of marriage, but soon thereafter she married the other supervisor, Richeson Whitby, who proved to be a disastrous manager.[40] Nashoba and New Harmony were cursed across the United States as iniquitous dens of free love. The outrage against Nashoba was also increased by Wright's explicit advocacy of the amalgamation of the races, her tirade in print against organized religion, and her open advocacy of sexual freedom. But despite its poor performance and its "bad" reputation kept alive by the press, Maclure remained impressed with Nashoba and dismissed the denunciations as born of "prejudice."

Nashoba's end came in January 1830, when Wright accompanied approximately thirty slaves to the black Republic of Haiti, where through the influence of her friend Lafayette they were permitted to live as free people on a gift of land.[41] Another communitarian experiment had come to a sad end, living on only as an object of gossipy scandal, godlessness, and sexual transgression. With the end of Nashoba (foreseen by Lafayette) and the grave troubles confronting New Harmony, Maclure had little to be cheerful about. In despair he brooded on the failure of communes to change the behavior of society because of the greed and intransigence of humankind, a view in keeping with his declining enthusiasm for supporting noble causes. At best, reform was a painfully slow process.

Maclure despised slavery ("the horror of nature") and the greed, cruelty, and stupidities of humankind that sustained it, and he fulminated against "prejudices against color, arising from the false supposition of superiority being in the skin." Slavery was not only immoral, "a disgrace to the civilization and knowledge of the day,"[42] it was also economically inefficient. Although three-quarters of Americans were aware of the "vast injury and destructive consequences" of slavery, they allowed their representatives to support it by subsidizing the sugar trade, which depended heavily on slave labor. According to Maclure, slavery was so inefficient that "the knowledge and exertions of one free man is worth the labor of ten slaves," obliging the U.S. government to pay sugar growers a subsidy of four dollars per 100 pounds of sugar produced by slaves, to make the enterprise profitable, the money coming from taxation. To Maclure, slavery meant that laborers were not getting their fair share of what they produced—an extreme example of the "ignorance, misery, and wretchedness of the many, and the despotism, injustice, and tyranny of the few." The "diffusion of knowledge" as the remedy for inequality and injustice in a free society still applied to a slave population, but would be far more difficult to achieve.[43]

Despite Maclure's vehemence on the subjects of inequality and slavery, when it came to publishing the radical tracts of Owen and Wright, as well as his own, he was concerned about their reception by the public and the resulting damage they would have on the welfare of New Harmony in general and his educational and publication efforts in particular. Frances Wright infuriated most Americans with her belief in the fusion of the races and her claim that George Washington was not a Christian.[44] The survival of Maclure's publication was of paramount importance to him. He did not want to alienate the public whose sympathy he desired, and so in 1827, after Frances Wright submitted an extremely provocative article to the *Disseminator of Useful Knowledge* on the "ticklish" subject of marriage, he wrote to Madame Fretageot: "You must exercise your prudence on the article of marriage, which she discusses in her usual stile, and may perhaps injure with some the circulation of your sheet." He felt that the public was not yet ready for this kind of openness. Notwithstanding his caution, and not without guile, he lectured Madame Fretageot in the same letter that "the present mairage is a priest's trap to catch all gentle and simple, and subject mankind to their control at birth, Death, and mairage in the midday of life."[45] His criticism was bitter, but it was private, not broadcast, and so he did not create a furor like those that followed Owen and Wright.

The career of the brilliant Frances Wright, an agitator of national and international fame, was inspired at least in part by Maclure's schools in New Harmony, with advice and guidance provided by Maclure and Robert Owen. She thought Owen's provocative Fourth of July speech marked him as the prophet of the coming age.

Maclure provided Frances Wright with a haven in New Harmony, where she wrote and maintained her lecturing career. A spellbinding speaker, she captivated audiences, including those whose beliefs were wildly different from her own. Wright published many articles in the *New-Harmony Gazette,* and after taking over its financial burden, which the Owens could no longer support, she combined her *Nashoba Gazette* with the *New-Harmony Gazette* to form the *Free Inquirer.* But she was too concerned with great issues to isolate herself in New Harmony, and she was certainly too ambitious to bury herself in a failing Nashoba. And so she and Robert Dale Owen, two voices of the Enlightenment, moved to New York in January 1829, taking with them her *Free Enquirer,* the major liberal voice for working people.[46] Madame Fretageot, a close friend and admirer of Frances, was not unhappy about the departure of a radical sheet from New Harmony, for "if I am not mistaken it will prove beneficial to our establishment in removing the [unfavorable] public opinion from our place."[47]

Along with Wright and Robert Dale Owen went Phiquepal with his students, who printed the *Free Enquirer,* Robert Dale's two younger brothers, Richard and David Dale, and Camilla Wright and her small son. They all lived comfortably in a large house near New York City, rented by Frances. William was left behind in New Harmony, where he tended to what remained of the Owen estate, burdened with debts. To raise cash, he transported about $20,000 worth of goods remaining in Owen's store to New Orleans, where he intended to sell them, but Owen's debtors (including Maclure) seized them and threatened William with jail. The crisis was averted by Robert Dale Owen, who borrowed money from Frances and Camilla Wright to satisfy the creditors.

FOURTEEN

⁂

Trouble in Paradise

When Owen returned to New Harmony in January 1826, in advance of the *Boatload of Knowledge,* he looked about and was pleased with what he saw, impressed by the vitality of the settlement. Believing that many of the pur- ported troubles of New Harmony sprang from the fact that its members came from disparate backgrounds, he believed it was only a matter of time before people became used to each other in the new environment. Clashing opinions would subside, and harmony would prevail because adults were capable of changing for the better. The education of children would also play a part in the process. Wondrously, he did not seem to notice that the opera- tion of New Harmony was seriously flawed and was losing a considerable amount of money—his money. Responsible members of the commune were living a grim existence, working long hours with little gain, and some of the best people were leaving. The enterprise was failing, and yet, while Owen was optimistic that he would be able to recoup the money he had invested, many inhabitants doubted that New Harmony could even survive.[1]

Owen was regarded as a messiah of sorts, a philanthropic guiding spirit willing to risk his own fortune on the success of New Harmony.[2] Now that their hero had returned, members were confidant that he would set things right. When his plans were fully revealed and developed, factories would be humming, well-managed farms would become profitable, and craftsmen would provide all sorts of wares for the community's benefit.

In a letter dated March 21, 1826, Thomas Pears wrote to his uncle in Pittsburgh about Owen's return: "Mr. Owen came. He praised us; told us we had not suffered as he anticipated; that we had reached the 'half-way house'; and then all was pleasant. . . . We had experienced all the evil of the individual and Social System [Owen's] without the benefit of either."[3] On the other hand, Pears's wife, Sally, revealed in a letter to her relatives: "Mr. Pears tells you that our government is an aristocracy. He ought to have called it a despotism. Our feelings are perpetually irritated by some or other of their acts and Resolutions; and if we should unfortunately be so bold as to express our sentiments upon them, we are told that we are liable to expulsion. It makes my blood boil within me to think that the citizens of a free and independent nation should be collected here to be made slaves of. . . . Ah my dear Uncle, how I do regret that we ever left Pittsburgh."[4]

As the situation worsened, Owen seemed to become ever more buoyant and aggressive. So enthusiastic was he about the advances made since his last departure (June 1825), he decided to honor his promise that if there was sufficient progress, he would advance the old schedule pertaining to the governance of New Harmony. Instead of waiting three years before abolishing the existing, appointed Preliminary Committee and creating a new, elected body to govern a new community of "perfect equality," the reorganization was to take place almost immediately—two years ahead of schedule.[5] This early period was considered by Owen to be merely a preliminary learning phase, a test to determine when the experiment was ready to proceed to the next level. Food, clothing, and education were to be provided equally to all members of New Harmony, and the plan was to accelerate the elimination of private property and its attendant evils. All land and buildings were to be held in a perpetual trust by and for the entire community with members of the commune purchasing leases so that all would share common property and assume responsibility for it (while he would recoup his original investment). Suddenly sprung upon this ailing community, the proposed reforms were unsettling and disruptive. In fact, the proposals constituted a clear, sudden change in Owen's thinking, for it expressed an egalitarian view that was new to him, as was the idea of communal property.

Undoubtedly, a major reason for Owen's advancement of the schedule was to rid himself of a growing financial burden by being bought out by members of the commune who were using the land he owned. He seems to have envisioned under the first constitution the generation of enough capital to enable individual members to purchase from him shares of a New Harmony joint stock company, and by so doing, Owen would recoup his original investment with a surplus to be used to found new communes. At present, Owen was the proprietor, "leasing" shares of the land and buildings of the commune at no expense to members. New Harmony was barely surviving, and instead of generating income, it was suffering losses that were covered by Owen. To make matters worse for Owen, at the time of his return in January 1826, the economy of Britain, the source of Owen's wealth, was depressed, while his debt in sustaining New Harmony was growing.

With the creation of a new community of "perfect equality," and the adoption of a new constitution, members of the commune would be obliged to purchase leases, but not own land privately (as Owen did), and if all went well, and with increased efficiency, the commune would be free of Owen's dominance—an important step in attaining true communal ownership.[6] According to the plan, Owen would make a handsome profit on his original investment as his control of the commune diminished.

Within a few weeks, reorganization had taken place, the old Preliminary Committee ceased to exist, and a new committee of seven members had been elected to draft a new constitution. William Maclure just missed being elected, which suggests that despite his wealth and generosity, he was not regarded as a popular hero and leader, central to the success of the commune. He seems to have been an aloof, shadowy figure who did not participate in disputes. Nor was he an official member of any group or committee, and he never asserted himself or exercised any political authority that could easily have been his; this did not seem to be his style. Wanting to avoid involvement in any debilitating conflict, he kept a low profile, choosing to leave the organizational aspects to Owen. By his own desire, his role was limited— confined to education and science.

The new committee, which met weekly with an assembly of all members of the community, had the power to make laws and decide who could join the community and who should be ejected, at a time when housing was grossly inadequate and the commune was overflowing with people, many of whom were lazy and disruptive. By February 1826, after a series of meetings, a constitutional convention had produced a document of "practical utility" that reflected the highest of Enlightenment aspirations. The new constitution, published in the *New-Harmony Gazette* for all to study, was adopted, over the protests of many dissenting voices.

The new constitution was a noble document that codified ideal behavior of humans in an ideal world, but in fact it was born at a time of mounting debt when a desperate Owen was trying to save himself by insisting that each member be held financially accountable, thereby condemning them to a frugal life of deprivation. Its purpose was to promote the happiness of the individual in a perfectly egalitarian society where sincerity, courtesy, kindness, and order would prevail, and education of both children and adults would be the highest priority. There would be free speech and perfect equality of rights and duties that applied to both women and men, although women could not vote in the assembly. Thus was born at this great historic moment the New Harmony Community of Equality, in which every member of the community would be considered a member of a family. Food, clothing, housing, and education would be the same for all, and no one would be held in higher regard because of his or her occupation.[7]

The principle of communal property was written into law; money or property brought in by members was to be returned if they left the community.[8] In reality, economic matters were left in a confused and undefined state—the source of future discord. What was to be done with the expected surplus once New Harmony really got under way? Was the land, all of which was owned by Owen, to be given, leased, or sold to community members? Were members to become employees? Statements by both Owen and Maclure implied that they were for communal property, but in fact they never threw their own money into a common pot beyond their personal control as was demanded by Paul Brown, a disputatious, troublemaking member of the commune.[9] Neither Owen nor Maclure was so unrealistic that they would allow their fortunes to rest in the hands of a community of disparate, captious individuals.

From the moment the constitution was adopted, discord in New Harmony was heightened. As Robert Dale Owen wrote: "Liberty, equality, and fraternity, in downright earnest! It found favor with that heterogeneous collections of radicals, enthusiastic devotees to principle, honest latitudinarians, and lazy theorists, with a sprinkling of unprincipled sharpers thrown in."[10] A socialist commune provided fertile ground for cheats and swindlers. Some members of the commune were reasonably happy to escape the intense competition and the harshness of the world outside, sheltered by the munificence of Owen, who was trapped financing a money-losing enterprise. Some were willing to give Owen sole authority and full responsibility.[11] But others felt cheated and were further embittered because they were not allotted sufficient credit for their efforts. Few were satisfied.[12]

The unrealistic expectations of Owen's return failed to be realized, and his attempt to reorganize an unstable governing structure only aggravated a bad situation.[13] Disillusionment accelerated due to economic problems, clashing ideologies, and troublesome personalities. Maclure felt that the commune was too large, with too many people of different backgrounds, interests, and beliefs. Although no one was starving, many members were working very hard with little return, while the task of expelling the lazy, alcoholic, and incompetent was difficult and becoming intolerable. In the final analysis, the New Harmony experiment failed because it never became a properly functioning, profitable working community.

While equality was preached, in practice there was segregation of New Harmonites on the basis of class and religion. A visitor wrote in his diary that at a Saturday evening lecture by Owen, "somewhat ragged members" were sitting together, separate from "the better educated members" who also gathered together and did not mix with the others, while members of the "affluent class" were "the only ones wearing their uniforms and formed their own group."[14] In a letter to her relatives back home, Sally Pears, a middle-class woman, confessed: "Oh, if you could see some of the rough uncouth creatures here, I think you would find it rather hard to look upon them exactly in the light of brothers and sisters. Mr. Owen says we have been speaking falsehoods all our lives, and that here only we shall be enabled to speak the truth. I am sure I cannot in sincerity look upon them as my equals."[15] The idea of taking her turn spending six weeks in a communal kitchen made her ill. She felt that her regimented life was intolerable, and she was shocked when her daughter was placed in a boarding school in which boys and girls were housed in the same building. A family with a two-year-old was then quartered in her home. The deliberate breaking up of the family was part of a plan to achieve a society of "perfect equality," for the bonds that held the family together were antithetical to the welfare of society as a whole. Yet, amidst all the drudgery, some relief was provided by lectures, concerts, and, ludicrously, weekly balls with cotillions, reels, and waltzes, held in the large brick building that had once been devoted to George Rapp's religious services. All this was in keeping with the spirit of Enlightenment for those who had wandered into the wilderness of Indiana.

For various reasons, groups with common grievances began to split away from the mother commune of New Harmony.[16] A group of about 150 devout Christians, "respectable" backwoodsmen and their families, refused to agree to the terms of a constitution written by deists, and they certainly did not want to be part of a community that harbored skeptics and, worst of all, atheists. Feeling that they would not be able to worship in peace, they separated from the main group, settling on 1,200 acres of land two miles from New Harmony, willingly provided by Owen for $5,000. By their removal, the deistic and atheistic elements of the parent commune became more prominent. Hoping to curry favor with the wealthy Maclure, an obvious alternative benefactor to the outspoken Owen, and apparently ignorant of his hostility toward religion, they named this community Macluria. Their ignorance suggests that Maclure was not a vocal participant in the commune's governance or in the local broadcasting of all of his views. Disputes were many within the new commune. It defaulted on its payment of principal and interest, and it ceased to exist within one year.

A second splinter group, seventy strong, consisting of English farmers who had moved en masse from Illinois to New Harmony, found the agricultural practices of New Harmony unproductive and chose to leave. Owen provided them with 1,400 acres, for which he charged $7,000. This community was called Feiba-Peveli, a name based on a bizarre system of nomenclature devised by Owen's architect, Stedman Whitwell, in which longitude and latitude were translated into letters of the alphabet so that a town could be located by its name. While this community far outlived its parent, New Harmony, largely because of its national identity (English), it soon lost its idealistic base, as the land gradually became privately owned, as did the land controlled by Macluria. Duke Bernhard of Saxe-Weimar-Eisenach pointed out that one of these groups had been founded on the basis of religious intolerance and the other on national intolerance—both evil. The spirit of dissension prevailed as the most useful and talented of New Harmony's citizens departed, leaving behind the incompetents, drifters, and malcontents.

The creations of the two new communities were surgical separations of disparate elements which damaged New Harmony but did not tear it apart. Apologists even claimed that these splinter groups relieved the congestion of the mother colony, but the defections had deprived New

Harmony of important food producers. Still, people kept coming; entire families presented themselves at the gate hoping for entry to escape the difficult world outside. Indeed, New Harmony was so besieged, notices were again placed in newspapers warning that newcomers would not be accepted because there was no housing for them.

But most important of all, the commune was threatened from within, when the "literati," the resident intellectuals of New Harmony, imbued with notions of what a commune should be, dedicated their efforts to the creation of a rather exclusive community of "perfect union" within the existing framework. Owen's two sons, Robert Dale and William, Robert L. Jennings, a former Universalist minister, and the Philadelphia group, who had arrived on the *Boatload of Knowledge,* were leaders of this aggressively idealistic clique, willing to endanger the very existence of New Harmony to realize their dream. Fired by high principles, this zealous band was intolerant of backsliders—"ordinary" people who brought with them their former habits and beliefs to which they adhered. Thus was born an elitist community with its stringent demands and high standards for entry, but lacking the necessary talent for labor and crafts. They and the other group, the excluded, consisting of people of "inferior" social and intellectual attainments, lived together within the confines of New Harmony in a state of war. In the backwoods, the elite promoted cotillions and insisted that a new form of dress be worn by all the men and women of this new society—pantaloons tied at the ankle, and a boy's jacket without collar for men, and bloomers for women—which, however ridiculous in appearance, soon became the emblem of social distinction, one that marked the superiority of those who wore the costume. Both Maclure and Owen approved of the unifying element of a uniform dress for all, inspired by the garb of the Quakers, whom they admired.

Owen strongly disapproved of the divisiveness that had arisen within the commune and quickly put an end to it by insisting that the elitist group accept wooded land elsewhere, which they would have to clear to establish their very own paradise, a task they were not willing or able to undertake. Despite the dissension, Owen's messianic fervor was unshaken, and he declared that the communitarian movement was catching on, as shown by the fact that communes like New Harmony were being established in New York, Kentucky, Pennsylvania, Ohio, Indiana, and Illinois.

For a man of affairs, a successful manufacturer and businessman, Owen seemed to be remarkably naïve and careless about the finances and operation of New Harmony. A good-hearted man of generous spirit, intoxicated with his ideas, he sank the better part of his considerable fortune into a venture without properly safeguarding his investment. He rarely spelled out costs or just what the financial contribution of New Harmonites should or could be; most of these people were happy to go along with him as long as he was paying the bills. According to one estimate, he had already spent $140,000 on the venture, over half his fortune, and by March 1826, with growing debts, and his realization of just how precarious his financial situation was, he asked members of New Harmony (including members of Macluria and Feiba-Peveli), to buy the commune from him for approximately $160,000, to be paid over twelve years with an annual interest of 5 percent. Most members refused to take on such a debt, for they knew that the productivity of the commune was low and that they would be permanently ruined by the commitment. Indeed, the critical problem of New Harmony had always been that consumption exceeded production so that repayment of the debt would be impossible. William Pears's response was probably typical: "Whatever may be the terms I have no intention of making myself responsible, for I can see no prospect of producing enough to maintain us."[17]

The poor prospect prompted the departure of some members, but most remained and hoped for the best. A young Frenchman who visited New Harmony with the intent of becoming a member was quickly disabused of the plan. In April 1826 he wrote that of the 750 members in the town, 600 were women and children, and the men worked at jobs they knew nothing about. All regretted having come and would have left if they were able. He quoted Madame Fretageot as saying the reason why things were going badly was that "there are more heads than arms."[18] With a mounting debt of $20,000 to $30,000 for the year owed to merchants in the vicinity of New Harmony, Owen was worried.

With disaster looming, once again the governance of New Harmony was reorganized to implement a new plan. Hastily, a "nucleus" of twenty-four men was formed, bestowed with considerable authority by Owen to decide on membership and, most difficult of all, to assign a monetary value to each member's labor, based on the total hours worked and his or her rate of productivity. From the start, the new arrangement was a source of grave dissension in a community dedicated to nominal equality, common property, and equal rights. Was an hour of work done by a laborer equal in value to an hour of work by a skilled craftsman or a teacher? Judgments could only be wildly subjective, leading to the dissatisfaction of those who felt their work was insufficiently valued. The experience at New Harmony provided convincing evidence that a society based on equal remuneration to all, whether hard worker or slacker, whether skilled or not, will fail, for soon the skilled and the conscientious will depart, leaving only the incompetent. On the other hand, in such a society the creation of privileged positions where some are favored economically also elicits protest and is equally disruptive. This was Owen's dilemma, one he did not seem to fully comprehend as he struggled to recoup his investment in New Harmony, which was rapidly falling in value.

Indeed, another round of defections by those who could afford to leave began almost immediately, the situation becoming so serious that within two weeks Owen was asked by the remaining stalwarts of the commune (by unanimous vote) to take on the sole direction of the community for one year. With a constitution still in place (but not rigidly adhered to), the business of the commune was now carried out more rigorously, with the keeping of accounts and records, and in this way New Harmony continued to operate, with frequent changes of rules, still teetering on the brink of ruin.

Another reason for defection is revealed in a letter from Maclure to Madame Fretageot. Some "respectable" families were leaving new Harmony because Owen was "amourouse. . . . The wives of the greatest part of those who have left you lately have declared to their husbands that it was in consequence of the freedom that Mr O took with them that they could not think of remaining under such dreadfull risk of their virtue." Knowing Owen's views on marriage, and his wife on the other side of the Atlantic Ocean, his alleged dalliances come as no surprise.[19] Yet Maclure did not believe the allegations, calling them "lies," and he defended Owen, whom in some perverse way he still admired.

Instead of the promised three- or four-hour workday envisioned in theory, those who remained labored from dawn to dusk, obeying the ringing of a bell to break off from work to eat food that was poor and unsatisfying ("below all review"). Many worked at tasks under protest for which they were poorly suited. A visitor was surprised to find that the naturalist Thomas Say, "appeared quite comical, dressed in the uniform of the Society . . . with his hands full of calluses and blisters."[20] Robert Dale Owen, reminiscing about his experiences in New Harmony, wrote of his useless right arm after sowing wheat for a day, and his utter unsuitability for tearing down derelict cabins, baking bread, or "wielding the axe or holding the plough-handles." No wonder he escaped by becoming a teacher and an editor.[21] Regimentation was the order of the day, and the amount of work done per week and the value of goods drawn from the stores became a measure of a person's worth—almost a moral judgment. To encourage the troops to do better and to identify slackers, public evaluation of members took place at Sunday evening meetings, with Owen presiding,[22] but Maclure disapproved of this practice, calling it "invidious."

The system by which there was to be "equality of remuneration" was not practicable, for it gave rise to mistrust between people who hardly knew each other. By what system could the work of the mind be compared to that of the physical laborer or the skilled worker? The notion was widespread, especially among mechanics and farmers, that work done by the brain was not as productive or consequential as that done by hands. Maclure suggested that a more workable approach would be to divide workers into communities according to occupation, each forming a federation that would enhance the common good. Members of each of these smaller, friendlier groups would have common interests and could make better evaluations. Payments of each community would depend on the area of land actually used.[23] Owen saw much merit in the plan, and accordingly New Harmony underwent yet another reorganization, the third in five months, in which three groups were identified—the Agricultural and Pastoral Society, the Mechanic and Manufacturing Society, and closest to Maclure's interest, a School or Education Society (to be financed by Maclure and run by Madame Fretageot), all overseen by a Board of Union, with trade between the groups mediated through "labor notes."

In this division, the New Harmony tavern and store, with its $30,000 worth of goods bought by Owen, was kept by him, a not unreasonable plan, approved by Maclure. However, the mechanics and agriculturists insisted that these lucrative sources of income belonged to them and the community at large. Owen capitulated to their demands, ceding the profits from the tavern to the agriculturists and half the profits of the store to the mechanics, but even this did not assuage them. The commune was rife with dissatisfaction on all sides. Maclure felt that Owen had succumbed to pressure too easily and should not have yielded anything to the "incorrigible" agriculturists and mechanics because they were motivated by greed.[24]

As much as he could, Maclure dissociated himself and the Education Society from the vagaries of Owen's New Harmony. By this time, Owen was so desperate for cash that he offered Maclure a lease for Rapp's former home, other structures on the property, and 900 acres of land, for "10,000 years." Maclure accepted the offer, despite his long-held misgivings about doing business with Owen, and agreed to pay Owen $35,500, with $11,000 more to be paid in the future, and he assumed responsibility for half of any debt incurred by Owen for up to $10,000. A legal document was drawn up, with terms clearly stated, in which Maclure also promised to support the educational and research efforts of the Society. He made Rapp's home his own, another building was used as a boarding school, and a large Rapp church was converted into a workshop. This was the first arrangement between Owen and Maclure that was formally set down in writing, but it did not quell a growing hostility between the two men. Their differing views on education were becoming even more apparent, as was Owen's anxiety about the further decline of his capital, a decline from which Maclure attempted to disengage himself with only partial success, despite a written agreement. The relationship between the two men was difficult, with Maclure striving for separation from a clinging Owen. Responding to a gaffe made by Madame Fretageot, who referred to the two men as "partners," Maclure wrote, "I have not the smallest connection with anything he has done. Every purchase or sale he has made has been either against my will or unknowing to me, for which I cannot for a moment consider myself responsible. When I objected he said he must have his own way."[25]

While Owen entertained big ideas and dealt with large sums of money, his personal wants were very modest. He was living simply, boarding in the New Harmony tavern. Maclure lived on a grander scale in the former Rapp home, an imposing brick structure that he shared with Madame Fretageot, undoubtedly giving rise to gossip. For a time it also housed Thomas Say and his wife, Lucy. Characteristically, Maclure arranged for students to live in the house, and he converted the larger rooms into classrooms, as he had done in his home in Paris.

Adding to his troubles, Owen could not escape the harassment of the zealot Paul Brown, who was uncompromising in his belief in total communal ownership. As far as Brown was concerned, the bitter dispute between Owen and Maclure which attended the downfall of Owen's Utopia was merely a "squabble about individual property between two rich men." He had recently arrived from the failing commune at Yellow Springs, where he had contributed to its upheaval. Brown considered Owen and Maclure frauds for not handing over all their property and fortunes outright to the community. On several occasions, at meetings, and in the pages of the *New-Harmony Gazette,* Owen was challenged to state clearly his views on private property—a put up or shut up approach; his response was unsatisfactory. Communications from Brown were so frequent and lengthy, the editor refused to accept more of them. For holding back, Owen was excoriated by Brown, a constant torment who accused Owen of not living up to the high principles expounded in his speeches and published writings. "When any man who, having presented himself in the character of a philanthropist, and professed it his sole aim to substantiate an actual precedent of the true order of society, asks pay for his land or houses, the foundation of such establishment, either principal or interest, to be secured as private property to himself or to his heirs, from that moment he forfeits the confidence of all considerate persons who are in pursuit of realizing a true commonwealth upon earth. This was the beginning of Robert Owen's iniquities."[26]

Following the announcement of one of Owen's reorganizations, Brown had shouted, "Doomsday!" Brown also criticized Maclure for attaching conditions to his gifts of books and specimens, which if not met would result in their removal. He objected to expenditures on frivolities such as musical instruments, and he railed against Maclure's industrial schools. Brown accused Madame Fretageot of exercising an inordinate influence on both Owen and Maclure for her own gain. His harsh judgments, ascetic tastes, and constant outrage suggest that if he had somehow assumed control, he would have been another Robespierre.

FIFTEEN

✳

Out of the Ashes

Scarcely half a year after the arrival of the *Boatload of Knowledge,* the very survival of New Harmony was in doubt. Just when it needed a helpful word, Owen delivered his provocative "Declaration of Mental Independence," an important Fourth of July oration on the fiftieth anniversary of the founding of the republic (1826).[1] The occasion was used to denounce "absurd and irrational SYSTEMS OF RELIGION," private property, and the institution of marriage—everything that Americans held dear—thereby embarrassing friends, infuriating foes, and creating a whole new set of enemies. Latitude in religious belief was tolerable, but outright condemnation was unacceptable. Henceforth, 1826 was to be called "the first year of mental independence," echoing the revised calendar devised by the zealots of the French Revolution. Owen fervently believed that his oration was the opening salvo that heralded the coming of a new era.

The widely reported speech created a furor, with further rejection of Owen and his commune. But in truth it had little effect on the people of New Harmony, for they had heard it all before. The declaration was a "truly preposterous composition," according to a national journal. "A community proclaimed to rest on Atheism and Libertinism, cannot fail to be viewed, with mingled horror and pity."[2] New Harmony's infamy as a hotbed of atheism, antireligious sentiment, and licentiousness was further enhanced by another member of New Harmony, Robert L. Jennings, a former Universalist minister from Philadelphia, who countered the religious sermons of itinerant preach-ers in and around New Harmony with devastating sermons of his own.[3]

While Maclure had no argument with Owen's "trinity of the most monstrous evils" ("superstition, Commerce, and mairage"), he felt that the speech was badly timed, a distraction that damaged their cause—so much so that he felt compelled to dissociate himself from Owen's public state-ments. He instructed Madame Fretageot how to answer parents' questions and assuage their alarm by assuring them of the high moral tone of New Harmony, that what Owen said was his own private opinion, and that Owen had nothing to do with how their children were cared for and taught by the Education Society.[4] Still, the public, fed by a hostile press, was alarmed by stories of sexual impropriety, including the alleged freedom Owen took with the wives of New Harmonites—sinful behavior in a godless community.

Owen, a deist, kept making bold, antireligious, antisectarian statements that alienated many who could have been helpful to his cause. Maclure con-fessed to ignorance of any world but the one he lived in, but whether he was an atheist or an agnostic is not really known—although he did use the word *Creator*. Since he was extremely skeptical of "higher powers," the term *Creator* meant little more than did his employment of Latin quotations. Maclure's quarrel was largely with the Catholic Church, which was closely allied to political leadership. That said, he was against the banning of religion by gov-ernmental decree.[5] To Maclure, the enforcement of Sunday blue laws was nothing less than persecution of Jews and those with other beliefs. In Spain, he learned firsthand about the raw power of a Crown and Church that had crushed his plans, threatened his life, and cost him a fortune. In America, he refused to sell land or rent houses to religious groups, and he was explicitly against founding churches in New Harmony. Thus the young commune ac-quired an unsavory reputation for ungodliness, one it could hardly afford.

Maclure admired the Quakers, who were pragmatic and like himself had simple tastes, kept to themselves, operated apart from governmental agencies, and were guided by their experience rather than by slavishly fol-lowing authority—consistent with a basic principle of science.[6] According to Maclure, "The Quakers laid the axe to the root of the evils of both laws and re-ligion by abolishing the trades of both lawyer and priest, taking management of their own affairs, both in this and the other world into their own hands."[7]

In late 1826, there was another round of defections, so that at least three-quarters of the remaining members fell into the incompetent category, according to Maclure. The architect Stedman Whitwell, who had "many usefull properties," proved to be a troublemaker and left to participate in the operation of a new "English" commune in Illinois. Thomas Pears, an earnest communitarian, had come to New Harmony with his family filled with hope, but was now leaving disillusioned, haunted by a dismal lack of fulfillment of Owen's visions and failed promises. There were no gardens or grand palaces, and there was no evidence of thriving manufacturing. The official response to Pears's detailed complaints was that more time was needed. An unhappy Mrs. Pears wrote her aunt: "Mr. Owen is growing very unpopular even with the greatest sticklers of the System. I assure you that Mr. Owen of New Harmony is a very different personage from Mr. Owen in Pittsburgh, Washington, etc."[8]

The Education Society operated three schools that provided instruction to the children of the farmers and mechanics in the other two societies, even as they disputed the lands abutting each other's territory. While farmers and mechanics made a profit providing goods and services, the Education Society did not charge them for the education of their children; only students from the outside paid tuition. However, after Owen's Fourth of July speech, many parents removed their children from the schools, drastically reducing their income and forcing the Society to charge New Harmonites for their services. Those farmers and mechanics who remained then objected, refused to pay, and withdrew their children.

In this crisis, Robert Owen's conduct was shocking. Rather than defend and support the existing schools and defuse the situation, he joined the chorus of criticism, questioned the competency of the system, and justified the withdrawals of pupils.[9] Because the schools had not fulfilled their promise, he was stepping in to provide his own system of education. Owen's new system of education was announced in talks that dazzled his audience. With his emphasis on educating and reforming adults, he proposed that a superior educational process must be extended to everyone in the community—adults and children over three years of age, male and female—a preparation for participating in a society where property and wealth were to be shared. Owen's proposal was adopted unanimously by New Harmonites, who were now obliged to assemble three evenings a week for a global educational experience, while children were to attend Owen's schools during the day. The plan, which deprived Maclure's Education Society schools of any function, was denounced by Maclure as misguided.[10]

By setting up a school in competition with Maclure, Owen brazenly put an end to any sort of rapprochement between the two men. It was a hostile act in perilous times in the life of a small community, justified in Owen's discourses by his differing approach to education. It can more accurately be described as supremely undiplomatic and a destructive lunacy. Further, Owen forbade members of the Education Society to harvest crops on the land Maclure had leased, claiming that the harvest belonged to the entire community, as though he, Owen, still had control of the land. This was the final break between the two men.

Maclure, who was traveling at the time, could hardly believe that Owen's attack was serious, and he resolved to proceed with his own plan. Maclure vowed that Owen would not get another penny from him—a statement he had made several times before. The Education Society, which included Robert Dale Owen, was torn apart, giving rise to wildly conflicting accounts by irate members of both camps.

Owen's increasing dissatisfaction with Maclure's schools was now known to all.[11] To overcome the deficiencies of Maclure's Pestalozzian schools, Owen brazenly set up a new school in a former shoe factory (which had been leased by Maclure),[12] and Madame Fretageot was persuaded to teach a class. In Maclure's absence, Madame Fretageot had been in charge, guarding Maclure's interests, and nasty conflicts had flared up with Phiquepal, the Neefs, and others. Her life was one of extreme anxiety at a time when the steadying hand of Maclure should have been present. At one point, Madame Fretageot was so bitterly in conflict with the members of the Education Committee, she refused to take a teaching assignment and was expelled from the Society. It was at this time that she actively entertained the notion of becoming a regular teacher in Owen's schools, something Maclure would not abide.[13] Maclure was irked by Madame Fretageot's attachment to Owen, who he claimed had "bewitched" her. However, the entire crisis was short-lived because the two new schools started by Owen—a school for boys and girls, and a boarding school for older boys—ended almost immediately, as did Madame's willingness to participate in Owen's program.[14]

In the midst of all the uproar, Phiquepal shifted his classes from Maclure's school, with its teaching workshops in a converted church, to space provided by Owen, taking with him books and instruments purchased by Maclure. Phiquepal, always a loose cannon, had shown little appreciation for Maclure's generous support over the years, and now he brazenly transferred his loyalty to Owen. Robert Dale Owen judged Phiquepal to be "a wrong-headed genius, whose extravagance and willfulness and inordinate self-conceit destroyed his usefulness . . . he gained neither the goodwill nor the respect of his pupils."[15] Gerhard Troost, the chemist, whom Maclure believed to be "useful" but with too many "religious prejudices founded on ignorance," departed to become a professor of chemistry at the University of Nashville. Joseph Neef could no longer abide Madame Fretageot, and he left New Harmony for Cincinnati, despite Maclure's pleas and offer of support. Maclure regarded him as "a good old man," a favorite of students and grownups, "simple, straight-forward, and cordial," and he never forgot how well Neef's Pestalozzian school had succeeded in Philadelphia—for a while. When Neef was denounced by Owen, Maclure defended him as a skilled Pestalozzian teacher. But in this stressful time, Neef accused Maclure of being under Madame's spell. In fact, Maclure had no choice but to side with his partner, Madame Fretageot, for not only was she a trusted manager, indispensable for the entire educational operation, but he sincerely believed that women were better teachers of children than men—and it was loyalty to her that prevailed.

In his attempt to maintain an effective organization while traveling about during the summer and early autumn of 1826, Maclure was either soothing or admonishing. At one time, from distant Mexico, he had harsh words for Madame: "What a humiliating situation your ambition and love of power has brought you to." But this was soon followed by a conciliatory confession: "I acknowledge that you have been heretofore exceedingly usefull in improving education," and he would regret losing her services, admitting that she was the best of all the teachers, worth more than all the other teachers combined. He warned her that when Owen has met with total failure, as he surely would, there would be no one to protect her. It did not take much for her to relent, and once again they were good friends.[16]

Maclure's next letter to Madame Fretageot was amiable and soothing, beginning with "Your last letter . . . gave me much pleasure," and in answer to a litany of her complaints, Maclure urged, "Patience, things will find their level. . . . Give yourself no uneasiness about the fate of the schools. As soon as you have all organized you will have pupils enough."[17] As she returned to Maclure's camp and calm was restored, Owen's luster seemed to fade. While the troubled schools of New Harmony had been a constant worry to Maclure, what he encountered upon his return from his travels

(October 1826) only confirmed his darkest fears. Relations between Madame, the Neefs, and Phiquepal were still at a boil. Maclure had no alternative but to side with Madame on all points, for she was most certainly his indispensable, steadfast support.

Owen's venture in education came to an end within two months, but incredibly, this rapid failure of his schools did not deter him from making the outrageous claim that the grave faults of Maclure's schools had been remedied—students were now punctual, industrious, and no longer given to wild conduct.[18] In fact, Maclure's educational organization was in disarray, and the New Harmony store was now almost bare, a situation that Maclure ascribed to waste and extravagance. Some people had special privileges at the store (relatives and friends of the trustees), and Owen himself seemed to bestow favors on the select, allowing them to receive from the stores what they wanted at favorable prices, while denying others the same privilege. Owen also was accused of exempting his favorites (from "aristocratic families") from arduous labors that should have been shared by all in this egalitarian society.[19]

To insulate education at New Harmony from Owen's influence and bring some sort of peace to New Harmony, Maclure petitioned the Indiana legislature to grant the Education Society a charter, an act that would ensure its legitimacy and independence and would further remove the schools from Owen's meddling. Alas, the petition was rejected by a vote of fifteen to four by that august body, which was hardly sympathetic to new forms of education in an antireligious commune. Maclure ascribed this defeat to "religious bigotry."[20]

In February 1827, with Maclure in New Orleans, Owen tried another scheme to raise money. Those who did not fit into the working of the main commune (the central town of New Harmony) would be given, leased, or sold land, with enough provisions to survive in regions where they could establish outlying communes. The offer was one they had to accept; otherwise, they would be given their "walking papers." The "doomsday" edict, which was to take effect immediately, led to what was mockingly called separating the sheep from the goats, and it resulted in the expulsion of twenty families. This latest crisis was yet another added to the many others that had bedeviled the fragile community since January 1826, when Owen had returned so triumphantly.

Maclure was critical of the proposal, and the zealous Paul Brown was once again aflame. To Brown, the selling of land outright to individuals was a "complete betrayal of the original social system" so earnestly espoused by Owen. In response to Owen's various financial schemes to recoup his fortune, Brown had hard words: "Thus has Mr. Owen gone on selling and buying, doing and undoing, taking and retaking, turning and overturning and re-overturning, bargaining, bantering, scheming, and maneuvering, and keeping the whole town in a perpetual agitation."[21] Owen always had great plans for establishing outlying communities— "Ten Social Colonies of Equality and Common Property"—but none was ever successful, and most never went beyond the planning stage.

Owen's troubles increased when, to raise cash, he sold 1,500 acres of land, several buildings in New Harmony, a cotton factory, a store, and a tavern to William J. Taylor, whose plan was to start a new community. The bill of sale stated that all that was on the land (cattle, machinery) would be included in the transfer. The night before the agreement was to take effect, Taylor secretly transferred equipment and drove a large number of cattle from the surrounding areas onto what was to become his land, leaving New Harmony itself bereft of livestock and farm implements. Further, according to the agreement, Taylor was to have a monopoly of trade in New Harmony, but Owen had permitted others to operate stores, and so he sued Owen for breach of contract. He lost, but the fiasco ended with a legal battle, costly for Owen. In the end, Taylor, a psychopath, was fated to spend many days in the Ohio penitentiary for dishonest dealings.[22]

Agonizing and complex financial warfare between Owen and Maclure in the first five months of 1827 marked the sad end of Owen's great social experiment.[23] No sooner had Maclure departed for New Orleans at the end of November 1826 than Owen demanded the return of some of the 900 acres of land he had leased to Maclure, calling their arrangement a "misconception" about the boundaries they had established that purportedly gave the Education Society too much land, despite the clarity of the legal agreement recently signed by both parties.[24] The *New-Harmony Gazette* refused to print a protest written by Joseph Neef, in which he declared that the boundaries had been fixed and were without dispute.[25] Further, with Maclure away, Owen tried to obtain money deceptively from Maclure's brother Alexander, as if Owen and Maclure were still full partners.

The *New-Harmony Gazette* proved to be an Owenite house organ; protests against Owen's highhanded, illegal actions were refused publication, and in fact, the entire breakdown period of New Harmony went virtually unrecorded. When Neef and others informed Maclure about what had happened, the battle lines were drawn, and he determined to settle matters and put a complete end to his relationship with Owen (as he had attempted several times before). He would not pay the $10,000 forfeiture he was obligated to pay Owen, and he insisted that Madame Fretageot and the others keep exact accounts of the services provided to the community, so that Owen would be charged for use of Education Society goods, labor, and property.[26] Disentangling from Owen was a confounding, never-ending process, but Maclure was relentless, as the dance approached its end.

Soon after Maclure returned from New Orleans in April 1827, bonds issued by Owen to purchase Harmonie from George Rapp, and held by him, were coming due (the last remaining indebtedness). Wisely, Maclure had been careful not to advance "one dollar" to New Harmony for fear that a desperate Owen might commandeer it for payment of the mortgage. Since Owen was unwilling or unable to make any payment, Maclure's strategy was to buy the bonds from Rapp for $40,000, and by so doing, Owen became legally indebted to Maclure, who then demanded the deed to the property. When Owen refused, because he insisted on additional money and on a stipulation that the land continue to be used to further his social objectives, Maclure took legal action to collect his money or the deed; he would have none of Owen's conditions. Maclure went so far as to attempt to have Owen arrested by the local sheriff, which Owen was barely able to avoid.

The situation was fraught with unbearable conflict. At the Posey County seat, the gentle Thomas Say registered Maclure's request for the arrest of Robert Owen at the same time that his colleague William Owen registered an intent to sue Maclure for $90,000 on behalf of his father. To the enjoyment of many, this painful, rancorous dispute was now out in the open. On April 30, Maclure posted a sign: "Notice is hereby given to all whom it may concern, forewarning them not to trust Robert Owen on my account, as I am determined not to pay any debts of his, or in any way be responsible for any transaction he may have done or may attempt to do in my name." The very same day, Owen posted a rejoinder: "Having just now seen a very extraordinary advertisement put upon some of the houses in this place and signed Wm. M'Clure, it becomes necessary in my own defense to inform the public that the partnership between Wm. M'Clure and myself is in full force, and that I shall pay any contract made either by Wm. M'Clure or myself on the partnership account." By the next day, both notices had disappeared.

It is difficult to believe that at this late date, Owen could assert that Maclure was still his partner, but this desperate act in the end served Owen well, for the matter was taken out of the courts and settled by an arbitration board that assumed that a kind of partnership had in fact existed between the two men. Accordingly, they ruled that Maclure should pay $40,000 to Rapp for the bonds, and $5,000 extra to Owen, and in turn receive outright the deed for 490 acres of land. Poor Owen was also bedeviled by a complex of lawsuits, one by Taylor for breach of contract, and some for nonpayment of goods and supplies, as neighboring merchants demanded to be paid. The events of the previous year had so strained the finances of the entire Owen family that they were forced to sell their holdings in the cotton mills at New Lanark.

The idealistic New Harmony venture cost Owen much of his fortune. He escaped with a capital of $50,000 that had once been $250,000.[27] The money he had retained later "melted away" in support of social reform in Great Britain, so that in the end, he was supported by his sons in the United States to whom he had transferred the deed of trust for his remaining holdings at New Harmony. The cost to Maclure was about $82,500, but he had acquired land and real estate that was worth about $40,000, leaving him with a sufficiently ample fortune to support the Education Society for the remainder of his life and beyond.

Robert Owen's involvement in the great social experiment was rapidly coming to a close, announced by an editorial in the March 28 edition of the *New-Harmony Gazette*. Because it was written by Robert Dale and William Owen (and only scanned by their father), there is some rigor in its account of the downward spiral of the commune, with repeated reorganizations of its governing body (seven constitutions had failed). Hope of establishing a society based on human equality and common property had been constantly thwarted by overpopulation, improper selection of members, discord, and above all "deficiency of production." They asserted that the social theory upon which New Harmony was founded was perfect, and failure to implement the theory was due to the imperfection of people.[28] Nothing was said about Robert Owen's own failings or about the shifting, uncertain status of private and common property in the commune, in clear contrast to Rapp's successful Harmonie, in which there was true, common ownership and Rapp's absolute authority.

A cynical view of New Harmony's inhabitants was expressed by an English visitor who had studied the commune and was sympathetic with its aims: "The community was composed of a heterogeneous mass, collected together by public advertisement, which may be divided into three classes. The first class was composed of a number of well-educated persons, who occupied their time in eating and drinking—dressing and promenading—attending balls, and *improving the habits* of society; and they may be termed the *aristocracy* of this Utopian republic. The second class was composed of practical co-operators, who were well inclined to work, but who had no share, or voice, in the management of affairs. The third and last class was a body of theoretical philosophers—Stoics, Platonics, Pythagoreans, Epicureans, Peripatetics, and Cynics, who amused themselves in *striking out plans*—exposing the errors of those in operation —caricaturing—and turning the whole procedure into ridicule."[29]

On May 6, 1827, Robert Owen addressed the citizens of New Harmony before his departure for Great Britain. The speech is remarkable for what it does not say and how it softened and clouded the reality of the situation. Somehow, Owen came to believe that he was leaving a commune full of promise, with eight thriving satellite colonies that included Taylor's community and outlying clusters of German settlers, but in fact Macluria lay abandoned, and only New Harmony and Feiba-Peveli were functioning, and these had distanced themselves from Owen. To him, the many satellite colonies were all according to plan and evidence that his Social System was spreading. Owen's concern was that the people of New Harmony "trained in the individual system . . . have not acquired those characteristics of forbearance and charity for confidence and harmony," and they do not "understand the principles" necessary for communal life.

His major disappointment was in the field of education, where "the chief difficulty at this time arose from the difference of opinion among the professors and teachers brought here by Mr. M'Clure, relative to the education of the children." Their method of teaching would not contribute to a feeling among students that they were "one large family" because they would be taught in small, separate groups. The recent battle between Owen and Maclure had arisen "from some extraordinary misconception in the minds of some of our well meaning friends" that led to great publicity, which, however negative, was a good thing because it would reduce the number of new arrivals at New Harmony, thus relieving the pressing problem of a housing shortage. In Owen's opinion, a major cause of failure could be laid at Ma-clure's doorstep. Although events had not taken place as he had expected, the experiment was on the whole successful, and he was leaving with all debts paid, heartened by evidence that now "nothing can prevent the rapid spread of the [New Harmony] social system over the United States."[30]

Owen's extraordinary testimony could not be allowed to pass un-challenged. It was countered by some angry members in the audience, especially by an incensed Joseph Neef. Owen had stated that Maclure and associated professors and teachers were responsible for the "miscarriage" of his plans in education. Neef protested that "the sole and only source of this abortion" was "Your conduct, Sir." Neef continued that, while Owen's speeches and writings about equality and common property were lofty and noble and perceived by all to be right, practice was another matter. When he arrived at New Harmony, the first thing that struck Neef with "astonishment and dismay was to hear of nothing but valuation of houses, barns, stables, land; of making bargains and contracts, of 'buying cheap and selling dear,' of capital and its interest.... The first thing that you at-tempted after my arrival was to saddle us with a debt of $160,000 and an annual interest of $8,000." Short of finding gold on the land, this was a debt that no combination of settlers could ever repay. The ideals espoused by Owen had little meaning unless he was willing to drastically reduce the price of land to a level that people could pay; otherwise, they would be permanently indentured, with as little interest in the enterprise as black slaves have in plantations. Owen was trying to create a "feudal barony." Neef's rebuttal went on, and point by point, along with Paul Brown's ti-rade, reduced Owen's position to ashes.[31] While those in New Harmony agonized, there were many on the outside who rejoiced.

Owen, while often of modest demeanor, could act imperiously—the "feudal barony" label was not entirely inaccurate. He was brilliant and high-minded, believing in a society of justice, equality, and common prop-erty. But his attempts to devise an ideal economic arrangement that would still allow him to retrieve the fortune he had invested prompted behavior that compromised his principles, made him vulnerable to attack, and left his utopia foundering. He could not have his fortune and his ideal com-mune, too. In the aftermath, some called Owen a fool, while others could not forgive him for enticing people to come to a New Harmony that he must have sensed was rapidly failing.[32]

Still, Owen was a man of great vision and an inspired social reformer. His honorable intention was to usher in "a millennium of peace and plenty, brotherhood and happiness."[33] He had sustained New Harmony and its people for two years, a beneficent effort that cost him dearly. Owen was addicted to swaying large audiences, but in fact he was carried away by his own rhetoric and his craving to be an oracle. This autointoxication led to such high hopes for the future of society that disappointment and disillusionment inevitably followed. What must have confounded his contemporaries was how such a successful, wealthy manufacturer could be so unrealistically optimistic. (The same could be said for Maclure.) One wonders how Owen could make so many bad judgments and why he could not be more selective in choosing those who peopled New Harmony. But perhaps it was his faith in the capacity of humans to redeem themselves in an appropriate environment that served him so badly.

It took Maclure, a shrewd, hardheaded merchant, always wary of Owen, to bring him halfway down to earth without too much room for maneuvering, very much like Owen's partners had done in New Lanark, where he was left with no alternative but to depart. With all his brilliant achievements and good intentions, his dealings with Maclure and New Harmony had revealed a desperate, muddled niche in a person capable of self-deception on a grand scale. He left New Harmony indebted to local suppliers and merchants and a mortgage that had to be paid off—a legacy for his sons. Before departing for England in a state of disarray, as a final, grand gesture he arranged for a teacher from Ohio, a Mr. Dorsey, to supervise his imaginary schools in New Harmony that would compete with those of the Education Society. Mr. Dorsey was authorized to use $3,000 of the nonexistent earnings of the foundering satellite settlements of New Harmony.

The fact remains, however, that the venture ended with Maclure as a victor of sorts, owning most of New Harmony's real estate and with much of his fortune intact, while Owen lost most of his wealth and was left with only a fraction of New Harmony property. Perhaps Owen's greatest gifts to New Harmony and the United States were his sons and daughter, who chose to stay in America, where they prospered in science, education, and politics.

Before sailing from New York to Liverpool (July 1, 1827), Owen spent a week in Philadelphia, where he spoke at a crowded public meeting in the Franklin Institute. He was surprised by the keen interest Americans expressed in the recent troubles at New Harmony. While dismissing the troubled state of New Harmony as merely transitional in nature, on its way to a great future, he made specific arguments when it came to dealing with Maclure, a subject in which all were interested. Owen presented a sanitized view of his understanding with Maclure, and their financial transactions. Maclure, who aimed to control the entire town of New Harmony, had been a disappointment to him because his educational plans had promised so much, but he "could not organize his operations," which justified Owen's own intrusion into education: "I had, I suppose, somewhat irritated Mr. Maclure; for I had commenced a system of education different from his own." As for their bitter legal battles: "You all know Mr. Maclure—He is an old man, a rich man, and a man who has done a great deal of good; but he is sometimes unfortunate, and the state of his mind becomes irritable, and his feelings are worked up by those around him, into a state very much beyond rationality: And I have no hesitation in stating that his advertisement was written under some such excitement."[34]

The address marked the end of Owen's involvement with New Harmony. Thereafter, he never took any real interest in his Indiana dream, although he visited New Harmony briefly in the spring of 1828, in 1829, and in the 1840s, mainly to visit his children and grandchildren. Undaunted, he returned to England to become an advocate for the working class, a major player in the founding of the British labor movement, and a leader in the reform movement of the 1830s. Perhaps Emerson said it best when he described Owen and his fellow theoreticians as reducing everything to problems of logic and overlooking real life.

Just after the New Harmony experiment fell apart, it was visited by an English barrister, Simon Ferrall, who did extensive interviews and wrote letters to his friends about what he saw and about the judgments rendered by the people remaining in New Harmony. These included "literary and scientific characters" and others who "still linger here, and may be seen stalking through the streets of Harmony, like Marius among the ruins of Carthage." The writing has the ring of competent investigative reportage. Ferrall's comments about the ordeal of getting to New Harmony on dreadful roads were a reminder of the burdensome isolation of New Harmony— clearly a detriment to active development.

According to Ferrall, there were many conflicting opinions about why New Harmony had failed, and in the end he sided with those who were critical of Owen. Owen had "too great confidence in the power of the system which he advocates to *reform* character," and he felt that Owen was "totally incompetent" to carry out his grand plans. He condemned Owen for enticing people to throw up their lives and come to a failing New Harmony, and he disagreed with Owen's statements that Americans were not capable of governing themselves and that there was nothing wrong with the system he advocated, only with the commune's flawed citizens. Ferrall could hardly believe Owen's statement that New Harmony had "exceeded his most sanguine expectations" when he and all others could still see the smoking ruins. In answer to the view held by Owen's friends that the commune began to fall apart when Owen relinquished his command, Ferrall claims that he never did abdicate and that he was constantly meddling and interfering. Owen could not abide independent views, and he would refuse to answer difficult questions: those who disagreed with him were dismissed as ignorant of his system. This highhanded, *ipse dixit* approach did not go over well with New Harmonists. In New Lanark he had had great success among Scottish working people (really, peasantry) who were responsive to authority, while he completely misjudged the independent, individualistic nature of Americans.[35]

Owen was certainly not a totalitarian demon, but he did manifest strong authoritarian impulses, emphasizing "loyalty" in his education. He was willing to sacrifice the well-being of people for a principle, in order to attain an egalitarian society that was not particularly democratic. But nothing remotely resembling a totalitarian state could ever come about in New Harmony because Americans were too diverse in origin and too individualistic in spirit. They were desperate people, but not sufficiently so to remain immobilized in such a vast, rich country of promise.

An intellectual construct such as an ideal society based on Enlightenment principles of rationality and equality had little lasting power because personal preferences and self-interest always asserted themselves effectively, and thoughtful people could always find alternative ways of doing things. If not satisfied, they were always free to leave. Maclure understood this: "The most ignorant of them both thinks and acts in more cases for themselves and may be deluded by quakery for a little, but when they bring things to a scale of common sence and utility they can and will judge."[36] Still, there is a more cynical view that people can be more effectively disciplined by an intense, coercive faith such as the one practiced by Rapp and his followers— ecclesiastic autocracies tend to have a greater capacity for survival.

Owen had created havoc in Maclure's life, and yet Maclure himself confessed that he had been so charmed by Owen that he acted against his own better judgment, and in the end he paid for the error, without losing an element of admiration and fascination for the man. Although the two men had similar views on the nature of the ideal society, in many ways they were different. Owen was expansive and explosive in his drive and ambitions. He made up his own rules as he went along, while Maclure was private and circumspect.

With the departure of Owen, and New Harmony in a state of disarray, all pretense at building a new, secular, communitarian society came to an end, a fate that had befallen all other such settlements in the United States patterned after it.[37] New Harmony was to begin a new chapter in its history that was not without interest and importance, for it played an important role in the establishment of free, coeducational public schools in America, in government-sponsored geological surveys, and in the study of natural history.

Maclure was now the dominant player, free to reorder most of the community according to his lights, while the Owen boys tended to their part of the town. He had retained enough of his fortune, sufficient to carry out his plans, and he owned most of the property, while the Owens still had a modest financial interest in New Harmony (as did a number of other individuals), but they were all relatively impoverished.[38] Although Maclure survived, he never failed to rue his involvement with Owen, forced to spend his money in ways that could have been used to greater advantage elsewhere.

The operation, diminished in scale, was placed on a businesslike footing, with the land divided into lots for sale without restrictions at the price the market would bear, and houses were rented or used for schools. Unabashed capitalism was now the order. No longer was there talk of socialism and common ownership or of New Harmony as a model for a reformed society, nor were there innumerable committees holding endless meetings and discussions; political and social rhetoric was mercifully muted. If there was to be an improvement of society, it would be through education of the children. Individual initiative asserted itself. The town seemed to brighten up as houses were repaired and painted, fences were built, and in the Owen sector no fewer than five stores opened for business, with Madame planning to open a general store.

The commune in the wilderness ceased to have a special, ideological attraction for settlers, and since there was little to hold many of those who had remained, they departed, singly and in groups, abandoning their cherished hopes, which had been aroused by Owen's siren song. They had come from all parts of the country, some disrupting their lives, and they were now trying to salvage what little they had. Many went west where land was cheaper and better. Maclure said he was glad to see the shrinkage, for the community was now more manageable, and in the winnowing process, New Harmony rid itself of the unfit—a Panglossian perspective. Blessed relief was afforded by the departure of Paul Brown for greener pastures where he could skewer the wayward for falling short of his exalted standards. Phiquepal, reviled by both Maclure and Madame Fretageot, set himself apart in his own school with eighty boys, well stocked with supplies "looted" from Maclure's school. There were also a few newcomers who contributed to the general welfare of New Harmony.

Many of those who remained had brought almost nothing, and so they lost little. The most prominent of these were Say and Lesueur, who must have felt stranded in the marches, but with a sense of loyalty to their benefactor, they continued to do research, teach, and publish. Say's wife, Lucy, wanted to return to the East, but Say felt too obligated to Maclure to leave him. She taught small children, made their clothing, and assisted her husband in his scientific work by drawing and coloring his illustrations.[39]

There remained a shortage of currency, so a system of barter prevailed as the community's ability to generate wealth (cash) for amenities continued to be marginal. The survival of New Harmony depended on William Maclure's generosity, but the cost, he felt, was manageable, perhaps $700 or $800 per year, since the entire scope of the enterprise had been greatly reduced. The printing press contributed to the upkeep, and a modest profit was generated by a garden farm, although much of the food had to be transported from New Orleans at great expense. New Harmony gradually settled down to become an isolated midwestern frontier town, far from any great center of population and difficult to reach, placing the community at a great economic disadvantage. Still, it was in the unusual position of having Maclure's wonderful library and a remarkable group of citizens—scientists, artists, teachers, mechanics, farmers, engravers, and ex-soldiers. But unquestionably New Harmony had lost its luster, and there hung over it a sense of decline and uncertainty regarding its future. Owen's drive and provocation were lacking.

In May 1827, Maclure was in New Harmony actively engaged in devising means by which education could be made more effective. But with the arrival of the cold in December, he departed for New Orleans and Mexico with Thomas Say, leaving his educational creations in the hands of others. As the dominant force in New Harmony, Maclure was free to set up any kind of school he wanted. His greatest desire was to provide an appropriate education for every kind of student, gifted or not, affluent or poor—a salvaging and tailoring process that is modern by present-day standards. A group of institutions were planned that would provide instruction on how to grow food, make clothes, and build houses, but these proposals hardly saw the light of day. Earlier he had spoken of an agricultural college on 900 acres of land, probably similar to the one he hoped to found in Spain before he fled the country, but little came of it. An orphans manual training school was announced in May 1827, and a society for mutual instruction was planned, complete with laboratories of chemistry and physics.

An industrial school on a diminished scale was ultimately formed according to his plan, the motto of the school proclaiming, "Utility shall be the scale on which we shall endeavor to measure the value of everything."[40] The program offered free instruction for young men and women who would be provided with food, lodgings, and clothing, and by adhering to a rigorous schedule of instruction and manual work, they would pay for themselves.[41] In the end, one of Maclure's major achievements was to introduce a multiple track system of education into the United States—a trade school approach, and a progressive, more intellectual education, grounded in observation and rational analysis, with a modern understanding of science. The consequences of this new approach would be the creation of "productive, useful, and necessary" people by the millions who would insist on being governed by a responsive, representative government. Freedom would follow that is "necessary for the full development of that quantum of happiness, men are capable of enjoying."[42]

The staff consisted of Madame Fretageot, Say, Lesueur, and Maclure's brothers and sisters. Maclure planned to fill the school with orphans (free of parental corruption),[43] but as much as he tried, he could not recruit enough of them. Robert Owen persisted in denigrating Maclure's efforts, making it difficult for Maclure to attract students.

About fifteen children learned to read, write, calculate, draw, and master trades. But even with the modest numbers of students, there were too many for the limited number of occupations for which training could be provided. The making of textiles was planned so that students would not only learn how to weave but would also make their own clothes and earn money for themselves and their school.[44] For the purpose of research and education, Maclure provided an outstanding library of about 2,000 volumes, and New Harmony could also boast of a collection of specimens, rocks, minerals, and fossils, chemical apparatus, and instruments (such as air pumps and an "electric machine"), purchased by Maclure during his travels in Europe and North America.

Maclure advocated an education of a "plain simple narrative of facts" and of "calculations." His ideal, "productive" education included drawing, botany, zoology, arithmetic, geology, chemistry, geography, and astronomy, by the method of teaching prescribed by Pestalozzi, based on demonstration and the use of material aids and objects. His desire was to prevent "the captivating briliencey of imagination from enslaving young minds." Maclure believed that the teaching of "improper subjects . . . literature, very properly called Belles Letters," which promotes an "imagination of false delicacy," was useless. To guard against this, he emphasized that the young should be subjected to "constant and uninterrupted occupation from morning to night with the properties and nature of realities, leaving no time for the reading of romances, or Poetry." Soon they would be happily in agreement. Maclure was convinced that this system was most effective and that students would soon realize it and be the happier for it.[45]

Boys and girls over twelve years of age worked seven hours each day in what was formerly Rapp's church, where they were taught carpentry, cabinet making, tin plating, and shoemaking. One of the student projects, supervised by adults, was the printing and publishing of a new journal, established by Maclure, the *New-Harmony Disseminator,* emblazoned with the banner "Ignorance is the fruitful cause of Human Misery." The journal was dedicated to providing "useful knowledge," practical advice, and "hints for the youths of the United States." An ideal vehicle to broadcast Maclure's views on politics and education, it also provided lessons in geometry and botany, advice to stammerers, and the rules for making conversation, baking bread baking, extracting oils, cleaning stone stairs, removing stains, cutting out shirts from whole cloth, and making sheet lead, soap, soup from bones, and paper. Pages were filled with maxims and short biographies of successful people as well as essays by Maclure and Robert Dale Owen, and papers on natural history by Thomas Say. Several chapters on the laws of motion were taken from Mirabeau's *System of Nature.* A number of Maclure's articles in the *Disseminator* were republished in his three-volume work, *Opinions,* whose publication was a major project of the School of Industry Press of New Harmony, supervised by Phiquepal. Maclure made sure that copies of *Opinions* were sent to libraries, institutions, and influential people, and he was pleased that it was of sufficient importance to be reviewed by a London journal.

New Harmony was now the shelter of Maclure's siblings, all of whom were troublesome dependants. His two brothers, John and Alexander, joined him in 1826 after being extricated from some difficulties; his two sisters, who had hitherto been living very well in Scotland supported by Maclure, were brought to New Harmony to reduce expenses when financial problems arose in New Harmony. He derived little pleasure from his family, and perhaps this dissatisfaction, as well as considerations of health, kept him away from them. Anna had little sympathy with her brother's societal and educational ambitions, and she was resentful of Madame Fretageot's close relationship with him and of her influence on him—a sister should have been his confidant. Religion was important to Anna, and through her, church groups tried to influence her brother, but with little success.[46] Margaret, who was "unmanageable," resented the dominance of her sister, Anna, and chose to live apart from her. According to Madame Fretageot, John, occasionally in tears, was at times "absolutely deranged" and tormenting his sisters;[47] he died in a mental institution in 1834. Alexander, who seems to have been an idler with an inflated view of himself, was rescued from a failing business in Virginia by William, who provided him (and his other siblings) with a pension, which Alexander felt was owed to him. In New Harmony, he operated a tannery, a business that failed—costly to himself and to Anna. According to William, he was "one of the most incorigible, obstinate, prejudiced individuals I have ever come across," and for a long time Maclure deliberately excluded Alexander from management and the handling of finances.[48] After the deaths of the reliable Madame Fretageot and Say in 1833 and 1834, respectively, Maclure was left to the mercy of Alexander and Anna to manage his estate—a precarious situation indeed.

For the time being, Maclure depended on Madame Fretageot and Say to manage his affairs, promote his educational philosophy, and serve as a buffer between him and his siblings. Fortunately, the two managers got along well. Madame had a head for business, while Say, somewhat otherworldly, refused a salary for his work and lived a pauper's life, working on his mollusks and insects and editing the *Disseminator*.[49] Lesueur continued with his natural history studies and his drawings of birds, fish, and plants. Although the relationship between Phiquepal and Maclure was irreparably broken, he continued to teach his boys in a school set apart from the rest, where the *Gazette*, the *Disseminator*, and other publications were printed at Maclure's behest.

Madame Fretageot's willingness to be Maclure's agent permitted him to reside in Mexico with its admirable climate and people, beginning in late 1828. A strong-minded, stubborn, intelligent person, Madame was capable of making hard choices and bearing the brunt of local criticism and complaint. She was a devoted protector of Maclure's interests and the central figure in his operation. By one of Maclure's rough calculations, he had lost as much as $100,000 in his philanthropic adventures, and he was in no mood to lose more, and so Madame's job was made more difficult. He insisted that New Harmony support itself as much as possible, without incurring significant debt, by operating frugally. Always on the lookout for ways to save money and make the farm and orchard yield a profit, he even suggested that poppies be grown for producing opium. As she watched the pennies, her brusque manner alienated her colleagues, and as a woman making decisions that concerned men's affairs, she suffered an extra measure of abuse.[50]

As the guardian of Maclure's fortune, Madame Fretageot antagonized Troost, Neef, Phiquepal, and Anna Maclure by turning down some of their financial requests. In her letters to Maclure she had a bad word for almost everyone, and all Maclure could do from a distance was soften her censure and make allowances for them. Whether true or not, the widely publicized discord must have been disheartening to Maclure, especially when he was bitterly criticized for being controlled and misled by Madame. Having few places to turn, Madame Fretageot on her part complained to Maclure that "everyone is against me," and in fact she had little support from those in New Harmony. However, Maclure still regarded Madame Fretageot tenderly, as a true partner, and clearly saw that without her, all would be lost. While he had complete confidence in her ability and integrity, and continued to support her through all the controversies and squabbles, his friends, associates, and certainly his own family made their complaints known. Ludicrously, although she was frugal and efficient, she was deficient in bookkeeping skills. To Say, her accounts were incomprehensible. Her devotion to Maclure was total as she worked herself to death, rising at 4, teaching until 6:30, cooking and serving breakfast, then further teaching and tending to the publishing effort of New Harmony, managing business, and making the "family" dinner, usually without help.[51]

Throughout the turmoil, Madame Fretageot's declared love and admiration for Maclure continued undiminished. While his letters to her were admiring and complimentary, they were somewhat impersonal, filled with advice and warnings such as to be wary in dealing with his brother Alexander: "You must put him into such a situation that he cannot injure our plans."[52] The demands made on her never abated. In a letter to Maclure in Mexico dated September 6, 1830, a time when she was beset by managerial and financial problems that threatened to overwhelm her, she presented a detailed summary of Maclure's complex financial obligations pertaining to New Harmony. She listed the decisions she had made and attempted to justify them. She asked for advice and begged him to return, for only he could make the right decisions. Her letter ends on a plaintive note: "I think you will render justice to my attention in your affairs, and in my wish of pleasing you in every thing I have done; and if you decide to replace me, do not preserve in your mind any unpleasant feelings towards me. I will remain satisfied with any thing you please to do in that account, and shall never forget what kindness you have shewn me in a time that I was without means to undertake any kind of buseness; and not only have you lended me money, but when I offered to return it, you refused it and made a present to me. Also what is more yet: you care for Achilles' education."[53]

The departure of key Pestalozzian teachers, troublesome to Madame Fretageot, put an end to the Education Society. A relative calm had descended on New Harmony after 1828, but pressing problems, great and small, arose in the day-to-day maintenance of an aging plant, and Say was always too busy with his scientific investigations to help. George Rapp and his flock had constructed buildings that looked substantial, but in fact they had neglected to place them on solid foundations. As members of a millennial sect, they were awaiting the imminent Second Coming—the end—so they felt there was no need to build anything that would last. Serious structural defects began to appear, and buildings were showing signs of wear. The floors and foundations were rotting and desperately in need of repair. New Harmony was taking on a shabby appearance. Where would they get the money to pay carpenters and masons?[54] Madame Fretageot was being worn down, trying to manage.[55]

Maclure always maintained a strong interest in science and publishing. There is little question that the United States was Maclure's adopted land. His values were thoroughly American, and his desire was to promote American science. He was proud of the arguable "fact" that "we can count more naturalists scattered over every corner of our Union, than are to be found in all Europe."[56] New Harmony had been blessed with first-rate naturalists. Thomas Say produced two classics, *American Entomology* (1824–28) and *American Conchology* (seven volumes, 1830–37),[57] and Charles-Alexandre Lesueur published *Fish of North America,* the first account of fish of the Great Lakes. Maclure had provided them with a printing press and copperplates for engraving, and he brought to New Harmony a fine engraver and expert in color printing, Cornelius Tiebout.[58] Over the years New Harmony became a self-sufficient publishing center, whose triumphs were the publication of Maclure's *Opinions* and a magnificent edition of Michaux's *North American Sylva,* from plates that Maclure had bought in Europe. His aim was to provide the public with editions of high quality at a low price by keeping expenses down—"all for the diffusion and equalization of useful knowledge." Students in Maclure's School of Industry did the printing at a fraction of the usual cost as they learned their trade. A prospectus was published to advertise publications, and friends in Philadelphia, New York, and New Haven were urged to promote the venture.[59] To further publicize his views, Maclure published the *Disseminator of Useful Knowledge.* As a man with a mercantile background, he encouraged venders to travel the country by wagon to sell books and printed material to the people—in keeping with the tradition of peddling in the early United States. Of all Maclure's mighty efforts, publishing was perhaps the most successful.

SIXTEEN

✳

Withdrawal to Mexico

In December 1827, Maclure visited Mexico for the first time, leaving Madame Fretageot in New Harmony in charge of finances, education, and publications—an ominous responsibility indeed. He was accompanied by Thomas Say, who had left his young bride in New Harmony preparing illustrations for his *American Conchology.* A quiet, solicitous man, Say was an ideal companion for his benefactor because he was not only a superb naturalist with liberal views, admired by all, but he was also a good listener, a sounding board for Maclure who had strong opinions on all subjects.

After a stormy passage to Vera Cruz from New Orleans, they came upon a Philadelphia friend, Lardner Vanuxem, a naturalist who managed a silver mine in Mexico. Accompanying them on their trip from the coast to Mexico City, he was able to observe Maclure closely, and while he had the warmest of feelings toward Say, he was critical of Maclure, a "dogmatic . . . bore," and "much changed" from what he knew of him in earlier times. Pleased when the journey ended, in a letter home he made the derogatory remarks that Neef, Troost and others whom Maclure had brought to New Harmony had "deserted" him, and that while Say admired and respected Maclure, he remained only for the financial support he provided.[1]

In the early nineteenth century, Mexico and much of Spanish America suffered revolutions to free themselves of oppressive and corrupt Spanish control, uprisings that were the echoes of the French Revolution and the great movement toward liberalism. With the French invasion of Spain, Napoleon's brother Joseph was placed on the throne of Mexico, but after Waterloo, he was replaced by a Bourbon king. With weak governments in unstable times, New Spain found it impossible to contain erupting independence movements.[2]

Mexico became an independent nation in 1821. An uneven succession of governments, some liberal and others despotic, followed each other (no fewer than seventy-four over the next fifty years). By 1828, the time of Maclure's visit, an independent republican state, federalist in nature, led by a government with a president and upper and lower houses of parliament, had come into existence.[3] Promising an end to tyranny, the spirit of idealism was evident in a state that would not tolerate abusive, arrogant officials. While Catholicism remained the official state religion, its authority was curtailed, all Spanish-born priests were expelled, and the Church no longer collected tithes or held a monopoly on education. Maclure was elated by all this and the legal reform based on the Napoleonic Code: "All these improvements are hints at civilization, and will no doubt show the vast advantage of a population, emerging immediately from the simplicity of barbarism and despotism, free from the intrigues and prejudices of a half state of civilization." Maclure wrote of universal suffrage, and was moved by "the great humanity, mildness, and aversion to shedding blood" of the natives (in contrast to the genocide that was going on in the United States). According to Maclure, such a great advance at the expense of the powerful, elicited a countercampaign of lies and vilification "as in the French revolution and all other changes for the benefit of the producers." In the face of widely quoted falsehoods and horror stories, Maclure saw no disorder and anarchy, no murder, robbery, or cruelty. He deplored the fact that important visitors to Mexico inevitably first came in contact with the "most corrupt and vicious part of the population" (aristocracy and rich owners), and were misled by their lies.[4] According to Maclure, "a new epoch opened to the progress of human happiness, when civilization crossed the Atlantic" to settle in bountiful lands. The young United States of Mexico could be compared more than favorably with the young United States of America with respect to finances, commerce, and education.[5]

Traveling in a carriage drawn by ten mules, the 335 miles from Vera Cruz to Mexico City, with rests stops at Jalapa and Puebla, were memorable. Maclure was enchanted with all that he encountered in "this favorite country," leaving him in "excellent health and spirits."[6] The perfect climate, the quality and variety of natural foods, the simple domestic cuisine, the luxuriant vegetation, and the "good tempered, mild, serious and reserved" character of the people (who, however, could be improved by "a cross with the Negro") pleased him. He judged them as not at the level of the average American ("the most enlightened people on earth") but superior to the Spaniards of the "old country." Indeed, Maclure believed that "those who compare any part of the globe with our Union in a moral, religious, or political point of view do that country an injustice" because of the deficiencies in all other countries.

As they proceeded at a leisurely pace, Maclure was taken with "the romantic variety of the land," which he regretted not being able to draw, and he commented extensively on the volcanic nature of the landscape, acquiring samples of rocks and minerals and studying the natives. Say collected insects, shells, and plants unknown in the north. In their travels, they came upon Aztec artifacts that were reported on by Say in the *Disseminator*,[7] but Maclure had little sympathy for the acquisition of antiquities, just as he disparaged classical studies, which he saw as useless agents of oppression: "I see nothing worth the trouble, in searching for antiquities, and studying the learned disquisitions of antiquarians. The only use of both is to retard the progress of the age, by neglecting the useful arts.... I do not ever remember having occasion to examine the results of either, of antiquities or antiquarians, but to find them in opposition to the general good.... I would not give a single new fact of the operations of the laws of nature, for all the antiquities that exist.[8]

Well disposed toward an emerging Mexico, he was pleased with every change he saw,[9] and if there was any unpleasant element, he ascribed it to the continuing influence of the old regime, which in time would disappear as the country emerged from "barbarism." He noted that beggars on the street "fed by the false charity of the church" were now being taught useful trades, and attempts were being made to provide them with constant employment such as the building of a hospital, and houses for the poor, something previously unheard of. Newly built inns made the trip pleasurable, their architecture was functional and agreeable, the public buildings were "numerous, elegant, and superb," and the cuisine was simple and excellent.[10] He saw nothing but good.

Eleven days after departure from Vera Cruz, Maclure and his friends arrived at Mexico City, having crossed volcanic plains. As they approached their destination, they came upon streets of hovels, the hallmarks of former despotism, reminiscent of the approaches to St. Petersburg and Madrid, and once again Maclure was aware of the contrast between the "external superfluities of the church, state and other non-productives, with the ragged misery of the class of productive laborers." A customary round of visits took him to the mint, the botanical gardens, palaces, and the university. Some institutions he visited were found in a degraded state because they had little financial support, and their leadership lacked vigor—a hangover from European control. Maclure, with boundless optimism, regarded the situation merely as a transitional phase that would improve as Europeans departed and control fell into the hands of natives.

In Mexico City they befriended Joel Roberts Poinsett, American minister to Mexico, and later secretary of war. Through Poinsett, a man with botanical interests, Say received seeds or cuttings of an attractive plant that he later brought back to Philadelphia, the first plants being cultivated in the nursery of Say's great-grandfather, John Bartram, and first shown in the Philadelphia Flower Show of 1829. Say named the plant *Poinsettia,* and at Maclure's behest, he proposed Poinsett for membership in the Academy of Natural Sciences of Philadelphia. On his last visit to Philadelphia in November 1828, Maclure had visited the Bartram gardens, where in his usual role of facilitator, arranged for various kinds of seeds to be sent to Say for cultivation in New Harmony.

Following the civil wars that took place in virtually every state of Mexico and many countries in South America, a federation of governments, broadly based on universal suffrage, was established. The new arrangement was deemed creditable by Maclure, for it was the means by which the corruption left by "Spanish despotism" would be wiped away. In some peculiar way, Maclure was not frightened by revolution in this sunny land,[11] blessed with a fertile soil, a good climate, geographical advantages, and an admirable native population, destined to be the dominant force through sheer weight of numbers. Maclure foresaw a favored land of as many as 300 million people.[12] Although corruption persisted, and the old order remained a threat, a key step was to ensure an end to the "collusion" between the state and the church with its outrageous tithes and its control of education.

Of the greatest importance to Maclure was the establishment of a representative government, with as little treasury as possible—"an empty treasury at the commencement of a free government, is one of the most effectual means of eradicating the corruption, patronage and pensions, instituted for the support of arbitrary power." Maclure prescribed the return of the riches of the Church to the people, the holding of frequent elections, and single terms for the elected so that structural corruption could not take hold and patronage would be kept to a minimum. By contrast, in monarchies, where there was great centralization of power in the hands of a chief executive, an empty treasury would lead only to revolution when the demands of the "unproductive" supplicants were not gratified. Maclure preferred multiple sites of power and patronage, as did Jefferson.

He was pleased with the "frankness" he found among legislators, and he looked forward to the time when the wealth accumulated by the Church and others in power would be used to build "museums of natural history, gymnasiums, schools and seminaries of all kinds" rather than "magnificent churches and convents."[13] The newly formed government of Mexico had set aside money for a survey of the country, essential for the development of the nation; even the United States, which was far more advanced than Mexico, had not yet instituted such an official overview.

Maclure was impressed with the progressive schools that had been set up based on the Lancastrian platoon system of education, free of Church influence. In such an environment, Pestalozzian schools would be welcomed, and so Maclure decided that he would focus his efforts and money on their establishment in Mexico, recognizing that in the United States his "individual exertion against national prejudices" had met with little success.[14]

What troubled him and threatened Mexico's future was that property and knowledge still remained "in the hands of the few," that "the millions are the last to benefit from the revolution." He worried that the entire revolution, beset with external and internal enemies, might go the way of the French and the Spanish revolutions and "finish merely by a change of masters," but he saw more hope for Mexico because the old colonial powers were so far away.[15] Mexico, on this side of the Atlantic Ocean, adjoined the United States, which was a fine model for a democratic federation with representative government, an arrangement which in turn might best serve American interests, and to this end he recommended financial investment in Mexico. Maclure envisioned a healthy rivalry rather than one that would foment belligerency.[16]

Spain persisted in its attempt to regain control of Mexico by military force, but this failed. News that a Mexican brig "beat off two Spanish brigs, and afterward fought a Spanish frigate of sixty guns," was considered by

Maclure to be "a singular proof of the great superiority of freedom over despotism—of freemen over slaves."[17]

While he ascribed the many fine qualities of native Mexicans to the ideal climate in which they lived, of concern to Maclure was that the country's "perpetual spring" could also be detrimental to the creation of a democratic state, for he was convinced that no democracy had ever flourished in a warm climate with its abundance of food and easy life, leading to "indolence" and a ready submission to "injustice, tyrrany and oppression." Maclure's answer to this danger was universal education.[18]

In contrast to Europeans in Mexico, most of whom he condemned because they were intent on making a fortune in a hurry, Maclure admired the native Indians—the laborers of Mexico—whom he considered to be "by far the best, most industrious and moral" of all people; his hope was that someday they would run the country "to astonish the old world."[19] Although the institution of slavery did not exist in the country, Indians were so ignorant and egregiously exploited by the French and Spanish that they were unable to buy property. It was imperative that this vast majority (approximately 80 percent) be enlightened, for they would have the greatest say if universal suffrage prevailed; the future of Mexico resided with these admirable people.[20] Maclure also believed that those of mixed ancestry, a sizeable group, would also play an important part in Mexico's destiny, while rich Europeans were the "inveterate enemies of freedom," villains who had to be watched, as they fought against any change or development that might threaten their power and income.

He found native Indians to be good-natured, pliable, "quick in comprehension," and very capable. Their history, before their degradation by the Spanish and their adoption of the worst characteristics of their masters, showed them to be industrious builders, with great political skills, so that under the right conditions there was little doubt they could function well in a modern democracy.[21] While Maclure never failed to praise the Mexican Indian, he had a poor opinion of the North American Indian, with whom he must have had dealings. Due to "the inclemency of our rough climate," these people were "animal[s] of slow comprehension, slow of intellect, morose, taciturn, cruel, suspicious, unsociable, obstinate, riveted to their savage habits, unchangeable; when intoxicated with their favourite liquor, vicious in the extreme and indiscriminately cruel." The Mexican Indian was at least "tractable when drunk.[22]

In truth, great advances had been made in Mexico after throwing off the Spanish yoke, but critical analysis suggests that Maclure in his zeal painted an excessively rosy picture of the country, its people, and its future, just as Robert Owen had done in describing his Utopia. Both men had difficulty distinguishing between reality and the ideal image that they craved to make a reality. His account of a first trip to Mexico confirms that he was a reformer, so zealous in his convictions that there was little nuance in his judgments. He praised the new order in the most glowing terms—ceaselessly, inaccurately—and made excessive allowances for any shortcomings. Still, it is apparent from his writings that he was an important geopolitical thinker, whose geological observations and ethnological accounts of the Mexican people added to an ever increasing store of knowledge that informed the curious in Europe and America.

With the New Harmony winter at an end, Maclure and Say began their trip home, just as Mexicans "were fixing a post to shoot the priest Martinez for rebellion." A drunken driver fell under the wheels of their carriage, and the dead man was simply left behind as the carriage rolled on. Without a word of sympathy for the deceased, the only consequence of the tragedy was Maclure's sanctimonious sermon on the evils of drink and its social and political consequences.[23] The incident reveals a curious and disturbing lack of empathy for the individual. Maclure's interest in humankind and injustice was confined to the abstract masses.

Passing from one semi-independent Mexican state to another, escorted by a mounted guard for fear of bandits, they were treated well by local officials, but disconcertingly they encountered numerous corrupt guards and customhouse men who had to be bribed to allow passage.[24] The experience prompted a denunciation of the "despotic oppression of passports" and of indirect taxation—on food, clothing and imports—that still persisted in Mexico, inherited from the Spanish. Not only did indirect taxation place a heavier burden on the poor and spare the rich. It also gave rise to the criminal activity of smuggling and created a need for a body of officials to protect the public at great expense. Even worse, it placed officials in a position of power whereby they too could extort money, the corrupt faring far better than the honest.[25]

When the travelers reached New Orleans in April, Say, never robust, was too ill to proceed further, and so they remained until he recovered. It is no wonder that Maclure returned to Mexico as soon as he was able, for

Mexico showed more promise than any other place of fulfilling his dream of reform. It was here that the authorities were investing in education, and so there was the greatest chance of success of Pestalozzian schools. Maclure and Say were effusive in their praise of the country. Maclure wrote, "I never have been in any place where I have found more to agree with me in opinion; it is a novelty for one trained in the turmoil of opposition, eternally counteracted by all the powers, physical and moral, to find such toleration where the least expected. I shall leave their fine climate, their urbanity, civility, and friendly toleration, with regret, though both SAY and myself, are cooped up in a small room not ten feet square, I never spent my time more agreeably, nor more to my own satisfaction."[26] Maclure went to great lengths to gather Mexican Indian boys and orphans for schooling in New Harmony, appealing for help from influential people such as Joel Poinsett, but he met with little success. However, on his return he managed to bring two Mexican orphans for schooling in New Harmony; Madame Fretageot was enthralled with these "brown little creatures."

After returning from Mexico, Maclure spent the summer of 1828 in New Harmony supervising his affairs and acquainting himself with newcomers, one of whom was Robert Owen's son David Dale, whose interest in science and geology increased through direct contact with Maclure and his impressive collection of rocks and minerals. After Maclure's death, David Dale became the curator of the collection, cataloging, and arranging the geological specimens for display and shipping them to museums and colleges throughout the United States. This was the beginning of David Dale Owen's illustrious career in geology. His center of operation was New Harmony, where his laboratory and mineral and rock collections were housed in a great stone Rappite building, given to him by Anna Maclure.[27] Married to Joseph Neef's daughter Caroline, he played an important role in the establishment of governmental geological surveys.[28]

At the time, Madame Fretageot, Say, and Lesueur, along with Maclure's siblings, were the core of one of the two groups in New Harmony, which, while not openly hostile to the Owen clan as a consequence of the recently resolved great quarrel, operated somewhat apart from this second group, which ran its own schools. It consisted of Owen's sons, Mr. and Mrs. Chase, Robert Jennings and William Phiquepal, all of whom, according to Madame, were deficient in common sense and were constantly in disagreement with one another. There were also skilled craftsmen in the town, including the engraver and printer Cornelius Tiebout, associated with the publishing effort carried out by Phiquepal and his boys, who did the bidding of all.

In October 1828, after about four months in New Harmony, Maclure was off again on a second visit to Mexico, from which he never returned. He was now sixty-five and suffering from arthritis. Choosing a meandering route, rather than heading for the nearest port of departure, he ascended the Ohio River to reach Detroit, traveled by steamboat to Buffalo, visited Niagara Falls, traversed the Erie Canal to Albany, then boarded a steamboat on the Hudson River to West Point and New York City before reaching Philadelphia. In November, he visited New Haven, Connecticut, to see his old friend, Benjamin Silliman of Yale University, and attended a meeting of the American Geological Society, where he was reelected president.[29] Perhaps Maclure made this whirlwind tour of the United States because he sensed that he might never return to his adopted land.

On the way, he tried to recruit skilled workers and students for New Harmony, purchased copper plates and special items for Madame Fretageot (pencils, crayons, instruments, etc.), visited schools, and spread the word about the publications of the School of Industry press. Zealously pursuing the difficult task of seeking students for his schools and seeking subscribers to the *Disseminator,* he usually ended up paying for the subscriptions he "sold." Never wanting to travel alone, Maclure was accompanied by one of Madame's students, Allen Tuck Ward, a bright young man who, soon after reaching Mexico, returned to New Harmony with the complaint that there had been little time for him to see the sights because Maclure rushed from one city to another, keeping him too busy packing and shipping mineral specimens.[30]

Maclure was in Philadelphia when, to his great satisfaction, Andrew Jackson was elected president of the United States. But unlike Madame Fretageot in New Harmony (where Jackson was heavily favored), he never commented on it in his letters written the week of the election. Maclure seemed to avoid American partisan politics, perhaps because passions were uncomfortably high, and argument would alienate too many of his friends and associates with opposing views. To avoid direct conflict, Maclure advised Madame to place the more controversial articles submitted to the *Disseminator* at the back of the journal, and to omit some of the most inflammatory writing, such as that of the assertive atheist Baron Holbach. Oddly, while Maclure expounded at length on his strongly held views, he was not a confrontational advocate.

Leaving New York on November 21, 1828, the travelers arrived at Vera Cruz in mid-December and proceeded to Mexico City. For the remainder of his life he directed the affairs of New Harmony by correspondence with Madame Fretageot and the Academy of Natural Sciences of Philadelphia through correspondence with Samuel G. Morton. Maclure's letters to Morton were mostly of a general nature, with advice and suggestions that could easily be set aside, but this did not dampen his generosity toward the Academy. Say was left with the task of editing the *Disseminator,* which continued to print Maclure's essays until the journal came to an end (June 1831) because of Say's declining health. Madame Fretageot (assigned Maclure's power of attorney) ran the business and educational affairs of the town, and both Say and Madame were jointly entrusted to satisfy the demands of Maclure's siblings. Keeping the peace between the squabbling brothers and sisters was burdensome, as was nursing Say and his wife, Lucy, through various illnesses. Say's health broke down periodically, requiring intensive nursing by this overworked mother confessor.[31]

As if to reassure Maclure that the management of his money was in good hands, Madame told of turning down requests for loans, denying pay raises, and detailing various financial matters, usually to the penny.[32] It is evident from her letters that Madame Fretageot was an entrepreneur who learned fast, and with experience and increasing confidence she was becoming proficient at running the affairs of New Harmony—capable of wheeling and dealing with astute businessmen. An effective manager, she assumed broad responsibilities ranging from cooking meals to teaching, hiring teachers, repairing buildings, constructing fences, encouraging textile manufactories, and farming. Eager for New Harmony to be more than self-sustaining, she thought she could do it by employing students more fully, but Maclure cautiously dampened her enthusiasm for her "chariccature manufactory." Wanting to start a distillery, she arranged to send local produce on flat boats to New Orleans, and she attempted to have the law court moved from nearby Mount Vernon to New Harmony to bring business to the town, but this ambitious scheme fell through. Maclure urged her to concentrate on the existing printing facility with its printers, engravers, and student help, not only to make a modest profit but also to publish journals and books that promoted natural science and his ideas. To help Madame manage the complex affairs of New Harmony, he asked Reuben Haines to act as a business agent and the banker Stephen Girard to assist and advise her in important financial transactions.

In addition to business matters, his letters to Madame would suddenly burst into an impassioned screed about the shortfalls of humankind, replete with aphorisms, seemingly from out of nowhere. Such outbursts suggest the growing despair of an isolated, restless ideologue beginning to lose faith and wondering about what he had accomplished. Perhaps this mood was thrust upon him by deteriorating conditions in his idealized Mexico. The growing presence of government officials and the military, a declining economy, and a weak, ineffective president at the helm were troubling. The pandering of politicians to the mob, domestic intrigue, and the search for power and influence by corrupt means disgusted him.[33] His beloved Mexico was showing signs of the disease that beset all peoples, and his worst opinions about humankind were being confirmed.

By return mail (which was by no means dependable), Say appealed to him to collect shells and plant seeds, and from Madame he received an account of the schools, the business transactions taking place in New Harmony, and baleful news about his brothers and sisters, whose requests for extra money were being denied. Maclure's siblings could not live with each other or with their cooks and servants, who they insisted eat separately—an unacceptable slight in a community that prided itself in its egalitarianism. Madame, always eager to impress Maclure with how well she was guarding his assets, usually ended her letters with a variation on "I long for your return; the time passes very quick, yet it seems long when in expectation. I am yours."[34]

Living in an easygoing Mexico and a bucolic New Harmony made Maclure aware of the unsettled nature of the United States and the restless activities of its citizens; there was always a drumbeat of complaint about tension and greed in his every letter. Reading about exploitative and monopolistic practices in the United States, he was outraged. He had been appalled by the "confusion, crowd, noise and busle, by strive and competition" of Philadelphia, labeling the city a "speculative mad town." He described the making of money as "the god of this country," and New York City as "founded on the artificial base of paper."[35] Maclure was deeply offended when someone innocently asked him if he was making money from his New Harmony venture. The look of "care and anxiety" of the citizens on American city streets bothered him, and he was resolved that he would never live in such places. He was critical of all the road, house, and canal building going on—all "unproductive"—mostly at public expense, and he disapproved of the introduction of public transportation in

New York as a ridiculous luxury.[36] Did all this really mean he would never return to live in the United States?[37]

Perhaps Maclure was so ill-disposed toward Philadelphia and the East because he met there with so much questioning and criticism of New Harmony, for the furor over the Owen affair was still fresh in people's minds, and the angry defections of Neef and Troost, who were known and admired by many Philadelphians, had not been adequately explained. While in Philadelphia, Maclure had received a letter from a disconsolate Lesueur threatening to sue him for lack of payment of his expenses, and he was questioned about this in Philadelphia.[38] It was no secret that George Ord and others at the Academy of Natural Sciences wanted Lesueur and Say back, convinced that these admirable naturalists were being wasted in New Harmony. Maclure scoffed at their hypocrisy, for when Say and Lesueur worked in Philadelphia, they had received virtually no compensation for their efforts; Say had slept and cooked in the building that housed the Academy and lived on ten cents per day.

After Owen returned to England, his concern for the betterment of society continued unabated, especially in the field of labor. He was a famous man, regarded as a hero by many. Although his means were now limited, his weakness for immense schemes remained undiminished as he strove to establish utopian settlements in Texas (which belonged to Mexico), to be financed by Rothschild and Baring, who owned large tracts of land. Maclure, recently arrived in Mexico, heard of these great plans from Owen himself, for he happened to be in Jalapa when Owen dropped in on him in January 1829, on his way to Mexico City to promote his scheme.[39] Apparently the meeting was cordial, for money was not involved, and in fact Madame still regarded Owen as a "good friend" of Maclure's, despite his letters to Madame stating that he had been "swindled" and "shamefully deceived" and that he felt "terribly cheated" by that "fool" Owen. Maclure, bewildered by how Owen could have garnered such glowing letters of recommendation from high officials in London in support of his Texas scheme,[40] wrote to Madame: "So long as he stops at theory all will do well. But should he attempt practice, the second edition of New Harmony will most probably be published to the world contradicting his theories and bringing loss and disappointment on all that have placed faith and confidence in him."[41] In fact, Owen's great plan came to a sudden end when his proposal was rejected by the Mexican government.

A constitutional government was in power in Mexico, but it was being challenged by a growing military presence that worried Maclure. The interests of an expanding, standing army would inevitably diverge from those of the people, become a threat to democracy, and in a time of unrest would usurp the civil power.[42] One government followed another—liberal and conservative—as the country suffered uprisings fomented by potential dictators and adventurers, while corruption steadily increased. No sooner had an election taken place than a violent uprising followed.

During these decades, Mexico and other Latin American countries were beset with revolutions and counterrevolutions as dictators, heading groups of insurgents, seized power or were deposed, with leaders killed or forced into exile. Foreigners and Spanish were looked upon with suspicion, and travel was risky because the roads were terrorized by bandits. Maclure was well informed about the political situation in Central and South America. He denounced Simon Bolivar (usually looked upon as a liberating hero) as a dictator, who condemned "all liberal opinions as destructive of good order (that is, his order)," with views on education that were outmoded—"a complete retrograde of two centuries."[43] On the other hand Maclure thought that Bolivar might possibly be able to create an effective democratic government; he would certainly be a hero if he gave power back to the people.[44] The constant struggle for power between rivals and factions unsettled him and certainly made the execution of his plans for education of the Indians most difficult, if not impossible.

Maclure's letters to Madame Fretageot continued, invariably passionate about such matters as the governance of nations, how it is corrupted, and how it can be set right. But in practice his indictments were tempered by a caution that reveals how he operated. He wrote with the expectation that what he had to say was to be published in the *Disseminator,* and yet he instructed Madame (and others) who were editing his letters to delete the more inflammatory parts as they saw them, and not to assign his name to some of his reports.[45] However, he complained that some of his essays for the *Disseminator* did not appear in print, suspecting censorship by "young editors" (who certainly must have been responsible for cleaning up his grammar and spelling).[46] Considering Maclure's vulnerability in Mexico, it was a wise move, for his denunciations would have offended powerful Mexicans at a time in the mid-1830s when General Santa Anna became a virtual dictator. Perhaps he had learned a lesson in Spain when he was obliged to flee the country. Although Maclure himself was not fearful, the word about Mexico was that it was a dangerous place, especially for foreigners, causing Madame to worry and to urge caution, begging him to return. Particularly threatening to Maclure was the possibility of a Spanish invasion to reclaim its lost colony; he was already a fugitive from Spain. An invasion had already taken place in the summer of 1829, but yellow fever devastated the invaders, and happily for Maclure, a Mexican army under Santa Anna defeated the survivors at Tampico.

In March 1829, Maclure was in Mexico City, attempting to recruit Indian and orphan children for schooling in New Harmony. Despite promises from authorities, prospects were discouraging, and in the United States, only a few young students were added to the roll. Frustrated and despondent, Maclure wrote of the "appathy of the Millions," and "Every time I ref[l]ect on the School, and the mode it is treated, puts me in mind of Burks [Edmund Burke] name given to the people of Britain, the Swinish multitude, and adds to the contemp I have long felt for my species, but they may serve to amuse us even if they render all our attempts at benefiting them abortive." These were bitter words from an optimist dedicated to reform, who brooded about a generation "with its venom of mony making, avaritious Speculation, luxury, dissapations," which was rotting the foundations of the country. "Spanish wickedness and the climate has lef[t] this place a sink of corruption."[47]

The postal service was unreliable, leaving Maclure to worry when there was no news from New Harmony. When there was news, it was bad, and this made him worry all the more. The continuing strife in Mexico, rooted in hostility between classes, was portrayed in the worst possible light by the foreign press. More hopeful were events taking place in the United States, where Andrew Jackson was president, to the consternation of the Federalists, a ray of hope that brightened Maclure's prospects—for the present time.[48]

In October 1829, Maclure met Frédéric August Ismar in Mexico City, a young man who was ideally suited to teach school and assist Madame Fretageot. According to Ismar, until the age of seventeen, he had been educated in the schools of Pestalozzi and of Fellenberg. Then he had obtained a medical degree at the University at Göttingen, become a surgeon in Paris, and was now in Mexico, where he was brought by the government to establish a school for boys along Fellenbergian lines. Regrettably, "indolent, appathetic rulers" and political instability had blocked the creation of a new school, stranding him without prospects. Ismar was offered a position by Maclure in New Harmony to assist an overworked Madame Fretageot, and in so doing, he would learn about the operation of Pestalozzian schools in the New World. After two or three years he could return to head a school for young Indians in Mexico, if conditions permitted. Before embarking for New Harmony, he tried to recruit Indian boys and collect specimens of birds, fish, and insects for Say and Lesueur. Maclure was impressed with Ismar, the "proper person," who "does everything *con amore*, not for money."⁴⁹ He could use 1,000 Ismars. In November, Maclure wrote Madame that Ismar was on his way: "You will find him gay and lively; perhaps a little too quick in deciding a fault."⁵⁰

Ismar had entered the lives of Maclure and Madame Fretageot, and soon he revealed himself to be an Iago, a disruptive, dark angel who created poisonous stories (mostly untrue) about the disaffected members of New Harmony and related them to Maclure, who began to believe some of his tales. Puzzling events such as the disappearance and the irregularity of mail and the lack of sales of New Harmony publications in New Orleans were explained. Arriving in New Orleans, Ismar related what he had heard about the very low regard people had for both New Harmony and Madame Fretageot, resulting in a decision by the Mexican government not to send 200 Indian boys to New Harmony.⁵¹

Upon arriving at New Harmony, this purveyor of false information gave Madame distressing news that she immediately reported to Maclure. Ismar claimed he had spoken to a Mr. Ogilvie, Maclure's agent in New Orleans, who had told him "there was no school at all, and when in existence, the students were encoraged to steal, and commit so many depradations that they were the scourge of the country; that the woman at the head of your school [Madame Fretageot] had abondened her own child at Paris etc. and was consequently unfit for such a philanthropic [undertaking] as yours."⁵² Mr. Ogilvie also reported that the press was no longer functioning, and he told Miss Carroll, a New Orleans bookseller engaged to promote the sale of publications and prints from the New Harmony press, that publishing would not resume until Madame had left. Miss Carroll disliked Madame Fretageot, which explains why she had been inexplicably difficult and uncooperative in her dealing with New Harmony and was in fact happy to discourage sales of its publications.

The trail of this twisted plot ends with Alexander Maclure who, however cordial he was to Madame, bitterly resented the fact that his brother had such complete trust in her (and so little in him) and that she had been given sole control of the finances of New Harmony, due no doubt to Alexander's history of disastrous sorties in the world of finance. It was from Alexander that Mr. Ogilvie received his information, obviously designed to discredit and get rid of Madame. All mail to and from Maclure passed through Alexander's hands, since the New Orleans agent who forwarded mail was beholden to him, and so Alexander must have decided which letters were to disappear and which were to be delayed; Ismar claimed that he had seen some of these letters.

The result was confusion, misunderstanding, and repeated accusations by Maclure that Madame never read his letters or that she ignored them. While the correspondence between Maclure and Madame was filled with recriminations about not writing, Anna Maclure's letters were received without interference. Madame was aware of the fact that she was intruding in Maclure's family affairs, and she pleaded with him to return to New Harmony to clear up matters and to rid himself of Mr. Ogilvie. Maclure's letters to Madame suggest that he did not respond appropriately to her urgent and alarming revelations of betrayal and double-dealing, especially those implicating his brother.

Investigation of the situation by Maclure led him to the misbegotten conclusion that some of the mischief had been perpetrated by "that quack and hypocrite, Phiquepal, amplified by the Neefs," and others at New Harmony. Mr. Ogilvie was a mere "ploding Scotch man" who was only "negligent." The real villain had to be Ogilvie's partner, a Mr. Klein, a good friend of Alexander whom he had manipulated with the aim of gaining control of Maclure's fortune. According to Maclure, Alexander was "totally unfit to do anything either for himself or others." He was without any sense at all and incapable of such a "dastardly" scheme.

In fact, the postmaster of New Harmony had done Alexander's bidding, opening, delaying, and discarding letters. A story that the Mexican government refused to send students to New Harmony, based on the findings of a Mexican investigator, was a complete fabrication, and Joel Poinsett had not been involved in the affair. Ismar, the conduit of lies and misinformation, had been taken in by the New Orleans crowd because he was so "young and volatile."[53] In the face of such an intricate, tangled problem, Maclure felt powerless and utterly unable to get to the bottom of the intrigue; his response was feeble.

Within weeks of Ismar's arrival, Madame was finding him troublesome, another querulous Phiquepal, fomenting dissension among the students and faculty, and lacking "wisdom." She often wished him "to the Devil." Claiming to be familiar with printing, he proved ignorant and incompetent, and it took weeks to straighten out the affairs of the printing shop after his removal. He submitted costly, extravagant proposals to Maclure, who dismissed them as the product of too "speculative" a mind—"perhaps Literature is his fort."

As early as 1830, Maclure had shown signs of a flagging enthusiasm for New Harmony, writing about "the mortifications of our school establishment," and "even our *Disseminator* fell dead from our press."[54] Utopia aroused bad memories; it had cost him a fortune, and it was costing him another small fortune to repair the decaying infrastructure of a town that was beginning to show its age. Most discouraging was an inability to find students, even orphans, to fill his school and to make people aware of the school's existence in the surrounding area. The "diffusion of knowledge" through the printed word at the least possible cost was now becoming his primary interest, even greater than the operation of schools.

His grand program to bring justice to the world was contracting in scope. Surprisingly, though a successful merchant, he was now remarkably unassertive, remiss in not taking measures to increase the number of outlets for the New Harmony press, nor did he build an organization to promote and sell its publications. These essential efforts were desultory and haphazard—a wagon loaded with printed material that two young men, William Bennett and Mark Penrose, peddled about the country. Maclure was so skeptical about the integrity of booksellers, he would have little to do with them, and yet he strove to enjoy a wide circulation of books and journals and retain his vision of achieving great social reforms through books and the *Disseminator*. His emphasis was shifting from the education of the young to the enlightenment of worthy adults, a task that he had formerly thought unpromising, if not hopeless.

Maclure began complaining that he was not receiving copies of his "child," the *Disseminator*, and he was irritated by misprints and errors in the text—undoubtedly caused by his illegible handwriting. Delay in publication and in his receipt of issues was not the result of negligence on Madame's part or a faulty postal service. The *Disseminator* was not being printed, resulting at one point in a pileup of over 100 of his essays. Thomas Say, who edited Maclure's essays, was often seriously ill or too immersed in his own studies, and Madame was overworked. It was no wonder that at times the printing shop was hardly functioning, frequently in need of paper and ink. Such mundane problems, however, were beneath Maclure's regard.

He could not understand why Frances Wright's radical sheet, the *Free Enquirer,* blaring its inflammatory proclamations, was so popular, for it only contained what he had written the previous year in the *Disseminator,* "deluted into an ocean of words." Maclure asserted that jealousy was not a factor, for it was not in his nature to be envious. He frequently questioned himself in his writing whether egotism was involved in his decisions, because it was something unacceptable to him. Still, he could not remain unmoved by Frances Wright's claim that the *Free Enquirer* was so much more popular than the *Disseminator*—it was the *only* press in the country with "pretensions to freedom." To increase the circulation of his journal, he sent packets of the *Disseminator* to institutions and to President Jackson. Maclure seemed to think that all the problems publishing the *Disseminator,* its numerous typographical errors and its small circulation, were due to the fact that those in New Harmony, including Madame, "despised" it. He was convinced that the *Disseminator* was filled with interesting and important essays, and though it was almost unread, he would not change a word of what he had written. In truth, neither Maclure's nor Wright's bold ideas were original, but reflected the radical thinking of the time, much of it originating with Thomas Paine.

There seemed to be little promise that Maclure's investment in the United States would render dividends. Aside from conflicts within the community, the ongoing deterioration of its buildings, and the machinations of his siblings, many of Maclure's affairs were in the hands of uncooperative and even treacherous agents—Mr. Ogilvie and Miss Carroll in New Orleans, and Andrew B. Spence in Philadelphia (the successor to his deceased partner, William Robertson). Whereas Robertson had been helpful to Madame, Spence ignored her requests for information, did not carry out her orders for payment according to Maclure's wishes, and was undoubtedly mismanaging funds. Despite the downward spiral, of which he must have been aware, Maclure continued to struggle with his affairs from a distance at a time of imperfect communication. Mexico provided an agreeable escape from the "intrigues, villany, and hypocracy" of a distant New Harmony. Answering Madame's repeated pleas to return to set things right, which only he could do, he replied, "I have no intention of leaving soon, as I could be of no use to you, having sufficient confidence in your perseverance to be entirely easy on that score."[55]

To add to his misery, his plan for Pestalozzian education in Mexico was at the mercy of the unstable revolutionary politics of Mexico, the opposition of the Church, and of a powerful group of wealthy men. Maclure was attempting to establish a stable institution in an unstable land. No wonder that Maclure, in his late sixties, was becoming increasingly suspicious of philanthropic appeals. He was withdrawing, content to pontificate from a sunny distance, writing essays on Mexico, the betterment of humankind, geopolitics, and an array of other subjects, all of which were published in the *Disseminator* and later included in his *Opinions*. He praised Madame's "courage, patience, and sang froid" and was "perfectly convinced that [she had] done everything that could be done." He emphasized that she was not responsible for what was happening in New Harmony. But by adding that "the disagreeable affairs . . . [are] much more than I could bear," and that "times must change very much before I can have any wish to be nearer you," he was possibly admitting defeat. Still, he exhorted Madame to do even better if she wanted him to return.[56] Although surrounded by growing anarchy and confusion in Mexico, he still saw progress there, and he remained hopeful that the Indians would take control by weight of numbers—if properly educated in schools such as the ones he planned.

Ismar, a "charming," lively fellow, involved in the musical life of the community, had settled into the life of New Harmony, living in the same house as Madame. After two months of disruptive activities that tested Madame's patience, he informed her that he was intent on removing her from a position of authority because it was rightfully his. He was writing an exposé of her that he was sending to Maclure and was planning to publish. His research had convinced him that the destruction of Phiquepal's reputation was Madame's work. A furious Madame insisted that this "madman" move out of the house.

Ismar fought with everyone. He claimed that Maclure had sent him to New Harmony with the promise that he would have important responsibilities, which included the running of the school, but the plan was frustrated by an overbearing Madame who was making herself rich with Maclure's money. He moved into another house with the Owens and Mrs. Chase—the other camp. Welcomed at first, he again proved so troublesome that he was evicted, taking with him valuable books and engravings, stolen from the Maclure and Owen library. The thievery discovered, he was forced to return most of the loot, but some he sold to provide for his travel expenses.[57] It was apparent that he was mentally unstable, paranoid, and suffering marked mood swings, one moment gay, the next, brooding and morose. A little investigation by Maclure revealed that he had never gone to the schools of Pestalozzi or Fellenberg as he claimed nor to medical school.[58] He knew little about Fellenberg's school when quizzed by Robert Dale Owen, a graduate of the school, and he was more ignorant of human anatomy than was Madame. Considered a "rogue" by New Harmony, he left, demanding money, which Madame refused.[59]

Ismar attempted to blackmail Maclure by threatening to publish a letter revealing all, an exposé of New Harmony and Madame, if Maclure did not honor a draft for $1,127. Maclure declined, and a lengthy open letter by Ismar to Maclure appeared in April 1830, relating a detailed history of their relationship and of Ismar's efforts to improve New Harmony. He criticized Maclure and the school system, and advised him to return to New Harmony and run the communal venture himself. (Actually, there was merit in this suggestion.) The denunciation of Madame Fretageot and her school was total and indeed libelous. She was accused of being dictatorial, incompetent, greedy, and dishonest. Maclure called it "the essence of . . . malice, scandal, envy, malignity."[60]

Ismar's publication was such a scurrilous tract, it elicited feelings of sympathy for Madame, and everyone came to her defense, with the result that enrollment in the school actually increased. Robert Dale Owen, a member of the "other" group with which Ismar was identified, wrote that he was convinced that Ismar was a "wretch," and a "rascal" who should be put in jail. He had left New Harmony without paying his debts, refused to pay his fare after passage to New Orleans, and was drunk the entire trip. William Owen reported that in New Orleans Ismar was "plunged in every form of debauchery."[61] With the departure of Ismar, the tempest subsided, though he never ceased his slander as he traveled about the country. He kept writing to Maclure, heaping abuse on Madame, and over the years his critique took on a life of its own and was quoted from time to time by the naïve, the ignorant, and the enemies of New Harmony as a thoughtful evaluation of the commune—the inside story—which in the end actually survived the Robert Owen and Ismar paroxysms.[62]

The sense of complacency and well-being of New Harmony's residents kept changing, turning one way or another with events and petty squabbles. According to Madame, by 1830 New Harmony was showing signs of success, its reputation was growing, and her standing had greatly improved. The fields of corn were well tended, a grocery store and carpentry and blacksmith shops were operating successfully, the printing office was well run by a Mr. Kellogg and was accepting new orders, buildings were slowly being repaired and painted, and fences were being built. There was some rapprochement between the two camps in New Harmony—between Madame of the Maclure faction, and the Owen family and Phiquepal; some of the Owen sons were beginning to work at the press again. Madame reveled in the achievement, which was in no small part due to her intelligence and hard work, and she chided Maclure for losing faith in his schools.[63] Many saw Madame as shrill and tough, but with Maclure she was modest and devoted, admitting that "I am always so frightened not to do well." Touchingly, she wrote to him: "The little good I do satisfy me fully of my cares, and when you are satisfied, it is the height of my happiness," and in return he reassured her of his complete trust in her.[64]

Madame's letters to Maclure are endearing, and if they reflect reality, she was an angel. Her efforts and effectiveness were exemplary, but in the light of the host of enemies she made and the criticism by so many citizens of New Harmony, the question arises whether everyone was misguided or motivated by unworthy passions. Whatever the complaints about Madame, they had little effect on Maclure, who dismissed them as originating in base jealousy of a woman who had "command of half a town," a school, and 8,000 acres of land.[65] A young woman living in New Harmony wrote to Maclure that though she "had no enmity to any party," except for a nasty argument she had with Madame, she found that Madame's "conduct is not admired in New Harmony and the country around," that she didn't keep her word, and that she was "universally disliked."[66] However, there is no doubt that she was honest and loyal, and as a woman making important decisions about the welfare of men (doing Maclure's dirty work), with people dependent on her judgments, she was accused of being avaricious and overly ambitious. She was a special target for resentment, for she collected rents and turned down requests for money from Alexander and Anna Maclure, among others. Although she depicted herself as the perfect diplomat, one suspects that she could be stubborn and irritatingly self-righteous.

She vigorously defended the status of education at New Harmony, convinced that her school would withstand Maclure's scrutiny. Still, her competence as a teacher and as a school administrator was questioned, and her understanding of the Pestalozzian philosophy was suspect, so the quality of the education she provided is really unknown. Madame Fretageot's brother was outraged that his two sons had been badly taught. She had terrible battles with teachers who were known to be competent; among them was William Phiquepal, admittedly a wild man, and Joseph Neef, whose teaching had been highly praised by Maclure. Certainly, she had little knowledge or appreciation of natural history and science. She also antagonized Lucy Say, Miss Carroll in New Orleans, Charles-Alexan-dre Lesueur, Reuben Haines in Philadelphia, and others. Despite all this, New Harmony could not have done without her.

Madame Fretageot, imbued with Maclure's ideas, and determined to demonstrate her loyalty to him, was resolute in her actions. Her letters pro-vide convincing evidence that she was entirely in accord with Maclure's social and political philosophy. Proud of the fact that she had turned down the requests of religious groups to preach in the New Harmony hall, she followed his instructions not to sell property to them—much to the cha-grin of Anna Maclure, an "ill-natured and capricious. . . . cats paw of the priestcraft," who actively supported the church. Malicious rumors were spread about Madame, especially among the growing number of religious people in New Harmony, including missionaries who established a Sun-day school and distributed Bibles.[67]

Talk of mortgages, business, prospects for money-making ventures, notes coming due, buying, selling, and renting properties took up a large portion of their letters. There was, however, one recurrent theme: Maclure complained persistently that the press, his great hope for reform, continued to be treated with "indifference," and efforts to sell publications and prints were wanting. He ignored the fact that there was virtually no organization to distribute and sell the publications, and there were few skilled workers, printers, engravers, and bookbinders available to produce them. Skilled workers seemed to come and go, and suitable paper for the press was always difficult to find.

Madame, lacking expertise in English and without a suitable literary background, was forced to run the press, while Say, a most capable editor who should have taken over publications, neglected this responsibility in order to pursue his scientific studies. He did not like to write letters or handle money matters, and he was often seriously ill. His wife, Lucy, disliked Madame, and some of this dislike rubbed off on Say, so that he was not fully cooperative. All the while Maclure kept presenting his grand ideas for publishing children's books for Mexican children, which would require hiring a Spanish editor.

In his letters, Maclure expounded on the thought of the moment: "Given for nothing, goes for nothing is the maxim of mankind. A thing being worth what it will bring, what brings nothing, is worth nothing" was a preface to criticism that prints and books provided to schools without charge were not being used and were actually being destroyed. He decided that parents who were reasonably well off should pay tuition for their children's education, and they would be better off for it. To feed, clothe, and educate the children of "independent" parents is "a fit of presumption. . . . It is an insult to offer it, which their avarice might temp them to accept."[68] Only orphans and the truly poor should not be charged. When this dictate was implemented, school enrollment dropped to a critically low level, from a desired fifty or sixty pupils to about nine. People who could pay removed their children, while the poor were so "appallingly ignorant," they saw no use in schooling and questioned whether their children were wasting their time in school. These were discouraging moments that gave rise to the issue of whether the entire venture should be scrapped.

Although Maclure kept reassuring Madame that he had complete faith in her, a critical note crept into his letters. His letters now included "you should have . . ." or "had you paid the least attention to my letters, you must have seen that . . ." or "I hope you have not been so negligent in following my directions as you have been in informing me of what you have done . . ."[69] Remarks such as these from her "only friend" pained this overworked woman, who was "surrounded by enemies," and her responses were touching. She cried, "You wrong me," and she begged him to come home to see for himself what was going on, to take charge, and show her how to do things correctly. Humbling herself, she said, she was doing her best, and if he wanted to remove her, she would still be grateful for all he had done for her.

But accusations that she was "a bad correspondent" who gave "little satisfaction" were not easily forgotten, although she kept addressing him as "my dear friend," declaring that she was passionately devoted to him. She ended one letter with: "I am so much yours that any thing which concerns you seems to be my own concern. I need not say that I am affectionately."[70] Madame, a fortress in defense of Maclure's interests, revealed in her letters an amalgam of love, defiance, and abject obedience. She was often unable to sleep, was plagued by headaches, gained weight, and was beginning to feel middle-aged, but she persevered because she believed that all misunderstandings would be swept away when her hero returned. Could this precarious situation continue for long?

The fortunes of New Harmony, or at least Madame's perception of them, seemed to shift—rising and falling, and rising again. But in the outside world, the pervading opinion was that it was an abysmal failure. By December 1830, Maclure's letters took on a more kindly tone, and Madame, the Says, and Anna Maclure were living together harmoniously. Madame was pleased with the press, which kept students so busy that they had little time for lessons. Say's classic work, *American Conchology*, appeared; Michaux's *Sylva* and Lesueur's work were being readied, and prospects were good that *Condillac's Logic*, two books by Neef, and Maclure's *Geological Observations* and his *Opinions* would soon go into production. It would appear that Maclure's strategy for the diffusion of knowledge through inexpensive books was achieving some success, but against all reason he continued to emphasize the role of the *Disseminator* in his plan. The journal was important to him because he felt that this voice from New Harmony and Wright's *Free Enquirer* were the rare, if not the only, progressive voices in America. The small circulation of the *Disseminator* was troubling, but Madame reassured Maclure that it was read by many of her pupils.[71]

Perhaps the main reason for the general lack of interest was that the articles were too dense and unrelentingly strident, tiring readers and eventually boring them. Maclure was beginning to believe that despite his attempt to simplify articles in the *Disseminator*, they were "too far above the comprehension of the workers,"[72] and he was losing "trust in the worker," an admission that his hope for the reorganization of society might not be realized. Yet there was the occasional heartening event, such as the uprising of the Spanish against King Ferdinand VII. A liberal government might soon be in power that would enable Maclure to reacquire his confiscated properties and continue with his plan for an "orphan school of industry" in Spain. He had already communicated with some English teachers with an interest in the project. Alas, within a few months his hope was again shattered when Spanish liberals met with defeat, and despotic forces regained control of the nation.

✳

SEVENTEEN

Crippling Losses of Madame Fretageot and Thomas Say

To the casual eye, New Harmony appeared serene, a small town in a charming pastoral setting on the Wabash River, its remarkable inhabitants busying themselves with various crafts, farming, teaching, publishing, and studying nature. But New Harmony's reputation was tarnished, a failure founded on visionary notions, and almost destroyed by incompetent practice. New Harmony had been denounced as a hotbed of sin and socialism and as a threat to Christianity, morality, and American capitalism.

Closer inspection reveals a town filled with rather unhappy people who were recuperating from the pandemonium of recurrent crises, trapped in a venture that had failed to realize its utopian aims and, even now, struggling to support itself. The rhetoric ended, an important segment of the town was managed in the name of its absentee owner, William Maclure, who gave the town purpose and financial support. For whatever reasons, he refused to return from Mexico to resolve the many conflicts that beset the community, and so a malaise weighed heavily on the community. By 1831, when Robert Dale Owen returned to New Harmony to join his youngest brother, Richard, the town itself had taken on a sad, shabby appearance.

As the great and small problems within New Harmony multiplied, Maclure's manager, Madame Fretageot, was tested beyond endurance, and by November of 1831 she had decided to leave—for a period of time.[1] She had not fully recovered from a recent illness lasting two months in which she was delirious with fever. Even Say, a tender reed ("as timorous as a mouse"), under the influence of his wife, Lucy, who was at odds with Madame at the time, had not been helpful, nor had Say been attentive to the business of the town; as Madame wrote, they "wished her dead."

Thoroughly depressed and aggravated by an unreliable communication with Maclure (due to tampering of the mail by the local assistant postmaster),[2] she precipitately informed Maclure that she was returning to France, leaving Say in charge. Like everyone else, she admired Say, and she assured Maclure that he could take over from her, but in fact she knew he was neither able nor willing to manage this kind of enterprise. Madame was fleeing from an intolerable situation, but the professed reason for her departure was that she was returning to France to claim a modest legacy of 800 francs per year, left to her by a friend, a claim that had to be made in person. Another matter compelled her to visit France: she wanted to make suitable arrangements for her ailing husband with money inherited from her father. Surprisingly, her letter to Maclure was cordial, businesslike, without reproach or recrimination, and in return his letters continued as if nothing unusual had happened—she was merely taking a short, well-deserved vacation. Indeed, except for an increasingly tender appreciation of her in his letters, there seemed to be no discernable change in the temper of their communications. They were soul mates. Later from Paris, in high spirits, she wrote "My dear friend, I am yours until my last . . . your affectionate . . ."

Madame was soon in Philadelphia on her way to Paris, surprised and heartened by the love and high esteem of her former Philadelphia students (now young women), and in this environment, where she was fussed over and every need was taken care of, her health improved. With increased energy, her thoughts turned to New Harmony and its needs. More than anyone, she knew what was lacking, and so she began purchasing various goods for the store and items requested by Say.[3]

By Christmas she was in Paris, warmly greeted and enjoying the food and the society. She was taken up by her old friends Mesdames Couture and d'Aubigny, solid people of wealth and breeding. No doubt they were fascinated by Madame's adventurous life in the wilderness of the American frontier, surely the stuff of Romance in the age of Chateaubriand, but in fact they were the very people who roused the suspicions of Maclure.[4] Madame Couture insisted that Madame Fretageot live in her home, and from time to time she vacationed at their country estate in Normandy. Joining the circle was another good friend, M. Zédé, who had a particular interest in Madame's son, Achille Fretageot, because he was probably the boy's biological father.[5] All insisted that Achille should live in France for a few years, while Maclure, a surrogate father, generous with advice, had plans to have Achille learn the printing trade and the Spanish language and become his secretary in Mexico, where he could edit liberal Spanish publications.[6] Whatever happened, Madame wanted her son to be looked after—preferably to be adopted by Maclure.

Madame Fretageot was thriving. She slept well, lost excess weight, no longer suffered from periodic fevers, and felt years younger. With characteristic energy she looked after her affairs and wrote long, thoughtful, well-informed letters about social and political conditions in France, her comments reflecting those of an American observer. Both she and Maclure felt that an American kind of democracy in France was not feasible at the time because of the overwhelming corruption and the "ignorance" and lack of "sense" of the French people; anarchy would ensue if they attempted to establish a republican form of government. Not being "wise enough," the French required a "strong ruler."[7]

Madame arranged for her invalid husband, Joseph, to live and work comfortably in a hospital, and she bought a small house for him when he was well enough to leave the hospital. The money she had inherited was transferred to him, sufficient for the remainder of his life.[8] Through her friend Lafayette she learned that Frances Wright was living in Paris, and upon visiting her, she was appalled to find that as the abused wife of the detested William Phiquepal, she was worn out caring for their infant in what seemed to be a tawdry garret. Madame was shocked at how Phiquepal had wrung the life out of this vital, free woman. Probably, embarrassed by being found in such a compromised state, an exhausted Wright received her friend coldly.

Under Maclure's guidance, Madame purchased supplies, books, and journals requested by Say, to be sent to New Harmony, and she sent a truss, syringes, books (secondhand if possible), and newspapers to Mexico. He also wanted her to distribute copies of his *Opinions* to friends and seek out recruits for New Harmony—students, teachers, bookbinders, and farmers. He was enthusiastic about producing mother-of-pearl buttons from the abundant shells found around New Harmony, and he urged her to find craftsmen capable of working the material. Silk producers in Lyon had fallen on hard times, prompting Madame to suggest that silk workers be enticed to New Harmony where mulberry trees could be grown. But Maclure disparaged the idea. In case Madame might enjoy Paris too much, he kept her busy, but he provided all the money she needed and kept reminding her that her rightful place was in New Harmony where she was needed. She did not need much convincing.

Maclure was not optimistic about New Harmony ever being self-sustaining, let alone profitable in the long run, and since its social promise was flagging, he was not unreceptive to ridding himself of this burden and trying his luck elsewhere.[9] According to Madame, recent enrollment in the New Harmony school was so low that she could not see it continuing in its present state, not only burdened by the legacy of Owen but also the victim of Owen's constant barrage of disparaging criticism about education at New Harmony. Such publicity discouraged parents from enrolling their children in Maclure's school. On several occasions Madame and Maclure discussed the possibility of selling his interest in New Harmony outright to a Count de Leon, a German mystic of questionable history (Bernhard Muller, also called Archduke Maximilian of the Stem of Judah) who had plans to establish a religious commune. Fortunately, nothing ever came of it, for the "count" turned out to be a fraud.[10]

It was apparent that by 1832–33 Maclure's energy was declining, and his interest was faltering. Surely the inadequacy of his control over such a complex enterprise through less than ideal intermediaries was becoming apparent to him. While remote control may have been acceptable in business, where the dealings, the incentive, and the criterion of success were relatively simple—profit and loss in numerical terms—the complex operation of a commune, peopled by individuals with different motivations and temperaments, required a firm hand and a watchful presence.

To add to Maclure's discouragement, Mexico and the various republics of South America were increasingly besieged by the forces of reaction. Clutching at straws, Maclure felt the situation was not nearly as hopeless as in France and Spain, for as he claimed, more progress had been made in the Americas in 10 years than in 1,000 years in Europe. To his dismay, civil war had erupted in Mexico between state and federal authorities, both "sinks of corruption" run by the "consuming class" and increasingly controlled by the military and the Catholic Church.[11]

World-weary and disillusioned with humankind, his thoughts turned increasingly to science and natural history, which yield to observation and rational analysis, and he recommended greater emphasis at New Harmony on "exploring, collecting, and explaining the natural productions." In a letter to Madame, he said of her, "Your maxim is 'the noblest study of mankind is man.' I begin to think it is like many other of the nobles, not the most profitable, and so full of crosses and dissapointments as to afford poor amusement. Civilization, as far as it has yet gone is a state out of nature, of artifice, pretensions, and hypocracy."[12]

In the spring of 1832, a deadly outbreak of cholera occurred in Europe. Paris was brought to a standstill as people of every class died, including Madame Couture's daughter and some friends of Madame Fretageot. They fled to Madame d'Aubigny's estate in Caen, Normandy, only to find that cholera had spread to that area, and so they returned to Paris, where there was greater medical help. The epidemic had apparently begun in the East Indies and had now reached Europe, where Madame reported there were 1,800 to 2,000 deaths per day in Paris alone, and by the summer of 1832, the disease had spread to New York and Philadelphia. On April 22, Madame wrote to Maclure telling him that she had come down with cholera and that Madame Couture was nursing her back to health.[13]

By fall, 1832, Madame's business in Paris was concluded, and prodded by Maclure, she prepared to return to New Harmony. Maclure complained that since she had left New Harmony, he hardly knew what was going on there; her place was in New Harmony managing its affairs. She had been too long with her aristocratic friends in Paris and was beginning to be influenced by them, but in the end he admitted that her "spirit of activity and independence would not brook long that idle, trivial, and uncertain life of the rich." Madame was pleased with Maclure's request and would comply.

Despite the irritations and hostilities of the past, soon after Madame's departure, her absence from New Harmony had been acutely felt, and everyone quickly realized how indispensible she was; they were eager, perhaps desperate, for her return. In a letter to Maclure, Say and Alexander Maclure freely admitted all this, and Say sent Madame a letter affirming that she was indispensible; all recriminations, bitter and trivial, were forgotten.[14] Alexander wrote his brother that Achille Fretageot was in charge of Madame's store while she was away but was managing it badly; debts were not being collected, and losses were mounting.[15]

In his letters, Maclure's mood was increasingly dark. Violent clashes between groups, many renegade, were now the dominating characteristic of Mexican politics. Constitutional government could hardly survive such turmoil; social and political reform was virtually impossible, and the establishment of good schools was a hopeless task. At this point, Maclure seemed convinced that there was sufficient reason to return to New Harmony, for he could see new opportunities there. Perhaps if he returned, he could realize his plans for education through schools and appropriate publications, with the participation of the Owens. He received a long, chatty letter filled with discussion about Pestalozzian education from Joseph Neef and his wife ("my old rib"), both of whom returned to New Harmony in 1834 to teach.[16] Encouraged, Maclure cautiously suggested that the New Harmony school might be enlarged and publication of the *Free Inquirer* recommenced. In this time of heightened expectations at New Harmony, Maclure began planning his departure from Mexico, prompted by his vulnerability to swindlers lusting after his considerable wealth. As a foreigner, he felt threatened by shady lawyers and a corrupt judiciary, prevalent in Mexico.[17]

Madame sailed from Le Havre on December 31, 1832, and arrived in good health one and a half months later at Vera Cruz. Rather than sail directly for New York or Philadelphia as was expected, she chose a southern route to Mexico to visit Maclure, ostensibly to discuss with him complicated matters of business and family. Maclure must have been surprised when without warning, he received a note informing him of Madame's arrival in Mexico, and within a few days, a letter arrived from Madame herself, dated February 17, 1833, from Vera Cruz, almost at his doorstep. This was an impulsive but calculated action, although perhaps it was really not surprising considering her constant expressions of yearning for him; clearly, she wanted to be with him after a separation of four years. Maclure was not displeased because, by chance, her arrival coincided with his decision to leave Mexico. She was "in good time to convey an old man to New Harmony."

In Madame's absence from New Harmony, her unstable, disputatious brother Jean Duclos sued her and Maclure because they had failed to prop-

erly educate his two sons in New Harmony schools, and in their absence
he seized the school furniture which he erroneously claimed was owned
by his sister. Her crazed brother was also writing an insulting biography of
Madame to humiliate her.[18] Maclure wished to attend the trial that would
soon be coming up, for he thought, Jean Duclos was a "maniac" who would
lose the case trumped up by lawyers and be jailed by them for not being
able to pay court costs. In New Harmony, a disconcerted Thomas Say did
his best to handle the matter, and he was able to hold off the seizure of
furniture by the sheriff by posting a personal bond. He begged Madame to
return and suggested that perhaps Duclos should be paid off to bring the
affair to an end.[19] The fact that William Owen, serving as Duclos's lawyer,
seemed to take such great delight in this affair suggests that the old antagonism between the Owen and Maclure camps was still very much alive.

Despite the many good reasons for returning to New Harmony without delay, Maclure and Madame lingered in Mexico to enjoy the beauty
and the balmy weather. Madame wrote to a friend that they planned to
stay for a year. Her son was to join them and would then proceed to France
after they left Mexico.[20] Almost nothing is known of this sojourn, but one
would like to think of it as an idyll, an escape from their frustrations and
entanglements, where they could leisurely consider Maclure's ideas about
the "diffusion and equalization of knowledge," and how these could be
brought to fruition. It is not possible to say whether they were lovers, but
most probably it was the happiest time of their lives.

Alas, all this was prelude to the sudden and tragic end of Marie Fretageot, for six months after her arrival, she contracted cholera and died on
August 24, 1833. A thirteen-year relationship had ended abruptly, leaving
Maclure in a state of despair for his terrible loss, the greatest he had ever
known. Having lived seven decades, he was conscious of his declining
vigor, and he had looked upon his devoted companion as his "moral and
physical nurse." He let his feelings be known to those of his friends whom
he trusted and who would understand his relationship with her. One correspondent, Alexander Greaves, a teacher of Spanish who had lived in
Maclure's house, comforted Maclure on his great loss with kind words that
had actually originated with Maclure: "She was a cheerful companion, attentive nurse, kind friend, and disinterested manager, all in one person."[21]
Greaves also commiserated that Maclure had been suddenly deprived of
"renewed comforts."

The sudden and unexpected death of Madame was painful to many (but not all) of her colleagues. Her selfless life had been a "useful" one, but one senses that it was a life of sacrifice to please Maclure. It distressed Maclure that Madame was often unpopular in New Harmony and had aroused hostility in others who were jealous of her privileged relationship with him while doing his work. George Ord of the ANSP, no friend of Maclure's, upon hearing of Madame's death, commented that she had been a "brazen strumpet who played the part of a mistress to the community, and who ruled the chiefs with a rod of iron."[22] But Maclure defended her vigorously, rebutting her detractors, refusing to write to his sister Anna, who had "calumniated the person of all others I esteemed and confided in."[23]

After this catastrophe, there was no one left at New Harmony who could be relied upon to operate Maclure's schools, and for the time being Pestalozzian education in Indiana, which Madame had set on course, came to an end without her further direction. It was a system that had been transplanted, but never fully Americanized, and so this highly praised effort faded away, leaving no trained teachers or influence. However, in the coming years, progressive education along Pestalozzian lines was established by A. Bronson Alcott in Boston, and after the Civil War, a new generation of progressive educators, strongly influenced by Pestalozzi (Henry Barnard, Horace Mann, Thomas Gallaudet, Lowell Mason, and Emma Willard) founded schools to which they brought real and permanent reform to American education.[24]

Maclure, crushed, decided to remain in Mexico, knowing that without Madame, all hope for the success of his schemes in New Harmony was gone. Unrealistically, he entertained the thought that soon Achille would become his agent, as reliable and dedicated as his mother had been. Maclure planned to bring him to Mexico just as he would a son, and in return Achille would become a companion and an assistant.[25]

With his heavy sense of responsibility and loyalty to Maclure, Say was incapable of deserting him, especially after the death of Madame Fretageot. Passionately devoted to natural history and the collecting of specimens, he had looked forward to the relief that would follow Madame's return, but with her death, he was devastated, trapped in New Harmony, incapable of handling its business matters and printing establishment—at the expense of his true calling. He remained, despite the advice and encouragement of others, including his wife, that he return to the East,[26] and members of the Academy of Natural Sciences of Philadelphia, who insisted that he stop wasting his time in the wilderness. Say had even less time now for his work, which had suffered from his separation from a major scientific center with its libraries and knowledgeable professionals. Yet despite this, his achievement is impressive, attesting to his brilliance.

Management of Maclure's interests in New Harmony fell hard on an ailing Say, but even a healthy Say was no Madame Fretageot, and Maclure's enterprise continued its decline, faltering in its educational efforts. When David Dale Owen returned to settle in New Harmony, he noted that the place was drab, without spirit, and in a state of disrepair. It had no economic base, for the farmers in the region were bringing their produce to other towns in the region, including Mount Vernon and Evansville.

In October 1834, one year after Madame's death, Alexander informed Maclure that Thomas Say, "our good and valued friend," had died.[27] Most probably he was suffering from chronic disease of the gallbladder when there was little to be done for it and surgery of the gallbladder was fearful, if not impossible. He seems to have suffered recurrent attacks of obstruction and inflammation of the biliary tract with dire effects on the liver.[28] An extremely frugal diet (probably inspired by Maclure), lack of sleep, and recurrent bouts of fever and dysentery had drained him. One cannot rule out malaria as a cause of death, which Say may have contracted on the Long expedition or in the environs of New Harmony.

Maclure was deeply moved by the loss of his dearest friend, and at his request Say was buried in a vault on the grounds of the imposing Rapp-Maclure home in which Say had lived for a time. A monument of pure white marble ("as befits his character") marked the gravesite which later held the remains of Maclure's brother and sisters. Thereafter, Maclure treated Lucy Say generously, with an allowance of $200 per year, and in his will he left her a Pennsylvania bond worth $5,000, yielding 5 percent interest.

George Ord, a Philadelphian in the hierarchy of the ANSP, resented Maclure's removal of the city's best naturalists to the West.[29] On several occasions Say had declined offers to leave Maclure for positions in Philadelphia and the East, a loyalty to Maclure that was repayment for Maclure's unstinting support over the years. The two men had great affection for each other and held similar liberal views on the methods and uses of education. Maclure's press had assured Say that his major works would be published. Madame also had the warmest feelings toward Say despite sharply differing attitudes toward science, money, and business.

It was now impossible for New Harmony to become a model for reform through education, and Maclure made no attempt to engage anyone upon whom he could depend. Just as Madame's death seemed to diminish his participation in education in New Harmony, Say's death signaled a waning of interest in the promotion of natural history. Without Say, he decided that his precious library of 2,000 books in New Harmony would be better used by members of the Academy of Natural Sciences in Philadelphia.

A member of the original *Boatload of Knowledge,* Charles-Alexandre Lesueur, remained, but he now faced the prospect of waning support, and after the death of his close friend Say, there was nothing left to retain Lesueur on the frontier. Because Maclure was not sympathetic to his demand for compensation for all the years he had spent in New Harmony, he left, embittered. After a stay in Paris, he returned to his hometown of Le Havre in 1845 as the curator of its Museum of Natural History, the repository of his numerous drawings and watercolors, an illuminating record of life on the *Boatload of Knowledge* and in New Harmony.

With Madame Fretageot and Say gone, Maclure's assets were now increasingly at the mercy of his brother Alexander and his sister Anna. He had no choice but to manage his affairs through them, but even Alexander's repeated mishandling did not goad Maclure into leaving Mexico. Their communications were filled with such matters as the repair of roofs and fences, the buying and selling of mortgages, and speculation on land around New Harmony ("the rage of the day"). To Anna, he sent advice about publishing, and he complained that he could not make heads or tails of her accounts.[30] There is nothing warm or personal in the messages, only bitter complaints about "the deplorable state of legislators and banks that have bought the country." In return, Alexander's contempt for William and his writings, and Anna's lack of sympathy for his views on religion and the state of society, were barely disguised. Clearly, Maclure's ability to manage his interests in New Harmony effectively became almost nonexistent.

EIGHTEEN

✳

New Harmony Adrift

Those who survived the storm that had beset New Harmony now lived together without the noxious discord of the recent past. The financial status of the commune, though not without worry, was no longer a source of conflict, nor were philosophic differences the fount of controversy. Alexander and Anna Maclure managed their brother's estate, which encompassed half the land and properties of New Harmony, while much of the remainder of the town centered around Robert Owen's sons and daughter, who in return for a much-needed 300 pounds per year had been given in trust the title to their father's remaining possessions in New Harmony.[1] In the pursuit of their various careers, Owen's sons spent years away from New Harmony, coming and going, but by the mid-1830s, now American citizens, they were all located in Indiana, as was their sister, Jane Dale Owen.[2] Robert Dale Owen, the eldest, assumed a leadership role in the community, while his brother William, who died young in 1842, was more concerned with commerce.

The year 1837 saw a triple wedding, in which William Owen married the daughter of a former member of the Preliminary Committee, and David Dale and Richard Owen, the two younger brothers, married the daughters of Joseph Neef, the crusty Pestalozzian teacher whom Maclure had brought to America and New Harmony. Neef had left the commune bitterly critical of Robert Owen, who now became family. Neef and his wife, Eloisa, were induced to return, and they ended their days in New Harmony as teachers. The town seemed to exert an attraction for those who had attended its schools, for many of Phiquepal's former students, including Achille Fretageot, chose to settle in New Harmony, and a few of the original inhabitants from the *Boatload of Knowledge* still remained. By choice or by chance, the remarkable Owens seemed to create unusual situations for themselves. A closely knit family, at one time all five Owens with their spouses and children lived in a single dwelling in New Harmony. Evenings were filled with discussion, readings, amateur theatricals, and musicales, for there were several pianists among them, and William played the violin, Richard the cello, and Jane the harp.

With visions of reform all but gone, Maclure's siblings tended to his interests in New Harmony, and to their credit they were always generous in making their brother's library and collections available for instruction and scholarship. Maclure's contributions to the community now lay in the support of studies in geology and natural history, an excellent library (despite the removal of some of its most precious books to the ANSP) that was open to all, and a publishing house. Although Maclure was the major proprietor of New Harmony, his influence was weakened from remote Mexico. Anna and Alexander Maclure were not effective administrators, and they certainly were no match for the dynamic, entrepreneurial Robert Dale Owen, who increasingly set the Owen stamp on New Harmony. The Owens dominated the life of the community, creating its sociable environment and giving it its flavor. Robert Dale's hope was to create a lively center of culture and learning on the Wabash River, promoting lectures and public entertainments under the aegis of the New Harmony Institute, a new lyceum which met in a building provided by the Owens—shades of the father—but unlike earlier days, no burning social and political agenda lit up the assembly.[3] Robert Dale penned articles for the *Free Enquirer* and the *Disseminator of Useful Knowledge*, which were avidly read in local circles and which imparted a welcomed sense of unity and identity to the community. The *Disseminator* also featured interesting articles for the young, scientific papers, and essays and letters by Maclure that acquired a new life when they were republished in his three-volume work, *Opinions.*

Maclure stated many times that adults had been corrupted by their life experiences and that changing the thinking of adults was almost impossible. Still, he wanted to provide these lost souls with enlightening publications at a price they could afford—a penny press, as it existed in England. Maclure was greatly pleased when Madame produced and sold a pamphlet on temperance for a quarter of the usual price. However, the New Harmony Press, reflecting the values of Say, Lesueur, and Troost, became less the flaming voice of reform directed toward the education of the masses and more the publisher of books and monographs of a scientific nature. The output of Maclure's press was remarkable, even after his death, for it produced several seminal classics and made a significant contribution to American natural history.[4] Using F. A. Michaux's exquisite copperplate engravings, which Maclure had purchased in France, Michaux's *North American Sylva* was produced by an expert English printer and New Harmony resident, William Amphlett. Among many publications, Say produced his classics, *American Conchology* and *American Entomology.* Several other monographs were published by Lesueur (*American Ichthyology*), David Dale Owen, and Alexander Maclure (*Code Napoléon*), as well as acknowledged classics such as *Aesop's Fables* and Benjamin Franklin's *Way to Wealth.* That all this enlightenment emanated from a small town in the wilds of America is truly remarkable, and it would not have happened without Maclure's vision and drive. Maclure provided the necessary financial backing, but his efforts to sell and distribute publications remained hopelessly limited (from roving carts or at book fairs).[5]

While Maclure was always concerned with the "diffusion of knowledge" to benefit the workingman and the poor, he made no allowances for their ability to understand what he wrote. He was aware of the fact, but because he was utterly convinced of the correctness of his views (which ultimately would prevail), he was not concerned that the books and articles he was publishing really targeted an affluent, middle-class audience who were not in sympathy with his social, economic, and religious views. Deemed by an ill-disposed critic as "utopian, childish, foolish," in fact, they were far too weighty and analytic for the workingman, and they were too radical, repetitive, and haranguing for the educated. On several occasions he shrugged off the lack of popularity (and sales) of his works, remarking that he was not surprised by the rejection, for his message was one of harsh truth, and it was not pleasant.

Through Robert Dale Owen's leadership from 1834 on, the overwhelming task of maintaining the town in good repair was only moderately successful. Roads were improved, gardens were created, and buildings were painted, but to one newcomer, New Harmony in 1839 was a sorry place. Insufficient care had been taken of buildings, so the town had "rather a ruinous than an improving appearance." Although some residents were of a "better class," living in presentable homes, there still remained too many of the "dregs" without a commitment to the community. They did not take proper care of their houses, and their children were delinquent in behavior. The great hall, which housed two schools, a theater, and the Mechanics' Institute, where lectures were held, lay almost in ruins. The schools and their teachers were inadequate, so New Harmony was judged by one observer to be an "entirely unfit place for a growing and cultivated young family."[6]

The ambitious plans of Robert Dale Owen to make New Harmony an industrial and agricultural educational center by establishing a manual labor college collapsed, as had a Pestalozzian school system for children (after the deaths of Madame Fretageot and Say). In their ambitious attempt to establish a regional college, the Owens donated land and appealed to Maclure and the state government for support. While the state legislature granted the Owens a charter, it did little else, and there was almost no public interest in the project. An increasingly cautious Maclure was wary of spending money on a new venture that he deemed to be without reliable management (despite the urging of his brother Alexander), and so the project withered.

In his plan to attract lively intellects to New Harmony, Robert Dale Owen tried to bring Frances Wright, a star attraction, and her husband, William Phiquepal, from Paris, but they declined the offer to resettle. Instead, the Owens were shocked when Phiquepal, handling Wright's financial affairs, demanded the immediate repayment of $10,000 that the Owens had borrowed from Frances when they were in desperate need of money. A settlement was made after Phiquepal threatened to take William and Robert Dale to court, in which the brothers agreed to pay off the debt over fifteen years at a high rate of interest—an unpleasant arrangement that elicited hard feelings. This debt, and the obligation to pay their father, Robert Owen, 300 pounds per year, became an almost unbearable burden that forced Robert Dale to speculate on land and to enter into various dubious business arrangements, such as raising horses and establishing a general store. All these ventures were unsuccessful, if not disastrous. Rents on their lands were inadequate for economic survival, and William's trading in commodities also met with great difficulties. None of the Owens seemed suited for this kind of activity: not only did they lack talent for business, they were simply unlucky.

Robert Dale Owen and his fellow townspeople soon learned that, without political influence, a small, isolated community such as New Harmony missed out on lucrative government contracts. Favorable decisions could only come about if citizens of New Harmony and surrounding Posey County were represented politically, when public work projects were being approved or delayed. To ensure that they would get their fair share, Robert Dale entered the political arena in 1836 and was elected a Democratic representative of Posey County in the Indiana legislature at Indianapolis. He remained there until 1842, when he went to Washington as a congressman in the House of Representatives until 1853. In the 1850s, he helped write the constitution of Indiana and the laws establishing public schools and township libraries, in the spirit of his father and of Maclure. As a legislator who faithfully tended to the interests of his community, he was a tireless and effective politician. But to the dismay of the colleagues of his early years, especially Frances Wright, he was now a cautious soul, no longer the radical reformer they once knew. Owen opposed the abolitionists before the Civil War, reflecting the sentiments of his constituents, and he favored the annexation of Texas, a jingoist, expansionist act that led to war with Mexico. To his credit, however, during the Civil War he was a strong supporter of Lincoln and advocated the freeing of slaves even before the Emancipation Proclamation. Following his second term in Congress, Robert Dale became a diplomat posted to Naples, and after returning to New Harmony from his European venture, this former freethinker ended his days fervently religious, his faith linked to a lively interest in spiritualism to which he had been introduced in Naples.[7] Spiritualism seemed to run in the family, for his father, after leaving New Harmony, became a confirmed spiritualist while striving to make the world a better place. On the other hand, two of Robert's sons, David Dale and Richard, became scientists. They must have been pained and embarrassed that both their brother and father professed a belief in spiritualism, and one can only imagine the contempt Maclure would have expressed for these most unscientific beliefs.

David Dale Owen, the third son, had arrived at New Harmony from Europe in the spring of 1828, and over the summer months he probably had friendly contact with Maclure, despite the hostility between this master geologist and David Dale's father. It was only at this time that they could have met, because that autumn Maclure departed for Mexico, never to return. David Dale was drawn to Maclure's collections of rocks, minerals, stuffed animals, and precious scientific instruments, all of which were made freely available by Maclure. Pursuing a career in chemistry and geology, David Dale prepared himself by attending the University of London, and to broaden his education he proceeded to a degree in medicine at the Ohio Medical College in Cincinnati. He had no intention of practicing medicine, but intensive study of human anatomy, a major part of the curriculum, would be indispensible, he reasoned, for paleontological studies. During these years he classified and arranged Maclure's collection of minerals and rocks, and he set up a laboratory, his first in the old "granary" provided by the Maclures, and later, in a new, castlelike structure he built nearby. Returning from Cincinnati, he pursued his interest in geology and paleontology, particularly their practical and "useful" aspects, to become the foremost American authority on midwestern geology. A strong advocate of geological study, he summarized his thinking in a series of reports on his geological surveys of the Midwest.

Following the example of Maclure two decades earlier, he completed a geological survey of the region as state geologist of Indiana, and under the auspices of the U.S. General Land Office, he headed a team of surveyors that covered Wisconsin, Iowa, Minnesota, and Nebraska, gathering reliable information for the government upon which it could make intelligent policy decisions pertaining to the sale of public lands for agriculture and mining at a time of vigorous westward expansion. Based on this model, the U.S. Geological Survey was born, with its headquarters in New Harmony, until it was removed to the Smithsonian Institution in Washington, which was established in no small measure through the efforts of Robert Dale and David Dale Owen.[8] They transferred a large part of Maclure's collections there.[9] With David Dale as head of the Survey, working with Robert Dale, who was an influential politician in Indianapolis and Washington, opportunities were created for this small community in Posey County. New Harmony became a major site for American geology in the 1840s and 1850s. Having become successful and a leading citizen of New Harmony, David Dale bought Maclure's grand home (formerly George Rapp's) from Anna and Alexander Maclure.

He was assisted by the youngest Owen, Richard, an officer in the Mexican and Civil wars, who was also trained as a doctor and a geologist. He later became the official geologist of Indiana, professor of natural history at Indiana University in Bloomington, and the first president of Purdue University. All these achievements were the consequences of what Maclure had set in motion.

As a center of geological study, New Harmony became the thriving town Maclure had envisioned—a secular, businesslike, self-sustaining community filled with scientists and other workers. This was the kind of community that could seed the nation with enlightened, "useful" citizens, molded by a system of progressive education in a setting where science and nature were cherished. In reality, after 1834, with the deaths of Madame Fretageot and Say, the education of New Harmony youth became rather conventional, without any defining philosophy. The reform of education to achieve specific social ends, as in the days of Maclure and Robert Owen, had come to an end. For many years, while Maclure's town of New Harmony was steeped in the lore of geology and paleontology, its children were fascinated by unearthed wonders such as a fossil brachiopod *Chonetes maclurea,* named in honor of the late William Maclure. These were happy days, as remembered by former pupils.

Unfortunately, New Harmony was far removed from the great centers of population and was difficult to reach. After the transfer of the Geological Survey to Washington, and without special financial backing, the town operated at a subsistence level. Inevitably its influence waned, its great collections were lost to the museums of large cities, and it ceased attracting naturalists and scientists. New Harmony settled down to the quiet life of a small, sleepy midwestern town.

During the 1830s Maclure kept informing Samuel George Morton, corresponding secretary of the Academy of Natural Science of Philadelphia, of his plan to leave almost everything to the Academy.[10] As a generous patron of an institution that expected a windfall when Maclure died, Morton kept him fully informed of Academy affairs. It so happened that Maclure's friend and agent in Vera Cruz, Dr. Marmaduke Burrough, who tended his business affairs, was in correspondence with Morton, so Morton knew precisely how Maclure was faring and his concerns about the disposal of his estate after his death. The two men tried to assuage Maclure's anxieties as they listened with sympathy to laments about his health, aging, greedy lawyers, failure of his schools, the lack of sales of his books, and the deplorable state of Mexican politics.[11]

In the last decade of his life, Maclure gave the proceeds of a $5,000 mortgage with the accrued interest of five years to the Academy, $1,000 of which was to be set aside for the Academy press, and another $1,000 was to be sent to Benjamin Silliman, president of the American Geological Society in New Haven.[12] Maclure assured Morton that he would provide funds for the building of a new home for the Academy, although he felt that leasing an existing building was preferable because big cities like Philadelphia had no future and were dying, citing the fact that the rate of crime in cities was now alarming. When he was young, there was less crime in the entire Union in a year than there was presently in New York in a month. Accepting the inevitable, he urged that if there was to be a new building, fireproof materials were to be used and library shelving should be made of iron. When the Academy moved to new quarters at Broad and Sansom streets in 1836, he contributed $15,000 to the building fund—a munificent benefaction, despite his inability to understand the "frenzy" about new buildings.

Fifty boxes of mineral and geological specimens Maclure had collected in Europe and the United States were sent to the Academy and to a number of museums and geological societies, and he transferred the bulk of his precious library from New Harmony to the Academy.[13] As a result 70 percent of the Academy's considerable library, now one of the best in the country, was the gift of Maclure. The New Harmony library still had a considerable number of Maclure's books and stood to gain support from his legacy.

Maclure's earthly possessions in New Harmony and the surrounding counties were valued at $44,600 in real property, $36,600 in personal property, and a library worth $30,000.[14] He also owned 10,000 acres of land near Alicante, three convents, his house, and various properties in Spain whose worth he estimated at $200,000. Unfortunately, all this had been confiscated by those who had overthrown the legitimate Spanish government, and the matter was at present under litigation.[15] Operating through agents in the Spanish court, Maclure had some hope of regaining his property if a democratic government was restored. Not surprisingly, the various estimates of his wealth differ from one another, even as determined by Maclure himself, being in many forms (properties, buildings, investments, debts, bonds, mortgages, etc.), with a variety of possessions in New Harmony, Great Britain, France, Illinois, Virginia, and Pennsylvania. Among other estimates, at one point he declared that he had lost $60,000 in Spain and had $90,000 "sunk in an unproductive property at New Harmony in consequence of attempting to aid Mr. Owen."[16]

During his last years in Mexico, Maclure's insecurity about the fate of his estate and his disgust with lawyers were apparent in the frequent changes he made in his will and in the people who were entrusted to stand guard over its provisions. He was most anxious that after his death, his fortune was to be used largely for the education of children of poor and working people. He was well aware of how the terms of the Stephen Girard Trust in Philadelphia had been disregarded and how lawyers and clergy "switched the funds from the poor to the rich."[17] In contrast to medical doctors and priests, who could be avoided by simply not consulting them, "lawyers, armed with authority, [can] interfere with your affairs at the instigation of any one that chooses to sue you . . . clothing falsehoods with all the reverence and dignity that can be attached to the forms of law and justice."[18] He wrote of an experience that could have come from Charles Dickens's *Bleak House,* in which legal haggling over the disposition of an estate went on for so long that by the time of its settlement, its value was negligible—frittered away in legal fees. In Maclure's case, his attempt to foreclose on a $5,000 mortgage on a Virginia property resulted in costly litigation that lasted fifteen years, with his lawyer charging $150 per year.[19]

Maclure's first will, which dates from 1827, bequeathed $1,000 per year to his sister Anna and to Madame, and $600 annually to Alexander, Margaret, and John. His property, real and personal, was to be used by members of his family as long as they lived, and then it would revert to the estate. The revenue of the property was to be administered by Madame Fretageot to support an orphans school of industry and any other school she might see fit to establish.

Maclure was convinced that the terms of wills entrusted to males were invariably perverted, and so he chose females—Madame Fretageot and Frances Wright—as "lawful trustees and executrices," who he believed would be "faithful" to the provisions he set forth. They were given the authority to appoint other trustees. His decision to use women trustees was also based on his belief that by their nature, women were more committed to the Pestalozzian education of children than were men, that they were better teachers, and that they were more sympathetic to the education of women. But Frances Wright left New Harmony to marry the detested William Phiquepal, and so she was removed as a trustee. Maclure then gave Madame Fretageot the major responsibility for overseeing the execution of his will, fully confident that she would be able to withstand the demands of his siblings.[20] A statement was added by Maclure that in any dispute, an independent "umpire" would make a final judgment on specific challenges. Anyone "not conforming with such decision, [would] cease to receive any benefit from this last Will and testament," clearly a pointed warning to his siblings, who had been bequeathed an adequate annual stipend but still had other ideas about how to spend their brother's money. Unfortunately, Maclure's plan was confounded by Madame's death in 1833.

A provision was made in Maclure's will for ridding the nation of slavery. One-third of the revenue of his land was to be used "for the purpose of establishing, maintaining, and supporting a colony of free colored People" on his land near New Harmony—presumably inspired by Frances Wright's Nashoba experiment. But little came of this proposal, just as it did in Nashoba, for want of suitable personnel, organization, and hands-on management. Maclure despised the institution of slavery. He referred to New Orleans as "that sink of corruption and slavery," and he was shocked by the violence of racial riots in South Baltimore and the "hatred aggravated by the existence of slavery." He warned that such violence and lawlessness, supported by aristocrats and the banks, could spread to the streets of Philadelphia, New York, and Boston.[21] Maclure wrote many articles about slavery, stressing the evil influence it had on the education of both black and white children, perpetuating the iniquity from one generation to the next. Since "children, as well as all other animals, commence their instruction the moment they begin to make use of their senses," children exposed to slavery mimic both "the high-handed violence" of the master and the "low, deceitful cunning" of the slave. Each kind of instructor sends the wrong message to the young so that the "imitative minds" of the progeny of master and slave are "corrupted and vitiated" by their experience.[22] Beyond the humanitarian aspect of slavery—its immorality and cruelty—was the fact that it was inefficient and economically wasteful.

Maclure had always believed that the major function of the Academy was to enlighten people and that its museum and library should be freely available to the public for the "diffusion of useful knowledge." But by the mid-1830s, the Academy, with its members from the Philadelphia establishment, was becoming an elitist research organization that charged admission fees and annual dues, which largely excluded the very people Maclure wanted to educate; the Academy was becoming "a monopoly to favor the rich."[23] Maclure also felt that too many members of the Academy were religious, which roused fears that his gifts would be used for ends that he could not abide. Negotiations with the Academy to ensure that public education would be stressed, with ready access to all, proved discouraging. Members of the Academy were willing to compromise to a point, but after much deliberation, they decided that they were unwilling to alter its charter to turn it into an educational institution for the common man at the expense of its program of scholarly research. Maclure reluctantly withdrew his offer to leave almost his entire estate to the Academy, but as consolation he gave the Academy a generous $10,000 in addition to $15,000 for a building fund, and most of his library.[24] The latter action seems to have signified that there were some books that the workingman would never understand or appreciate.

By the time of his death in 1840, Maclure had made many revisions in his will. The final version was written in January 1839, with codicils added in September 1839 and in January 1840, two months before his death, all reflecting the fact that after 1827 much had changed—the death of trusted friends, the state of his affairs, and his anxious and depressed state of mind. With little faith in the reliability of potential trustees and administrators to carry out his wishes, Maclure was deeply troubled as he brooded far away in Mexico. To whom could he turn to administer his estate, and who should be the inheritor?

The final version of the will was vulnerable to mischief, and it proved disastrous despite its apparent straightforward nature.[25] In this version, in addition to each sibling's annuity, "the use and revenue of all his property, real and personal, was to be equally divided between his brother and two sisters during their lifetimes, and upon their deaths all moneys would be returned to the estate, which would then be dedicated to the establishment and support of libraries in working men's institutes.

Surprisingly, in early 1840, the three trustees of the will, George W. Erving, John Wilbanks, and John Speakman, all old, reliable friends of Maclure who could be depended upon to insist that the terms of the will be honored, were dismissed. According to Maclure, even they could not be trusted, for they were too identified with the Academy, and so an ailing, paranoid Maclure in faraway Mexico, with too much time to brood, made the radical move of removing the three, lest his entire fortune end up at the Academy, despite all his specifically designated preferences.

He seemed to reason that little damage could be done because the will was now unambiguous regarding the way the money was to be used and that his siblings would behave reasonably and ethically. His decision is surprising, for he had on many occasions declared that his siblings were incompetent and selfish and could not be relied upon to carry out his plans, with which they had little sympathy. They did not approve of their brother's interest in social and educational reform, and he knew it.[26] Yet he went ahead, removing known, trustworthy guardians who could be relied upon to supervise known, unreliable agents. This was a desperate change in course by a man with faltering judgment.

Despondent and brooding, Maclure wrote from Mexico: "I have ceased all gratification from the physical appetites, all my pleasures, [and] pastimes." His aim was "to have as many friends and as few enemies as possible" and "to do as much good and as little harm as possible." Beset by his own "self-conceit and vanity" and "ego," he was given to beating his breast and embracing the values of the ascetic. He could not spend money on himself, and his threadbare diet was as severe as ever. In effect he was a poor man with money. Conditions were so uncertain that uncharacteristically he was close to admitting defeat, confessing that his hope of reforming schools was too great a task for one man, and he even concluded that a penny press in Philadelphia for the diffusion of "useful" knowledge was not feasible at the present time.

As his energy and enthusiasm flagged in the last years of his life in Mexico, his openhanded philanthropic spirit declined. He was not receptive to requests by Robert Dale Owen to participate in admirable causes, such as support for the *New York Daily Sentinel*, a workingman's newspaper that was ailing financially. The *Sentinel* could have provided Maclure with an opportunity to have his voice heard across the nation.[27] Perhaps Maclure feared wide acclaim. As it was, the *Disseminator*, in which he did publish his essays, did not have wide readership and influence. Quite simply, he was deeply suspicious of new ventures and did not want to get involved with them. Sensing that everyone was after his money, he now replied to letters of request only after inordinate lengths of time (a message in itself), or he did not reply at all.

This not unjustified temper was perhaps reinforced by Robert Dale Owen's brash, insistent requests that Maclure provide many thousands of dollars for the *Sentinel's* survival. Owen's scarcely disguised message was that Owen knew better than Maclure what should be done with Maclure's money. His patronizing attitude is evident in a letter to Reuben Haines in which he writes, "The good old man's *money will be lost to society* if it remains as at present."[28] Maclure also declined Owen's suggestion that he take advantage of a golden opportunity to underwrite a new manual labor school in New Harmony. Similarly he rejected his brother Alexander's requests for loans to operate his businesses, which Maclure was certain would fail (they did).[29] He also turned down a dubious request by two former New Harmony students (one of whom was Madame Fretageot's son, Achille) that they be given land around New Harmony for farming. Maclure was now a cautious businessman, and if he was to make an investment, it had to be sound and as risk-free as possible.

Although at times his thinking seemed to be orderly and clear, deterioration is evident in his letters. While some of them dealt with business and educational matters in an appropriate manner, his handwriting, always bad, was becoming smaller and less legible, sometimes lacking punctuation and capitalization. In places, paragraphs run together, sentences tumble onto the page in an incoherent sequence, and at times he launches into oft-repeated rants (against the rich, priests, lawyers, cheating the poor, etc.) without preamble.[30] His regrettable grammar and spelling were worse than ever at a time when the rules were becoming standardized.

❋

NINETEEN

The Working Men's Institute and the Death of William Maclure

As early as 1828, the Society for Mutual Instruction, which Maclure had founded, met in one of the larger rooms in a major building in New Harmony. Coupled with the Society was a Mechanics' Atheneum, located in a nearby building that contained workshops with benches and tools for the training of carpenters, shoemakers, cabinet makers, and metal workers. The purpose of the Society, which was based on the English mechanics' institutes, so admired by Maclure, was to facilitate self-instruction, learning through experience, without dependency on professors or superiors, and "to communicate a general knowledge of the arts and sciences to those persons who hitherto have been excluded from a scientific or general education by the erroneous and narrow-minded policies of colleges and public schools, who have invariably endeavoured to confine learning to the *few* rich, so that they might tyrranize over the uneducated *many*."[1] However admirable the Society was in its intent, with Maclure in Mexico, it languished. But it came to life again in 1838 with the founding of the Working Men's Institute in New Harmony, where it exists to this day.[2]

The revival was initiated by Maclure himself, who was in contact with Achille Fretageot in New Harmony. He asked Achille to find out whether there were working-class people in New Harmony who would be willing to promote an institute as configured by Maclure. If such an institute could be founded, it would be endowed with a house, land, books, and supplies as long as the organization had at least thirty members and maintained a library of 100 volumes.[3] It was to be a model for all others he intended to establish in the United States, really the very first realistic proposal for a national library system. Eager to take advantage of Maclure's largesse, and knowing his views from his writings, a group of working men established a "Society for Mutual Instruction by Means of Reading, Lectures, Experiments, &c," fashioned a constitution, chose a president, secretary, and treasurer, and formed a Committee of Trustees and of Management to oversee education—all to be elected by secret ballot.[4] Anyone over eighteen years of age who had read the constitution and signed it was eligible. Persons of all religious denominations were eligible, and while members were expected to lecture or read to each other, religious instruction on the property was forbidden. Wives, children, and apprentices were invited to weekly meetings, as well as Alexander and Anna, who kept Maclure informed about how the organization was faring. In return, through them Maclure was able to have his opinions heard and his instructions followed. Maclure was careful to suggest that the committee should not make a big issue of religion or politics lest it detract from its primary aim of promoting education.[5] There was every hope that an act of incorporation of the Working Men's Institute by the Indiana legislature would be approved, since Robert Dale Owen was their state representative in Indianapolis.

The constitution, with its articles, sections, and bylaws, carefully crafted in every detail to please Maclure, was signed by twenty-six people and sent off to him for his approval, with the hope that he would become their generous patron. After four months they had heard nothing from Mexico, and so a second letter was sent seeking his advice on various matters. This message was filled with news about the progress being made, the growth of the library, and the strides being made in self-education. In keeping with Maclure's ideas about the ruin of minds by the bad education of the very young, efforts were being made to establish a "Juvenile library."

When he did reply, the response was favorable but guarded. The delay itself was uncharacteristic of him, perhaps due to illness. He seemed tired and reluctant to become involved in yet another costly scheme, which like so many others would probably fail. His hesitation is in fact surprising, because the New Harmony proposal was closely in line with his plans for the ultimate disposal of his fortune. Maclure permitted them to use one of his houses near the town's center, and there were others if they were needed. His collection of instruments and his remaining library of 1,800 books were made available for instruction, provided they were not abused by students. He was generous with advice, but for the present he would not promise an endowment, nor would he hand over his property outright to anyone. Fearing entrenchment of power and the patronage and corruption that follow prolonged authority by individuals, he advised that members should hold office for only one term at a time and that business transactions be open and known to all. From his earlier experience with Owen, he warned them against the indiscriminate admittance of members and the possibility of splintering into rival groups. He exhorted them to unite in their vote against the rich to be effective, and to this end he insisted that membership consist largely of laborers or farmers—those who work with their hands. They complied with his wish and sent him a complete list of members and their occupations. With his trusted Madame Fretageot and Benjamin Say gone, Maclure was cautiously placing his trust in the hands of "informed laborers" who truly worked for a living.

Members soon replied that they were grateful for the building, books, and instruments, and that the constitution had been amended to include all his suggestions. Currying favor and accommodating Maclure in every way, they reported that the Society was now truly democratic and functioning well. At the next meeting a member was to "give a discourse on the classification of animals, preparatory to something on Geology."[6] Maclure's next letter expressed approval of the progress made at New Harmony and suggested that if they needed help in establishing a warm and well-lit reading room, they should consult his brother and sister. Mention of the education of the very young prompted him to expound on the need to minimize the role of the parent and on the virtues of the Pestalozzian system of education and his role in its promotion. He encouraged them to try to set up such a school, implying that he would support it.[7] His interest in New Harmony seemed to be reviving as evidenced by a document entitled "Conditions of Bequest from William Maclure," which was communicated to the members by Anna Maclure. There was nothing in the list of conditions that had not been insisted upon and discussed many times and was now part of the constitution, which suggests that Maclure wanted all agreements clearly understood and codified before he would even think of proceeding. He was pleased when the

Indiana legislature finally incorporated the Working Men's Institute, which added a further level of oversight to the operation.

An understanding was growing between Maclure and members of the Institute, and evident progress had been made, but he must have been struck by the obsequious, importuning nature of their requests, which no doubt put him on his guard. Communications continued, and those from the Institute (president John Beal, secretary W. G. Macy, and treasurer Achille Fretageot) were still deferential, but they became more specific in listing their needs. Beal, a master carpenter, had witnessed the entire history of the town, for he had arrived at New Harmony on the *Boatload of Knowledge.* Indeed, most of the active members had come to New Harmony in the 1820s, and despite differences in their financial and social status, there was no conflict among them in the planning or operation of the Institute.

Many locals were eager to establish a common day school, and if Maclure wanted it, it would be along Pestalozzian lines. But money was lacking, and they required more space, which entailed using another of Maclure's houses in addition to the large building with its hall that they were already using. For lack of funds they could not retain a teacher, and since members of the Institute worked all day, they were unavailable to take on this task. Hints were dropped, but no explicit demands were made, and no direct response was proffered by Maclure, except for his decision to divide the space of the large building already being used into smaller rooms that would satisfy their needs; his brother Alexander would assist them.

Letters went back and forth. Those from New Harmony were immediate replies, unabashed in their flattery, detailing progress being made despite the numerous problems encountered, while those from Mexico were long in coming and overly generous in advice and discourse on social theory, but restrained about meeting the needs of the Institute. Maclure would not part with property or buildings outright, something the committee desperately wanted. Too often he had seen gifts and loans claimed as the personal property of those in charge of his schools, an abuse that he found particularly aggravating, and he was determined to prevent its recurrence. Maclure insisted that the Working Men's Institute be more of a cooperative venture, with members contributing, to show their sincerity; both sides seemed to be leading each other on. While Maclure asserted that the committee should be bold and independent, he made demands concerning every aspect of their organization if they were to obtain an endowment.

In fact, steady progress had been made. Enrollment of working men increased, the library and reading room were busy, and lectures were given, but Maclure was still reluctant to deed his property outright. From his usual rhetoric, there arose a new, despondent note in his letters about the overwhelming ability of parents to misguide their children and a doubt that perhaps working men were as corruptible as anyone else and might be incapable of taking advantage of their potential power.

Quite clearly, Maclure's skittish behavior reflected an insecurity, born of repeated disappointments, which he attributed to the shortcomings and perversity of humankind. In the past, the promising ventures of this aging, ailing man had foundered, even with the oversight of faithful agents, and now he was being asked to sponsor a costly project without supervision by someone he could rely upon—and he in Mexico. He wanted assurances, but even when they were given, they did little to calm him. The committee in New Harmony might grumble, but they had to watch their step, for there was a wavering on his part along with new expressions of skepticism.

The committee openly expressed its disappointment and complained about the forlorn state of the buildings that Maclure was making available to them. Arguments were advanced that they had done everything he had wanted, and that since he was getting on in years he should deed them the properties now.[8] They never received answers to their requests, perhaps due to Maclure's state of health, but their alarm soon turned to elation when they heard that he planned to return to New Harmony to make a liberal and permanent settlement that would ensure the future of the Institute. They were confident that when they confronted Maclure directly, he would see the justice of their claims.[9] In fact, they were shrewd in their belief that Maclure would be pliable and openhanded if faced directly. While he could be careful, evasive, and businesslike in his affairs when dealing with people indirectly, in person he was agreeable and compromising. Maclure could harangue his opponents as a faceless group, but he rarely criticized individuals, and when they showed any sign of agreement or concession, he became most accommodating and reasonable. Instinctively he wished to please.

Maclure, now seventy-seven, looked old, and his health was rapidly declining, according to Dr. Marmaduke Burrough, who tended to many of Maclure's business needs. He had heard alarming reports that Maclure was suffering from a "faultering of speech" and legs so swollen that he required the help of a servant to walk. He was probably suffering from a failing heart in addition to urinary malfunction. But when Burrough saw him, Maclure looked better than "he had reason to expect." His memory and conversation seemed unimpaired, and he showed great interest in the new building of the Academy.[10]

Maclure sensed that if he was ever to see Philadelphia and New Harmony again to straighten out his affairs, this was the time. He decided to undertake the perilous voyage in the spring of 1840, knowing that he might not survive the strain of travel. Arrangements were made for him to be carried by litter from Mexico City to Jalapa on the coast, where Dr. Burrough was to meet him. But Maclure never arrived. He soon became so ill and weakened that he could travel no further, and while he was attempting to return to Mexico City, his condition deteriorated even more. He was taken to the home of a friend, a former president of Mexico, in the small town of San Angel, where he soon died on March 23, 1840. An Episcopal church burial service read by Thomas H. Ellis, acting U.S. consul, took place in the English cemetery at San Angel. The elation felt upon hearing that Maclure was returning to New Harmony quickly vanished with news of his death.

What had been accomplished in Maclure's thirteen years in Mexico? It would seem relatively little. There was the occasional philanthropic gesture, but little else. He had been unable to establish a working school to educate Indian and poor children, for the promising halcyon days that followed the revolution just after his arrival were short-lived. The founding of Pestalozzian schools was rendered impossible because of corruption, turmoil, and political instability. There was a shortage of suitable teachers and even of pupils. His advanced age and poor health prevented him from pursuing his educational goals with vigor, nor could he muster sufficient energy for geological explorations. His tolerance was waning for the strife and the problems of New Harmony, created he thought by human perversity, especially when he himself saw things so clearly. From his perspective there was no better place to witness the tumult than from afar—in Mexico. Prone to expound on the corrupting effect of fine weather ("eternal spring") on the vigor and productivity of people, perhaps he was one of its victims. After a lifetime of travel, he ended up a sedentary letter writer, journalist, and essayist whose commentaries were published in the *Disseminator* and in *Opinions;* he seems to have withdrawn from the battle.

The memorial service for William Maclure, conducted by members of the Institute, began with appropriate words of condolence and was quickly followed by an undisguised appeal for support addressed to Alexander and Anna Maclure, now the executors of Maclure's estate, in whose hands the future of the Institute lay.[11] The committee listed the successes of the Institute, and they emphasized that every condition and wish of Maclure had been faithfully followed. The request was made that the buildings housing their school, lecture hall, and reading room should be leased or deeded to the board of trustees of the Institute so long as all the conditions of the constitution were met and were consistent with the intent (and promise) of the founder, William Maclure; the understanding should remain unchanged with Alexander and Anna in control. Alexander declined to give them the deed to the property, so central to their wishes, which they claimed his brother had planned to do. But he permitted the continued use of the buildings for meetings and other functions, for neither Alexander nor Anna had any desire to change the ongoing situation. The decision was final, and all efforts to make them change their minds failed.

Despite the disappointment, the Society continued to function, but members were unwilling to invest too much of themselves into buildings that were not theirs. Still, it can be said that they operated with some courage, for as managers they refused Anna Maclure's request to use the hall for visiting preachers, a refusal that would have pleased her brother.[12] The dream of establishing a chain of these societies across the land, however, was all but dead as the Institute quietly struggled through the nineteenth century.

By an almost miraculous turn of events, the fortune of the New Harmony Working Men's Institute was unexpectedly bettered in 1894 by a generous bequest from Dr. Edward Murphy that made possible the survival of the Institute to the present day. Born in 1813, Murphy arrived at New Harmony as a lonely, starving Irish orphan, and here he found a home and friends. He was enrolled in the School of Industry in 1826, and several years later, after making his fortune as a physician and investor, he showed his appreciation by supporting the Working Men's Institute with gifts amounting to $150,000—far more than William and his siblings had provided. Through Dr. Murphy's bounty, a handsome brick building was constructed that housed a library, an archive related to New Harmony's history, and Dr. Murphy's collection of art and artifacts. Adjoining the main building is an auditorium.

Maclure's definitive plan for the ultimate disposition of his wealth had been set down in his final will, drawn up and signed in Mexico City.

His family was allowed the use of his property and the revenue it might provide, but upon their deaths all their holdings would revert to the estate whose charge was "the diffusion of useful knowledge" and the education of working men who lived by the "sweat of their brow." To achieve this aim, he was prepared to entertain only one substantive philanthropic venture—the establishment of as many libraries as possible.[13] The entire estate was to be dispensed with as gifts of $500 to "any institute, club, or society of laborers who worked with their hands, which established anywhere in the United States a reading and lecture room with a library of at least 100 volumes, none of which were to be of a trivial nature."[14]

The task of distribution was, in fact, not completed until almost two decades after Maclure's death, because Alexander and Anna, unsympathetic to their brother's plans and his "misguided" notion of spending good money on libraries for working people, consulted lawyers who pointed out that no such libraries actually existed to which they could give money, and so the siblings were sole inheritors of his fortune, to do with as they pleased. Maclure had made generous provision for his sister and brother, but they wanted more. Living very well, as if they were of "the moneyed aristocracy," Anna would have dismayed William by her largesse, supporting religious causes and Scottish charities. Land was sold to the Episcopalian ministry to establish a church with an adjacent cemetery in New Harmony. This sale of land was expressly forbidden by the terms of the will, and Maclure's (and Owen's) cherished belief that New Harmony should be free of churches was violated. Further, by law, trustees of the estate were required to report on any settlements or other transactions taking place. This was not done, and the little information provided by Alexander and Anna in the years following Maclure's death revealed gross mismanagement and irregularities.

Quite simply, they looted the estate and were freely spending Maclure's fortune with little regard for the terms of the will, thus breaking the law. And so in 1849, management of the estate was taken out of their hands by the state court, which appointed a lively young attorney, Alvin P. Hovey, to be the administrator of the will.[15] The move was challenged by the executors and their lawyers, with the case ending in the supreme court of Indiana, which decided against the executors.[16] An accounting of Maclure's land, property, and finances, and all the transactions that had resulted in the dissipation of the estate, was carried out by Hovey, who then instituted over sixty lawsuits to reacquire land and properties that had been sold or given away illegally, according to the terms of the will, and from this he realized over $75,000 from the resale of what had been repossessed. One of the recipients of Anna and Alexander's largesse was David Dale Owen, who was required to pay for the Rapp brick granary, which he had converted into a laboratory, and the large Rapp-Maclure mansion, in which he now lived. He had received these gifts "in good faith," and under protest he agreed to pay the estate $3,592.50, a fraction of their worth, and for $34 he bought the adjoining lot on which Thomas Say was buried.[17]

Maclure's reconstituted fortune was then used for the support of working men's libraries, just as he had intended, and by 1855, $80,000 had been distributed to 144 libraries, working men's institutes, and literary societies in Indiana, and 11 had been established or aided in Illinois. Justice had prevailed, and Hovey became well known as a conscientious advocate of the people. After serving in the Civil War with distinction, he became governor of Indiana.[18]

Unfortunately, the initial explosive growth of libraries for working people was followed within a few years by their equally rapid disappearance.[19] With the enticement of a $500 gift, many libraries were hastily created without stable management or adequate space for books, and they often lacked personnel with library experience. By 1876 only eighteen of the libraries still existed, and by the end of the century only one, the New Harmony Working Men's Institute, remained—as it does today. Still, despite the scattering of the books, many found their way into schools and private libraries and were read by young and old, so some good came of them. The New Harmony library was a herald of the free library system in the United States that had its origins in the fertile mind of William Maclure. Within the walls of New Harmony's Working Men's Institute rests an invaluable record of the state of Indiana, and preserved in innumerable documents is the story of New Harmony, a great social experiment that failed but might have been the model for an earthly paradise.

The memory of working men's libraries faded, and with it remembrance of Maclure, his beneficence, and his dream of educating working people and the children of the poor. Maclure's last great hope had consumed his fortune. Poorly organized and managed, the project was dependent on people whose agenda ran counter to his own. His wishes were thwarted, and failure was almost inevitable. Alas, Maclure's philanthropy was not all that it could have been. Still, a deeper analysis might show that Maclure's efforts had hidden, easily overlooked consequences. Maclure's efforts had an impact on the establishment of the state public school system in Indiana and with it, associated township libraries, largely brought about by a younger member of the commune, Robert Dale Owen, whose ideas on education must have been molded to a significant extent by Maclure.

Epilogue

His views were noble; his fellow-creatures were his family, and to carry out his large plans his ample means were munificently bestowed. His own personal wants were few and simple, and a very small part of his revenue sufficed to supply them. Although some of his views were visionary, they were benevolent, and he was one of the benefactors of his race.

Benjamin Silliman

A man larger than life, William Maclure was beset by contradictions. While he prided himself on his gruff, almost anti-intellectual pragmatism, he indulged in extravagant dreaming, steeped in the liberal ideas of the Enlightenment in a Romantic age. An endlessly curious and energetic traveler, he lived an uncommonly eventful life. Surviving a schooling that he felt did not prepare him for the real world, he emerged an able, robust young man, steeped in the mercantile tradition of his family, who amassed a fortune that assured him a life of boundless possibilities. But commerce was not a sufficient challenge to fulfill his life, and so he sought something more. With remarkable courage, he changed the direction of his life by retiring in his early thirties to devote his days to science and technology and the reform of society.

He began by making a serious study of geology, a branch of natural history that was in the formative stages of becoming a science of practical and theoretical interest. The subject appealed to Maclure because geological knowledge could be exploited for commercial and agricultural purposes, which interested him as a former businessman and suited his propensity for a descriptive, rather than an experimental, approach to science. Geological fieldwork obliged him to roam, and this he did relentlessly because he hungered for travel and new experiences that provided him with a sense of authority and mission. After assiduous exploration of the United States, he published a landmark work that merited him the enviable reputation as "father of American geology" and the time in which he worked as the "Maclurean era of American geology."

In Maclure's time, when the American republic was young and burgeoning and had little time or will to indulge in such a "useless," esoteric interest as science, there was almost no support for those willing to devote their lives to its study, and only those with a private income could do so. Maclure recognized the importance of science to the welfare and prosperity of the nation, and so he brought foreign investigators and geologists to the United States and supported them, as he did many native-born Americans. He filled libraries with books and glass cases with specimens of rocks and minerals, and he bought scientific equipment for those who could use them. He provided financial support for organizations of scientists such as the Academy of Natural Sciences of Philadelphia, which might not have survived without him, and he furnished printing presses, which enabled them to print some of the first American scientific journals in which investigators could publish their results. In short, Maclure was an entire philanthropic foundation, at a time when there were none. However generous he was, he was rather impetuous and unsystematic in his giving, which was confined to the field of science and social reform through education.

What he had accomplished would have been reason enough to rest and to assume the role of the munificent, grand old man of geology and the foreteller of the U.S. Geological Survey. But he harbored a greater ambition, more impossibly complex than he knew, for he believed that irrational man was perfectible. Maclure was a man of high moral principles and strongly held opinions who was influenced by the social thinkers of the day and the revolutions he had witnessed. He was outraged by the social injustice in Europe and America perpetrated by the wealthy and the Catholic Church, who used their power to abuse the great majority of the poor and the vulnerable. Having little or no "useful" education, the majority of citizens (whom he deemed "useful producers") did not know where their best interests lay and were easily duped. In an age of reason, believing that human beings behave rationally, his solution to the problem was to educate the masses about their own interests so that in democratic countries with universal suffrage they would vote intelligently and prevail because of their numbers. Moreover, they would be the leading group in society because they would be effective, expert, and productive, in contrast to the "useless" rich. The goal was to redistribute knowledge, power, and the wealth of the nation so that everyone received their fair share. After maintaining progressive schools in Paris, and attempting to do so in Spain, Maclure was the very first to bring a new, progressive Pestalozzian education to the United States to teach children to be "useful," thinking citizens, establishing schools in Philadelphia and later in New Harmony that he stocked with special teachers, both American and European.

Unfortunately, Maclure's efforts to correct the egregious imperfections of society through education faltered for many reasons, and his hopes were far from realized. His great program depended on people with different competencies, motivations, and ideas about how to proceed; some were corruptible. Maclure's undoing in the social sphere, which he himself acknowledged, was his partnership with Robert Owen, a leader of English socialism and the labor movement. The victim of Owen's bizarre machinations, Maclure allowed much money and effort to be tied up in Owen's vastly ambitious New Harmony in southwestern Indiana, a utopian commune, which struggled and ultimately failed.

An aging Maclure had come upon hard times, his health was failing, and so he craved the seductive climate of Mexico. Had he repaired to New Harmony to salvage the remains of his dream, and had he proceeded to oversee its management closely, he might have succeeded, but this was not his style, and his attempt to unravel the complex problems of society from a distance failed. He found it difficult to contend with the weakness, fallibility, and perverseness of people with whom he dealt, and bad luck deprived him of his most trusted agents. Still, though disillusioned and far away, he was never resigned to failure, and he struggled to the end.

Young people in their formative years were attracted to him, because he was a brilliant, kindly man who offered financial support in an ungenerous world. He was also eager to share his immense knowledge with them, and in so doing he was remembered as a generous teacher and beneficent patron. To the casual observer, so many of his achievements are taken for granted today in geology, public education for both boys and girls, publishing, and printing. He established public libraries and was a munificent philanthropist in support of scientific institutions and expeditions—all part of Maclure's desire to better this world.

New Harmony today, by the Wabash River, is an utterly pleasing town of 900 people. Several decades ago it would have been described as ramshackle and decaying, similar to many of the surrounding towns in the region, all set in verdant, rolling countryside. However, a descendent of Robert Owen, Kenneth Dale Owen, an oil geologist, and his wife, Jane, having made their fortune elsewhere, returned to New Harmony to restore the town to its former promising self, and in this marvelous venture they have been largely successful. New Harmony is now a charming community laid out in its original form as a grid. All is peace and quiet, without a trace of the social unrest and rancor that marked its history. Many of the buildings and homes have been restored, and a conference center has been built. At the edge of the town sits a gleaming white tourist center and museum, a superb building designed by Richard Meier, and nearby one can pass through monumental gates, fashioned by Jacques Lipshitz, into a great church open to the sky, designed by Philip Johnson. A few steps away is a haunting grove of pines, the grave site of the theologian Paul Tillich, his bust forever brooding in the cool shade, his remains hidden under a great rock of granite. This new New Harmony is an Owen product, and many of the Owens sleep forever in Maple Hill Cemetery overlooking the town. Here and there, headstones bearing the names *Fretageot* and *Duclos* can be found, but nowhere does one see *Robert Owen* or *William Maclure*—absent, as usual.

Maclure is memorialized in the town by a small, rather undistinguished park, one side of which is dominated by a church, while nearby, a large, multipurpose open space is dedicated to the memory of Dr. Edward Murphy. At its center is a magnificent five-globed, cast-iron street lamp that bears a plaque informing the stroller that it once resided in Maclure Park but that after renovation it was transferred to its present location— symbolic of Maclure's eclipse. Only in the imposing Working Men's Institute is one reminded that William Maclure passed this way.

NOTES

Acronyms

ANSP Academy of Natural Sciences of Philadelphia
APS American Philosophical Society, Philadelphia
WMI New Harmony Working Men's Institute

1. Origins and the Making of a Life

1. I. E. Dunlop, ed., *The Royal Burgh of Ayr: Seven Hundred and Fifty Years of History* (Edinburgh: Oliver and Boyd, 1953); Raymond Bentman, *Robert Burns* (Boston: Twayne, 1987).

2. John L. Sanders, "Ayr Mount on the Eno River, near Hillsborough, North Carolina," *Antiques* 135 (1989): 1191–92.

3. Maclure to Reuben Haines, February 9, 1831, APS.

4. Charles Keyes, "William Maclure: Father of Modern Geology," *Pan-American Geologist* 44 (September 1925): 86.

5. Incoherent letters to William were sent by John (Sept. 11, 1833, WMI) and Margaret (Nov. 24, 1833, WMI), attesting to their mental instability.

6. Josephine M. Elliott, *Partnership for Posterity: The Correspondence of William Maclure and Marie Duclos Fretageot, 1820–1833* (Indianapolis: Indiana Historical Society, 1994), 12.

7. Some information about Maclure's early life is revealed in a letter from Alexander Maclure to Samuel George Morton (Feb. 17, 1841) that helped Morton write the memoir that was first published in *Proceedings of the American Philosophical Society* 1 (1841) and then included in the 1887 reprint of Maclure's *Opinions*, 1:7–33. The letter itself appears in J. Percy Moore, "William Maclure—Scientist and Humanitarian," *Proceedings of the American Philosophical Society* 91 (1947). Other information coming from Maclure's letters to Reuben Haines and information housed in the New Harmony Working Men's Institute can be found in the introduction to Elliott, *Partnership*, and in Josephine M. Elliott, "William Maclure: Patron Saint of Indiana Libraries," *Indiana Magazine of History* 94 (1998): 178–90.

8. Maclure to Marie Duclos Fretageot, Jan. 28, 1828, in *Partnership*, 486–87.

9. J. C. Herold, *The Age of Napoleon* (New York: Harper and Row, 1963), 94–95.

10. Maclure to Benjamin Silliman, Oct. 19, 1822, in George P. Fisher, *Life of Benjamin Silliman,* 2 vols. (New York: C. Scribner, 1866).

11. Maclure to R. Haines, Jan. 12, 1822, APS.

12. Fortunately, many of his letters have been faithfully transcribed in *Partnership* and in Arthur E. Bestor Jr., ed., *Education and Reform at New Harmony: Correspondence of William Maclure and Marie Duclos Fretageot, 1820–1833* (Indianapolis: Indiana Historical Society, 1948). For his diaries, see John S. Doskey, *The European Journals of William Maclure* (Philadelphia: American Philosophical Society, 1988). Maclure's errors in spelling have not been corrected.

13. Maclure to Thomas Say, Nov. 7, 1833, WMI.

14. William R. Brock and C. Helen Brock, *Scotus Americanus: A Survey of the Sources for Links between Scotland and America in the Eighteenth Century* (Edinburgh: Edinburgh University Press, 1982); Arthur Herman, *How the Scots Invented the Modern World* (New York: Crown, 2001).

15. Thomas H. Ellis to Charles J. Stillé, in *Pennsylvania Magazine of Biography and History* 12 (1888): 483–84.

16. Maclure to Fretageot, Apr. 25, 1824, *Partnership,* 275–78.

17. William Maclure, *Opinions on Various Subjects, Dedicated to the Industrious Producers,* 3 vols. (New Harmony, Ind.: School of Industry Press, 1831, 1837, 1838), 2:176 (hereafter cited as *Opinions*).

18. Maclure to Silliman, Oct. 19, 1822. Doskey, *European Journals,* xviii, states that he retired in 1797.

19. George P. Merrill, *Contributions to the History of American Geology* (Washington, D.C.: Government Printing Office, 1906), 218.

20. Maclure to Thomas Jefferson, Nov. 20, 1801, Jefferson Papers, Library of Congress.

21. Samuel G. Morton, "Memoir of William Maclure, Esq.," in Maclure, *Opinions,* 1:32.

22. The most complete chronology of Maclure's life was constructed by Josephine Elliott in *Partnership for Prosperity.*

23. Doskey, *European Journals,* appendixes P, T, V, W, X, and Z.

24. Maclure, *Opinions,* 2:153.

25. These were the American, French, and Mexican revolutions, the Spanish rebellion against the French, and the Mexican rebellion of 1820. Maclure to S. G. Morton, Dec. 27, 1836 (APS); Maclure, *Opinions,* 1:628–29.

26. Maclure to Silliman, June 30, 1824, *American Journal of Science* 9 (1825): 157–61.

27. Maclure to W. Gower, May 10, 1821, WMI.

28. John H. Jensen has discussed the origin of the Maclure Collection, now housed in the Van Pelt Library of the University of Pennsylvania. It is believed that Maclure did little collecting. Rather, he purchased the collection from his friend Marc-Antoine Jullien de Paris, a writer, editor, and poet who assembled the massive documentary record and probably tutored Maclure about matters pertaining to the revolution. See Jensen, "Collector and Collection: A Note," in James D. Hardy Jr., John H. Jensen, and Martin Wolfe, eds. *The Maclure Collection of French Revolutionary Materials* (Philadelphia: University of Pennsylvania Press, 1966), xix–xx; and *Partnership,* 3–4.

29. Stephen L. Gwynn, *History of Ireland* (London: Macmillan, 1923), 3.

30. Morton, "Memoir," in Maclure, *Opinions,* 1:29.

31. Fisher, *Life of Benjamin Silliman,* 284–86.

32. Eleanor Nicholson, "The Radical Scot: The Educational Ideas and Philanthropies of William Maclure (1763–1840)" (PhD diss., Loyola University, Chicago, 1995), 20.

33. Patricia T. Stroud, *Thomas Say, New World Naturalist* (Philadelphia: University of

Pennsylvania Press, 1992), 34; Anne Taylor, *Visions of Harmony: A Study in Nineteenth-Century Millenarianism* (New York: Oxford University Press, 1987), 124, 201.

34. Morton, "Memoir," 1:29.

35. Martin Garrett, *George Gordon, Lord Byron* (New York: Oxford University Press, 2000).

36. Maclure to Fretageot, Nov. 28, 1828, in *Partnership,* 532–33.

37. Alexander's letter was reprinted in full in Moore, "William Maclure—Scientist and Humanitarian." William set Alexander up in business in Norfolk, Virginia. Alexander spent his last years at New Harmony with his two sisters and was the executor of William's estate.

38. Morton, "Memoir," in Maclure, *Opinions,* 1:13–14.

39. Maclure to S. G. Morton, Dec. 27, 1836, APS.

40. Bestor, *Education and Reform,* 293.

41. Maclure, *Opinions,* 2:174–78.

42. *Partnership,* 5.

43. Maclure, *Opinions,* 2:153.

2. Philadelphia (1796–1800)

1. Philip Chadwick Smith, "Philadelphia Displays the 'Flowery Red Flag,'" in Jean Gordon Lee, *Philadelphians and the China Trade, 1784–1844* (Philadelphia: Philadelphia Museum of Art, 1984), 12–21.

2. Francois-Alexandre-Frédéric, duc de la Rochefoucauld-Liancourt, *Voyage dans les États Unis d'Amerique; fait en 1795, 1796, et 1797,* 8 vols. (1799), 6:312–36.

3. Van Wyck Brooks, *The World of Washington Irving* (New York: Dutton, 1944), 3–6.

4. Isaac Weld Jr., *Travels through the States of North America, and the Provinces of Upper and Lower Canada during the Years 1795, 1796, and 1797,* 2 vols. (London, 1800), 1:21.

5. Julian Ursyn Niemcewicz, *Under Their Vine and Fig Tree: Travels through America in 1797–1799, 1805, with Some Further Account of Life in New Jersey,* trans. and ed. Metchie J. E. Budka (Elizabeth, N.J.: Grassmann, 1965), 46–47; Andrew Hook, *Scotland and America: A Study of Cultural Relations, 1750–1835* (Glasgow: Blackie, 1975).

6. Jefferson to Maclure, Nov. 20, 1801, Jefferson Papers, LC.

7. William Maclure, "Observations on the Geology of the United States Explanatory for Geological Map," *Transactions of the American Philosophical Society* 6 (1809): 411–28.

8. Maclure, *Opinions,* 2:100.

9. George H. Daniels, "The Process of Professionalization in American Science: The Emergent Period, 1820–1860," *Isis* 58 (1967): 151–66; Nathan Reingold, "Definitions and Speculations: The Professionalization of Science in America in the Nineteenth Century," in Alexandra Oleson and Sanborn C. Brown, eds., *The Pursuit of Knowledge in the Early American Republic* (Baltimore: Johns Hopkins University Press, 1976), 33–69.

10. Niemcewicz, *Under Their Vine and Fig Tree,* 214–15.

11. Maclure, *Opinions,* 2:100.

12. Ibid., 2:151–52.

13. Latrobe to Scandella, April 3, 1798, cited in Edward C. Carter II, Angeline Polites, Lee W. Formwalt, and John C. Van Horne, eds., *The Virginia Journals of Benjamin Henry Latrobe, 1795–1798,* 2 vols. (New Haven: Published for the Maryland Historical Society by Yale University Press, 1977), 2:381–83. See also Edward C. Carter II, "Benjamin Henry Latrobe, 'Learned Engineer': The American Philosophical Society and the Promotion of Useful Knowledge and Works, 1798–1809," in R. S. Klein, ed., *Science and Society in Early*

America: Essays in Honor of Whitfield J. Bell Jr. (Philadelphia: American Philosophical Society, 1986), 201–23.

14. Carter et al., *Virginia Journals*, 2:453.

3. Political and Economic Philosophy

1. Doskey, *European Journals*, 123–24.
2. See Stephen Copley and Kathryn Sutherland, *Adam Smith's Wealth of Nations: New Interdisciplinary Essays* (Manchester: Manchester University Press, 1995); David Harris, *Socialist Origins in the United States: American Forerunners of Marx, 1817–1832* (Assen, the Netherlands: Van Gorcum, 1966), 56–81; *Opinions*, 1:1–22, 258, 2:50–63; John Humphrey Noyes, *History of American Socialisms* (1870; reprint, New York: Dover, 1966).
3. *Opinions*, 1:258.
4. John Gray, *Lecture on Human Happiness,* quoted by Harris, *Socialist Origins*, 58.
5. *Opinions*, 1:1–6.
6. *Opinions*, 2:554–56.
7. *Opinions*, 1:19.
8. *Opinions*, 2:414.
9. *Opinions*, 2:414–15.
10. *Opinions*, 1:19, 68, 366–67.
11. *Opinions*, 2:537.
12. *Opinions*, 1:102–3, 2:570, 3:155.
13. *Opinions*, 1:458.
14. *Opinions*, 2:570.
15. Maclure to Morton, April 3, 1830, APS; *Opinions*, 3:58.
16. *Opinions*, 3:27.
17. *Opinions*, 1:199.
18. *Opinions*, 1:37, 130, 2:226.
19. Maclure to Morton, Mar. 26, 1835, APS.
20 Opinions, 2:670.
21. Harris, *Socialist Origins*, 54–81; M. J. Waserman, "A Bio-bibliography of William Maclure (1763–1840)" (master's diss., Catholic University of America, Washington, D.C., 1963), 27–32.
22. Maclure to Fretageot, May 7, 1822, in Elliott, *Partnership*, 182–85.
23. Jensen, "Collector and Collection: A Note," xvii.
24. Nicholson, "The Radical Scot," 67–80; Brooks, *Washington Irving*, 106–9.
25. Maurice Margarot, *The Trial of Maurice Margarot: Before the High Court of Judiciary, at Edinburgh, on the 13th and 14th of January, 1794* (New York: James Carey, 1794); Hook, *Scotland and America*, 232–37.
26. William Godwin, *Enquiry Concerning Social Justice,* ed. K. C. Carter (New York: Oxford University Press, 1971), xii–xxxv, 13–16.
27. *Opinions*, 1:12; Nicholson, "The Radical Scot," chaps. 4–6.
28. *Opinions*, 1:19, 158–61, 2:6–10.
29. *Opinions*, 1:66.
30. *Opinions*, 1:37–42, 79–80; 3:445–47.
31. *Opinions*, 1:461–62.
32. *Opinions*, 1:454–55.

33. Gordon S. Wood, *The American Revolution: A History* (New York: Modern Library, 2002), 139–66.

34. *Opinions,* 2:51–56, 89–91.

35. *Opinions,* 1:178–84, 2:21–25, 2:195, 3:56.

36. *Opinions,* 2:5.

37. *Opinions,* 2:590.

38. *Opinions,* 1:476–77.

39. *Opinions,* 2:51–56.

40. *Opinions,* 1:18–22, 2:89–91.

41. *Opinions,* 1:452–58.

42. Maclure to Morton, Mar. 26, 1835, APS.

43. Harris, *Socialist Origins,* 1–19. An excellent summary of Maclure's views on politics, economics, social conflict, and education (which I have used as a guide) can be found in Harris, *Socialist Origins,* 54–81. For a more extensive description of the antidemocratic views of Federalist spokesmen, see Brooks, *Washington Irving,* 44–65.

44. Doskey, *European Journals,* 660–62.

45. *Opinions,* 2:411–15.

46. Nicholson, "The Radical Scot," 10–106.

47. *Opinions,* 2:59.

48. *Opinions,* 2:174–78.

49. *Opinions,* 2:33–36.

50. *Opinions,* 2:402–6.

51. Maclure to Morton, Mar. 26, 1835, APS.

52. Maclure to Morton, Aug. 1835, APS.

53. *Opinions,* 2:362–65.

54. *Opinions,* 1:25–35.

4. European Sojourn (1800–1808)

1. Maclure to Samuel G. Morton, Mar. 26, 1835, as cited in Nathan Reingold, ed., *Science in Nineteenth-Century America: A Documentary History* (Chicago: University of Chicago Press, 1964), 52.

2. Maclure to Jefferson, July 3, Nov. 20, 1801, Jefferson Papers, Library of Congress.

3. Edward Peters, "The Desire to Know the Secrets of the World," *Journal of the History of Ideas* 62 (2001): 593–610.

4. Frederick Hall, "Modern Paris—Letters," letter 8, August 21, 1807, in *The Literary and Philosophical Repertory: Embracing Discoveries and Improvements in the Physical Sciences, the Liberal and Fine Arts* 1 (1812): 258. American Periodical Series, 1800–1825, reel 126. Middlebury, Vt.: printed for S. Swift by T. C. Strong, 1812–17.

5. T. H. Ellis to C. J. Stillé, in *Pennsylvania Magazine of History and Biography* 12 (1888): 483–84.

6. In 1803, Monroe also assisted Livingston in negotiations for the purchase of Louisiana from the French.

7. Accounts of the proceedings can be found in John Bassett Moore, *History and Digest of the International Arbitrations to Which the United States Has Been a Party,* 6 vols. (Washington: Government Printing Office, 1898), 5:4436, and Henry Adams, *History of the United States of America* (New York: C. Scribner's Sons, 1904–9), 2:48–50.

8. Maclure to Reuben Haines, Oct. 10, 1823, APS.

9. A cabriolet is a two-wheeled carriage driven by a postillion, drawn by two horses that are changed every ten miles.

10. All of the extant journals of Maclure, and those of Cabell which have a day-to-day correspondence with those of Maclure, have been arranged and edited by John S. Doskey.

11. Doskey, *European Journals,* 1–81.

12. Hall, "Modern Paris—Letters," *Literary and Philosophical Repertory,* 1:260–61.

13. Doskey, *European Journals,* journal no. 3, 83–111.

14. In fact, the water in regions of endemic goiter usually do have low iodine content. Certain deep valleys of France, Germany, and Switzerland are areas of high incidence of endemic goiter, which result from an iodine deficiency or the ingestion of food and water containing goitrogens. The routine addition of an "iodized" salt to the diet has largely eliminated such thyroid pathology. As a medical student I was taught that during formation of the earth's crust, in regions where goiter was common, molten rock (which became soil) had solidified before iodine-containing materials and had excluded them. Iodine-containing materials are quite soluble in water, and so, when exposed, they were leached away. Maclure noted that there was "no goiter" in Spain. He found a high incidence of goiter in women living in deep valleys in Switzerland that were subject to flooding. Doskey, *European Journals,* 339–40. Perhaps flood water removed materials containing iodine.

15. Novales, *William Maclure in Spain,* 23–41; Doskey, *European Journals,* 99–109.

16. Maclure, Feb. 9, 1808, in *European Journals,* 124.

17. Maclure, Feb. 20, 1808, *European Journals,* 132.

18. Maclure, Feb. 24, 1808, *European Journals,* 133.

19. Maclure, May 8, 1808, *European Journals,* 153.

20. Maclure, May 23–28, 1808, *European Journals,* 161.

5. The Maclurean Era of American Geology

1. Maclure, *American Journal of Science* 4 (1821): 363.

2. Alexis de Tocqueville, *Democracy in America* (New York: Colonial Press, 1900), 1:442, 2:399.

3. Jefferson to Volney, 1805, cited in John H. Wells, "Notes on the Earliest Geological Maps of the United States, 1756–1832," *Journal of the Washington Academy of Sciences* 49 (1959): 201; Jefferson to Maclure, Nov. 2, 1817, Jefferson Papers, Library of Congress.

4. William Maclure, *Observations on the Geology of the United States* (Philadelphia: printed for the author by A. Small, 1817), iii–iv.

5. A. H. Dupree, "The Pursuit of Knowledge in the Early American Republic," in Alexandra Oleson and Sanborn C. Brown, eds., *The Pursuit of Knowledge in the Early American Republic* (Baltimore: Johns Hopkins University Press, 1976), 21–32; Rebecca B. Bedell, *The Anatomy of Nature: Geology and American Landscape Painting, 1825–1875* (Princeton, N.J.: Princeton University Press, 2001), introduction.

6. Maclure to Samuel G. Morton, Mar. 26, 1835, as cited in Reingold, *Science,* 52.

7. Keyes, "William Maclure," 85.

8. Karl J. R. Arndt, *Harmony on the Wabash in Transition, 1824–1826* (Worcester, Mass.: Harmony Society Press, 1982), 801.

9. Doskey, *European Journals,* xxii–xxiii; Maclure to Thomas Jefferson, Nov. 20, 1801, Jefferson Papers.

10. George P. Merrill, *The First One Hundred Years of American Geology* (New Haven:

Yale University Press, 1924), 35; Charles C. Gillespie, *Genesis and Geology* (Cambridge: Harvard University Press, 1951).

11. R. H. Dott Jr., in Cecil J. Schneer, ed., *Toward a History of Geology* (Cambridge: MIT Press, 1967), 121–42.

12. Charles Lyell, *Principles of Geology* (London: J. Murray, 1853); W. F. Cannon, in Schneer, *Toward a History of Geology*, 78–79.

13. Maclure, "Observations on the Geology of the United States Explanatory for Geological Map," *Transactions of the American Philosophical Society* 6 (1809): 427.

14. Maclure to Silliman from Spain, Apr. 29, 1823. Published as "Miscellaneous Remarks on the Systematic Arrangement of Rocks, and on Their Probable Origin, Especially of the Secondary," *American Journal of Science* 7 (1824): 261–64.

15. Wells, "Notes," 201; *Medical Repository*, 1809.

16. Maclure, "Observations sur la géologie des États-Unis, servant à expliquer une carte géographique," *Journal de physique* 69 (1809): 204–13; see also *Journal de physique* 72 (1811): 137–65. "Observations" ranks with Jean-Etienne Guettard's mineralogical *Map of Louisiana and Canada* (1752), which contained the very first geological map of North America. C.-F. Volney, *A View of the Soil and Climate of the United States of America* (Paris, 1803; Philadelphia: J. Conrad, 1804).

17. The five sections are (1) across Lake Champlain and the White Hills, (2) from Plymouth to Lake Erie, (3) from Egg Harbor to Pittsburgh, (4) from Cape Henry to Abingdon, and (5) from Cape Fear to the Warm Springs. Merrill, *Contributions to the History of American Geology*, 228.

18. Maclure, *Opinions*, 3:175–78; George W. White, "William Maclure's Maps of the Geology of the United States," *Journal of the Society for the Bibliography of Natural History* 8 (1977): 266–69; E. M. Spieker, "Schöpf, Maclure, Werner, and the Earliest Work on American Geology," *Science* 172 (1971): 1333–34.

19. Maclure, *Observations*, iii.

20. Maclure, "Miscellaneous Remarks on the Systematic Arrangement of Rocks."

21. Maclure, "Essay on the Formation of Rocks, or An Inquiry into the Probable Origin of Their Present Form and Structure," *Journal of the Academy of Natural Sciences of Philadelphia* 1 (1818): 261–76, 285–310, 327–45; Maclure, "Observations on the Geology of the United States of North America." *Transactions of the American Philosophical Society* 1 (1818): 1–91; Maclure, "Miscellaneous Remarks on the Systematic Arrangement of Rocks; Doskey, *European Journals*, 755–58.

22. B. Silliman's editorial preface to a letter from Maclure in *American Journal of Science* 1 (1819): 209–13.

23. Maclure, "Miscellaneous Remarks on the Systematic Arrangement of Rocks."

24. Doskey, *European Journals*, 13–33.

25. Maclure, "Miscellaneous Remarks on the Systematic Arrangement of Rocks," 262.

26. Maclure, *American Journal of Science* 16 (1829): 352.

27. Ibid., 351–52.

28. Maclure, *Observations*, 28.

29. Maclure, "Miscellaneous Remarks on the Systematic Arrangement of Rocks," 261.

30. Maclure, *American Journal of Science* 10 (1826): 205.

31. Maclure, *Observations*, viii.

32. Ibid., 87.

33. Maclure to Jefferson, July 3, Nov. 20, 1801, APS.

34. Maclure, *Observations*, 126–27.

35. Brooks, *Washington Irving*, 84–103.

36. Maclure to Morton, Nov. 24, 1835, Jan. 31, 1836, J. Percy Moore Papers, ANSP.

37. Jefferson to Maclure, Nov. 2, 1817, Jefferson Papers, Library of Congress.

38. Eaton to John Torrey, Oct. 5, 1817, NYBG. This and other relevant letters (Sept. 29, 1818; Eaton to Silliman letters) are cited in Ethel M. McAllister, *Amos Eaton, Scientist and Educator, 1776–1842* (Philadelphia: University of Pennsylvania Press, 1941), 283, 285, 331; Markes E. Johnson, "Geology in American Education, 1820–1860," *Geological Society of America Bulletin* 88 (1977): 1192–98; Markes E. Johnson, "The Parallel Impacts of William Maclure and Amos Eaton on American Geology, Education, and Public Service," *Indiana Magazine of History* 94 (1998): 151–66.

39. Silliman, *American Journal of Science* 1 (1818): 209–11.

40. *Edinburgh Review* 30 (1818): 375–88.

41. C. S. Rafinesque, *American Monthly Magazine and Critical Review* 3 (1818): 41–44; Wells, "Notes," 203. See Leonard Warren, *Constantine Samuel Rafinesque: A Voice in the American Wilderness* (Lexington: University Press of Kentucky, 2004), 67.

42. In the United States, the first stratigraphic studies were reported by S. Van Rensselaer and Amos Eaton. Lardner Vanuxem has been credited with first correlating fossils with the geologic strata in which they are found. See Maclure to Morton, Apr. 29, 1823, J. Percy Moore Papers, ANSP.

43. Maclure, "Observations on the Geology of the United States of North America," *Transactions of the American Philosophical Society* 1 (1818): 1–91.

44. Maclure, *American Journal of Science* 9 (1829).

45. Morton, "Memoir of William Maclure, Esq."

46. Merrill, *First One Hundred Years of American Geology*, 207–49; Johnson, "Parallel Impacts."

47. Maclure, "Observations on the Geology of the West India Islands, from Barbadoes to Santa Cruz, Inclusive," *Journal of the Academy of Natural Sciences of Philadelphia* 1 (1817): 134–49. Maclure's report was read at a meeting of the APS on Oct. 28, 1817, and also published in the *Transactions of the American Philosophical Society*, Nov. 1817; it was reprinted in New Harmony for the author in 1832.

48. Maclure, "Essay on the Formation of Rocks, or An Inquiry into the Probable Origin of Their Present Form and Structure," *Journal of the Academy of Natural Sciences of Philadelphia* 1 (1818): 261–76, 285–310, 327–45.

49. Merrill, *The First One Hundred Years of American Geology*, 23–24; Chandos Michael Brown, *Benjamin Silliman: A Life in the Young Republic* (Princeton, N.J.: Princeton University Press, 1989).

50. Maclure, *Opinions*, 2:152.

51. H. Struve, *Beiträge zur Meneralogie und Geologie des Nördliche Amerikas* (Hamburg, 1822). For an excellent account of early American geology and mineralogy, see John C. Greene and John G. Burke, *The Science of Minerals in the Age of Jefferson* (Philadelphia: American Philosophical Society, 1978).

52. Maclure to Silliman, Jan. 10, 1825, in *American Journal of Science* 9 (1825): 253–55.

53. William B. Rogers and Henry D. Rogers, "On the Physical Structure of the Appalachian Chain, as Exemplifying the Laws Which Have Regulated the Elevation of Great Mountain Chains, Generally, in *Reports of the First, Second, and Third Meetings of the Association of American Geologists and Naturalists* (Boston: Gould, Kendall, and Lincoln, 1843), 474–531.

54. *Opinions*, 3:175–78.

55. Doskey, *European Journals*, 343; Maclure, *Opinions*, 3:175–78.

56. Maclure to S. G. Morton, 1835, APS.
57. Steven J. Gould, *The Mismeasure of Man* (New York: Norton, 1981).

6. Introduction of Progressive Education to the United States

1. *Opinions,* 1:149–51.
2. Maclure states that he "stumbled by accident" upon Pestalozzi's school, but in fact it was Neef who advised him to look into the school during his visit to Switzerland.
3. For the rest of his life Neef carried a bullet lodged in his head that caused him much pain. At autopsy, a ball was found resting on his palate.
4. Käte Silber, *Pestalozzi, the Man and His Work* (London: Routledge and Kegan Paul, 1960), 119–33. Several books on the life and pedagogy of Pestalozzi have been written, including Henry Barnard's *Pestalozzi and the Education System* (Syracuse, N.Y.: Bardeen, 1881). Pestalozzi is discussed extensively in books on the history of American education by Stuart G. Noble, *A History of American Education* (Westwood, Conn.: Greenwood Press, 1954), H. G. Good, *A History of American Education,* 2nd ed. (New York: Macmillan, 1962), and Will S. Monroe, *History of the Pestalozzian Movement in the United States* (Syracuse, N.Y.: C. W. Bardeen, 1907).
5. Maclure, cited in Doskey, *European Journals,* 75.
6. *Opinions,* 1:60–63.
7. Silber, *Pestalozzi,* 309.
8. Ibid., 120–33. Maclure's views on education are detailed in his *Opinions,* 1:48–105.
9. *Opinions,* 1:4, 2:511.
10. *Opinions,* 1:60–61.
11. Gerald Lee Gutek, "Robert Owen's New Harmony Community: An Example of Communitarian Education," *Journal of the Midwest History of Education Society* 3 (1975): 100–109; Gerald Lee Gutek, *Joseph Neef: The Americanization of Pestalozzianism* (University: University of Alabama Press, 1978), 3–29; Dieter Jedan, "Joseph Neef: Innovator or Imitator?" *Indiana Magazine of History* 78 (December 1982): 323–40.
12. Joseph Neef, *Sketch of a Plan and Method of Education Founded on an Analysis of the Human Faculties and Natural Reason, Suitable for the Offspring of a Free People and for All Rational Human Beings* (Philadelphia, 1808), 3; Joseph Neef, *The Method of Instructing Children Rationally in the Arts of Writing and Reading* (Philadelphia, 1813).
13. *Opinions,* 1:122, 2:209.
14. Johann Heinrich Pestalozzi, *How Gertrude Teaches Her Children,* trans. Lucy E. Holland and Francis C. Turner, ed. Ebenezer Cooke (London: Swann Sonnenschein, 1894), 139.
15. William Maclure, "An Epitome of the Improved Pestalozzian System of Education," *American Journal of Science* 10 (1826): 146–47. See Jedan, "Joseph Neef: Innovator or Imitator?"
16. Neef, *Sketch,* 6.
17. A. M. Kellogg, *Pestalozzi: His Educational Work and Principles* (New York: Kellogg, 1894), 13.
18. Ibid., 22, 23.
19. Pestalozzi, from a letter written in 1807, in Kellogg, *Pestalozzi,* 16–17.
20. *Opinions,* 1:48–57, 60–63; Maclure, "Epitome," 145–51.
21. For further discussion of the ideas presented, see Silber, *Pestalozzi,* 133–50.
22. *Opinions,* 1:219.
23. Silber, *Pestalozzi;* Gerald Lee Gutek, *Joseph Neef,* 3–29.

24. Kellogg, *Pestalozzi*, 5–6; a street in Berlin is named after Pestalozzi.

25. Monroe, *Pestalozzian Movement*, 1.

26. *Opinions*, 1:87–89; John A. Griscom, *A Year in Europe*, 2 vols. (New York, 1823), 2:383.

27. Arthur E. Bestor Jr., *Backwoods Utopias: The Sectarian Origins and Owenite Phases of Communitarian Socialism in America, 1663–1829* (Philadelphia: University of Pennsylvania Press, 1970), 137–39, 144.

28. Robert Dale Owen, *Threading My Way*, 121–49.

29. This Marxian point of view (before Marx) was presented in *Opinions*, 1:87–88.

30. *Opinions*, 1:479.

31. *Opinions*, 1:79–80, 3:198; Maclure to Fretageot, May 22, 1820, in Elliott, *Partnership*, 26.

32. *Opinions*, 3:67.

33. Nicholson, "The Radical Scot," 130–70; *Opinions*, 1:57–59, 2:214–18.

34. Maclure to Fretageot, May 24, 1822, in *Partnership*, 183–88.

35. *Opinions*, 1:48–59.

36. Maclure to Silliman, *American Journal of Science* 9 (1825): 384.

37. Maclure to Morton, August 1835, APS.

38. Maclure to Morton, Oct. 30, 1835, APS.

39. J. Ramsauer, in C. H. Wood, *Indiana School Journal* 37 (1892): 659–65, quoted by Monroe, *Pestalozzian Movement*, 63–64.

40. Monroe, *Pestalozzian Movement*, 67. A fictionalized account of the visit is given in Caroline Dale Snedeker, *The Town of the Fearless* (Garden City, N.Y.: Doubleday, Doran, 1931), 71.

41. Gutek, *Joseph Neef*, 16–17.

42. Maclure, *National Intelligencer and Washington Advertiser*, June 6, 9, and 30, 1806; Monroe, *Pestalozzian Movement*, 44–45; Maclure, "Epitome"; *New-Harmony Gazette*, Feb. 15, 1826, 166–67.

43. Good, *A History of American Education*, 172; Monroe, *Pestalozzian Movement*, 89.

44. Maclure to Silliman, Nov. 9, 1824, in *American Journal of Science* 9 (1825): 163–64.

45. Gutek, *Joseph Neef*; Jedan, "Joseph Neef: Innovator or Imitator?"

46. Gutek, *Joseph Neef*, 23; Monroe, *Pestalozzian Movement*, 97–108.

47. Maclure Papers, microfilm 740 D, APS. The original is owned by the Working Men's Institute, New Harmony, Ind.

48. Maclure to Fretageot, Apr. 29, 1823, in *Partnership*, 226–28.

49. Maclure to Fretageot, Feb. 18, 1824, in *Partnership*, 264–67.

50. Noble, *A History of American Education*, 189–91; Amos Bronson Alcott, *Conversations with Children on the Gospels*, vol. 1 (Boston: J. Munroe, 1836).

51. Doskey, *European Journals*, 685.

52. Fisher, *Life of Benjamin Silliman*, 2:43.

53. *Opinions*, 2:386.

54. Maclure to Fretageot, July 9, 1820, in *Partnership*, 29.

55. Fretageot to Maclure, Jan. 18, 1821, in *Partnership*, 31–33.

56. Their letters, about 350 in number with 65 fragments, were published by Bestor in *Education and Reform* and by Elliott in *Partnership*.

57. Frances Trollope, *Domestic Manners of the Americans* (New York: Knopf, 1949), 10–12. This gossip seems to have been initiated by the malicious Trollope. She also stated that Madame Fretageot made off with the earnings of pupils in the school she ran.

58. Fretageot to Maclure, Apr. 1824, in *Partnership,* 278–80. Josephine Elliott discusses the close relationship of Fretageot and Maclure in *Partnership,* 16–17.

59. Maclure to Fretageot, Mar. 21, 1822; Doskey, *European Journals,* xxxvii–xxxviii.

60. Maclure, "Epitome," 145–51.

61. Maclure to Fretageot, July 5, 1821, in *Partnership,* 120–22.

62. Fretageot to Maclure, Mar. 20, 1821, in *Partnership,* 48–49. Madame's writing in English showed great improvement in only a few months.

63. Fretageot to Maclure, Mar. 30, 1821, in *Partnership,* 54–55.

64. Fretageot to Maclure, July 22, 1821, in *Partnership,* 131–33.

65. *Partnership,* appendix A, 1045–48.

66. Maclure to Fretageot, Mar. 12, 1821, in *Partnership,* 45–46. Next to Philadelphia, he preferred New York. Advising Madame as to which ship to take to America, he told her to choose one built in Philadelphia. These were the best, while those from Boston were the worst.

67. Maclure to Fretageot, Nov. 30, 1823, in *Partnership,* 250–52.

68. Maclure to Fretageot, May 24, 1821, in *Partnership,* 84–87.

69. Maclure to Fretageot, Jan. 18, 1824, in *Partnership,* 260–62; *Opinions,* 1:479–80.

70. *Opinions,* 1:479–80.

71. For a list of the school's students and their favorable comments by them, see *Partnership,* appendix A, 1045–48.

72. Fretageot to Maclure, Oct. 16, 1821, in *Partnership,* 150–51.

73. Maclure to Fretageot, Dec. 4, 1821, in *Partnership,* 155–58.

74. *Partnership,* 141, 1047.

75. The original school, located at 240 Filbert Street, was moved to a larger building at Chestnut Street between 12th and 13th Streets.

76. Bestor, *Backwoods Utopias,* 154. Madame Fretageot introduced Drs. William and Philip Price to *New Views of Mr. Owen of Lanark Impartially Examined* by Henry Grey Macnab, and it is probable that the book was read by several members of the Academy of Natural Sciences of Philadelphia who later settled in New Harmony.

77. Maclure to Fretageot, Aug. 6, Sept. 16, 1822, in *Partnership,* 198–201, 204–6.

78. Maclure to Fretageot, Feb. 15, 1824, in *Partnership,* 264–67.

7. The Grand Tour of Europe (1809–1815)

1. Maclure, "Observations on the Geology of the United States Explanatory for Geological Map," *Transactions of the American Philosophical Society* 6 (1809): 411–28.

2. *Opinions,* 1:151–54.

3. Doskey, *European Journals,* 231. Maclure recorded his Swedish experiences in journals no. 7 and 8, which appear in *European Journals,* 163–253; his Russian travels are described in journal 10, *European Journals,* 258–311. This chapter also draws on Maclure, *American Journal of Science* 9 (1825): 158.

4. Doskey, *European Journals,* 163.

5. Ibid., 227–28.

6. Ibid., 255.

7. Ibid., 265.

8. *Opinions,* 3:91–94.

9. Doskey, *European Journals,* 294.

10. Ibid., 309.

11. Ibid., 307.

12. Doskey, *European Journals,* xxxi. Doskey cites a letter from Jefferson to Niemcewicz stating that he had seen Maclure during the winter and that Maclure then returned to Paris. Journal 11 begins on p. 339.

13. Ibid., 343–44.

14. Ibid., 345–46.

15. Ibid., 358.

16. Ibid., 369.

17. Ibid., 446–48.

18. Ibid., 438.

19. Ibid., 371.

20. Ibid., 429.

21. Ibid., 454–55.

22. Ibid., 454.

23. Ibid., 455.

24. Ibid., 468.

25. Ibid., 484.

26. Ibid., 491.

27. Ibid., 499.

28. Ibid., 583.

29. Ibid., 524.

30. Ibid., 583–84, 591.

31. Ibid., 573.

32. Ibid., 572–73.

33. Ibid., 583.

34. Ibid., 613–63 (journal 18).

35. Ibid., 665–66.

36. Ibid., 624.

37. Ibid., 660–62.

38. William Maclure, "Observations on the Geology of the West India Islands, from Barbadoes to Santa Cruz, Inclusive," *Journal of the Academy of Natural Sciences of Philadelphia* 1 (1817): 134–49.

39. Maclure, Nov. 16, 1820, in Doskey, *European Journals,* 675 (journal no. 20).

40. Maclure, June 29, 1821, ibid., 677–78.

41. Maclure to Fretageot, Nov. 22, 1820, in Elliott, *Partnership,* 30–31.

8. Patron of the Natural Sciences

1. Minutes of the Preliminary Meeting, ANSP. The history of the ANSP has been told many times. The present account is drawn from Edward James Nolan, *A Short History of the Academy of Natural Sciences of Philadelphia* (Philadelphia: Academy of Natural Sciences, 1909); Patsy Gerstner, "The Academy of Natural Sciences of Philadelphia, 1812–1850," in Alexandra Oleson and Sanborn C. Brown, eds., *The Pursuit of Knowledge in the Early American Republic* (Baltimore: Johns Hopkins University Press, 1976), 174–93; Charlotte M. Porter, *The Eagle's Nest: Natural History and American Ideas, 1812–1842* (University: University of Alabama Press, 1986); Simon Baatz, "Patronage, Science, and Ideol-

ogy in an American City: Patrician Philadelphia, 1800–1860" (PhD diss., University of Pennsylvania, 1986), 1–110; Simon Baatz, "Philadelphia Patronage: The Institutional Structure of Natural History in the New Republic, 1800–1833," *Journal of the Early Republic* 8, no. 2 (1988): 111–38; Maurice E. Phillips, "The Academy of Natural Sciences of Philadelphia," *Proceedings of the American Philosophical Society*, n.s., 43, no. 1 (1953): 266–74; John C. Greene, *American Science in the Age of Jefferson* (Ames: Iowa State University Press, 1984), 57–59, 225–35.

2. Trollope, *Domestic Manners*, 10. Her visit began in 1827, and her account was first published in 1832 and republished in 1949 by Knopf.

3. Nolan, *Short History*, 9; Morton, "Memoir," in *Opinions*, 1:31.

4. Maclure to Morton, June 15, 1839, in the Morton Papers at the APS; minutes of ANSP, Aug. 13, 1839.

5. Maclure to Morton, Apr. 10, 1826, APS.

6. Maclure to Fretageot, Sept. 1830, in Elliott, *Partnership*, 802–5.

7. The printing press was located in Maclure's home at 104 South Front Street. Between 1818 and 1821, the years when the journal's editor and driving force, Thomas Say, was away on expeditions, there were no publications; upon his return, they recommenced. Eight volumes of the journal were published sporadically by 1842.

8. Thomas Nuttall, *The Genera of North American Plants, and a Catalogue of the Species, to the Year 1817,* 2 vols. (Philadelphia: printed for the author by D. Heartt, 1818), 2:115.

9. Morton, "Memoir."

10. Stroud, *Thomas Say,* 34.

11. See ibid., 59–68; T. P. Bennett, "The 1817 Florida Exposition of the Academy of Natural Sciences," *Proceedings of the Academy of Natural Sciences of Philadelphia* 152 (2002): 1–21; Charlotte M. Porter, "Following Bartram's 'Track': Titian Ramsey Peale's Florida Journey," *Florida Historical Quarterly* 61 (1983): 431–44.

12. T. Say to J. Gilliams, Jan. 30, 1818, Historical Society of Pennsylvania.

13. Ibid.; Bennett, "1817 Florida Exposition."

14. Jessie Poesch, *Titian Ramsey Peale, 1799–1885, and His Journals of the Wilkes Expedition* (Philadelphia: American Philosophical Society, 1961), 20–22.

15. T. Say to G. Ord, Apr. 11, 1818, Historical Society of Pennsylvania.

16. Maclure, journal 20, June 29, 1821, Madrid, in Doskey, *European Journals, 677.*

17. Porter, "Following Bartram's 'Track'"; Porter, *The Eagle's Nest,* 91–93.

18. Stroud, *Thomas Say,* 60.

19. See Nathan Reingold, "American Indifference to Basic Research: A Reappraisal," in George H. Daniels, *Nineteenth-Century American Science: A Reappraisal* (Evanston, Ill.: Northwestern University Press, 1972), 38–62.

20. Baatz, "Patronage, Science, and Ideology," 78–80.

21. Warren, *Rafinesque,* 54–55.

22. George H. Daniels, *American Science in the Age of Jackson* (New York: Columbia University Press, 1968), and "The Process of Professionalization."

23. Gerstner, "Academy," 55–56. See also Patricia Tyson Stroud, *The Emperor of Nature: Charles-Lucien Bonaparte and His World* (Philadelphia: University of Pennsylvania Press, 2000).

24. Ibid., 87–89.

25. Ord to T. R. Peale, Jan. 8, 1830, Ord papers, Historical Society of Pennsylvania; Ord to Charles Waterton, Nov. 15, 1834, Ord papers, APS.

9. Spanish Years and Return to America

1. A. Gil Novales, *William Maclure in Spain* (Madrid: Indec, Iniciativas de Cultura, 1981), 44; A. Gil Novales, "The Spain William Maclure Knew," *Indiana Magazine of History* 94 (1998): 99–109; Maclure, June 29 and 30, 1821, in Doskey, *European Journals,* 677–80.

2. Maclure to Fretageot, Oct. 19, 1822, in Elliott, *Partnership,* 208–11.

3. Maclure to Silliman, in *American Journal of Science* 8 (1824): 187.

4. Novales, *William Maclure in Spain,* 48, 52–53.

5. Maclure to Fretageot, Apr. 29, 1823, in *Partnership,* 226–28.

6. The striking exception was Jacobo Maria y Puga, whom he encountered in Madrid.

7. *Opinions,* 1:6–11, 222–26, 420–23.

8. Fretageot to Maclure, Apr. 21, 1821, in *Partnership,* 64–65.

9. Novales, "The Spain William Maclure Knew," 76–79, 104–5.

10. Maclure to Silliman, *American Journal of Science* 9 (1825): 157.

11. Maclure to Fretageot, Dec. 25, 1823, Feb. 18, 1824, Mar. 14, 1824, in *Partnership,* 258–60, 264–67, 267–70.

12. Maclure to Fretageot, July 12, 1822, in *Partnership,* 194–96.

13. Novales, *William Maclure in Spain,* 57–58, 64–65, 105; Erving to Maclure, Oct. 8, 1821, WMI. Erving was sent by President Madison to negotiate the transfer of Florida to the jurisdiction of the United States.

14. Maclure to Fretageot, Feb. 18, 1824, in *Partnership,* 264–66.

15. *Opinions,* 1:109–12, 247–49, 2:370–73.

16. Maclure to Fretageot, Jan. 28, 1823, in *Partnership,* 218–20.

17. Maclure to Fretageot, Jan. 21, 1822, in *Partnership,* 166–68.

18. Doskey, *European Journals,* 681. Joseph Lancaster (1778–1838), an English Quaker educator, devised a widely heralded school system in which older students instructed the younger ones.

19. Maclure to Fretageot, Dec. 19, 1822, Doskey, *European Journals,* 214–16.

20. Maclure to Fretageot, Jan. 28, 1823, Doskey, *European Journals,* 218–20. Maclure's Spanish properties are also listed in his 1827 will, reproduced by Elliott in *Partnership,* appendix H, 1083–90.

21. Doskey, *European Journals,* 682–84.

22. Maclure to Silliman, Oct. 19, 1822, in Fisher, *Life of Benjamin Silliman,* 2:41–43. Some of Maclure's essays that had been banned in France had been translated into Spanish and presumably were available in Spain.

23. Maclure to Fretageot, July 5, 1823, in *Partnership,* 232–34.

24. An extensive correspondence between Maclure and Erving discussing political and economic matters is quoted in Novales, *William Maclure in Spain,* 57–67.

25. *Opinions,* 1:87–89; Novales, *William Maclure in Spain,* 91–94.

26. Edwin Emerson Jr., *A History of the Nineteenth Century, Year by Year* (New York: P. F. Collier and Son, 1901), 2:701–5.

27. Maclure to Fretageot, Jan. 18, 1824, in *Partnership,* 260–62.

28. Maclure to Morton, Dec. 26, 1836, APS.

29. Novales, *William Maclure in Spain,* 105–10.

30. Maclure to Fretageot, Apr. 25, 1824, in *Partnership,* 275–78.

31. Maclure, *American Journal of Science* 9 (1825): 157.

32. Doskey, *European Journals,* 696–97.

33. Ibid., 698–700.

34. Ibid., 709–10.

35. Ibid., 714–15.

36. Maclure, *American Journal of Science* 9 (1825): 383–84.

37. Doskey, *European Journals*, 721–24.

38. Ibid., 728–29.

39. Ibid., 739.

40. Ibid., 730–33.

41. Ibid., 734.

42. Maclure, *American Journal of Science* 9 (1825): 163–64.

43. Doskey, *European Journals*, 741. The mineral was found to have been identified earlier by Thomas Nuttall and was called brucite; the Seybert collection of minerals is now held by the ANSP.

44. Maclure to Silliman, Mar. 16, 1824, *American Journal of Science* 8 (1824): 187–90.

45. *Opinions*, 1:221.

46. *Opinions*, 2:150–54.

47. Bestor, *Backwoods Utopias*, 154.

48. Reuben Haines to Jane B. Haines, Aug. 25, 1825, APS.

10. Robert Owen, Maclure, and the Utopian Commune

1. G. D. H. Cole, *Socialist Thought: The Forerunners, 1789–1850* (London: Macmillan, 1959), 1–10; W. H. G. Armytage, *Heavens Below: Utopian Experiments in England, 1560–1960* (London: Routledge and Kegan Paul, 1961).

2. Richard Pankhurst, *The Saint Simonians, Mill, and Carlyle: A Preface to Modern Thought* (London: Sidgwick and Jackson, 1957), 37–71.

3. Maclure to Fretageot, Jan. 19, 1831, in Elliott, *Partnership*, 879.

4. George B. Lockwood, *The New Harmony Movement* (New York: D. Appleton, 1905), 12.

5. Pankhurst, prologue to *Saint Simonians*, 1–36; Jonathan Beecher, *Charles Fourier: The Visionary and His World* (Berkeley: University of California Press, 1986), 364–71, 497–502.

6. Maclure to Silliman, in *American Journal of Science* 9 (1825): 383.

7. *Opinions*, 1:1, 2:50.

8. Articles of Agreement Drawn Up and Recommended by the London Co-Operative Society, 1925, in John Gray, *A Lecture on Human Happiness* (Philadelphia: Vertical Press, 1825).

9. Maclure to B. Silliman, May 2, 1825, *American Journal of Science* 9 (1825): 165–66.

10. A short and excellent summary of his life was written by Joseph Clayton in 1908. Other biographical sources are Lockwood, *New Harmony Movement*; Bestor, *Backwoods Utopias*; and Edward Royle, *Robert Owen and the Commencement of the Millennium: A Study of the Harmony Community* (Manchester: Manchester University Press, 1998). His son Robert Dale Owen wrote of him in his memoir: "He had been received, respectfully and sometimes with distinction, by those highest in position; by Lords Liverpool, Sidmouth, Castlereagh, and by Mr. Canning; by the Royal Dukes York, Cumberland, Sussex, Cambridge, and especially by the Duke of Kent; by the Archbishop of Canterbury (Sutton) and the Bishops of London, St. David's, Durham, Peterborough, and Norwich. Besides Bentham, his partner, he was more or less intimate with Godwin, Ricardo, Malthus, Bowring, Francis Place, Joseph Hume, James Mill, O'Connell, Roscoe, Clarkson, Cobbett, Vansittart, Sir Francis Burdett, the Edgeworths, the statistician Colquhoun, Wilberforce, Coke of Norfolk, Macaulay (father

of the historian), and Nathan Rothschild, the founder of his house. . . . In Europe he made the acquaintance of La Place, Humboldt, La Rochefoucauld, Boissy d'Anglas, Camille Jourdain, Pestalozzi, Madame de Staël, Pastor Oberlin, and many other celebrities." Robert Dale Owen, *Threading My Way: Twenty-seven Years of Autobiography* (London: Trübner, 1874), 165.

11. Engels cited in George B. Lockwood, *The New Harmony Communities* (Marion, Ind.: Chronicle Company, 1902), 61.

12. Maclure to Silliman, *American Journal of Science* 9 (1825): 383.

13. Bestor, *Backwoods Utopias*, 61.

14. Owen, *Threading My Way*, 215–18.

15. Ibid., 166–67; *Opinions*, 1:158–61.

16. *Opinions*, 1:172–75, 2:51–56, 590, 3:150–53, 229–32.

17. William E. Wilson, *The Angel and the Serpent: The Story of New Harmony* (Bloomington: Indiana University Press, 1964), 184–87.

18. Bestor, *Backwoods Utopias*, 62.

19. For an account of Owen's philosophy and his reception in America, see Bestor, *Backwoods Utopias,* chapters 4 and 5.

20. Maclure to Fretageot, Aug. 25, 1824, in *Partnership*, 296–97.

21. Ibid.; Maclure to Fretageot, Sept. 10, 1824, in *Partnership*, 299–300.

22. J. F. C. Harrison in Donald E. Pitzer, ed., *Robert Owen's American Legacy: Proceedings of the Robert Owen Bicentennial Conference* (Indianapolis: Indiana Historical Society, 1972), 29–41.

11. Harmonie to New Harmony

1. Owen, *Threading My Way*, 210–11; Lockwood, *New Harmony Communities,* 31, 47–48; Frank Podmore, *Robert Owen: A Biography* (New York: D. Appleton, 1906), 284–90. The Harmonists had built two communes called Harmonie. To distinguish them, the second, which Owen purchased, was called Neu Harmonie. The abbreviated form is used in this work. Richard Flower was a great admirer of Rapp, and for serving as Rapp's agent he pocketed $5,000. An outspoken abolitionist, he and his son Edward fled for their lives to England. Edward remained in England, a staunch supporter of the Union during the Civil War. His daughter, Sarah Flower Adams, wrote "Nearer My God to Thee."

2. Owen, *Threading My Way*, 237–60.

3. Duke Bernhard, quoted in Arndt, *Harmony on the Wabash in Transition*, 802. Information about the enemies of the commune was kindly provided by Dr. Donald E. Pitzer.

4. Wilson, *The Angel and the Serpent,* 5–113; Arndt, *Harmony on the Wabash in Transition;* Donald E. Pitzer and Josephine M. Elliot, "New Harmony's First Utopians, 1814–1824," *Indiana Magazine of History* 75 (September 1979): 225–300; Elinor Lander Horwitz, *Communes in America: The Place Just Right* (Philadelphia: J. B. Lippincott, 1972), 55–72; C. J. Jeronimus, ed., *Travels by His Highness Duke Bernhard of Saxe-Weimar-Eisenach through North America in the Years 1825 and 1826,* trans. William Jeronimus (Lanham, Md.: University Press of America, 2001), 395–401; Daniel Cohen, *Not of the World: A History of the Commune in America* (Chicago: Follett, 1969); Mark Holloway, *Heaven on Earth: Utopian Communities in America, 1680–1880* (New York: Dover, 1966); Anthony F. C. Wallace, *Rockdale: The Growth of an American Village in the Early Industrial Revolution* (New York: Norton, 1978), 273–74, 277–84.

5. William Owen, *Diary of William Owen from November 10, 1824, to April 20, 1825,* ed. Joel W. Hiatt (Indianapolis: Bobbs-Merrill, 1906), 53.

6. Donald Macdonald, *The Diaries of Donald Macdonald, 1824–1826* (Indianapolis: Indiana Historical Society, 1942).

7. Gilbert Seldes, *The Stammering Century* (New York: Harper and Row, 1965), 4.

8. Lockwood, *New Harmony Communities*, 55–61, 83, 132, 190–91.

9. Jeronimus, *Travels*, 396.

10. William W. Story, *Life and Letters of Joseph Story*, 2 vols. (Boston: C. C. Little and J. Brown, 1851), 1:485–86.

11. Stroud, *Thomas Say*; Harry B. Weiss and Grace M. Ziegler, *Thomas Say, Early American Naturalist* (Springfield, Ill.: C. C. Thomas, 1931).

12. Fretageot to Maclure, Mar. 9 and 13, 1825, in Elliott, *Partnership*, 333.

13. Fretageot to Maclure, Feb. 11, 1825, in *Partnership*, 325.

14. Thomas Say to Benjamin Tappan, Aug. 30, 1827, cited in Reingold, *Science*, 34; Maclure to S. G. Morton, cited in Reingold, *Science*, 53; Daniel Feller, "The Spirit of Improvement: The America of William Maclure and Robert Owen," *Indiana Magazine of History* 94 (June 1998): 92.

15. Fretageot to Maclure, Oct. 21, 1824, in *Partnership*, 304–5.

16. William Owen, *Diary*, 47–56; Arndt, *Harmony on the Wabash in Transition*, 326.

17. Owen, *Threading My Way*, 213; Lockwood, *New Harmony Movement*, 27–43.

18. According to Elfrieda Lang ("The Inhabitants of New Harmony According to the Federal Census of 1850," *Indiana Magazine of History* 42, no. 4 (December 1946): 355–94), he paid $125,000. Other reports vary from $50,000 to $190,000 for 32,000 acres to a recorded $125,000 for 20,000 acres. Wilson, *The Angel and the Serpent*, 110.

19. Maclure to Fretageot, July 21, 1826, in *Partnership*, 392.

20. The building, dating from 1822 to 1824, deteriorated over the years, and by 1874 it had been torn down. Its bricks were used to build a wall around the cemetery.

21. Owen, *Threading My Way*, 229.

22. *National Intelligencer*, Mar. 1, 1825, 2; Mar. 15, 1825, 2.

23. Owen, *Threading My Way*, 72–134, 254.

24. Jeronimus, *Travels*, 403.

25. Bestor, *Backwoods Utopias*, 114–32; Thomas Skidmore, *The Rights of Man to Property!* (New York: printed for the author by A. Ming, 1829).

26. *New-Harmony Gazette* 1 (1825): 102.

27. Thomas Clinton Pears Jr., *New Harmony, an Adventure in Happiness: Papers of Thomas and Sarah Pears* (Indianapolis: Indiana Historical Society, 1933; reprint, Clifton, N.J.: A. M. Kelley, 1973), 7; Lockwood, *New Harmony Communities*, 105.

28. *New-Harmony Gazette* 1 (1825): 1–3.

29. Wilson, *The Angel and the Serpent*, 95.

30. Lockwood, *New Harmony Movement*, 103–19.

31. William Owen to Robert Owen, Dec. 16, 1825. The letter was printed in the *New Harmony Times*, Aug. 6, 1906, and is cited in Bestor, *Backwoods Utopias*, 130.

32. Pears, *New Harmony*, 40–41.

33. William Pelham to his son, in Harlow Lindley, ed., *Indiana as Seen by Early Travellers* (Indianapolis: Indiana Historical Collections, 1916), 403.

34. Thomas Pears to Benjamin Bakewell, Sept. 2, 1825, and Mrs. Pears to Mrs. Bakewell, Jan. 6, 1826, in Pears, *New Harmony*, 25–26.

35. *Niles Register* 4 (July 9, 1824).

36. Jeronimus, *Travels*, 400.

37. Thomas Pears to Benjamin Bakewell, June 2, 1825, in Pears, *New Harmony*, 13.

38. Josephine M. Elliott, *To Holland and to New Harmony: Robert Dale Owen's Travel Journal, 1825–1826* (Indianapolis: Indiana Historical Society, 1969), 227–28, 233–34. David Dale Owen wrote his diary in English, but sensitive remarks were hidden in German, in which he was fluent, having attended Fellenberg's German-speaking school in Switzerland.

39. Owen, "Discourse in Washington," reported in the *New-Harmony Gazette* 2 (1827): 241–42.

12. A Boatload of Knowledge

1. Maclure to Fretageot, June 16, 1826, in Elliott, *Partnership,* 374–76.
2. Maclure to Fretageot, Sept. 10, 1824, in *Partnership,* 299.
3. Fretageot to Maclure, Mar. 9 and 13, 1825, in *Partnership,* 332–34.
4. Fretageot to Maclure, Mar. 27, 1825, in *Partnership,* 334–37.
5. Maclure to Fretageot, July 15, 1825, in *Partnership,* 339–40. Maclure's inadequate education is particularly evident.
6. Maclure to Fretageot, June 9, 1826, in *Partnership,* 373–74.
7. Say was the author of *American Entomology* and *American Conchology,* both classics. Stroud, *Thomas Say;* Bennett, "1817 Florida Exposition." In America, Lesueur was the first classifier of the fish of the Great Lakes. Before meeting Maclure, he had studied the natural history of Australia.
8. George Ord, "A Memoir of Charles-Alexandre Lesueur," *American Journal of Science and the Arts* 8 (1849): 212.
9. See Macdonald, *Diaries,* 333–37, for an account of the trip down the Ohio River; see also Arndt, *Harmony on the Wabash in Transition,* 782–94, from diaries of R. D. Owen and D. Macdonald.
10. Letter written by William Pelham, a member of the New Harmony colony, to his son, dated Jan. 6, 1826. Cited in Lindley, *Indiana,* 405.
11. Victor Colin Duclos (Madame Fretageot's nephew) in Lindley, *Indiana,* 536–48.
12. Donald E. Pitzer, "William Maclure's Boatload of Knowledge: Science and Education into the Midwest," *Indiana Magazine of History* 94 (1998): 117–27; a list of passengers can be found on 136–37. A list was also included in Robert Dale Owen's travel journal. Elliott, *To Holland and to New Harmony,* 265–68.
13. Snedeker, *The Town of the Fearless,* 234.
14. Macdonald, *Diaries,* 332.
15. Owen, *Threading My Way,* 236–38.
16. Elliott, *To Holland and to New Harmony,* 232, 247, 249.
17. The bulk of Lesueur's drawings are in the Musée d'Histoire Naturelle du Havre, Le Havre, France. Copies of some can be found at the APS. Lesueur produced 1,200 sketches, of which 127 were of the trip down the Ohio River. The Musée's extensive holdings of Lesueur's drawings and papers have been cataloged by Jacqueline Bonnemains and published in *Annales du Muséum D'Histoire Naturelle du Havre,* nos. 29 and 30 (1984).
18. Macdonald, *Diaries,* 335.
19. Lindley, *Indiana,* 410–11.

13. Education in New Harmony

1. For excellent discussions of the decline and fall of New Harmony, see Bestor, *Backwoods Utopias,* 160–201; Taylor, *Visions of Harmony,* 137–62; Charles Burgess, "A House

Divided: Robert Owen and William Maclure at New Harmony," *Journal of the Midwest History of Education Society* 3 (1975): 110–21; Charles Burgess, "The Boatload of Trouble: William Maclure and Robert Owen Revisited," *Indiana Magazine of History* 94 (1998): 138–50.

2. "View of New-Harmony," *New-Harmony Gazette*, Oct. 1825; Doskey, *European Journals*, 277–78. For a list of the major citizens of New Harmony and when they lived there, see D. F. Carmony and J. M. Elliott, "New Harmony, Indiana: Robert Owen's Seedbed for Utopia," *Indiana Magazine of History* 76 (1980): 161–261 (reprinted as a booklet, 1999), 217.

3. Lindley, *Indiana*, 409; Podmore, *Robert Owen*, 161, 162.

4. Maclure to Silliman, Mar. 16, 1826, *American Journal of Science* 11 (1826): 189–92.

5. Maclure to Fretageot, June 9, 1826, in Elliott, *Partnership*, 373–74.

6. There seems to be considerable uncertainty about Maclure's financial commitment to New Harmony.

7. Bestor, *Backwoods Utopias*, 134–36.

8. Maclure, *New-Harmony Gazette* 1 (1826): 166–67. This article also contains a reprint of Maclure's exposition of the Pestalozzian schools taught by Madame Fretageot and William Phiquepal in Paris and Philadelphia.

9. Maclure to Silliman, *American Journal of Science* 11 (1825): 189–92.

10. *New-Harmony Gazette* 1 (1826): 102.

11. A prospectus written by Maclure, found in a footnote on pp. 12–13 of Frances Trollope's *Domestic Manners*, describes a typical day: "Hours from five in the morning until eight in the evening, [are] divided as follows The scholars rise at five; at half past five each goes to his occupation; at seven the bell rings for breakfast; at eight they return to work; at eleven their lessons begin, continuing until half past two, including half an hour for luncheon; then they return to their occupations until five, when a bell calls them to dinner. Afterwards until half past six they exercise themselves in various ways; then the evening lesson begins and lasts until eight."

Henry's experience may have prompted Mrs. Trollope's sarcastic, gossipy criticism of New Harmony. She alleged that Maclure and Madame Fretageot were intimate and that Madame Fretageot was pocketing school funds—both baseless accusations.

12. Paul R. Bernard, "Irreconcilable Differences: The Social and Educational Theories of Robert Owen and William Maclure," *Journal of the Early Republic* 8 (1988): 21–22, 36–44. See also Charles Burgess, "William Maclure and Education for a Good Society," *History of Education Quarterly* 3 (1963): 58–76; Burgess, "A House Divided"; William A. Boram, "William Maclure: Response," *History of Education Quarterly* 3 (1963): 77–80; and Baron Roger de Guimps, *Pestalozzi: His Aim and Work,* trans. Margaret C. Crombie (Syracuse, N.Y.: C. W. Bardeen, 1889).

13. Gutek, "Robert Owen's New Harmony Community."

14. Beecher, *Charles Fourier,* 364–71, 497–500.

15. *New-Harmony Gazette* 1 (1827): 390.

16. Maclure to Silliman, *American Journal of Science* 11 (1826): 189–92; *Opinions,* 1:66.

17. Glowing reports about New Harmony schools appeared in the *American Journal of Education* 1 (June 1826): 587–92, and in Monroe, *Pestalozzian Movement,* 109–26.

18. Bestor, *Backwoods Utopias,* 182–83. A detailed report on the educational program at New Harmony was presented by Maclure in the *New-Harmony Gazette* 1 (Feb. 15, 1827): 166–67.

19. Victor Colin Duclos in Lindley, *Indiana,* 536–48.

20. Karl Bernard, Duke of Saxe-Weimar, in Lindley, *Indiana,* 418–37.

21. Maclure to friends, Mar. 14, 1824, Aug. 18–21, 1826, and Feb. 24, 1827, in *Partnership*, 267–70, 419–20, and 473–74.

22. Maclure to friends, Feb. 20, 1830, in *Partnership*, 688–92; Oct. 10, 1823, in *Partnership*, 244–46; Nov. 20, 1823, in *Partnership*, 248–50.

23. Maclure to Fretageot, June 9, June 20, 1826, in *Partnership*, 373–74, 376–79.

24. Maclure to Fretageot, Aug. 21, 1826 (second letter), Bestor, *Education and Reform*, 358–59.

25. Maclure to Fretageot, July 21, 1826, Feb. 24, 1827, in *Partnership*, 390–93, 469–75.

26. Maclure to Fretageot, Jan. 7, 1827, in *Partnership*, 451–54.

27. Maclure to Fretageot, Jan. 27, Feb. 8, 1827, in *Partnership*, 454, 459.

28. Fretageot to Maclure, Mar. 2, 1827, in *Partnership*, 476–78.

29. *New-Harmony Gazette* 1 (1826): 50–51, 57–58, 65–66, 73–75.

30. *New-Harmony Gazette* 2 (1827): 63.

31. *New-Harmony Gazette* 1 (1826): 36–37.

32. Maclure to Fretageot, July 24, 1826, in *Partnership*, 395–400.

33. Bestor, *Backwoods Utopias*, 211–13; Maclure to Fretageot, June 20, 1826, in *Partnership*, 376–79.

34. Maclure to Fretageot, Aug. 18–21, 1826, in *Partnership*, 418–21.

35. *New-Harmony Gazette* 3 (1828): 124–25, 132–33, 140–41; Celia Morris Eckhardt, *Fanny Wright, Rebel in America* (Cambridge, Mass.: Harvard University Press, 1984), 108–40.

36. Frances Wright, *Views of Society and Manners in America,* reprint of 1821 edition, ed. Paul R. Baker (Cambridge, Mass.: Belknap Press of Harvard University Press, 1963); Helen Elliott, "Frances Wright's Experiment with Negro Emancipation," *Indiana Magazine of History* 35 (1939): 141–57.

37. Maclure to Fretageot, Dec. 13, 1826, in *Partnership*, 438–40.

38. Maclure to Fretageot, Dec. 31, 1827, in *Partnership*, 478–80.

39. *Opinions,* 3:109–12, 154–56, 247–49.

40. Taylor, *Visions of Harmony,* 176–88.

41. F. Wright to Maclure, Jan. 3, 1830, WMI.

42. *Opinions,* 2:370.

43. *Opinions,* 1:30–31, 42–44, 3:109–12, 154–56, 247–49.

44. Trollope, *Domestic Manners,* 263.

45. Maclure to Fretageot, Dec. 31, 1827, in *Partnership*, 478–80.

46. Taylor, *Visions of Harmony,* 163–75, 198–99.

47. Fretageot to Maclure, Jan. 30, 1829, in *Partnership*, 555–56.

14. Trouble in Paradise

1. Benjamin Bakewell to Mrs. Pears, Jan. 2, 1826, in Pears, *New Harmony,* 50.

2. Lindley, *Indiana,* 421.

3. Ibid., 76.

4. Pears, *New Harmony,* 40–41.

5. Lindley, *Indiana,* 406–7.

6. Lockwood, *New Harmony Movement,* 121–28. An excellent, detailed account of the politics, economics, and educational organization of New Harmony is found in William Frank Kipnis, "Propagating the Pestalozzian: The Story of William Maclure's Involvement in Efforts to Affect Educational and Social Reforms in the Early Nineteenth Century" (PhD diss., Loyola University of Chicago, 1972), 169–210.

7. Pears, *New Harmony,* 56–59; Bestor, *Backwoods Utopias,* 170.

8. Lockwood, *New Harmony Communities,* 121–40.

9. Paul Brown, *Twelve Months in New Harmony; Presenting a Faithful Account of the Principal Occurrences Which Have Taken Place There within That Period; Interspersed with Remarks* (Cincinnati: W. H. Woodward, 1872; reprint, Philadelphia: Porcupine Press, 1972), 41–54.

10. Owen, *Threading My Way,* 254.

11. *New-Harmony Gazette* 1 (1826): 161–63.

12. Bestor, *Backwoods Utopias,* 165–67.

13. Owen, *Threading My Way,* 254–64.

14. Jeronimus, *Travels,* 404–5.

15. Pears, *New Harmony,* 60.

16. *New-Harmony Gazette* 1 (1826): 209, 225, 262–63; Thomas Pears to Benjamin Bakewell, Mar. 4, Mar. 21, 1826, in Pears, *New Harmony,* 66–69, 75–79.

17. *New-Harmony Gazette* 1 (1826): 77.

18. G. Rey to V. Du Pont, Apr. 13, 1826, in Elliott, *Partnership,* appendix D, 1059–66. The original letter is in the Winterthur collection of the Hagley Museum and Library, Wilmington, Del.

19. Maclure to Fretageot, Aug. 18–21, 1826, in *Partnership,* 418–21.

20. Jeronimus, *Travels,* 401.

21. Owen, *Threading My Way,* 245–46.

22. Pears, *New Harmony,* 83.

23. *New-Harmony Gazette* 1 (May 16, 1826): 268.

24. Brown, *Twelve Months in New Harmony,* 24, 25; Maclure to Fretageot, Aug. 21, 1826, in *Partnership,* 421–23.

25. Maclure to Fretageot, Aug. 21, 1826, in *Partnership,* 421–23.

26. Bernard, "Irreconcilable Differences."

15. Out of the Ashes

1. *New-Harmony Gazette* 1 (July 12, 1826): 329–32.

2. *National Gazette and Literary Register,* Aug. 27, 1826.

3. Wilson, *The Angel and the Serpent,* 129–32.

4. Maclure to Fretageot, July 24, Aug. 2 and 11, 1826, in Elliott, *Partnership,* 398, 406–8, 411–14; see also 360; Maclure in *National Gazette and Literary Register,* Oct. 4, 1826.

5. Maclure to Fretageot, Oct. 30, 1830, in *Partnership,* 819–21.

6. E. D. Baltzell, *Puritan Boston and Quaker Philadelphia* (New York: Free Press, 1979), 178.

7. *Opinions,* 2:463–67.

8. Pears, *New Harmony,* 85–94.

9. *New-Harmony Gazette* 2 (1826): 100. For criticism, see *New-Harmony Gazette* 1 (1826): 302–3, 309–10, 316–17; 2 (1826): 26–27, 100.

10. New-Harmony Gazette 1 (1826): 81; Maclure to an unknown gentleman, Sept. 20, 1826, in Bestor, Education and Reform, 347–48.

11. *New-Harmony Gazette* 1 (Aug. 1826).

12. *Opinions,* 1:366–67, 372–75, 382–83, 390–91.

13. Maclure to Fretageot, Aug. 30, 1826, in *Partnership,* 428–31.

14. Brown, *Twelve Months in New Harmony,* 82; Kipnis, "Propagating the Pestalozzian," 291–303.

15. Owen, *Threading My Way*, 252–53.
16. Maclure to Fretageot, Sept. 19, 1826, in *Partnership*, 431–33.
17. Maclure to Fretageot, Sept. 25, 1826, in *Partnership*, 433–35.
18. *New-Harmony Gazette* 2 (Oct. 11, 1826): 15.
19. Maclure to Fretageot, Nov. 28, 1826, in *Partnership*, 435.
20. *New-Harmony Gazette*, Feb. 14, 1827.
21. Maclure to Fretageot, Nov. 28, Dec. 22, 1826, in *Partnership*, 435–38, 440–42; Brown, *Twelve Months in New Harmony*, 76, 84–87, 116–17.
22. Bestor, *Backwoods Utopias*, 195–96.
23. Ibid., 197–99.
24. Ibid., 193–94; Owen in the *New-Harmony Gazette* 2 (Nov. 29, 1826): 70.
25. Brown, *Twelve Months in New Harmony*, 80–81.
26. Maclure to Fretageot, Jan. 3, 1827, in *Partnership*, 448–51.
27. Bestor, *Backwoods Utopias*, 197–99; *Partnership*, appendix G, 1081–82.
28. *New-Harmony Gazette* 2 (Mar. 28, 1827): 206–7.
29. Simon A. Ferrall, *A Ramble of Six Thousand Miles through the United States of America* (London: Effingham Wilson, 1832), 98.
30. Owen's speech can be found in Brown, *Twelve Months in New Harmony*, 98–106; *New-Harmony Gazette* 2 (May 9, 1827): 254, 2 (May 30, 1827): 278–79.
31. Brown, *Twelve Months in New Harmony*: Neef's response, 106–16; Brown's response, 118–28.
32. Ferrall, *Ramble*, 100.
33. William Bailie, *Josiah Warren, the First American Anarchist: A Sociological Study* (Boston: Small, Maynard, 1906), 4.
34. Weiss and Ziegler, *Thomas Say*, 126, 129.
35. Ferrall, *Ramble*, 88–107.
36. Maclure to Fretageot, Sept. 25, 1826, in *Partnership*, 434.
37. Kipnis, "Propagating the Pestalozzian," 340–56.
38. Maclure to Fretageot, Aug. 12, 1829, in *Partnership*, 607.
39. Weiss and Ziegler, *Thomas Say*, 213–20.
40. *New-Harmony Gazette* 2 (May 16, 1827).
41. Maclure, *American Journal of Science* 10 (1826): 145–51; Weiss and Ziegler, *Thomas Say*, 131.
42. *Opinions*, 1:45–117.
43. *New-Harmony Gazette* 2 (May 16, 1827): 263.
44. Fretageot to Maclure, Jan. 24, 1828, in *Partnership*, 481–86.
45. Maclure to Fretageot, Dec. 25, 1824, in *Partnership*, 312–14.
46. Maclure to Fretageot, Oct. 30, 1830, in *Partnership*, 819–21.
47. Fretageot to Maclure, Mar. 13, 1829, in *Partnership*, 571.
48. Maclure to Fretageot, Jan. 28, 1828, in *Partnership*, 486–87.
49. Fretageot to Maclure, Oct. 17 and Nov. 28, 1828, Nov. 29 and Dec. 13, 1830, in *Partnership*, 530–31, 834–37, 840–44.
50. Brown, *Twelve Months in New Harmony*, 82; Fretageot to Maclure, Sept. 29, 1830, *Partnership*, 796–801.
51. Fretageot to Maclure, Mar. 2, 1827, in *Partnership*, 476–77.
52. Maclure to Fretageot, Jan. 28, 1828, in *Partnership*, 486–87.
53. Fretageot to Maclure, Sept. 6, 1830, in *Partnership*, 786–89.

54. Fretageot to Maclure, Sept. 12, 1829, Sept. 29, 1830, in *Partnership,* 616–18, 796–801.

55. Fretageot to Maclure, Sept. 9, 1830, in *Partnership,* 789–92.

56. *Opinions,* 1:221.

57. *New-Harmony Gazette,* Nov. 29, 1827.

58. Maclure to Fretageot, July 31, 1826, in *Partnership,* 403–4.

59. Maclure to Haines, Aug. 9, 1827, APS; Maclure to Fretageot, Feb. 18, 1829, in *Partnership,* 561.

16. Withdrawal to Mexico

1. Lardner Vanuxem to Isaac Lea, Feb. 16, 1828, Sept. 10, 1828, ANSP.

2. *Encyclopaedia Britannica,* 1929, s.v. "Brief History of Mexico," 15:388–90.

3. Benjamin Keen and Mark Wasserman, *A History of Latin America,* 3rd ed. (Boston: Houghton Mifflin, 1988), 174–82.

4. *Opinions,* 1:207–15.

5. *Opinions,* 1:268, 300.

6. Maclure's experiences in Mexico were published as a series of letters in *Opinions,* 1:207–442.

7. *Disseminator,* June 25, 1831.

8. *Opinions,* 1:229.

9. Maclure to S. G. Morton, Apr. 3, 1830, APS.

10. *Opinions,* 1:214–15, 223, 227.

11. Maclure to Count Lasterie, Mar. 28, 1829, WMI.

12. *Opinions,* 1:281–85, 288–91.

13. *Opinions,* 1:225–26.

14. *Opinions,* 1:242–45.

15. *Opinions,* 1:299–319.

16. *Opinions,* 1:224–25.

17. *Opinions,* 1:237.

18. *Opinions,* 1:6–10; 222–23; Maclure to Fretageot, Dec. 19, 1828, in Elliott, *Partnership,* 539–41.

19. Maclure to G. W. Erving, Feb. 20, 1830, WMI.

20. *Opinions,* 1:288–91.

21. *Opinions,* 1:226–29, 232–34.

22. *Opinions,* 1:270–73, 311.

23. *Opinions,* 1:259.

24. *Opinions,* 1:259–60.

25. *Opinions,* 1:291–95.

26. *Opinions,* 1:242.

27. W. B. Hendrickson, *David Dale Owen, Pioneer Geologist of the Middle West,* Indiana Historical Collections, vol. 27 (Indianapolis: Indiana Historical Bureau, 1943), 13–14, 58–59.

28. Richard William Leopold, *Robert Dale Owen, a Biography* (Cambridge: Harvard University Press, 1940), 129, 223, 235.

29. Maclure to Fretageot, Oct. 24, 1828, in *Partnership,* 306–8.

30. Ward to Fretageot, Oct. 28, 1828, in *Partnership,* 510–11.

31. Fretageot to Maclure, Dec. 5, 1828, in *Partnership,* 533–35.

32. Fretageot to Maclure, Oct. 3, 1828, in *Partnership*, 495–97.

33. *Opinions*, 1:295–99.

34. Fretageot to Maclure, Jan. 9, 1829, in *Partnership*, 548–50.

35. Fretageot to Maclure, Nov. 28, 1828, in *Partnership*, 532–33.

36. Fretageot to Maclure, Nov. 13, 1828, in *Partnership*, 520–23.

37. Fretageot to Maclure, Oct. 24, 1828, in *Partnership*, 506–8.

38. Fretageot to Maclure, Nov. 2, 1828, in *Partnership*, 513–16.

39. Maclure to Fretageot, Jan. 28, 1829, in *Partnership*, 553–54.

40. Bestor, *Education and Reform*, 403–4.

41. Fretageot to Maclure, Jan. 9, 1829, in *Partnership*, 548–50; Maclure to Fretageot, Jan. 28, 1829, in *Partnership*, 553–54.

42. *Opinions*, 1:273–77.

43. Maclure to Fretageot, Feb. 18, 1829, in *Partnership*, 360–64.

44. *Opinions*, 1:345–48.

45. Maclure to Fretageot, Feb. 18, 1829, in *Partnership*, 560–64.

46. Maclure to Fretageot, June 10, 1829, in *Partnership*, 587–90.

47. Maclure to Fretageot, Mar. 23, and a following, undated letter, 1829, in *Partnership*, 575–78.

48. Maclure to Fretageot, no date, in *Partnership*, 643.

49. Maclure to Fretageot, Oct. 25, 1829, in *Partnership*, 626–27.

50. Maclure to Fretageot, Nov. 16, 1829, in *Partnership*, 638–39.

51. Ismar to Maclure, cited in *Partnership*, 673n1. Elliott offers an account of the Ismar affair in *Partnership*, 659–70.

52. Fretageot to Maclure, Jan. 6, 1830, in *Partnership*, 671–73.

53. Maclure to Fretageot, Mar. 3, 1830, in *Partnership*, 695–98.

54. Maclure to Fretageot, Mar. 20, 1830, in *Partnership*, 704–8.

55. Maclure to Fretageot, Jan. 16, 22, 23, 25, Feb. 1, 6, 7, Mar. 3, 1830, in *Partnership*, 676–81, 695–98.

56. Maclure to Fretageot, May 12, 1830, in *Partnership*, 727–28.

57. Fretageot to Maclure, May 5, 1830, in *Partnership*, 723–26.

58. Maclure to Fretageot, no date, in *Partnership*, 857–63.

59. Maclure to Fretageot, Apr. 1830, in *Partnership*, 716–17.

60. Maclure to Fretageot, June 4 and 5, 1830, in *Partnership*, 734–37; Ismar's libel, letter to Mr. Maclure, at Mexico concerning the state of his school at New Harmony, Mar. 5, 1830, in *Partnership*, appendix J, 1093–1104.

61. Fretageot to Maclure, June 7 and 10, 1830, in *Partnership*, 737–41; A. Ward to Maclure, July 8, 1830, WMI.

62. See *Partnership*, 660–62.

63. Fretageot to Maclure, no date, in *Partnership*, 859–61.

64. Fretageot to Maclure, Apr. 8, 1830, in *Partnership*, 714–16.

65. Maclure to George Erving, Feb. 20, 1830, WMI.

66. Martha Chase to Maclure, June 1, 1830, WMI.

67. Fretageot to Maclure, July 16 and 19, 1831, in *Partnership*, 928–31.

68. Maclure to Fretageot, June 30, 1830, in *Partnership*, 751–55.

69. Maclure to Fretageot, Aug. 21, 1830, in *Partnership*, 769–71.

70. Fretageot to Maclure, Apr. 18, 1831, in *Partnership*, 910–13.

71. Maclure to Fretageot, no date, in *Partnership*, 870–71.

72. Maclure to Fretageot, Mar. 30, 1831, in *Partnership*, 904–6.

17. Crippling Losses of Madame Fretageot and Thomas Say

1. Fretageot to Maclure, Nov. 8, 1831, in Elliott, *Partnership,* 966–69.
2. *Partnership,* 961–65.
3. Say to Fretageot, Nov. 21, 1831, WMI.
4. Fretageot to Maclure, Dec. 25, 26, 27, 1831, in *Partnership,* 873–77.
5. *Partnership,* 963.
6. Maclure to Achille Fretageot, Jan. 1832, in *Partnership,* 990–91.
7. Fretageot to Maclure, Feb.–Mar. 1832, in *Partnership,* 991–96.
8. Fretageot to Maclure, Dec. 30, 1831, in *Partnership,* 877–80.
9. Maclure to Fretageot, Jan. 7, 1832, in *Partnership,* 980–84.
10. Taylor, *Visions of Harmony,* 202.
11. Maclure to Fretageot, Feb. 18, 1832, in *Partnership,* 996–1002.
12. Maclure to Fretageot, July 5, 1832, in *Partnership,* 1017–22.
13. Fretageot to Maclure, Mar. 27–Apr. 25, 1832, in *Partnership,* 1002–5.
14. Say to Fretageot, Jan. 14, 1832, WMI.
15. Say and Alexander Maclure to Maclure, Feb. 2, 3, 4, 1832, WMI.
16. Monroe, *Pestalozzian Movement,* 61–96.
17. Maclure to Fretageot, Feb. 23, 1833, in *Partnership,* 1041–44.
18. Say and Achille Fretageot to Fretageot, Nov. 6, 1832, WMI.
19. Say to Maclure, Feb. 2, and 4, 1832, WMI.
20. Cited in *Partnership,* 962.
21. Alexander Greaves to Maclure, Nov. 1, 1833, WMI.
22. George Ord to Charles Waterton, Nov. 15, 1834, APS.
23. Maclure to Say, Oct. 3, 1833, series 1, WMI. Cited in *Partnership,* 965.
24. Monroe, *Pestalozzian Movement,* 123–26.
25. Maclure to Say, Nov. 7, 1833, WMI.
26. T. Say to Charles Lucien Bonaparte, Jan. 6, 1828, Dec. 1828, July 1830, APS.
27. Alexander Maclure to Maclure, Oct. 14, 1834, WMI.
28. Weiss and Ziegler, *Thomas Say,* 221–25.
29. George Ord to Reuben Haines, Aug. 21, 1820, Haverford College Library and Archives, Haverford, Pa.; Ord to L. Bonaparte, Oct. 14, 1838, APS.
30. Maclure to Anna Maclure, Apr. 20, 1838, WMI.

18. New Harmony Adrift

1. Leopold, *Robert Dale Owen,* 123–62, and Taylor, *Visions of Harmony,* 206–25, for accounts of the Owens' lives in New Harmony after the departure of Robert Owen.
2. Josephine M. Elliott, ed., "The Owen Family Papers," *Indiana Magazine of History* 60 (1964): 331–52.
3. Thomas J. De la Hunt, *History of the New Harmony Working Men's Institute, New Harmony, Indiana, Founded by William Maclure* (Evansville, Ind.: Burkert-Walton, 1927).
4. Ian MacPhail and Marjorie Sutton, "William Maclure as Publisher in the New Harmony Reform Tradition," *Indiana Magazine of History* 94 (1998): 167–77.
5. Maclure to Say, Nov. 7, 1833, WMI; *Opinions,* 1:462–63; Elliott, *Partnership,* 705.
6. J. D. Baldwin to Maclure, Aug. 19, 1839, WMI.
7. Robert Dale Owens, *Footfalls on the Boundary of Another World* (Philadelphia: J.

B. Lippincott, 1860); Robert Dale Owens, *The Debatable Land between This World and the Next* (New York: G. W. Carleton, 1872).

8. David Dale Owen, *Mineral Lands of the United States* (Washington, D.C.: Government Printing Office, 1845); David Dale Owen, *Report of a Geological Survey of Wisconsin, Iowa, and Minnesota, and Incidentally of a Portion of Nebraska Territory* (Philadelphia: Lippincott, Grambo, 1852; David Dale Owen, *Report of a Geological Reconnaissance of Indiana, Made during the Years 1859 and 1860* (Indianapolis: Dodd, 1862).

9. It has been said that the castlelike appearance of the Smithsonian Institution, complete with turrets, derives from the preferences of the Owen brothers and their selection of James Renwick Jr. as its architect. Part of Maclure's specimens went to New York museums.

10. Numerous letters from Maclure to Morton written during the 1830s to the last year of Maclure's life are found in the J. Percy Moore Papers, ANSP.

11. Marmaduke Burrough to Morton, Feb. 9, July 1, 1836, Oct. 1, 1837, Moore Papers, ANSP.

12. Maclure to Burrough, Aug. 19, 1836, APS.

13. Maclure to S. G. Morton, Aug. 1835, Oct. 30, 1835, Jan. 31, 1836, APS.

14. Elliott, "William Maclure."

15. J. P. Dunn, *The Libraries of Indiana* (Indianapolis: W. B. Burford, 1893), 12–13.

16. Maclure to S. G. Morton, Apr. 3, 1830, APS.

17. Maclure to S. G. Morton, Dec. 26, 1836, APS. Girard had left $2 million for the education of poor (white) children, which entailed the building of a school of simple structure. Nicholas Biddle, the aristocratic banker and chairman of the board of directors of the new college, hired the architect Thomas U. Walters to create a magnificent Greek Revival building, a grand monument of questionable function which when opened in 1846 was considered the finest building in the United States. The intent of Girard had been thwarted.

18. *Opinions,* 1:127.

19. Maclure to S. G. Morton, Aug. 12, 1836, APS.

20. Maclure to Reuben Haines, Feb. 9, 1831, Historical Society of Pennsylvania.

21. Maclure to Morton, Jan. 31, 1836, APS.

22. *New-Harmony Gazette* 3 (1827): 244, 260.

23. Maclure to S. G. Morton, Oct. 1, 1836, June 15, 1839, APS; J. Percy Moore, "William Maclure—Scientist and Humanitarian," *Proceedings of the American Philosophical Society* 91 (1947): 234–49.

24. Maclure to Morton, Oct. 30, 1835, APS.

25. De la Hunt, *Working Men's Institute,* 46.

26. Elliott, "William Maclure."

27. R. D. Owen to Maclure, Oct. 18, 1830, WMI.

28. R. D. Owen to Reuben Haines, Aug. 5, 1830, WMI.

29. A. Maclure to William Maclure, Aug. 15, Dec. 8, 1834, WMI.

30. Maclure to S. G. Morton, Mar. 26, 1835, Dec. 26, 1836, APS.

19. The Working Men's Institute and the Death of William Maclure

1. Maclure, *Disseminator* 1 (1828): 121.

2. De la Hunt, *Working Men's Institute,* 1; Waserman, "A Bio-bibliography," 21–24; Dan A. Williams, "The New Harmony Working Men's Institute," *Library Quarterly* 20 (1950): 109–18; Lockwood, *New Harmony Movement,* 330–35; Jeffrey Douglas, "William Maclure and the New Harmony Working Men's Institute," *Libraries and Culture* 26 (1991): 402–14.

3. Maclure to Achille Fretageot, undated letters, Sept. 2, 1837, WMI.

4. De la Hunt, *Working Men's Institute,* 2–6.

5. Ibid., 13–14.

6. Ibid., 19–20.

7. Ibid., 20–22.

8. Ibid., 34, 36–37.

9. Ibid., 38.

10. Burrough to Morton, Oct. 1, 1837, APS.

11. De la Hunt, *Working Men's Institute,* 41–42.

12. Ibid., 43.

13. *Reports of Cases Argued and Determined in the Supreme Court of Judicature of the State of Indiana* (1855), 5:467–69.

14. Dunn, *The Libraries of Indiana,* 13; Elliott, "William Maclure," 180; Lockwood, *New Harmony Movement,* 322–35.

15. See Elfrieda Lang, "Autobiography of Alvin P. Hovey's Early Life," *Indiana Magazine of History* 43 (Mar. 1952): 71–84.

16. *Reports of Cases Argued,* 5:465–78.

17. Hendrickson, *David Dale Owen,* 123; D. D. Owen to Lucy Say, Dec. 15, 1855, ANSP.

18. Elliott, "William Maclure," 182–86; Lockwood, *New Harmony Movement,* 325–27.

19. Dunn, *The Libraries of Indiana,* 13–15.

BIBLIOGRAPHY

Adams, Henry. *History of the United States of America.* 6 vols. New York: C. Scribner's Sons, 1904–1909.

Alcott, Amos Bronson. *Conversations with Children on the Gospels.* Vol. 1. Boston: J. Munroe, 1836.

Armytage, W. H. G. *Heavens Below: Utopian Experiments in England, 1560–1960.* London: Routledge and Kegan Paul, 1961.

Arndt, Karl J. R. *George Rapp's Harmony Society, 1785–1847.* Philadelphia: University of Pennsylvania Press, 1965.

———. *Harmony on the Wabash in Transition, 1824–1826.* Worcester, Mass.: Harmony Society Press, 1982.

Baatz, Simon. "Patronage, Science, and Ideology in an American City: Patrician Philadelphia, 1800–1860." Ph.D. diss., University of Pennsylvania, 1986.

———. "Philadelphia Patronage: The Institutional Structure of Natural History in the New Republic, 1800–1833." *Journal of the Early Republic* 8, no. 2 (1988): 111–38.

Bailie, William. *Josiah Warren, the First American Anarchist: A Sociological Study.* Boston: Small, Maynard, 1906.

Baltzell, E. D. *Puritan Boston and Quaker Philadelphia.* New York: Free Press, 1979.

Barnard, Henry. *Pestalozzi and the Education System.* Syracuse, N.Y.: Bardeen, 1881.

Bedell, Rebecca B. *The Anatomy of Nature: Geology and American Landscape Painting, 1825–1875.* Princeton: Princeton University Press, 2001.

Beecher, Jonathan. *Charles Fourier: The Visionary and His World.* Berkeley: University of California Press, 1986.

Bennett, T. P. "The 1817 Florida Exposition of the Academy of Natural Sciences." *Proceedings of the Academy of Natural Sciences of Philadelphia* 152 (2002): 1–21.

Bentman, Raymond. *Robert Burns.* Boston: Twayne, 1987.

Bernard, Paul R. "Irreconcilable Differences: The Social and Educational Theories of Robert Owen and William Maclure." *Journal of the Early Republic* 8 (1988): 21–44.

Bestor, Arthur E., Jr., ed. *Education and Reform at New Harmony: Correspondence of William Maclure and Marie Duclos Fretageot, 1820–1833.* Indianapolis: Indiana Historical Society, 1948.

————. *Backwoods Utopias: The Sectarian Origins and Owenite Phases of Communitarian Socialism in America, 1663–1829*. Philadelphia: University of Pennsylvania Press, 1970.

Boram, William A. "William Maclure: Response." *History of Education Quarterly* 3 (1963): 77–80.

Brock, William R., and C. Helen Brock. *Scotus Americanus: A Survey of the Sources for Links between Scotland and America in the Eighteenth Century*. Edinburgh: Edinburgh University Press, 1982.

Brooks, Van Wyck. *The World of Washington Irving*. New York: Dutton, 1944.

Brown, Chandos Michael. *Benjamin Silliman: A Life in the Young Republic*. Princeton: Princeton University Press, 1989.

Brown, Paul. *Twelve Months in New Harmony; Presenting a Faithful Account of the Principal Occurrences Which Have Taken Place There within That Period; Interspersed with Remarks*. Cincinnati: W. H. Woodward, 1872; reprint, Philadelphia: Porcupine Press, 1972.

Burgess, Charles. "William Maclure and Education for a Good Society." *History of Education Quarterly* 3 (1963): 58–76.

————. "A House Divided: Robert Owen and William Maclure at New Harmony." *Journal of the Midwest History of Education Society* 3 (1975): 110–21.

————. "The Boatload of Trouble: William Maclure and Robert Owen Revisited." *Indiana Magazine of History* 94 (1998): 138–50.

Carmony, D. F., and J. M. Elliott. "New Harmony, Indiana: Robert Owen's Seedbed for Utopia." *Indiana Magazine of History* 76 (1980): 161–261. Reprinted as a booklet, 1999.

Carter, Edward C., II. "Benjamin Henry Latrobe, 'Learned Engineer': The American Philosophical Society and the Promotion of Useful Knowledge and Works, 1798–1809." In R. S. Klein, ed., *Science and Society in Early America: Essays in Honor of Whitfield J. Bell Jr.* Philadelphia: American Philosophical Society, 1986.

Carter, Edward C., II, Angeline Polites, Lee W. Formwalt, and John C. Van Horne, eds. *The Virginia Journals of Benjamin Henry Latrobe, 1795–1798*. 2 vols. New Haven: Published for the Maryland Historical Society by Yale University Press, 1977.

Clayton, Joseph. *Robert Owen, Pioneer of Social Reform*. London: Fifield, 1908.

Cleaveland, Park. *An Elementary Treatise on Mineralogy and Geology, Being an Introduction to the Study of These Sciences, and Designed for the Use of Pupils,—for Persons Attending Lectures on These Subjects,—and as a Companion for Travellers in the United States of America*. Boston: Cummings, Hilliard, 1816.

Cohen, Daniel. *Not of the World: A History of the Commune in America*. Chicago: Follett, 1969.

Cole, G. D. H. *Socialist Thought: The Forerunners, 1789–1850*. London: Macmillan, 1959.

Copley, Stephen, and Kathryn Sutherland. *Adam Smith's Wealth of Nations: New Interdisciplinary Essays*. Manchester: Manchester University Press, 1995.

Daniels, George H. "The Process of Professionalization in American Science: The Emergent Period, 1820–1860." *Isis* 58 (1967): 151–66.

————. *American Science in the Age of Jackson*. New York: Columbia University Press, 1968.

————. *Nineteenth-Century American Science: A Reappraisal*. Evanston, Ill.: Northwestern University Press, 1972.

De la Hunt, Thomas J. *History of the New Harmony Working Men's Institute, New Harmony, Indiana, Founded by William Maclure*. Evansville, Ind.: Burkert-Walton, 1927.

Doskey, John S., ed. *The European Journals of William Maclure*. Philadelphia: American Philosophical Society, 1988.

Douglas, Jeffrey. "William Maclure and the New Harmony Working Men's Institute." *Libraries and Culture* 26 (1991): 402–14.

Dunlop, I. E., ed. *The Royal Burgh of Ayr: Seven Hundred and Fifty Years of History.* Edinburgh: Oliver and Boyd, 1953.

Dunn, J. P. *The Libraries of Indiana.* Indianapolis: W. B. Burford, 1893.

Dupree, A. H. "The Pursuit of Knowledge in the Early American Republic." In Alexandra Oleson and Sanborn C. Brown, eds., *The Pursuit of Knowledge in the Early American Republic,* 21–32. Baltimore: Johns Hopkins University Press, 1976.

Eckhardt, Celia Morris. *Fanny Wright, Rebel in America.* Cambridge: Harvard University Press, 1984.

Elliott, Helen. "Frances Wright's Experiment with Negro Emancipation." *Indiana Magazine of History* 35 (1939): 141–57.

Elliott, Josephine M., ed. "The Owen Family Papers." *Indiana Magazine of History* 60 (1964): 331–52.

———. *To Holland and to New Harmony: Robert Dale Owen's Travel Journal, 1825–1826.* Indianapolis: Indiana Historical Society, 1969.

———. *Partnership for Posterity: The Correspondence of William Maclure and Marie Duclos Fretageot, 1820–1833.* Indianapolis: Indiana Historical Society, 1994.

———. "William Maclure: Patron Saint of Indiana Libraries." *Indiana Magazine of History* 94 (1998): 178–90.

Emerson, Edwin, Jr. *A History of the Nineteenth Century, Year by Year.* 3 vols. New York: P. F. Collier and Son, 1901.

Feller, Daniel. "The Spirit of Improvement: The America of William Maclure and Robert Owen." *Indiana Magazine of History* 94 (June 1998): 89–98.

Ferrall, Simon A. *A Ramble of Six Thousand Miles through the United States of America.* London: Effingham Wilson, 1832.

Fisher, George P. *Life of Benjamin Silliman.* 2 vols. New York: C. Scribner, 1866.

Garrett, Martin. *George Gordon, Lord Byron.* New York: Oxford University Press, 2000.

Gerstner, Patsy. "The Academy of Natural Sciences of Philadelphia, 1812–1850." In Alexandra Oleson and Sanborn C. Brown, eds., *The Pursuit of Knowledge in the Early American Republic,* 174–93. Baltimore: Johns Hopkins University Press, 1976.

Gillespie, Charles C. *Genesis and Geology.* Cambridge: Harvard University Press, 1951.

Godwin, William. *Enquiry Concerning Social Justice.* Ed. K. C. Carter. New York: Oxford University Press, 1971.

Good, H. G. *A History of American Education.* 2nd ed. New York: Macmillan, 1962.

Gould, Steven J. *The Mismeasure of Man.* New York: Norton, 1981.

Gray, John. *A Lecture on Human Happiness.* Philadelphia: Vertical Press, 1825.

Greene, John C. *American Science in the Age of Jefferson.* Ames: Iowa State University Press, 1984.

Greene, John C., and John G. Burke. *The Science of Minerals in the Age of Jefferson.* Philadelphia: American Philosophical Society, 1978.

Griscom, John. *A Year in Europe.* 2 vols. New York, 1823.

Guimps, Roger de, Baron. *Pestalozzi: His Aim and Work.* Trans. Margaret C. Crombie. Syracuse, N.Y.: C. W. Bardeen, 1889.

Gutek, Gerald Lee. "Robert Owen's New Harmony Community: An Example of Communitarian Education." *Journal of the Midwest History of Education Society* 3 (1975): 100–109.

———. *Joseph Neef: The Americanization of Pestalozzianism.* University: University of Alabama Press, 1978.

Gwynn, Stephen L. *History of Ireland.* London: Macmillan, 1923.

Hall, Frederick. "Modern Paris—Letters." Letter 8, August 21, 1807, in *The Literary and Philo-*

sophical Repertory: Embracing Discoveries and Improvements in the Physical Sciences; the Liberal and Fine Arts 1 (1812): 258. Middlebury, Vt.: printed for S. Swift by T. C. Strong, 1812–17. American Periodical Series, 1800–1825, reel 126.

Hardy, James D., Jr., John H. Jensen, and Martin Wolfe, eds. *The Maclure Collection of French Revolutionary Materials*. Philadelphia: University of Pennsylvania Press, 1966.

Harlan, Richard. *Medical and Physical Researches, or Original Memoirs in Medicine, Surgery, Physiology, Geology, Zoology, and Comparative Anatomy*. Philadelphia: Lydia R. Bailey, 1835.

Harris, David. *Socialist Origins in the United States: American Forerunners of Marx, 1817–1832*. Assen, the Netherlands: Van Gorcum, 1966.

Hendrickson, W. B. *David Dale Owen, Pioneer Geologist of the Middle West*. Indiana Historical Collections, vol. 27. Indianapolis: Indiana Historical Bureau, 1943.

Herman, Arthur. *How the Scots Invented the Modern World*. New York: Crown, 2001.

Herold, J. C. *The Age of Napoleon*. New York: Harper and Row, 1963.

Holloway, Mark. *Heaven on Earth: Utopian Communities in America, 1680–1880*. New York: Dover, 1966.

Hook, Andrew. *Scotland and America: A Study of Cultural Relations, 1750–1835*. Glasgow: Blackie, 1975.

Horwitz, Elinor Lander. *Communes in America: The Place Just Right*. Philadelphia: J. B. Lippincott, 1972.

Jedan, Dieter. "Joseph Neef: Innovator or Imitator?" *Indiana Magazine of History* 78 (December 1982): 323-40.

Jefferson, Thomas. *Thomas Jefferson's Garden Book, 1766–1824*. Annotated by Edwin Morris Betts. Philadelphia: American Philosophical Society, 1944.

Jensen, John H. "Collector and Collection: A Note." In James D. Hardy Jr., John H. Jensen, and Martin Wolfe, eds. *The Maclure Collection of French Revolutionary Materials*. Philadelphia: University of Pennsylvania Press, 1966.

Jeronimus, C. J., ed. *Travels by His Highness Duke Bernhard of Saxe-Weimar-Eisenach through North America in the Years 1825 and 1826*. Trans. William Jeronimus. Lanham, Md.: University Press of America, 2001.

Johnson, Markes E. "Geology in American Education, 1820–1860." *Geological Society of America Bulletin* 88 (1977): 1192–98.

———. "The Parallel Impacts of William Maclure and Amos Eaton on American Geology, Education, and Public Service." *Indiana Magazine of History* 94 (1998): 151–66.

Keen, Benjamin, and Mark Wasserman. *A History of Latin America*. 3rd ed. Boston: Houghton Mifflin, 1988.

Kellogg, A. M. *Pestalozzi: His Educational Work and Principles*. New York: Kellogg, 1894.

Keyes, Charles. "William Maclure: Father of Modern Geology." *Pan-American Geologist* 44 (September 1925): 81–94.

Kipnis, William Frank. "Propagating the Pestalozzian: The Story of William Maclure's Involvement in Efforts to Affect Educational and Social Reforms in the Early Nineteenth Century." Ph.D. diss., Loyola University of Chicago, 1972.

Klein, R. S. *Science and Society in Early America: Essays in Honor of Whitfield J. Bell Jr.* Philadelphia: American Philosophical Society, 1986.

Lang, Elfrieda. "The Inhabitants of New Harmony According to the Federal Census of 1850." *Indiana Magazine of History* 42, no. 4 (December 1946): 355–94.

———. "Autobiography of Alvin P. Hovey's Early Life." *Indiana Magazine of History* 43 (Mar. 1952): 71–84.

La Rochefoucauld-Liancourt, Francois-Alexandre-Frédéric, duc de. *Voyage dans les États Unis d'Amerique; fait en 1795, 1796, et 1797.* 8 vols. 1799.

Leopold, Richard William. *Robert Dale Owen, a Biography.* Cambridge: Harvard University Press, 1940.

Lindley, Harlow, ed. *Indiana as Seen by Early Travellers.* Indianapolis: Indiana Historical Collections, 1916.

Lockwood, George B. *The New Harmony Movement.* New York: D. Appleton, 1905; reprint, New York, A. M. Kelley, 1970.

———. *The New Harmony Communities.* Marion, Ind.: Chronicle Company, 1902: reprint, New York: AMS Press, 1971.

Lyell, Charles. *Principles of Geology; or, The Modern Changes of the Earth and Its Inhabitants Considered as Illustrative of Geology.* 9th and entirely rev. ed. London: J. Murray, 1853.

Macdonald, Donald. *The Diaries of Donald Macdonald, 1824–1826.* Indianapolis: Indiana Historical Society, 1942.

Maclure, William. *To the People of the United States.* Philadelphia, 1807.

———. "Observations sur la géologie des États-Unis, servant à expliquer une carte géographique." *Journal de physique* 69 (1809): 204–13.

———. "Observations on the Geology of the United States Explanatory for Geological Map." *Transactions of the American Philosophical Society* 6 (1809): 411–28.

———. *Observations on the Geology of the United States; with Some Remarks on the Effect Produced on the Nature and Fertility of Soils, by the Decomposition of the Different Classes of Rocks; and an Application to the Fertility of Every State in the Union, in Reference to the Accompanying Geological Map.* Philadelphia: printed for the author by A. Small, 1817; reprint, Ulm/Donau: Werner Fritsch; New York: Stechert-Hafner, 1962.

———. "Observations on the Geology of the West India Islands, from Barbadoes to Santa Cruz, inclusive." *Journal of the Academy of Natural Sciences of Philadelphia* 1 (1817): 134–49.

———. "Essay on the Formation of Rocks, or An Inquiry into the Probable Origin of Their Present Form and Structure." *Journal of the Academy of Natural Sciences of Philadelphia* 1 (1818): 261–76, 285–310, 327–45.

———. "Observations on the Geology of the United States of North America." *Transactions of the American Philosophical Society* 1 (1818): 1–91.

———. "Miscellaneous Remarks on the Systematic Arrangement of Rocks, and on Their Probable Origin, Especially of the Secondary." *American Journal of Science* 7 (1824): 261–64.

———. "An Epitome of the Improved Pestalozzian System of Education." *American Journal of Science* 10 (1826): 145–56.

———. *Opinions on Various Subjects, Dedicated to the Industrious Producers.* 3 vols. New Harmony, Ind.: School of Industry Press, 1831, 1837, 1838; reprint, New York: A. M. Kelley, 1971.

MacPhail, Ian, and Marjorie Sutton. "William Maclure as Publisher in the New Harmony Reform Tradition." *Indiana Magazine of History* 94 (1998): 167–77.

Margarot, Maurice. *The Trial of Maurice Margarot: Before the High Court of Judiciary, at Edinburgh, on the 13th and 14th of January, 1794.* New York: James Carey, 1794. Early American imprints, 1st series, no 31173, microfiche 821.

McAllister, Ethel M. *Amos Eaton, Scientist and Educator, 1776–1842.* Philadelphia: University of Pennsylvania Press, 1941.

Medical Repository of Original Essays and Intelligence, Relative to Physic, Surgery, Chemistry, and Natural History. New York: E. Bliss and E. White, 1797–1824.

Merrill, George P. *Contributions to the History of American Geology.* Washington, D.C.: Government Printing Office, 1906.

———. *The First One Hundred Years of American Geology.* New Haven: Yale University Press, 1924.

Monroe, Will S. *History of the Pestalozzian Movement in the United States.* Syracuse, N.Y.: C. W. Bardeen, 1907; reprint, New York: Arno Press, 1969.

Moore, John Bassett. *History and Digest of the International Arbitrations to Which the United States Has Been a Party.* 6 vols. Washington: Government Printing Office, 1898.

Moore, J. Percy. "William Maclure—Scientist and Humanitarian." *Proceedings of the American Philosophical Society* 91 (1947): 234–49.

Morton, Samuel George. "A Memoir of William Maclure, Esq." In Maclure, *Opinions on Various Subjects,* 1:7–31. New York: A. M. Kelley, 1971.

Neef, Joseph. *Sketch of a Plan and Method of Education Founded on an Analysis of the Human Faculties and Natural Reason, Suitable for the Offspring of a Free People and for All Rational Human Beings.* Philadelphia, 1808.

———. *The Method of Instructing Children Rationally in the Arts of Writing and Reading.* Philadelphia, 1813.

Nicholson, Eleanor. "The Radical Scot: The Educational Ideas and Philanthropies of William Maclure, 1763–1840." Ph.D. diss., Loyola University, Chicago, 1995.

Niemcewicz, Julian Ursyn. *Pamietniki Dziennik pobytu za granicqi* (Memoirs and diary). Ed. J. K. Zupanski. Poznan, Poland, 1876.

———. *Under Their Vine and Fig Tree: Travels through America in 1797–1799, 1805, with Some Further Account of Life in New Jersey.* Trans. and ed. Metchie J. E. Budka. Elizabeth, N.J.: Grassmann, 1965.

Noble, Stuart G. *A History of American Education.* Westwood, Conn.: Greenwood Press, 1954.

Nolan, Edward James. *A Short History of the Academy of Natural Sciences of Philadelphia.* Philadelphia: Academy of Natural Sciences, 1909.

Novales, A. Gil. *William Maclure in Spain.* Madrid: Indec, Iniciativas de Cultura, 1981.

———. "The Spain William Maclure Knew." *Indiana Magazine of History* 94 (1998): 99–109.

Noyes, John Humphrey. *History of American Socialisms.* 1870; reprint, New York: Dover, 1966.

Nuttall, Thomas. *The Genera of North American Plants, and a Catalogue of the Species, to the Year 1817.* 2 vols. Philadelphia: printed for the author by D. Heartt, 1818.

Ord, George. "A Memoir of Charles-Alexandre Lesueur." *American Journal of Science and the Arts* 8 (1849): 189–216.

Owen, David Dale. *Mineral Lands of the United States.* Washington, D.C.: Government Printing Office, 1845.

———. *Report of a Geological Survey of Wisconsin, Iowa, and Minnesota, and Incidentally of a Portion of Nebraska Territory.* Philadelphia: Lippincott, Grambo, 1852.

———. *Report of a Geological Reconnaissance of Indiana, Made during the Years 1859 and 1860.* Indianapolis: Dodd, 1862.

Owen, Robert. *A New View of Society, or Essays on the Principles of the Formation of Human Character.* London: Cadell and Davies, 1813.

Owen, Robert Dale. *Footfalls on the Boundary of Another World.* Philadelphia: J. B. Lippincott, 1860.

———. *The Debatable Land between This World and the Next.* New York: G. W. Carleton, 1872.

————. *Threading My Way: Twenty-seven Years of Autobiography.* London: Trübner, 1874.

Owen, William. *Diary of William Owen from November 10, 1824, to April 20, 1825.* Ed. Joel W. Hiatt. Indianapolis: Bobbs-Merrill, 1906.

Pankhurst, Richard. *The Saint Simonians, Mill, and Carlyle: A Preface to Modern Thought.* London: Sidgwick and Jackson, 1957.

Pears, Thomas Clinton, Jr. *New Harmony, an Adventure in Happiness: Papers of Thomas and Sarah Pears.* Indianapolis: Indiana Historical Society, 1933; reprint, Clifton, N.J.: A. M. Kelley, 1973.

Pestalozzi, Johann Heinrich. *How Gertrude Teaches Her Children.* Trans. Lucy E. Holland and Francis C. Turner. Ed. Ebenezer Cooke. London: Swann Sonnenschein, 1894.

Peters, Edward. "The Desire to Know the Secrets of the World." *Journal of the History of Ideas* 62, no. 4 (2001): 593–610.

Phillips, Maurice E. "The Academy of Natural Sciences of Philadelphia." *Proceedings of the American Philosophical Society,* n.s., 43, no. 1 (1953): 266–74.

Pitzer, Donald E., ed. *Robert Owen's American Legacy: Proceedings of the Robert Owen Bicentennial Conference.* Indianapolis: Indiana Historical Society, 1972.

————. "William Maclure's Boatload of Knowledge: Science and Education into the Midwest." *Indiana Magazine of History* 94 (1998): 111–35.

Pitzer, Donald E., and Josephine M. Elliot. "New Harmony's First Utopians, 1814-1824." *Indiana Magazine of History* 75 (September 1979): 225–300.

Podmore, Frank. *Robert Owen: A Biography.* New York: D. Appleton, 1906.

Poesch, Jessie. *Titian Ramsey Peale, 1799–1885, and His Journals of the Wilkes Expedition.* Philadelphia: American Philosophical Society, 1961.

Porter, Charlotte M. "Following Bartram's 'Track': Titian Ramsey Peale's Florida Journey." *Florida Historical Quarterly* 61 (1983): 431–44.

————. *The Eagle's Nest: Natural History and American Ideas, 1812–1842.* University: University of Alabama Press, 1986.

Reingold, Nathan, ed. *Science in Nineteenth-Century America: A Documentary History.* Chicago: University of Chicago Press, 1964.

————. "American Indifference to Basic Research: A Reappraisal." In George H. Daniels, ed., *Nineteenth-Century American Science: A Reappraisal,* 38–62. Evanston, Ill.: Northwestern University Press, 1972.

————. "Definitions and Speculations: The Professionalization of Science in America in the Nineteenth Century." In Alexandra Oleson and Sanborn C. Brown, eds., *The Pursuit of Knowledge in the Early American Republic,* 33–69. Baltimore: Johns Hopkins University Press, 1976.

Rogers, William B., and Henry D. Rogers, "On the Physical Structure of the Appalachian Chain, as Exemplifying the Laws Which Have Regulated the Elevation of Great Mountain Chains, Generally," in *Reports of the First, Second, and Third Meetings of the Association of American Geologists and Naturalists,* 474–531. Boston: Gould, Kendall, and Lincoln, 1843.

Royle, Edward. *Robert Owen and the Commencement of the Millennium: A Study of the Harmony Community.* Manchester: Manchester University Press, 1998.

Sanders, John L. "Ayr Mount on the Eno River, near Hillsborough, North Carolina." *Antiques* 135 (May 1989): 1190–1201.

Schneer, Cecil J., ed. *Toward a History of Geology.* Proceedings of the New Hampshire Inter-disciplinary Conference on the History of Geology, September 7–12, 1967. Cambridge: MIT Press, 1967.

Seldes, Gilbert. *The Stammering Century.* New York: Harper and Row, 1965.

Silber, Käte. *Pestalozzi, the Man and His Work.* London: Routledge and Kegan Paul, 1960.

Skidmore, Thomas. *The Rights of Man to Property!* New York: printed for the author by A. Ming, 1829.

Smith, Philip Chadwick. "Philadelphia Displays the 'Flowery Red Flag.'" In Jean Gordon Lee, ed., *Philadelphians and the China Trade, 1784–1844,* 12–21. Philadelphia: Philadelphia Museum of Art, 1984.

Snedeker, Caroline Dale. *The Town of the Fearless.* Garden City, N.Y.: Doubleday, Doran, 1931.

Spieker, E. M. "Schöpf, Maclure, Werner, and the Earliest Work on American Geology." *Science* 172 (1971): 1333–34.

Story, William W. *Life and Letters of Joseph Story.* 2 vols. Boston: C. C. Little and J. Brown, 1851.

Stroud, Patricia Tyson. *Thomas Say: New World Naturalist.* Philadelphia: University of Pennsylvania Press, 1992.

———. *The Emperor of Nature: Charles-Lucien Bonaparte and His World.* Philadelphia: University of Pennsylvania Press, 2000.

Struve, H. *Beiträge zur Meneralogie und Geologie des Nördliche Amerika.* Hamburg, 1822.

Taylor, Anne. *Visions of Harmony: A Study in Nineteenth-Century Millenarianism.* New York: Oxford University Press, 1987.

Tocqueville, Alexis de. *Democracy in America.* New York: Colonial Press, 1900.

Trollope, Frances. *Domestic Manners of the Americans.* New York: Knopf, 1949.

Volney, C.-F. *A View of the Soil and Climate of the United States of America.* Paris, 1803; Philadelphia: J. Conrad, 1804.

Wallace, Anthony F. C. *Rockdale: The Growth of an American Village in the Early Industrial Revolution.* New York: Norton, 1978.

Warren, Leonard. *Constantine Samuel Rafinesque: A Voice in the American Wilderness.* Lexington: University Press of Kentucky, 2004.

Waserman, M. J. "A Bio-bibliography of William Maclure (1763–1840)." Master's thesis, Catholic University of America, Washington, D.C., 1963.

Weiss, Harry B., and Grace M. Ziegler. *Thomas Say, Early American Naturalist.* Springfield, Ill.: C. C. Thomas, 1931; reprint, New York: Arno Press, 1978.

Weld, Isaac, Jr. *Travels through the States of North America, and the Provinces of Upper and Lower Canada during the Years 1795, 1796, and 1797.* 2 vols. London, 1800.

Wells, John H. "Notes on the Earliest Geological Maps of the United States, 1756–1832." *Journal of the Washington Academy of Sciences* 49 (1959): 198–204.

White, George W. "William Maclure's Maps of the Geology of the United States." *Journal of the Society for the Bibliography of Natural History* 8 (1977): 266–69.

Williams, Dan A. "The New Harmony Working Men's Institute." *Library Quarterly* 20 (1950): 109–18.

Wilson, William E. *The Angel and the Serpent: The Story of New Harmony.* Bloomington: Indiana University Press, 1964.

Wood, Gordon S. *The American Revolution: A History.* New York: Modern Library, 2002.

Wright, Frances. *Views of Society and Manners in America.* London: Longman, Hurst, Rees, Orme, and Brown, 1821; reprint, ed. Paul R. Baker, Cambridge: Belknap Press of Harvard University Press, 1963.

INDEX

Academy of Natural Sciences of Philadelphia, 14–15, 20, 38; defection to
New Harmony, 181–182; founding
of, 125–130; journal of, 129; Maclure
as president, 126, 127, 134, 136; Ma-
clure wills wealth, 147; organizational
transformation, 134–136, 280–281;
Owen enthusiasts, 151–152, 162,
168–169; Pennsylvania/New Jersey/
New York expedition, 152; splinter
groups, 133–134
Adams, Abigail, 44
Adams, John, 16, 18, 36, 96, 169
adult education, 82, 217, 239, 272–273
Aesop's Fables, 273
African Americans, 105, 174, 198–202
Agassiz, Louis, 87
agriculture, 64–65
Alcott, Amos Bronson, 90, 268
American Conchology (Say), 236, 237, 260,
273
American Enlightenment principles, 13, 19,
27–28, 70
American Entomology (Say), 130, 236, 273
American Geological Society, 68; be-
queathed money, 278; foundation, 69;
Maclure president of, 122, 245
American Journal of Science, 68, 69, 86
American Philosophical Society, 124–125;
Maclure joins, 20; Wistar Party, 125

American Revolution, 9, 35
Amphlett, William, 273
Anna, General Santa, 249
anthracite, 64
Applegath, Joseph, 194
d'Aubigny, Madam, 262, 265
Audubon, John James, 97, 134
August, Karl, 101
Auvergne, France, 44–45
Ayr, Scotland, 3, 148
Aztec artifacts, 239

Barlow, Joel, 33
Barnet, Isaac Cox, 42, 92
Bartram, John, 131, 240
Bartram, William, 131
basalt, 44, 52, 56, 57, 62, 117
Beal, John, 183, 287
Beaver, Pennsylvania, 184
Bennett, William, 253
Bentham, Jeremy, 13, 33, 37, 105, 149–150
Berger, Jean-François, 46
Bernhard, Duke, 53, 167
Berzelius, Jöns Jacob, 41, 101
Birbeck, George, 149
Black, John, 149
Boatload of Knowledge (keelboat), 182–186
Bolivar, Simon, 249
Bonaparte, Joseph, 238
Bonaparte, Lucien, 134

Leonard Warren is Emeritus American Cancer Society Research Professor in the Department of Cell and Developmental Biology at the University of Pennsylvania and Institute Professor at the Wistar Institute. In addition to numerous published papers and books of a scientific nature, he is the author of *Joseph Leidy: The Last Man Who Knew Everything; Adele Marion Fielde: Feminist, Social Activist, Scientist;* and *Constantine Samuel Rafinesque: A Voice in the Wilderness.* He is currently writing a book on the impact of the immigrant on American science and medicine.

www.ingramcontent.com/pod-product-compliance
Lightning Source LLC
Chambersburg PA
CBHW070449100426
42812CB00004B/1252